Cultural Anthropology

Serena Nanda
John Jay College of Criminal Justice
City University of New York

D. Van Nostrand Company
New York Cincinnati Toronto London Melbourne

Cover photo: United Nations/Jerry Frank

D. Van Nostrand Company Regional Offices:
New York   Cincinnati

D. Van Nostrand Company International Offices:
London   Toronto   Melbourne

Library of Congress Catalog Card Number: 79-64466
ISBN: 0-442-25736-8

Published by D. Van Nostrand Company
135 West 50th Street, New York, N.Y. 10020

10 9 8 7 6 5 4 3 2

To Raj, Jai, and Paisley

Preface

Cultural Anthropology is intended for a one-semester course in introductory cultural anthropology. It has been designed with the idea that even though the majority of students in the course will not go on to major in anthropology, they will find it a fascinating and useful subject. The core concept of the text is *culture,* and the ethnographic data from our own and other cultures is organized around three major themes: (1) the impact of culture on human behavior; (2) the interrelationships between the different parts of a culture; and (3) the relations between culture as an adaptive system and cultural variation.

Students' understanding of these three themes will lead to their increasing awareness about themselves and the world they live in, about the past and the present, and about the unity and diversity that characterizes the human species. The study of cultural anthropology, as presented in this text, emphasizes that the forms and consequences of human behavior are only partly understood by the individual actor or the society. With an anthropological perspective, students can begin to "make sense" of the behavior of peoples unlike themselves as well as gain greater insight about their own behavior and society. This important contribution of the anthropological perspective is becoming increasingly necessary to deal with the plurality of cultures and life styles that characterizes the contemporary United States. For both the liberal-arts and pre-professional student, particularly those who will enter human service careers, anthropology is an essential intellectual, scientific, humanistic, and practical foundation.

Chapter Overview

Cultural Anthropology also introduces the fundamental concepts, theories, methods, data, and references that will enable the student to move successfully into more specialized and advanced anthropology courses. The topics included in the text cover the traditional scope of cultural anthropology, while drawing on the most recent anthropological research and presenting a number of different anthropological viewpoints and arguments. In Chapter 1, the focus is on "Anthropology as a Discipline" and the use of the anthropological perspective in understanding humankind. Part of this chapter is also devoted to an introduction to ethnography, the major research tool in cultural anthropology. The latter section of Chapter 1 introduces some recent research by anthropologists in the society of the United States and suggests some of

v

the ways in which the changes in the contemporary world are affecting both the theory and practice of anthropology.

Chapter 2, "Theory and Method in Cultural Anthropology," outlines each of the important theoretical perspectives cultural anthropologists have used in their understanding of culture and human behavior, beginning with the early period of classic evolutionary theory and including the more recent theoretical perspectives of cultural ecology and cognitive anthropology.

"The Culture Concept" is the main focus of Chapter 3. In addition to discussing various aspects and attributes of culture, concepts relating to culture change are introduced. This chapter provides the fundamental definitions and assumptions that are the foundation of later chapters. In Chapter 4, "The Cultural Context of Human Behavior," the emphasis is on the many aspects of human behavior that are patterned by culture. For example, perceptions of reality, space, and time; body movements and gestures, sex and gender, cognition, emotions, and attitudes are discussed in relation to the importance of cultural patterning. Chapters 1–4 make up Part One, "Anthropology and Culture," of the text.

Part Two, "Sociocultural Adaptations," examines variation in the major universal dimensions of human sociocultural systems. Chapter 5, "Language," explores both the special qualities of human language as a means of communication and the structural differences among different human languages. This chapter also includes a section on sociolinguistics, that is, the study of language in its social setting. In Chapter 6, "Learning Culture," the ways in which children are brought up to become functioning adults in a particular culture is emphasized. In addition to case studies of personality in adaptation, this chapter includes material on transitions from adolescence to adulthood.

Chapter 7, "Getting Food," brings cultural ecology into focus, describing the major preindustrial food-getting strategies through extended ethnographic cases. The emphasis here is on the relationship between cultural diversity and adaptation to environmental variation with different kinds of technologies. In Chapter 8, "Economics," different systems of production and exchange of goods are discussed, utilizing the ecological perspective on such classic anthropological topics as the Kula ring and the Potlatch. Chapter 9, "Social Ranking and Stratification," which deals with the basic differences between egalitarian and stratified societies, is also concerned with the ways in which goods and services are distributed in different societies and is thus a logical extension of Chapter 8.

"Marriage, Family, and Domestic Groups," Chapter 10, views both the functions and structures of different kinds of marriage rules and family groups, utilizing extended ethnographic examples of the major types. Chapter 11, "Kinship and Association," introduces the student to the major kinship ideologies and the kinds of extended groups formed by kinship. The chapter concludes with a section on forms of association other than kinship, such as age villages, sodalities, and modern voluntary associations. In Chapter 12, "Political Systems and Social Control," the focus is on the variation in political institutions and the control of behavior in band, tribal, chiefdom, and state level societies. The chapter concludes with a presentation of a variety of anthropological views on the origins of state societies in different sociocultural contexts.

"Religion," the subject of Chapter 13, is

viewed in light of its functions in human society as well as in regard to the variation in religious beliefs, practices, and organization that relate to other aspects of the sociocultural system. This chapter also includes a section on religious revitalization, using an example from our own society to emphasize the relationship between the lack of a positive personal identity and cultural loss. Chapter 14, "The Arts," emphasizes the universal functions of these cultural phenomona and the need to understand them in their particular cultural setting. Chapter 15, "Culture Change in the Contemporary World," focuses on sociocultural change as a result of the processes of urbanization, political modernization, and the entry of nonindustrial peoples into cash economies.

Study Aids

Cultural Anthropology is intended to increase the ability of the beginning student to absorb and understand the material. Although each chapter stands on its own and may be rearranged to fit individual teacher's preferences, the material is also integrated for greater comprehensibility. The substance of each chapter is organized so that the main ideas, secondary ideas, and ethnographic material stand out clearly. Ethnographic examples and extended ethnographic cases are presented with the aim of providing interesting and appropriate illumination of basic concepts, rather than in an attempt to cover the field of anthropological research exhaustively.

A concise summary of main points is provided at the end of each chapter. A glossary is included at the end of the book for easy reference to the definition of important concepts and terms used in the text. These are printed in bold type so

that they may be quickly identified by the student. Maps, charts, drawings, and photographs are used in appropriate places and are integrated with the main points of the chapter while providing additional, related information. A list of sources, in the notation system of the *American Anthropologist,* is included at the end of the book. A list of suggested readings that are both interesting and relatively accessible to the introductory student are at the end of each chapter. An Instructor's Manual includes multiple choice, short answer, and essay questions, film suggestions for each chapter, and student-oriented exercises for both class participation and assignments outside of class. A slide package that gives an overview of the concepts in the text is also available.

Acknowledgments

It gives me great pleasure to thank the many people who have helped me in many different ways in connection with this book. My colleagues and friends Anne Marie Cantwell and Owen Lynch have been particularly helpful with their suggestions and criticisms, all of which I found thoughtful and constructive. Beth Pacheco and Joan Gregg, who used the material in preparation with their students, also made many valuable comments and provided interesting suggestions for the Instructor's Manual. I also thank them for their enthusiastic support throughout. J. Scott Francher, Chairman of the Department of Anthropology at John Jay College of Criminal Justice, has been a continuing source of guidance. His commitment to the importance of teaching anthropology in a meaningful way to introductory students has been an important influence on my own teaching and on the text. I have also benefitted greatly

viii
PREFACE

from my discussions with Raymond Kennedy, whose commitment to humanistic anthropology and contributions to the field of popular music have benefitted both his colleagues and his students. To my colleagues in the interdisciplinary department of Thematic Studies, I feel much gratitude for their kindness in permitting me a teaching schedule that allowed me to work on the manuscript and for their consistent support of anthropology in our curriculum. I hope they have learned as much from my perspective as I have learned from theirs. Florence Grossman, supervisor of faculty services at John Jay College has my deep thanks for getting the manuscript typed and meeting my deadlines with grace and good humor. My students in anthropology have been my inspiration, and for all of them I have the sincerest gratitude. In this connection I also thank Jean Shapiro for her continued interest and excitement about the subject matter of the text as well as for reading portions of the manuscript for clarity. For assistance and generous use of their photographs I would like to thank Bernhard Krauss, Raymond Kennedy, David Klein, Joan Gregg, John Gregg, Tony Gahan, John Lenoir, Susan Locke, Christina Smith, at the United Nations Photo Library, the photo resources of the American Museum of Natural History and the Museum of the American Indian, and most especially Jane Hoffer. I would also like to thank Judith Joseph and Harriet Serenkin, at D. Van Nostrand Company, for their encouragement and assistance. Thanks are also due the reviewers who provided constructive criticism and many valuable suggestions.

My parents, Harry and Sylvia Young, have always been interested, encouraging, and enthusiastic about my projects, and this text is dedicated to them as well as to my children. Most of all, I thank Robin Nanda, my husband and my best friend, whose encouragement and helpful criticism made the completion of this book possible.

Critical Reviewers

The development of *Cultural Anthropology* was accomplished with the criticisms and suggestions of the following:

Joseph C. Berland, Northwestern University
Judith K. Brown, Oakland University
Anne Marie Cantwell, Rutgers University
George Epple, Rhode Island College
Michael Hoffman, University of Virginia
Susan Lees, Hunter College
Owen Lynch, New York University
William Millsap, Southwest Texas State University
Mary Lynn Morse, Montclair State College
Leonard W. Moss, Wayne State University
Ino Rossi, St. John's University
Dennis Shaw, Miami Dade Community College

Contents

Ethnographies

United Nations/Ray Witlin

Anthropology and Culture

The study of man and civilization is not only a matter of scientific interest, but at once passes into the practical business of life. We have in it the means of understanding our own lives and our place in the world, vaguely and imperfectly it is true, but at any rate more clearly than any former generation. The knowledge of man's course of life, from the remote past to the present, will not only help us to forecast the future, but may guide us in our duty of leaving the world better than we found it.

—E. B. Tylor

Serena Nanda

1
Anthropology as a Discipline

Anthropology is the comparative study of humankind; its aims are to describe, analyze, and explain both the similarities and differences among human groups. Anthropologists are interested in characteristics that are typical or shared in a particular human population, rather than what is abnormal and individually unique. In their study of human variation, then, anthropologists focus on the differences among human groups, rather than the differences among individuals within those groups. The groups traditionally studied by anthropologists are called **societies.** A society is a group of people who are dependent on each other for survival and/or well-being, and who share a way of life. But whether the unit of study is a particular society, a group within a society, or a whole human population, anthropologists look at what is typical for that group and how that group differs from others. Only by the study of humanity in its total variety can we understand the origins and development of our species.

PERSPECTIVES IN ANTHROPOLOGY

Anthropologists study our species from its beginnings several million years ago right up until the present. Anthropologists study human beings as they live in every corner of the earth, in all kinds of physical environments. Some anthropologists are now trying to project how human beings will live in outer space. It is this interest in humankind throughout time and in all parts of the world that distinguishes anthropology as a scientific and humanistic discipline. In other academic disciplines, human behavior is studied primarily from the point of view of Western society. "Human" nature is thought to be the same as the behavior of people as they exist in the modern industrial nations of Europe and the United States.

Human beings everywhere consider their own behavior not only right, but natural. For example, both "common sense" and Western economic theory see human beings as "naturally" individualistic and competitive. But in some societies, human beings are not competitive, and the group is more important than the individual. Anthropologists see the Western idea of "economic man"—the individual motivated by profit and rational self-interest—as the result of the particular socioeconomic and political system we live in. It is not an explanaton of the behavior of the Arapesh hunter in New Guinea, who makes sure he is not always the first to sight and claim the game, so that others will not leave him to hunt alone (Mead 1935:38). In anthropology, more than any other discipline, concepts of "human nature" and theories of human behavior are based on studies of human groups whose goals, values, views of reality, and environmental adaptations are very different from those of modern industrial Western societies.

In their attempts to explain human variation, anthropologists combine the study of both human biology and the learned and shared patterns of human behavior we call culture. Other academic disciplines focus on one factor—biology, psychology, physiology, society—as the explanation of human behavior. Anthropology seeks to understand human beings as total organisms who adapt to their environments through a complex interaction of both biology and culture.

Because anthropologists have this "holistic" approach to the study of the human experience, they are interested in the total range of human activity. They study the small dramas of daily living as well as dramatic events. They study the ways in which mothers hold their babies, or sons address their fathers. They want to know not only how a group gets its food, but the rules for eating it. Anthropologists are interested in how human societies think about time and space; how they see colors and how they name them. They are interested in health and illness, in the human body and the cultural significance of physical variation. Anthropologists are interested in sex and marriage, in giving birth and dying. They are interested in folklore and fairy tales, political speeches and everyday conversation. For the anthropologist, great ceremonies and the ordinary rituals of greeting a friend are all worth investigating. When presented out of context, some of the things anthropologists are interested in and write about seem strange or silly, but every aspect of human behavior is significant as part of the attempt to understand human life and society.

SPECIALIZATION IN ANTHROPOLOGY

The broad range of anthropological interest has led to some specialization of research and teaching. The major divisions of anthropology are cultural anthropology, archeology, and physical anthropology.

Cultural Anthropology

Cultural anthropology studies human behavior that is learned, rather than genetically transmitted, and that is typical of a particular human group. These learned and shared kinds of human behavior (including the material results of this behavior) are called **culture.**

Culture is the major way in which human beings adapt to their environ-

ments. Cultural anthropologists attempt to understand culture in this general sense: they study its origins, its development, its diversity as it changes through time and among peoples. They also examine its transmission through teaching and learning, and its relation to *Homo sapiens* as a biological species. Cultural anthropologists are also interested in particular cultures; they want to know how different societies adapt to their environments. In its comparative perspective, cultural anthropology attempts to discover what is specific and variable in human behavior and what is general and uniform. Cultural anthropologists ask questions like these: "Is religion universal?" "What kinds of family structures are found in different societies?" They are also interested in the relationships between the different subsystems of a culture—in particular, in their cause and effect relationship to culture change. The goal of cultural anthropology is to understand how culture change works so that we can predict and perhaps direct or control change in productive ways.

Anthropological **linguistics** is a subspecialty of cultural anthropology concerned with language, which is a part of culture. Anthropological linguists study linguistic variation, the ways in which human languages have developed, the ways in which they are related to each other, how language is learned, and the relationship between language and other aspects of culture. One aim of anthropological linguistics is ultimately to understand the process of thought and the organization of the human mind as this is expressed in language.

Archeology

Anthropological **archeology** specializes in understanding sociocultural systems that

Archeologists excavating a natural rock shelter in southern Connecticut, used by prehistoric Eastern Woodland hunters and gatherers as a temporary habitation. (Tony Gahan)

existed in the past, and for which there are either no written records or writing systems that have not yet been deciphered. The archeologist does not observe human behavior and culture directly, but reconstructs it from material remains: pottery, tools, garbage, ruins of houses and public buildings, burials, and whatever else a society has left behind. Archeology adds a vital time dimension to our understanding of how cultures change.

Up until about 1960, archeologists were mainly concerned with describing the artifacts, or material remains, of prehistoric sites. They would describe the procedures they followed, the relative frequency and locations of the artifacts, and compare those artifacts with similar ones in the same region. The "new archeology" re-

directs the interests of archeologists to new questions and research. The "new archeology" is interested not simply in describing prehistoric sites and artifacts, but in interpreting and explaining these data in terms of what they say about the culturally patterned behavior that produced them. The new archeology is primarily interested in questions of **culture process,** the rate and direction of culture change.

Physical Anthropology

Physical anthropology is the study of humankind from a biological perspective. A major task of physical anthropology is to study the evolution of the human species over time and the biological processes involved in human adaptation. **Paleontology** is the name given to the study of tracing human evolution in the fossil record. Paleontologists study the remains of the earli-

Physical anthropologist David Klein observes vervet monkeys in East Africa. Field observations of nonhuman primates have greatly added to our knowledge of the variety of primate behavior patterns, which up until about twenty years ago was obtained only from animals in captivity. (David Klein)

est human forms, as well as those nonhuman forms that can suggest something about our own origin and development. Paleontology is a particularly fascinating subject because it tries to answer the question, "Where did we come from?"

Figure 1.1 *Adaptive changes that are part of the evolutionary process are brought about by positive feedback systems. This figure shows a system of positive feedback that has occurred in the evolution of the human species. Notice that the positive changes in one component of the system bring about positive changes in other components of the system, which in turn feed back to reinforce the change in the initial component, which in this case is walking upright. Upright posture, which represents the most radical anatomical alteration experienced during human evolution—a major restructuring of the pelvis and the foot, is considered by most anthropologists to be the trigger of human evolution. In human evolution, biological and cultural components have both fed into and reinforced each other. The study of this interaction is one of the bases of a unified discipline of anthropology, bringing together physical anthropologists, cultural anthropologists, and archeologists.*

Physical anthropologists are also interested in the evolution of culture. In the evolution of the human species, physical and cultural evolution interacted in a complex feedback system; neither is independent of the other. The study of the complex interrelationship between physical and cultural evolution is the link between physical anthropology, cultural anthropology, and archeology (see Fig. 1.1).

Because early human populations were hunters and gatherers, physical anthropologists study contemporary foraging societies in order to fill in the fragmentary physical evidence left by early humans. In addition to studying living human groups, physical anthropologists also study living nonhuman **primates** (especially monkeys and apes) for the clues that their chemistry, physiology, morphology (physical structure), and behavior can give us in understanding our own species. Although at one time primates were mainly studied in

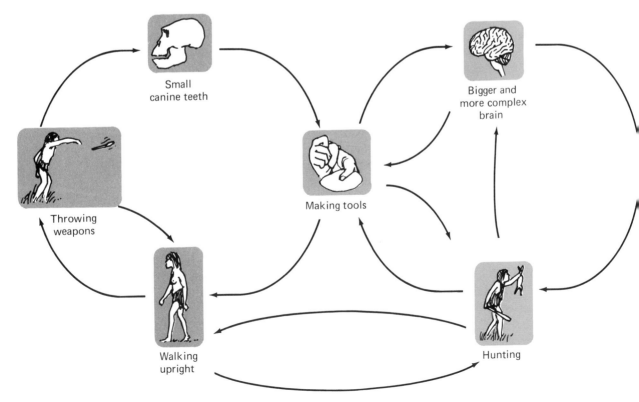

Small canine teeth

Bigger and more complex brain

Throwing weapons

Making tools

Walking upright

Hunting

the artificial settings of laboratories and zoos, now much of the work of physical anthropologists involves studying these animals in the wild.

Still another major interest of physical anthropologists is the study of differences among human groups that are transmitted genetically—for example, skin color, blood type, or certain kinds of diseases. In addition to the practical benefits of genetic analysis—for example, in the treatment and prevention of some harmful hereditary abnormalities—population genetics contributes to our understanding of human evolution and adaptation.

Interdisciplinary Specialties

As anthropologists develop special interests, they begin to work with scholars in other disciplines. The anthropology of law, for example, has led some anthropologists into a closer relationship with those in the legal and criminal justice fields. Medical anthropology, another new specialization, has led to a greater interest in medicine and public health in modern societies and also to a renewed interest in the healing practices of non-Western cultures. **Sociobiology** is a new interdisciplinary approach to the study of human behavior that brings together anthropologists, ethologists (people who study the behavior of many kinds of animals), geneticists, and biologists. They attempt to apply the perspective of evolutionary biology to human behavior. Cultural ecology (the relationship between culture and the physical environment) has led to interdisciplinary work by anthropologists, geographers, and botanists. Psychology overlaps with many anthropological interests: mental health, cognition (mental processes), learning theory, and cross-cultural studies of personality.

A good example of an interdisciplinary approach to the understanding of human behavior is a research project that was carried out to study a certain form of mental illness, called "Arctic hysteria," among the North Alaskan Eskimo (Foulks 1974). This project involved an anthropologist who had also trained as a psychiatrist, and a biologist specializing in the study of calcium deficiency. The causal factors considered in this study were the physical environment, population density, diet, body chemistry, sex roles, social pressures, and cultural change. Such studies draw specialists from many fields and use the theoretical understandings of several disciplines. This is an important trend in scientific research on human populations.

In spite of the various kinds of specialized and interdisciplinary interests among anthropologists, however, the discipline remains united in its interest in human beings as total organisms, and in its comparative approach to the understanding of the human species. Although anthropologists as individuals may specialize in physical or cultural anthropology, the aim of the discipline is to discover the nature of both biological and sociocultural processes and the relation between them.

DOING CULTURAL ANTHROPOLOGY: ETHNOGRAPHY

Anthropology uses the naturally existing diversity of human cultures as a substitute for the controlled experimental situation of the laboratory. For both technical and ethical reasons, the controlled laboratory experiment is of little use in gathering anthropological data and testing anthropological theories. Anthropologists can hardly go out and start a war somewhere to see its effect on family life. Nor can they control in a laboratory all the factors involved in examining the causes of "Arctic hysteria" among the Eskimos. In order to get information and test hypotheses, anthropologists, like natural scientists, go out into the field to observe their subject in a natural setting. This naturalistic approach to the study of human behavior is called **ethnography.** Ethnographic data are the evidence around which anthropological theories are built and tested.

In order to have the widest possible range of variation included in the data, anthropologists have been interested in the study of small-scale, technologically simpler societies whose cultures are very different from our own. These societies provide a valuable source of data on the interrelationships of different aspects of culture and the dynamics of culture change, because these interrelationships are easier to untangle in relatively isolated and integrated cultural systems.

Ethnography has two parts—fieldwork and writing up the results of the fieldwork. Fieldwork involves participating in and observing the lives of people in the group the anthropologist wishes to study. The writing up of the field data is aimed at presenting as authentic and coherent a picture of the cultural system as possible. The holistic perspective of anthropology developed through doing fieldwork. It is only by living with people, engaging in their activities and seeing things from their point of view, that we can see culture as a system of interrelated patterns. Good ethnography is not based only on the fieldworker's ability to see things from the other person's point of view; it is also based on the ability to see patterns, relationships, and meanings that may not be consciously understood by a person in that culture.

Anthropological Fieldwork: Participant Observation

Because an anthropologist is a human being studying other human beings, it is difficult—some say impossible—to make a completely objective study of another culture. An anthropologist's own culture, personality, sex, age, and theoretical approach can all be sources of ethnographic bias. Sex bias for example, has recently become a methodological issue in anthropology. Much fieldwork has been done by men who have had limited access to women's lives. Furthermore, even women anthropologists have been unconsciously biased by a male-oriented view of social structure and culture. In an attempt to correct this, anthropologists are taking a closer look at the lives of women, the meanings their culture has for them, the ways in which female personality is shaped, and the uses of power in the domestic as well as the public sphere (Rosaldo and Lamphere 1974). Because new data lead to new theory, awareness of ethnographic bias can not only give us a more accurate picture of a particular society, but more useful theories about the interrelationships between different aspects of culture.

Both participation and observation are necessary in good ethnographic fieldwork. The anthropologist observes, listens, asks questions, and attempts to find a way through which she or he can participate in the life of the society over an extended period of time. William Whyte (1955), who studied working-class Italian-Americans in Boston and was one of the first to do fieldwork in the United States, found that much of his most valuable data and theory came from observations of such "nonactivities" as "hanging around," going bowling, and going to dances. In order to make these observations, he had to move out of

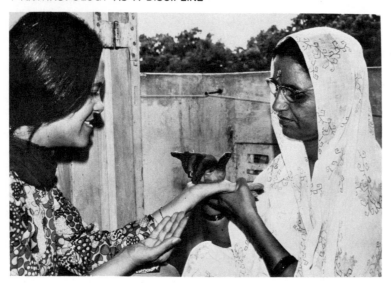

The author has her hands painted with vegetable dye as part of her participation in Karva Chowth, a ritual occasion in North India on which women observe a fast for their husband's welfare.
(Ravinder Nanda)

his college dorm and into an apartment in the neighborhood he was studying.

More than any other scientific enterprise, anthropological fieldwork is based on cooperation and trust between subjects and researcher. Long participation in the lives of other people is required for this trust to develop. Participation also forces the researcher to think about how to behave in a culturally approved manner and thus sharpens insight into right ways of behavior. Richard Lee (1974), for example, had this experience while working among the Bushmen of Africa. The Bushmen are a very egalitarian society. Their ecological adaptation requires a high degree of sharing and a minimum of individualism and competition. In order to thank them for the cooperation they had given him in the field, Lee presented the group with a large ox at Christmas. In telling the Bushmen about the gift, Lee stressed the large size of the animal and the great amount of meat it would provide. But the Bushmen did not thank him for it; they even insulted him by calling the ox skinny and unfit to eat. Only through continued fieldwork and growing friendship was he able to find out what he had done wrong. His gift had been very welcome, but his manner of presentation—boasting and expecting gratitude—had not. Bushmen values, in contrast to his, stressed generosity that does not call attention to itself.

Participant observation is the best way to understand the difference between what people say they do, feel, or think, and what kinds of action they take. It is not that people deliberately lie, but often when they are asked about some aspect of their culture, they will give the cultural ideal, not what actually happens. This is especially true when the outsider has a higher social status than the informant. For psychological or pragmatic reasons, the informant wishes to look good in the anthropologist's eyes.

In studying a culture different from his/her own, the main task of the anthropologist is to perceive things from the other person's point of view. Although training in the anthropological perspective is designed to help overcome cultural bias, even well-trained anthropologists slip into projecting their own culturally determined feelings and perceptions on other peoples, as Lee's experience among the Bushmen shows. In studying his/her own culture, the anthropologist must try to maintain the social distance of the outsider, because it is all too easy to take for granted what one knows. Remaining objective may be easier when studying cannibalism, kinship structure, or warfare in other cultures than when confronted with child neglect, corporate structure, or armed conflict in one's own society.

WHAT WE LEARN FROM ANTHROPOLOGY

Understanding Human Differences

Anthropology contributes to our understanding of genetically transmitted differences among human groups, as well as those that result from learning. By increasing our understanding of the importance of culture in human adaptation, anthropology enables us to look more critically at popular ideas about "human nature." Anthropology helps remove the blinders of **ethnocentrism,** the tendency to view the world through the narrow lens of one's own culture or social position. The American tourist who, when presented with a handful of Italian *lira,* asks "How much is this in *real* money?" is ethnocentric. An American anthropologist working in the Diribi society in New Guinea caused the people great confusion. The Diribi could not figure out what kind of "work" the anthropologist was doing. He was "not government, not mission and not doctor." Fi-

nally, they classified him as a "storimasta," someone interested in other people's ways of life, or "stories," but they could not believe anyone would pay him for such an activity. It did not fit any concept of "work" as they knew it (Wagner 1975). In my own anthropological fieldwork among women in India, I found myself pitied because my informants heard that "in America sons leave their parents' home when they marry." It was difficult to convince anyone that I would be pleased when my own two sons set up homes of their own.

All over the world, people are ethnocentric. They tend to see things from their own culturally patterned point of view, to value what they have been taught to value, to see the meaning of life in their own culturally defined purposes. But enthocentrism is more than just the biases of perception and knowledge; it is also the practice of judging other cultures by the standards of one's own. Most peoples in the world regard their own culture as superior and many consider peoples from other cultures as less than human. But although all peoples are ethnocentric, the ethnocentricity of Western societies has had greater consequences than that of smaller, less technologically advanced, and geographically isolated peoples. The historical circumstances that led to the spread of Western civilization have given us a very strong belief in its rightness and superiority. We have been in a position to impose our beliefs and practices on other peoples because of our superior military technology and because our industrial technology provides an abundance of consumer goods that other people quickly learn to want. Their acceptance of refrigerators and washing machines has led us to believe our values and other social institutions are also superior.

THE CONCEPT OF RACE

The complexity of the concept of race is illustrated in the following statements, which are part of a 1964 UNESCO proposal signed by many leading scientists throughout the world.

1. All humans living today belong to a single species, *Homo sapiens,* and are derived from a common stock. There are differences of opinion regarding how and when different groups diverged from this common stock.

2. Biological differences between human beings are due to differences in heredity, constitution, and to the influence of the environment on this genetic potential. In most cases, those differences are due to the *interaction* of these two sets of factors.

3. There is great genetic diversity within all human populations. Pure races—in the sense of genetically homogeneous populations—do not exist in the human species.

4. Many of the obvious physical differences in average appearance between populations living in different geographic areas of the world have a genetic component. Most often this consists of differences in the *frequency* of the same hereditary characteristics.

5. In humans as well as in other animals, the genetic composition of each population is subject to the modifying influence of such diverse factors as natural selection, tending towards adaptation to the environment, mutations, or random modifications in the frequency of qualitative hereditary characters. Certain physical characters have a universal biological value for the survival of the human species, irrespective of the environment. The differences on which racial classifications are based do not affect these characters and, therefore, it is not possible from the biological point of view to speak in any way whatsoever of a gen-

The paradox is that, although ethnocentrism gets in the way of understanding, some ethnocentrism seems necessary as a kind of glue to hold a society together. When a people's culture loses value for them, they may experience great emotional stress and even lose interest in living. To the extent that ethnocentrism prevents building bridges between cultures, however, it becomes maladaptive. Where one culture is motivated by ethnocentrism to trespass on another, the harm done can be enormous. From this kind of ethnocentrism to **racism** is but a short step, and one that has been made in both popular and

scientific thought in the West. The idea that cultural variation, and specifically cultural superiority, resulted from genetic or "racial" variation seemed to make sense: Peoples who looked different from each other also behaved differently. The theory that the peoples of Asia and Africa and those native to North and South America were biologically inferior was comforting to Europeans who exploited their natural resources, took over their lands, and used them as slaves and servants. Up until the late nineteenth century, even scientists believed in these ideas. This "scientific racism" was used as a justification for building eral inferiority or superiority of this or that racial group.

6. The human species, which is now spread over the whole world, has a past rich in migrations, in territorial expansions and contractions. Because of the mobility of human populations and of social factors, mating between members of different human groups has played a much more important role in human history than in that of animals. It has never been proved that interbreeding has biological disadvantages for mankind as a whole. On the contrary, interbreeding contributes to the maintenance of biological ties between human groups and thus to the unity of the species in its diversity.

7. Most racial classifications of mankind do not include mental traits or attributes as a criterion of classification. Heredity may have an influence in the variability shown by *individuals* within a given population in their responses to the psycho-

logical tests currently applied. However, no difference has ever been detected convincingly in the hereditary endowments of human groups in regard to what is measured by these tests. On the other hand, ample evidence attests to the influence of physical, cultural and social environment on differences in response to these tests.

8. Neither in the field of hereditary potentialities concerning the overall intelligence and the capacity for cultural development, nor in that of physical traits, is there any justification for the concept of "inferior" and "superior" races. The peoples of the world today appear to possess equal biological potentialities for attaining any civilizational level. Differences in the achievements of different peoples must be attributed solely to their cultural history.*

*Proposals on the Biological Aspects of Race. (Courtesy of UNESCO, 1964)

social, political and economic structures that favored the interests of the "superior" race. Even today, in spite of a century of scientific evidence to the contrary, racism and racial discrimination are still powerful factors in contemporary societies.

One of the most important things we can learn by studying anthropology is that the big differences among human groups are the result of culture, not biological inheritance or "race." The study of **race,** that is, the attempt to classify peoples in terms of shared physical characteristics, was a major concern of the early period of anthropology. A great deal of energy was spent on

measuring various kinds of physical attributes: skin color, head shape, height, body build, and hair texture. But many problems arose with the concept of racial classification. Some human populations—for example, the Polynesians, the inhabitants of South India, the African bushmen— were difficult to place in a group because they had the physical attributes of more than one "race." Many of the so-called diagnostic racial traits did not go together; a population might have a characteristic nose shape of one race and the skin color of another. Furthermore, some physical characteristics such as skin color and

Physical characteristics, language, and culture vary independently of each other. (United Nations)

met with complications. The more scientists learned about the factors responsible for the relative difference in gene frequencies among human groups, the more "races" they had to add to their classification schemes.

Because the biological similarities among human groups far outweigh the differences, and because racial classifications tell us very little or nothing about other kinds of variation, some anthropologists want to drop the word "race" altogether. They want to focus instead on studying variation among actual human populations. It is clear that all humans belong to the same species and that the biological features essential to human life are common to us all. We know that a human being from any part of the world can take on the behavioral and cultural patterns of any group into which he/she is born. The adaptation through culture, and the potential for cultural development and creativity, are part of a universal human heritage.

Cultural Relativity

Anthropology helps us understand peoples whose ways of life are different from our own but with whom we share a common human destiny. The idea that each culture must be approached on its own terms is called **cultural relativity.** Cultural relativity is a tool for understanding other cultures. With this attitude we understand cultural patterns in terms of the total culture of which they are a part. Cultural relativity does not mean that all patterns must be judged as equally "good"; everyone has a set of values that serve as criteria in judging human behavior. It does mean that other patterns make sense, even if we would not want them for ourselves.

But the value of anthropology is not sim-

height were found to be affected by the environment. They could not be used as indicators of racial classification or historical connections between different human populations. Even relatively recent attempts to use genetic traits such as blood type to define and classify human "races" ply that it teaches us to see cultures from the inside; anthropology demonstrates that cultural patterns have causes and effects that can be understood only from an objective, or outsider's, point of view. The ability to look at a culture objectively is the first step toward a better understanding of one's own society and behavior.

Understanding Ourselves

The critical perspective of anthropology gives us better insight into our own behavior. By introducing the idea that most human behavior is learned, and not biologically inherited, anthropology gives us the hope we can make changes in our culture. By introducing the idea that all parts of a culture are interrelated, anthropology also helps us understand why changes are often very difficult to make in one area only. And the anthropological idea that cultures are designs for living worked out over a long period of time helps us understand why people resist change, even if it is "for their own good." Anthropology also helps us understand ourselves as individuals influenced by our own cultural pattern, and by our society as a whole. The anthropological perspective—that is, the comparative study of whole cultures—contributes to a better understanding of contemporary social problems and conflicts. It can also lead to constructive ways to solve those problems. The anthropological perspective allows us to see that our own culture is only one design for living among many in the history of humankind. It is an adaptation to one kind of environment with a particular level of technology, and it is due to a particular set of historical circumstances. An outsider's view of ourselves and society is perhaps the most important contribution anthropology can make.

APPLIED ANTHROPOLOGY

Applied anthropology is the organized interaction between professional anthropologists and policy-making bodies, both public and private. I think, however, that the applications of anthropology go beyond the organized involvement of anthropologists, as anthropologists, in policy-making and administration. The anthropological perspective can be applied to any situation that involves research or intervention in the lives of people who will be affected by the outcome. Applied anthropology, as it has developed in the United States, has always emphasized the distinctive cultural traditions, values, and "felt needs" of the peoples toward whom various government policies were directed, and has stressed the "grassroots" participation of people in planning and directing their own lives.

Although few anthropologists have been directly involved in planning and administering policy involving development, their advice and counsel has been used in a number of different programs, including United States AID programs, UNESCO technical assistance efforts, and policy development in the United States regarding native Americans and other minority groups, such as the Equal Opportunity Program.

Many recent studies of American society indicate the usefulness of anthropology in our contemporary world. One of these, carried out by James Spradley (1970), concerns the enforcement of laws against being drunk in public and the rehabilitative efforts of the Criminal Justice System. Although Spradley's study took place in Seattle, Washington, its implications are useful throughout the United States.

Society's treatment of men arrested for

public drunkenness is based on the perception of these men as alcoholics or public drunks. The view these men have of themselves centers around their nomadic life style; they call themselves "tramps." Using the fieldwork approach of cultural anthropology, Spradley found that these men had a particular experience of time and space and that this shaped their experience in jails and rehabilitation centers. One of the justifications for incarcerating men found guilty of public drunkenness is to "dry out" and thus rehabilitate the individual. The period of incarceration thus increases proportionately with the number of previous convictions for this offense. The men arrested for public drunkenness, however, view the time spent in prison as punishment. Their perspective of time as something "to be done" dominates their prison experience. Whereas in American society we speak of work in the context of time, such as "part-time" or "full-time," for the public drunk, time is transformed from a commodity to a difficult task that must be performed. One is rewarded for working; if "doing time" is hard work, then "you owe yourself a drunk" when the job (time) is done. Spradley's study pointed out that not only has the criminal justice system not been successful in carrying out its rehabilitative function, but indeed the drunk's experience with this system actually increases the kind of behavior it is supposed to curb.

Taking into account a whole system includes studying and observing informal as well as formal social relationships. Robert Edgerton (1964), an anthropologist who has undertaken the unusual task of studying the mentally retarded, indicates how useful the anthropological perspective can be. Edgerton studied an institution for the mildly mentally retarded (IQs from 40 to 70) which had changed over the last fifteen years from primarily custodial care to a therapeutic orientation directed toward preparing at least some of the patients for life outside the institution. The therapy milieu resulted in much supervised activity; enjoyable recreation, some of which included male-female interaction; and vocational training. This institution, like others, however, is understaffed, so that much patient activity cannot be supervised. The "problem" of lack of supervision provided an opportunity for Edgerton to do research on how patients managed their unsupervised time.

He found that they used this time mainly for "dating"; male and female patients met in places on the grounds not accessible to staff supervision. Although this dating distracted from the vocational programs, Edgerton concluded it was very beneficial to the patients. Dating increased the patients' ability to control time and space; to utilize subtle verbal and nonverbal forms of communication; to understand the rules of behavior among members of the opposite sex; and to control sexual impulses. In most institutions that have a therapeutic orientation, the belief of the staff generally is that unprogrammed time, "if not wasted, [is] at least not so efficient therapeutically as it ought to be." In this study, at least, the data showed that the unsupervised activities of the patients, more than any other, produced improvements in social responsibility and competence that "good supervision had failed to accomplish." This is only one of the many anthropological studies of client populations of social services which show that "clients" are often much more capable of rational and complex social interaction than those who plan such systems believe them to be.

The anthropological perspective is also

useful in bringing to attention the fact that the values and traditional behavior patterns of different ethnic groups are an important element in understanding the way in which they respond to various programs developed by national governments. One important area of government intervention and planning is health care. Anthropologists know that health and illness are intimately connected with other aspects of culture. Theories of disease, treatment, and cure are all part of the culture of human groups: medical systems are one of

the adaptive responses humans make to disease and illness. Almost all the extensive research done on health care in the United States indicates that there is a difference in both the demand and supply of such services according to social class and ethnic background. Not only are different levels of health care facilities supplied to the poor contrasted with the non-poor, but there are different patterns of use of these facilities.

Among different ethnic groups, cultural values and traditional beliefs account for the inability of many present health care systems to serve their needs. One of many examples is provided by Margaret Clark's study of a Mexican-American community in California (1970). In discussing their

In complex societies, informal relationships become important as frameworks for social activity. The study of urban life, pictured here in San Juan, Puerto Rico, requires some rethinking of theory and method by cultural anthropologists. (Bernhard Krauss)

own ineffectiveness, Anglo (Western) medical personnel frequently complain that Mexican-American patients are not utilizing the services they provide. Anglo doctors say that the patient waits too long to come to the doctor or hospital and seems uncooperative in refusing to make an immediate decision about a further course of treatment. From a Western perspective, the Mexican-American patient seems irrational and irresponsible. From the point of view of the Mexican-American, however, to give in to sickness is a moral weakness, and thus a culturally valued stoicism inhibits seeking medical attention. Furthermore, for the Mexican-American patient it is impossible to make a quick decision about treatment, because such a decision involves family members and friends who will take over his/her responsibilities when he/she is hospitalized.

Mexican-Americans exhibit a lack of confidence in the Anglo health care system and are reluctant to use it except as a last resort for a number of reasons besides the high cost. One factor is the system of folk beliefs about causes and cures of various illnesses that is not recognized as valid by Anglo doctors. For example, the prevalence of the "evil eye" is "known" in this ethnic group; an Anglo doctor who dismisses this belief as irrelevant is not likely to be respected by people for whom it is a fact. In addition, Mexican-American cultural expectations about how curers should act are in direct contrast to Western conceptions. Within the ethnic community, curers are people who speak the same language as the patient; who are courteous and interested in the patient's personal relationships; who are willing to spend a great deal of time with the patient; and who do not generally charge high fees.

Given the "efficiency" orientation of Anglo medical personnel, the difficulty of the language barrier, and the high cost of care, it is not surprising that the Mexican-American population does not utilize the public health system very effectively. This example could be extended to many other groups within the United States and holds true not only for physical illness, but even more so for disruptions in health and functioning that have a psychological basis.

The essence of the anthropological perspective is, then, holism: taking into account the whole system within which groups of human beings carry on their lives. This holistic perspective can be applied to any system—a factory, a neighborhood, a city, a region, a nation, and even the world. It can be applied not just by anthropologists doing research or acting as consultants to those who have the power to make policy, but also by people working in capacities in which they are intervening in the lives of other human beings. There is no end to the kinds of work in which the anthropological perspective can be useful: law enforcement, health administration, corporation management, education, politics, urban planning, social work, architecture, and so on.

THE FUTURE OF ANTHROPOLOGY IN THE FUTURE OF HUMANKIND

In the past, anthropology has made its strongest contribution to the understanding of humankind by studying small-scale, relatively isolated, nonliterate, technologically simple societies whose cultural patterns were very different from the anthropologist's own. The world is changing, however. Such cultures are being altered, and many are disappearing altogether under the impact of modernization. The societies in which anthropologists have worked are no longer isolated (if they ever really were by the time anthropologists got to them), and they are being incorporated into larger societies and the emerging nation-states of Asia and Africa. The lives of people all over the world are becoming tied in to large organizations. Oppressed minorities and those who favor new life styles are demanding to be heard. They want a share in the power and economic structures of which they are a part. Public pressure is forcing leaders to reconsider goals, values, and methods.

In the past, when anthropologists were working among people who for the most part could not read Western languages and did not have access to published material, there was little political pressure to consider the feelings of informants in writing up ethnographies. This situation has now changed greatly. Not only have many groups being studied been interested in the accuracy of ethnographic accounts, but they have been demanding a share of the benefits—financial, professional, or political. This is true not only for various kinds of minority groups in the United States, but for national governments in the non-Western world as well. Leaders of new nations want their cultures written up in ways that are politically acceptable and fit newly created cultural images. A discussion of the degree to which ethnographers should or should not be political advocates of the people among whom they are working is motivated both by genuine ethical concern, and by the need to gain the trust and knowledge of informants for whom political activity has become an important part of life (Valentine and Valentine 1970). Ethnographers have traditionally tried to stay away from tribal or village conflicts,

but this is becoming more difficult to do. For many peoples being studied, and for many anthropologists, both ethnographer and ethnography are looked upon as a resource in the struggle for power.

Goals and Ethics

All these changes mean that the conditions under which anthropologists work are changing. The result has been some new directions in anthropology, and a reexamination of its goals and ethics. Anthropologists today do not agree about these directions. Some feel that anthropology must remain neutral in world affairs—that any kind of political commitment will undermine the scientific objectivity of the discipline. Others believe that without a commitment to human freedom and social justice, anthropology will become a study of exotica, an ivory tower diversion from the conflicts that are part of social life throughout the world today (Hymes 1972). Some anthropologists believe that the most urgent task is to preserve and record the few remaining relatively isolated non-Western cultures; others feel that more ethnography is not the answer. Still others believe that in order to be a useful science, anthropology must go back to studying human behavior in the framework of biological evolution. Only then, they say, will we have a basis on which to judge the value of different cultural patterns. Still others believe that the discipline must turn to the study of large-scale organizations and the social changes that are occurring in the contemporary world. Toward this end, more and more anthropologists are studying the culture and society of the United States.

Acting as an anthropologist in a professional capacity, however, means being committed to an ethical position. The professional situation of anthropologists is uniquely varied and complex. Anthropologists are involved with their discipline, the individuals and groups with whom they do fieldwork, governments, and the study of issues affecting human welfare. Such complex involvements mean making choices among conflicting values and generate ethical dilemmas. In some cases these dilemmas may be so intense as to lead to a decision to drop a piece of research altogether. The statement of ethics adopted by the Council of the American Anthropological Association in May 1971 holds that the anthropologist's paramount responsibility is to those he/she studies; the anthropologist must "do everything within his power to protect their physical, social and psychological welfare and to honor their dignity and privacy." This statement includes the obligation to allow informants to remain anonymous when they wish to do so and not to exploit them for personal gain. It also includes the responsibility to communicate the results of the research to the individuals and groups likely to be affected, as well as to the general public. Related to this obligation is the further one to reflect on the possible effects of one's research on the population being studied.

Thus, anthropologists are committed to taking responsibility for the policies that may be formulated by governments on the basis of their research and for how these policies may affect various groups in the society. Their obligations to the public include a positive responsibility to speak out, both as individuals and a collectivity, on what they believe as a result of their particular expertise in the study of human beings, and to contribute to an "adequate definition of reality" that may become the basis of public policy and public opinion. These ethical issues have become enormously complicated because of the cultural and social pluralism characteristic of the modern nation-states in which anthropologists carry out research. In almost all societies today, there is a plurality of interests, values, and demands. Although this makes the position of the anthropologist a more difficult one, ignoring the diversity may lead to irresponsible decisions that do not promote the welfare of those among whom anthropologists work and to whom they owe first allegiance in any conflict of interest.

SUMMARY

1. Anthropology is a comparative study of humankind. It studies human beings in the past and the present, and in every corner of the world.

2. Anthropology is holistic. It studies the whole range of human behavior, and the interrelationships between the different aspects of human behavior.

3. Anthropology focuses on what is typical and different within and between human groups, rather than individuals.

4. The aim of anthropology is to discover and explain the similarities and differences among human groups.

5. Physical anthropology focuses on human characteristics that are transmitted genetically.

6. Cultural anthroplogy focuses on culture, the learned and shared ways of

behaving typical of a particular human group. Anthropologists also study culture in general, and attempt to discover laws of cultural development that apply to the whole of humankind.

7. Two specialties in cultural anthropology are archeology and linguistics. Archeologists study societies that existed in the past and did not leave written records. Linguists study human speech and linguistic variation.

8. Anthropologists also participate in interdisciplinary research, in which specialists from different disciplines combine their knowledge to investigate a particular kind of behavior.

9. Anthropology uses the methods of the natural sciences rather than the controlled laboratory experiment. Ethnography is the naturalistic observation of human behavior. It is done by participant observation or fieldwork, and the written result of fieldwork is called an ethnography.

10. Various biases can get in the way of an anthropologist's objectivity. Among these are the anthropologist's age, sex, political values, cultural attitudes, and personality.

11. Both participation and observation are involved in good ethnography. Participation means living among and taking part in the ordinary life of the people being studied.

12. Although doing fieldwork in another culture presents different problems from doing fieldwork in one's own culture, the ideal of the anthropological fieldworker is to have both the insider's and the outsider's point of view.

13. By showing the importance of culture in human adaptation, anthropology makes us examine biological explanations of differences among human populations more critically.

14. Anthropology reduces ethnocentrism, which is looking at other people through the narrow perspective of one's own culture.

15. Anthropology introduces the concept of cultural relativity, which means understanding a culture from the point of view of its participants. Anthropology can thus present the "insider's" view of a particular culture.

16. Anthropology can also present an "outsider's" view of a culture; it can point out causes and consequences of particular patterns of which people in that culture may not be conscious.

17. By taking the "outsider" view of our own society and culture, we can understand it more objectively, and perhaps use this understanding to make more rational changes in our own lives.

18. In the contemporary world, anthropological concepts and research have an important place. They have not yet been fully utilized, particularly in the United States itself, although anthropologists have begun to work in such problem areas as public drunkenness, health care, and prisons and other institutions.

19. The complexity of contemporary societies, with their diversity of interests, demands, and values, present ethical dilemmas for anthropologists. But paramount responsibility is always to the people being studied; it is their welfare and dignity that must be preserved at all costs.

SUGGESTED READINGS

Campbell, Bernard G., ed.
  1976   *Humankind Emerging.* Boston: Little, Brown. A readable and comprehensive survey of human evolution, with outstanding illustrations.

Casagrande, J. B., ed.
  1960   *In the Company of Man: Twenty Portraits by Anthropologists.* New York: Harper & Row. Personal accounts of anthropologists and their informants from a wide variety of cultures.

Fagan, B.
  1975   *In the Beginning.* Boston: Little, Brown. An introduction to archeology for the beginning student.

Farb, Peter
  1978   *Humankind.* Boston: Houghton Mifflin. A book written as a "celebration of our species" by a literate and entertaining author who is a naturalist, linguist, and anthropologist.

Fried, Morton
  1972   *The Study of Anthropology.* New York: Crowell. An introduction to anthropology as a profession, directed toward undergraduates.

Hymes, Dell, ed.
  1972   *Reinventing Anthropology.* New York: Vintage. Provocative essays on the role of anthropology in the contemporary world.

Powdermaker, Hortense
  1966   *Stranger and Friend: The Way of an Anthropologist.* New York: Norton. An interesting, personal account of fieldwork in four different situations, including the United States.

Rynkiewich, Michael, and Spradley, James P.
  1976   *Ethics and Anthropology: Dilemmas in Fieldwork.* New York: Wiley. Personal accounts of particular problems of ethics that have come up in fieldwork. The articles represent a variety of fieldwork situations and include such topics as secrecy, nationalism, public service, studying elites, conflicting demands of interest groups, and personal values.

Raymond Kennedy

2
Theory and Method
in Cultural Anthropology

People have always been very aware of the differences in ideas, actions, clothing, morals, beliefs, and customs of other people with whom they have come into contact. Very often these contacts produced feelings of shock, awe, fear, hostility, and moral outrage; sometimes they resulted in interest and admiration. Ethnocentrism has always been the characteristic response of human beings to other human beings who are different from themselves. With few exceptions, contact did not lead to the systematic study of the ways of life of other people. In 1877, Edward Tylor, an Englishman, published a book called *Primitive Culture: Researches into the Development of Mythology, Philosophy, Religion, Language, Art, and Customs* in which he introduced the concept of culture as an explanation of variation in human behavior. Tylor defined culture as "that complex whole which includes knowledge, belief, art, law, morals, custom, and any other capabilities acquired by man as a member of society." He then defined anthropology as the "science of culture."

Every scientific discipline has a body of theory and a characteristic method by which it tests its theory. A **theory** is a general idea that guides the study of phenomena in any scientific discipline. A good theory should explain, that is, account for, and ultimately predict, interrelationships. Scientific objectivity is the willingness to match a theory against new data (evidence) and to accept a new theory that is more consistent with new facts.

THEORIES OF CULTURE

Cultural anthropology uses several different theories in its study of human behavior, culture, and society. In the history of anthropology as a discipline, different theories have been popular at different times. Sometimes, old theories have been revived in a modified way and applied to new data or tested by new methods. We will look here at some of the major theories in cultural anthropology.

Classic Evolutionary Theory

The sixteenth century was an age of discovery in which Europeans came in contact with peoples whose cultures were very different from their own and whose level of technology was much simpler. In the three centuries that followed, European philosophers interested in uncovering the origin and laws of development of human society had to deal with the question of these people's place in the scheme of human history. It was out of this background that anthropology developed as a science of culture.

The earliest anthropological theory tried to explain cultural development in terms of **cultural evolution,** the process in which new cultural forms emerged out of older ones. Each society in the world was believed to have moved through similar stages of culture, which followed each other in the same order. European civilization was viewed as the "top" of this evolutionary process, and the cultures of "primitive" peoples as earlier stages in the culture of mankind. In the nineteenth century, Lewis Henry Morgan in America and Edward Tylor in England developed this theory.

In 1877, Morgan published a book entitled *Ancient Society*. In it he proposed the idea that human society had passed through three major stages of cultural development. Each stage was marked by a major technological breakthrough and accompanied by changes in other aspects of culture such as the structure of the family and the ownership of property. The first stage, which he called "savagery," was marked by the acquisition of fire and the invention of the bow. Property was collectively owned, and brothers and sisters were allowed to mate with each other. The second stage, "barbarism," saw the beginnings of animal domestication, the use of iron tools in the Old World, and the invention of pottery and the development of agriculture in the New World. In this stage, accumulation of wealth was made possible by new technology and control of property fell into the hands of males. The patriarchal family (control by the father) emerged and private ownership of property replaced collective ownership. The third stage, "civilization," was marked by the use of the phonetic alphabet and writing. The monogamous family (one man married to one woman) is characteristic of this stage. The state, a form of society based on a politically organized territory, replaces the tribe, a form of society organized by kinship. Morgan's ideas were used by Frederick Engels and Karl Marx to refine their own evolutionary view of human society. Their theory, like Morgan's, is a materialistic one. All aspects of culture—law, government, family, religion—are affected by the ways in which a society is organized to satisfy its material needs. This organization, in turn, is affected by the level of technology.

The theory that cultural development proceeded by the same steps everywhere was based on the idea of the **psychic unity** of mankind: All human groups have the same mental capacities and the same ability to think logically. When faced with similar problems, they will invent similar solutions. If two societies were isolated from each other, **independent invention** was the explanation for similarities, while the developmental stage explained differences. The developmental stage was itself

influenced by contacts the society had with other cultures. Tylor recognized that culture contact led to the spread of elements from one society to another, a process which is known as **cultural diffusion.** The classic evolutionists were not interested in history, which is the study of the past through particular events, but rather in discovering the general laws by which cultural development occurred. Thus, although they recognized that diffusion did occur, they did not give it too much attention, believing that independent invention

This contemporary Mexican mural depicts the conversion of indigenous Mexo-American populations to Catholicism. When European peoples came into contact with non-Western peoples very different from themselves they often regarded them as primitives or savages and destroyed much of their culture in the attempt to bring them into the fold of "civilization."
(Serena Nanda)

accounted for most cultural similarities. The evolutionary schemes of Morgan and Tylor were based on poor ethnographic data used out of their cultural context. Their interpretations are no longer considered adequate explanations of cultural similarities and differences.

Figure 2.1 *Diffusion theorists believed that the Mayan temples (b) and native American burial mounds (c) of the New World were derived from the Egyptian pyramid (a), to which they bear a superficial similarity in shape. Most contemporary anthropologists take the view that these three kinds of structures were a result of independent invention rather than diffusion.*

(a)

(b)

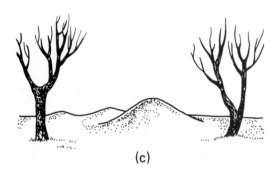

(c)

Diffusion Theory

The evolutionary theorists appeared to overestimate human inventiveness. In reaction, a new group of anthropologists in Europe and the United States turned to the study of cultural diffusion. In Europe, German and English ethnologists were still interested in the origins of human culture. They attempted to discover the earliest forms by mapping the distribution of cultural traits in nonliterate societies. The traits most widely distributed were presumed to be the oldest. Some diffusionists were determined to prove that all human culture originated in one place, and then spread through culture contact, or diffusion. For example, the similarities among the Egyptian pyramids, Mayan temples, and native American burial mounds led anthropologists like Elliott Smith and W. J. Perry to the conclusion that Egypt was the source of human civilization and culture (Figure 2.1).

The work of the European diffusionists is no longer of much interest to anthropologists. Both diffusion and independent invention are now recognized as contributing to the similarities between cultures. Furthermore, anthropology has largely moved away from the "bits and pieces" approach of the diffusionists, who were more interested in parts of culture (culture traits) than in cultures as wholes.

The American Historical Tradition

American diffusionists never reached the European extreme; they limited themselves mainly to tracing the origin and spread of specific cultural elements among the Indian tribes of North America. The anthropologists of the American historical tradition, among whom are Robert Lowie, Clark Wissler, Alfred Kroeber, and Franz Boas, believed that the laws of cultural process could best be discovered by reconstructing the particular cultural history of each society. Their efforts led to the designation of cultural areas for North America (Wissler 1926, Kroeber 1939) and some outstanding studies of American Indian culture (Lowie 1963).

Franz Boas, the leading American anthropologist of his time, was critical of both the deductive approach of the evolutionists and the piecemeal approach of the European diffusionists. Through intensive fieldwork among various North American Indian societies, Boas came to see that a cultural element—the design of a pot, the detail of a ritual—had to be understood in terms of the total culture of which it was a part. He began to insist on the study of cultures as wholes, as systems made up of many interrelated parts (1940). Boas also realized that diffusion was not an automatic result of cultural contact. People did not accept every new cultural element to which they were exposed. Even when elements did diffuse from one culture to another, they often changed meaning, and even form, when they became part of a preexisting cultural pattern. Boas became interested in the psychological as well as the historical influences that played a part in the similarities and differences in specific cultural patterns.

Boas became increasingly skeptical about the possibility of discovering laws underlying cultural process and regarded the search for cultural origins as fruitless. He urged anthropologists to do much more ethnographic fieldwork before they attempted to find cultural laws. He himself produced an enormous amount of ethnograpic data on native American cultures. For Boas, the status of anthropology as a science would depend on the most complete and objective gathering of ethnographic data on specific cultural systems, not on "discoveries" of cause and effect.

Critics accuse Boas of having held back the development of anthropology as a science by his outspoken hostility to the search for general laws of cultural development. But his contributions remain important. He shifted the focus of anthropology from cultural elements taken out of context to the study of culture as an interrelated system. He put anthropology on a sounder basis not only by his own ethnographic contributions, but by setting high standards in ethnography for future generations. His interest in psychology stimulated work in the field of culture and personality. His insistence on seeing culture in terms of the meaning it has for its participants led to important new work in linguistics and to an emphasis on cultural relativity as a necessary attitude in fieldwork.

Cultural Configurations

Ruth Benedict, a student of Boas, expanded his ideas in her book *Patterns of Culture* (1961). Benedict tried to account for cultural diversity by demonstrating that each culture is a unique **configuration** of interwoven parts, all of which are shaped by the particular theme, or **ethos,** of that culture. Religion, family life, economics, and political institutions all fit together to make up a unique configuration. Because the configurations result from particular historical processes, cultures cannot be measured against one another.

Drawing on ethnography from the Kwakiutl, Zuni, and Plains Indians of North America, and the Dobu of Melanesia, Benedict described these four culture configurations in psychological terms. She showed how cultural elements drew their meaning from the cultural ethos and the total configuration of which they were a part.

We can use the potlatch of the Kwakiutl Indians as an example. The **potlatch** was a feast in which many different kinds of wealth were distributed by the chief who hosted it to the people and chiefs from other villages who were his guests. Canoes, food, blankets, and fish oil were given away in great quantities and even destroyed as the chief tried to show how rich and generous he was. During these feasts, the host boasted about himself:

I am the great chief who vanquishes,
I am the great chief who vanquishes.
Oh, go on as you have done!
Only at those who continue to turn
    around in this world,
Working hard, losing their tails (like
    salmon), I sneer,
At the Chiefs under the true great
    chief.
Ha! have mercy on them! put oil on
    their dry brittle-haired heads,
The heads of those who do not comb
    their hair.
I sneer at the chiefs under the true
    great chief,
I am the great chief who makes people ashamed. (Benedict, 1961:192).

For Benedict, the potlatch made sense as an expression of the Kwakiutl ethos of social competition and individual rivalry.

Though cultural patterns and values remain basic anthropological topics, few anthropologists followed Benedict's theoretical approach, which was criticized as being

A speaker for the "Chief Who Gives Away Blankets," and who stands behind the pile of blankets, at Fort Rupert on the Northwest Coast of America. These "give-aways" called "potlatches" were an important feature of the social organization among Northwest Coast peoples. (Courtesy of the American Museum of Natural History)

too impressionistic. Furthermore, where Boas had stressed cultural relativity as part of the scientific method in anthropology, Benedict carried this concept to the extreme, where it seemed all cultural comparison must be abandoned. Nor did she suggest why a particular culture had developed a particular ethos, or what adaptive value an ethos had for a society. In spite of all the criticism, however, *Patterns of Culture* remains an anthropological classic.

Functionalism

In the early years of the twentieth century, American anthropologists were trying to describe traditional native American cultures using informants who were themselves being affected by the culture of the dominant white society. At the same time, Bronislaw Malinowski was doing fieldwork among the Trobriand Islanders of the New Guinea archipelago, a society whose cultural traditions were still very much alive. As a result of this fieldwork, he developed a theory of culture called **functionalism** (1944).

The central idea of functionalism was that culture serves the needs of individuals. In Malinowski's analysis culture is the outgrowth of three kinds of human needs: basic, derived, and integrative. Basic needs relate to the survival of human beings as biological organisms—the needs for food, shelter, and physical protection. Derived needs are the problems of social coordination humans must solve in order to satisfy their basic needs—the division of work, the distribution of food, defense, regulation of reproduction, and social control. Integrative needs are the human needs for psychological security, social harmony, and purpose in life that are met by systems of knowledge, law, religion, magic, myth, art. For example, magic functions to reassure people challenged by dangerous undertakings whose outcome is uncertain. Myth provides historical authority for the particular rules and values by which a society lives. Malinowski insisted that every aspect of a culture had a function in terms of one of these three needs.

Malinowski's idea that cultural elements and social institutions have functions which grow out of the needs of individuals in society is basic to much anthropological analysis. But because the human needs he talked about are universal, his theory does not serve as an explanation of cultural variation. For example, if all types of family systems serve the same human need, why do different societies have different systems?

Another aspect of Malinowski's functionalism was that the investigation of one aspect of culture would lead to a description of a whole cultural system. His own ethnography of the Trobriander Islanders (1961) is the best illustration of his theoretical approach. Among the Trobrianders, there was a cultural pattern called the **kula.** From their point of view, the most important aspect of kula was the trading of shell bracelets and necklaces, which took place between trading partners on the different islands that made up the kula ring. Malinowski showed that the kula was not an economic transaction like the impersonal money-goods exchanges in our own society, which are separated from other aspects of culture. Our norms and ethics in economic exchange are not expected to apply to friends and kin, nor are the ethics of personal relations between friends and kin supposed to apply in the marketplace. The kula, however, was related to many aspects of Trobriand life: kinship and political structure, magic, prestige, economy, technology, myth and feasting, friendship and alliance. Although kula appeared to be primarily an exchange of goods, it did not fill economic needs only. For the Trobriander, participation in the kula had important psychological functions. Participants derive prestige from generous behavior during the exchanges, and the kula gives them an opportunity to display their wealth. The kula's social functions were not consciously perceived by the participants. Through the preparations and activities, ties between participating local groups were reinforced, contributing to the integration of Trobriand society.

Structural Functionalism

Another kind of functional theory, **structural-functionalism,** was developed by

A. R. Radcliffe-Brown, who had been influenced by the French sociologist Emile Durkheim. Durkheim had rejected the psychological theories of his day, which attempted to explain social events in terms of individual needs and experiences. According to Durkheim, society, not the individual, must be the focus of study. Social events have an existence that goes beyond the individuals who take part in them. The origin and functions of religion, for example, are to be found in its contribution to social solidarity, not in its psychological functions for the individual. Durkheim's main interest was in social solidarity—the mechanisms by which societies are unified and maintained over time. Influenced by Durkheim's work, Radcliffe-Brown showed that norms, values, sentiments, and rituals have power over individuals and hold society together (1964).

Radcliffe-Brown's particular contribution to anthropology was showing that social systems are made up of structures and activities (1965). Social structures are the relatively persistent patterns by which people relate to one another and to the environment. Structures are inferred from social interaction and **norms,** or rules of behavior for social relationships. Although Radcliffe-Brown was interested in how social structures change, his work was mainly directed toward understanding the ways in which structural continuity and social solidarity are maintained. For him, the function of a structural element was the contribution it made to social solidarity and the continuity of a social system. Much of Radcliffe-Brown's own work, and that of other structural-functionalists, centered on kinship, because this is the most important principle of organization in nonliterate societies. An illustration of Radcliffe-Brown's theory is his explanation of "joking relations." Joking relationships are compounded of friendliness and hostility. They resemble what we call "teasing" in our own society. In many societies, joking relationships exist between persons occupying particular social statuses. An example of a joking relationship in our own society is that between a man and his mother-in-law. By presenting ethnographic data from several different societies, Radcliffe-Brown demonstrated that joking relationships exist between people who are tied together socially and yet have conflicting interests in the relationship. By acknowledging the conflict, and dealing with it formally, joking relationships reduce the possibility of open social conflict and contribute to the maintenance of the total social system.

The main criticism of structural-functionalism is that because of its focus on solidarity, integration, function, and stability, it ignores conflict, dysfunction, and change. This limits its usefulness in the study of complex societies; in looking back, it seems also to have imposed a false impression of stability and harmony on nonliterate societies as well. Nevertheless, **social function** is a basic concept in anthropological analysis. Many different cultural traits can be examined in terms of what they contribute to the solidarity of a group. A look at the potlatch from this perspective, for example, shows that it contributes to the maintenance of Kwakiutl society by publicly clarifying the social ranking system and by permitting an expression of hostility within the group that does not involve physical violence (Drucker and Heizer 1967).

Cognitive Anthropology

Another approach to the study of culture identifies it with rules, meanings, and classifications in language that give clues to the ways in which people perceive and understand their experience. In **cognitive anthropology,** culture is defined as a "blueprint for action," (not action itself), a "grammar" or system of rules for behavior, and a "code" it is the job of the anthropologist to break. What people learn when they learn "culture" is not just customs, but ways of organizing experience. From this perspective, anthropologists do not observe culture, but rather infer it from the behavior they observe in a particular society. A description of one particular culture is not merely a description of what people do, but a description of the rules or collective ideas behind that behavior. Sometimes members of a society know and can tell the anthropologist the pattern or rule underlying their behavior; sometimes they are not aware that an aspect of their behavior is culturally patterned. It is then the task of the anthropologist to find the pattern from observations and inquiries.

But although understanding the person's interpretation of experience is the aim of ethnography, not all anthropologists agree that it is the aim of anthropology. An important objection to the cognitive approach is that the overall results of cultural patterns are not necessarily part of one person's point of view or within her/his ability to grasp as an insider. The understanding of cultural process also depends on the ability of the outsider, the anthropologist, to see causes and effects that are different from, and perhaps even contrary to, the insider's view of experience.

Closely related to cognitive anthropology is **symbolic anthropology,** which treats culture as a system of shared symbols and meanings. An illustration from Clifford Geertz (1973) will make this clear:

> Consider . . . two boys rapidly contracting the eyelids of the right eyes.

In one, this is an involuntary twitch; in the other, a conspiratorial signal to a friend. The two movements are, as movements, identical . . . one could not tell which was twitch and which was wink. Yet the difference . . . between a twitch and wink is vast; as anyone unfortunate enough to have had the first taken for the second knows.

What Geertz is saying is that the winker is communicating. He is communicating deliberately, to someone in particular, according to a socially established code. A twitch of an eyelid is not culture—it is a physical movement that has no shared meaning. A wink is culture: it is a twitch of the eyelid that has meaning and communicates a special message. It is the patterned communication or symbolic aspects of human behavior that are of interest to the anthropologist describing a culture as a system of meaning.

Cultural Ecology

An ecological approach to culture sees cultural patterns as adaptive responses to the basic problems of survival and reproduction. Contemporary **cultural ecology** grows out of the theories of Leslie White (1949) and Julian Steward (1972) and has some links with evolutionary theory. White, like Morgan, was interested in the general evolution of culture. White's theory was that cultural development proceeds by an increasingly efficient transformation of energy, which leads in turn to population growth, increased productivity, and economic specialization. All other aspects of culture are secondary to this material base. White's theory was a universal one; it applied to human culture in general.

CULTURE AND PERSONALITY

Between 1920 and 1950, some anthropologists became interested in the relationship between culture and personality. This interest partly grew out of Freudian psychoanalytical theory, and partly out of the interest in the relationship between culture and psychology formulated by Ruth Benedict, Franz Boas, and Edward Sapir, a linguist and cultural anthropologist. Some of the early culture and personality studies were done to test specific Freudian theories in non-Western cultures. Malinowski (1927), for example, demonstrated that the Oedipus complex (defined by Freud as a sexual attachment of the male child to his mother, accompanied by hatred and jealousy toward his father), which Freud believed to be universal, did not exist in this form in the Trobriand Islands. The Trobriand society was matrilineal (the kinship group was organized around a woman and her descendants), and the mother's brother, rather than the father, was the primary authority in the family. Incest taboos in this society were strongest for brothers and sisters, not mothers and sons, and a boy's major unconscious rivalry was directed toward his maternal uncle, not his father.

Early culture and personality studies, having been influenced by Freudian theory, put particular emphasis on child-rearing practices such as feeding, weaning, and toilet training. Margaret Mead, who carried out some of the first studies among non-Western peoples, pointed out that what happened to an infant or child only partly accounted for later personality development. How a child was handled communicated cultural patterns as well as what it was taught. It did not matter so much whether a child was weaned early or late; the attitudes communicated in the process of weaning made all the difference. Although most culture and personality theoriests were interested in the influence culture had on personality, a group led by Abram Kardiner (1945) wanted to investigate the ways in which personality types might be reflected in patterns of culture. Kardiner and his associates believed that religion, folklore, and political systems might be seen as screens on which the basic personality orientation of a society was projected. They were interested in the relationship between child-rearing practices, the development of basic personality, and other aspects of culture. They saw a basic personality type as an adaptation that grew out of child-rearing practices that were themselves linked to the subsistence patterns of a society.

Later culture and personality theorists studied large "modernized" nations. National character studies, as they were called, appeared for Japan (Benedict 1946), the United States (Mead 1942), and Russia (Gorer 1949), among others. One of the problems with these studies was that it became difficult to generalize about personality in societies composed of several ethnic groups, social classes, and subcultures. Many of these national character studies also made connections between early child-rearing practices and later adult personality traits that were difficult to prove scientifically. Interest in the cultural patterning of personality also led to an interest in the effect of culture on the so-called abnormal or deviant person. The kind of personality most highly valued in one society might be labeled deviant or mentally abnormal in another (Benedict 1934). Furthermore, different societies had different ways of treating or responding to what we would call abnormal, and even within the history of Western culture, attitudes toward certain kinds of behavior, such as homosexuality, or trance, had changed over the centuries.

Because of the difficulty of proving many of the ideas of the early culture and personality theorists, this field of anthropology took new directions after 1950. There was a greater attempt to use statistics to prove the connections between child-rearing practices, personality, and other cultural patterns. John Whiting and Irwin Child (1953), for example, used a large cross-cultural sample in an attempt to demonstrate some of these interrelationships. One hypothesis they tested was that systems of curing illness would reflect techniques that had been sources of gratification in early child-rearing. Thus, a culture in which children were indulged in sources of oral gratification, such as feeding, would tend to use oral medicines for curing illness. Whiting and Child also hypothesized about the reverse of this relationship: They attempted to demonstrate that an aspect of child-rearing which was frustrating and promoted anxiety would be used to account for illness. If a culture frustrated a child's oral gratification—by withholding food, for example—that culture might be likely to see disease as something that enters the body through the mouth. Both hypotheses were validated statistically, and the

work proved to be a major step toward more refined methods of demonstrating the relationships between child-rearing practices, personality development, and other aspects of culture.

Whiting and his associates also tried to relate child-rearing patterns and subsequent personality development to the basic patterns of culture, food-getting, division of labor, and residence. This interest in the relation between ecology and personality has gained importance in culture and personality studies. In a recent study, for example, Robert Edgerton (1971) investigated four East African tribes who were divided into farmers and herders. He found personality differences not only among the four tribes, but also between the farmers and herders within each. Herders were more individualistic compared with farmers, who more often felt the need to consult others in making decisions. Edgerton concluded that the more an economy depends on herding, the more that society will value independence as a male personality trait.

Although psychologists are now entering the field of cross-cultural personality studies, anthropologists still tend to take a broader view of personality development. For the anthropologist, biological factors, family relations, cultural images, social roles, and specific situational factors all play a part in shaping personality. Contemporary psychological anthropology has also turned its attention in other directions, particularly to the relationship between culture and thought, and culture and perception.

Cultural ecologists help explain how some apparently irrational customs, such as the prohibition on eating beef in India, a country in which some people starve, makes sense as an adaptation to long run variation in the environment. (Serena Nanda)

In Julian Steward's multilinear evolutionary theory, cultures are primarily systems that evolved as adaptive responses to specific natural environments. Unlike White, he held that cultural evolution could move along a number of different paths, although societies in similar natural environments and with similar levels of technology would evolve in similar ways. This process of parallel evolution explains some general similarities in developmental stages among societies that are geographically distant from each other. It also explains similarities that cannot be explained by diffusion. According to Steward, the explanation of cultural forms or stages is to be found in the relationship between natural environment, level of technology, and patterns of work in a society.

Not all contemporary cultural ecologists agree with either White's or Steward's evolutionary emphasis on stages of development. They would generally agree however, that the question of how human societies develop particular patterns can best be approached by viewing culture as a system of socially transmitted behavior which serves to connect human communities to their ecological settings. The emphasis here is on culture as a behavior system that includes technology, ways of economic and political organization, settlement patterns, social groupings, religious beliefs and practices, values, and so on. From this perspective, the term **sociocultural system** seems better than culture, because the term sociocultural system includes the real-life expression of designs for living in particular environments, not just the design.

In emphasizing the adaptive nature of different aspects of a sociocultural system, cultural ecologists have been able to show that beliefs and practices which seem quite irrational may still result in rational utilization of the environment, given a particular level of technology. For example, the Hindu taboo on eating beef despite widespread poverty and periodic famine in India seems ridiculous to Westerners. Yet, according to Marvin Harris (1966) it does make sense as an adaptation. Cows are important in India not because they can be eaten, but because they provide bullocks, the draft animals that pull plows and carts and that are essential for agriculture. If a family was to eat its cows during a famine, it would deprive itself of the source of bullocks and could not continue farming. The religious taboo on eating beef strengthens the ability of the society to maintain itself in the long run.

The focus on the adaptive nature of sociocultural systems, rather than the ways such systems are transformed over time, has led to the criticism that cultural ecology is just another form of functionalism. It explains cultural variation in terms of "what is, is," with no real explanation of how it got that way. Nevertheless, cultural ecology does contribute to our understanding of the relationship of human populations to their physical and social environments. It is one of the dominant approaches in contemporary anthropology.

THEORIES OF CULTURE AND THE ETHNOGRAPHIC METHOD

The kinds of questions anthropologists are interested in cannot be answered by the methods used in the physical sciences. Anthropological theories cannot be tested in a laboratory under strictly controlled experimental conditions; the anthropological laboratory is the naturally existing diversity of cultural patterns in different parts of the world, in different natural environments, and at different times in history. The gathering of good ethnographic data through participant observation continues to be the hallmark of anthropology as a discipline and the foundation on which its theories are built and tested.

Although under the influence of Franz Boas the aim of anthropological fieldwork was the collection of detailed information on every aspect of life in a particular sociocultural system, today anthropologists tend to go into the field with some particular theoretical problem in mind, rather than with the idea of presenting the total picture of a culture. They may be interested in the relationship between subsistence and personality, or in symbolism, or in the role of voluntary associations in political participation, or in the relation of family type to economics.

An example is Margaret Mead's study in Samoa. In the 1920s in the United States, psychologists saw the stress experienced by adolescents as a universal and "natural" condition of growing up. Mead believed that the rebellion and emotional distress experienced by American adolescents was related to the particular difficulties of making the transition from childhood to adulthood in our society. She chose to study life in Samoa, where the transition from childhood to adulthood was known to be much easier. Mead found that the adolescent turmoil we know in the United States did not exist among this group of people. Her book, *Coming of Age in Samoa* (1961) is a now classic example of the use of ethnographic case study for testing a particular anthropological theory—in this case, that of the relation of specific emotional disturbances to specific cultural patterns.

Not all anthropologists use this method to test their theories. Some use a method called **controlled cross-cultural comparison,** which requires ethnographic data from many different societies. This method was used in a study of the relationship between family type and subsistence patterns carried out by M. F. Nimkoff and Russell Middleton (1960). Their aim was to test the hypothesis that family type is a function of the type of economy a society has. By using ethnographic data from over 500 societies, they examined whether the nuclear family (the family type based on husband-wife relationship and the kind we generally have in the United States) and the extended family (a family type based on blood ties and including more than one generation) were associated with different kinds of economies. They found that this was indeed true. Extended families are found more frequently in fishing and agricultural societies, and the nuclear family is associated with hunting societies. After discovering the important relations between several parts of a culture using cross-cultural comparison, the anthropologist then tries to account for why these relationships exist.

From a historical perspective, anthropological approaches to culture are somewhat like the seven blind men trying to describe the elephant. The one who caught the tail described the elephant as a rope, the one who caught the leg described the elephant as a tree, and so on. Anthropologists have approached culture from a number of different perspectives and have defined it in terms of what they think is most important to say about it. All the different approaches have something to contribute to our understanding of the human experience. Although at present there is a major division in the field between anthropologists who view culture as a system of ideas or symbols and those who emphasize the material basis of sociocultural systems, there are also attempts to integrate these two points of view. Unlike the seven blind men describing the elephant, anthropologists work with their eyes open: Human culture is a system and it is the understanding of this system in all its aspects that is the aim of anthropology as a discipline.

SUMMARY

1. For the anthropologist, culture is the major explanation of differences between human groups. Cultural anthropology is the systematic investigation of culture in both its general and specific forms.

2. A scientific theory is a general idea that attempts to explain the interrelationships among phenomena. Because theory in cultural anthropology attempts to explain the interrelationships in sociocultural phenom-

ena, it is most often classed with the social sciences.

3. Classic evolutionary theory attempted to uncover the origin and laws of development of culture. It viewed culture in terms of a uniform evolutionary process: the gradual emergence of new forms from previous ones followed the same sequence throughout the world. Cultural similarities were explained by independent invention, which rested

on the assumption of psychic unity, the idea that all humankind had the same mental capacities and would invent similar solutions when faced with similar problems.

4. Diffusion theory attempted to account for cultural similarities by the spread of culture traits from one society to another through historical contact.

5. The American historical tradition, led by Franz Boas, was first interested in diffusion and then turned to the study of whole cultures. Boas insisted on the study of particular cultures in their historical and psychological context as the first step toward finding general laws of culture.

6. Ruth Benedict, a student of Boas, tried to characterize whole cultures in terms of unique psychological configurations. She saw each culture as an interwoven pattern of traits, dominated by a particular ethos or theme.

7. In Europe, functionalist theory was developing from the study of whole societies. Bronislaw Malinowski's functional theory saw culture as functioning to meet the needs of individuals in society.

8. The structural functionalist theory of Radcliffe-Brown stressed the contribution that different parts of a social system make to the maintenance of the total society.

9. Between 1920 and 1950, anthropologists developed culture and personality studies. These attempted to understand the influence of culture on both normal and abnormal personality. At first done in small, traditional societies, these studies were expanded by the 1940s to national character studies. After 1950, such studies were more oriented toward an ecological approach to personality, and also used more sophisticated methodology, especially statistical analysis of ethnographic data from many societies.

10. Cognitive anthropology views culture as a blueprint for behavior, rather than behavior itself; symbolic anthropology emphasizes culture as a system of shared symbols and meanings.

11. Cultural ecologists are primarily interested in culture (or sociocultural systems) as systems of socially transmitted behavior that serve to connect human communities to their ecological settings.

12. Anthropologists may do ethnography to grasp the entire cultural pattern of a society, or to provide data on a more specific theoretical problem.

13. Some anthropologists examine theoretical problems by comparing ethnographic data from a large number of societies using controlled cross-cultural comparison.

14. Although there is a major difference between anthropologists who view culture as a system of ideas and those who emphasize its material base, each perspective makes a contribution to our understanding of the human experience.

SUGGESTED READINGS

Benedict, Ruth
1961   *Patterns of Culture.* Boston: Houghton Mifflin (orig. 1934). The presentation of the theory of cultural configurations, with a dètailed account of three different cultures. A best seller in its time.

Harris, Marvin
1974   *Cows, Pigs, Wars and Witches: The Riddle of Culture.* New York: Random House. A witty, fascinating look at such diverse topics as food prohibitions, warfare, messianic cults, and the counterculture in the United States from the standpoint of cultural materialism.

Kardiner, Abram, and Preble, Edward
1961   *They Studied Man.* New York: New American Library. Essays on the personalities and professional contributions of the most important social scientists of our century.

Netting, Robert McC.
1977   *Cultural Ecology.* Menlo Park, Calif.: Cummings. An excellent short book that looks at some classic ethnographic data from the standpoint of cultural ecology.

Spradley, James
1970   *You Owe Yourself a Drunk.* Boston: Little, Brown. A cognitive approach to the study of men arrested for public drunkenness in Seattle, Washington.

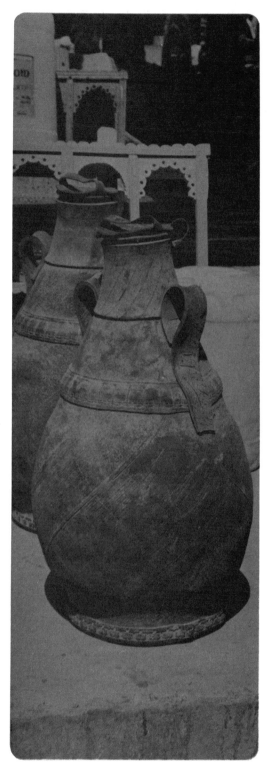

Joan Gregg

3
The Culture Concept

CULTURE IS LEARNED

Culture is learned through social interaction with other people in society. Humans, more than any other animal, depend on the social transmission of knowledge for survival. The learning processes through which human cultural traditions are passed on from one generation to another are called **socialization.** The difficulty in seeing the importance of learning in human behavior is that much of what is learned is not consciously taught, nor are we consciously aware of learning it. Culturally distinct ways of thinking, behaving, feeling, responding, become habitual very early in life. That is why much of what humans learn comes to seem "natural."

The importance of learning for humans is related to the prolonged dependency of the human infant and child. Although our complex brain gives us the capacity for learning, it also means that we develop more slowly and need the support of others in order to survive. Human social organization and group living thus provide the basic context in which we can learn from others at the same time that we are being protected by them. Although humans share this interrelated set of characteristics (a high capacity for learning, prolonged dependency, and group living) with other primates, no other species has as great a capacity for learning. And no other animal species depends so much on learned behavior for its adaptation to the environment.

The dependency of the human infant on human social organization provides the basic context in which human infants can learn from others at the same time they are protected by them. (United Nations)

CULTURE IS SHARED

To be considered part of culture, a way of thinking or interacting must be shared among a group of people. Some cultural patterns are shared by all people in a society. Societies in which important beliefs, values, and customs are shared by almost everyone are said to be homogeneous. Although anthropologists are now discovering that even small, traditional societies are less homogeneous than was previously believed, it is in the large, heterogeneous societies that discovering the degree of shared beliefs, values, and practices really becomes a problem. In heterogeneous societies, written law may be a useful guide to the most widely shared cultural traits.

One universally shared cultural pattern in the United States is driving a car on the right side of the road. This custom is not simply the result of law, but is built into our response system. Another cultural universal in the United States is our system of weights and measures. Here again, although this pattern is supported by formal teaching and law, it is a way of giving shape to the physical universe that is basic to the way we perceive the world.

Cultural Specialization

Some cultural patterns are shared only by people in certain social positions, or **statuses.** In most societies, for example, there is some cultural specialization between men and women. This specialization derives not only from the sexual division of labor, in which men customarily do different things than women, but also from cultural prohibitions on the kinds of activities women are allowed to engage in. Among the Arapesh of New Guinea, for example, women are not allowed to join the *tamberan* cult because the tamberan is the supernatural patron of adult men. Not only are women not permitted to see the tamberan, but they are not even allowed to think about what he might look like or the meaning of the activities that accompany his entry into the village. Margaret Mead, who studied the Arapesh, notes that the intellectual passivity women must accept regarding the tamberan soon becomes a habit. All that is "strange, uncharted and unnamed" becomes unfamiliar to them. This not only cuts women off from speculative thinking on many subjects, but also "from art, because among the Arapesh art and the supernatural are part and parcel of each other" (Mead 1963). Thus, intellec-

The celebration of Halloween is a part of children's culture in the United States. Losing its original religious meaning, this holiday has become an opportunity for the promotion of popular, contemporary culture heroes. (Serena Nanda)

tual and creative activity becomes a male cultural specialization.

Age is also a universal criterion of cultural specialization, though in most societies age specialization is not nearly as important as it is in the United States. In our own society, the degree to which cultural specialties—in language, music, and behavior—are associated with people between the ages of 12 and 20 has led to the label "youth culture" (Schwartz 1972).

Some occupational specialties exist in most societies. These cultural specialties are most often of a ritual kind. In some societies, they may be learned by anyone who wishes to engage in ritual activity and who seems to be successful at it. In others, ritual specialization may be limited to a few men or women who must first serve a long apprenticeship or join a secret association to learn ritual techniques and handle sacred materials. In India, most occupations are specialties of certain groups called castes, and only persons born into a particular caste may practice its traditional occupational specialty.

Subcultures

A **subculture** is a system of perceptions, values, beliefs, and customs that are significantly different from those of the dominant culture. Modern nations may contain many subcultures—based on region, religion, occupation, social class, ethnicity, or life style. One distinct subculture in the United States is the Old Order Amish, who number about 60,000 people and live mainly as farmers in the states of Pennsylvania, Ohio, and Indiana.

Amish religious beliefs require a simple life in a church community away from other influences. Their culture emphasizes learning through doing, a life of "goodness," the welfare of the community rather than individual competition, and separation from contemporary society. The Amish reject television, telephones, automobiles, radios, and other modern conveniences. Their distinctive dress and speech and their habits of manual work are symbolic of their cultural separateness and also contribute to the integration of the community. As an extension of their religious beliefs, the Amish reject formal education beyond elementary schooling. They believe this will alienate their children from Amish culture and remove them from the community at a time when they must take up important responsibilities.

The refusal to send their children for higher education has brought the Amish into conflict with the larger society. In the 1960s a school district administrator for the Wisconsin public schools brought suit against several Amish individuals for failing to obey the compulsory school attendance law, which requires children to attend public or private school until the age of 16. This case was later brought up to the Supreme Court of the United States (*Wisconsin* v. *Yoder* 1972). John Hostetler, an anthropologist who is an expert on Amish culture, testified for the defense. He held that formal higher education was not only in conflict with Amish religious beliefs, but would have negative effects on the integration of Amish culture and society. Impressed with Hostetler's argument, the Supreme Court decided that the school attendance law did interfere with the free exercise of religion in this case. Although the Amish were successful in this instance, it is only by constant efforts to isolate themselves from the larger society that they have been able to maintain their distinctive way of life.

The degree to which subcultural variation is allowed to flourish differs from society to society and depends to some degree on the values and behavior patterns of the subculture. The success of the Amish in preserving their culture is due partly to the fact that many of their values—thrift, hard work, honesty, and the importance of family and community life—are also values in the larger culture. They are also a nonviolent people who rarely come into conflict with the law. When subcultural values and customs are in opposition to those of the dominant culture, they may be suppressed, as was the case with polygyny (one man having more than one wife) among the Mormon community in the United States.

Individual Variation and Culture

Anthropology, because of its focus on what is typical of human groups, often leaves us with the impression that there is little or no choice or individual variation from cultural norms. Although it is true that culture affects every aspect of an individual's life, every culture allows some variation in behavior. As you participate in your anthropology class, you may be sitting with your legs crossed, your elbows on the table, your head in your hands, or your chair tilted back. Your eyes may be focused on the teacher, or on some of the other students. You may even have your eyes closed occasionally, a permissible alternative to keeping your eyes open because it can give the appearance of deep thought rather than sleep. You may hold a pencil in your hand, or take notes, or even doodle. All these behavioral variations are within the culturally acceptable limits for participation in an American college classroom. It is less likely that you will be knitting, taking apart your watch, or reading a newspaper. And it is completely unlikely that you will be standing on your chair, with your back to the teacher, whistling "I'm a Yankee Doodle Dandy."

Even in small, homogeneous societies, there is some scope for individual decision-making, for individual variation, and for creativity. Some of these societies are even described as highly individualistic. Among the Kamba of East Africa, for example, there is a "looseness" to the cultural pattern that allows for much individual choice. Many of the rules of Kamba culture are left open-ended; the individual is expected to make his/her own interpretation of "right action" (Oliver 1965). But however "loose" the cultural pattern, every culture puts limits on what it considers acceptable in a particular situation. When people share the same culture, they share an understanding of the range of variation the culture permits in different situations. Most people act within these limits without even thinking about it. It is only when the limits are overstepped that we become aware of them. We know limits have been reached when behavior calls forth censure. Expressions of disapproval may range from ridicule or avoidance, to publicly expressed criticism and legal proceedings.

CULTURE AS REAL AND IDEAL

Anthropologists have most often been concerned with culture as a system of **ideal norms.** Ideal norms are the ideas a society has about what *ought* to be done and the ways in which behavior *ought* to be carried out. A simple example of an ideal norm is the expectation in the United States that when two adult males are introduced to each other, they will shake hands.

Behavioral norms are what people actually do. These are only sometimes consistent with ideal norms. Thus, most men in the United States probably do shake hands when they are introduced. Other behavioral norms are not consistent with ideal norms. The Kinsey Report (1948) indicated that in such areas as extramarital sex and homosexual experience, there was a considerable gap between what people did and the ideal norms.

Deviance from ideal norms does not happen only in heterogeneous societies. In describing the sexual behavior of the Trobriand Islanders, Malinowski (1929) wrote:

From the statements of informants, you will arrive at a conclusion that marriage and sexual intercourse within the clan are neither allowed nor ever practiced and that they do not even constitute a serious temptation to the native. . . . It would be most improper and censured by an indignant public opinion. If discovered [a guilty couple] would commit suicide by jumping from a coconut palm.

Clan incest among the Trobrianders is not punished simply by public censure. There is a supernatural punishment as well, a disease in which the belly of the victim begins to swell, the skin becomes white and breaks out into sores, and the person fades away with a wasting sickness. Several people with this disease were pointed out to Malinowski. After questioning his informants, however, Malinowski discovered that cases of clan incest do occur. Furthermore, it was common knowledge that a particular magical ritual performed over a wild ginger root wrapped up in leaves would neutralize the supernatural punishment for this kind of behavior.

Two points emerge from Malinowski's findings. The first is that an understanding of a society cannot be based solely on informants' statements about ideal cultural norms. Malinowski argues that people in all societies are embarrassed to admit that behavior deviates from the ideal. In order to maintain their prestige, they will not easily disclose evidence of nonconformity. Second, this example illustrates that a body of behavioral norms develops as a way of evading the ideal norms. "Everyone knows" about the magic ritual to evade the supernatural sanctions for incest in the Trobriand Islands. Every society is apparently willing to pretend ignorance of certain kinds of deviance. But ideal norms do exert pressure on behavior, even when they are not formally and legally expressed. Culture, as a system of ideal norms, meanings, and expectations, does limit human behavior both by channeling it in culturally approved directions and by punishing known violations.

The Relationship between Ideal and Behavioral Norms

Both ideal and behavioral norms change. Ideal norms may change before behavioral

The plains Indian Chief represented the high ideals of bravery, wisdom, and generosity. Shown here is the Cheyenne Chief, Brave Bear. (Courtesy of the American Museum of Natural History)

norms. Among the upper middle-class Hindus living in large cities in India, for example, the ideal of social equality among all classes of society is widely accepted. This ideal is considerably in advance of actual behavior, which only rarely involves social interaction between individuals of the highest and lowest castes on a basis of equality. In other cases, a change in ideal norms follows a change in behavioral norms. The contemporary American cultural ideal of small families followed the actual limiting of the number of children by parents who wanted to move up the social ladder.

Ideal norms themselves may be contradictory in a particular society, so that people can justify their behavior in terms of more than one norm. In describing the political system among the Soga of Uganda, Lloyd Fallers (1955) shows the conflict of two opposing ideal norms. In traditional Soga society, political institutions emphasized personal rights and obligations. A person owed loyalty to his own kinsman, patron, and local ruler. The administrative staff of the state was recruited through kinship and maintained through personal loyalty. With the coming of the British and the rise of a civil service bureaucracy, an opposing value system came into being. A bureaucracy should ideally treat everyone alike without regard to status or personal relationships. Recruitment to a bureaucracy is based on merit. Fallers emphasizes that both these ideal norms now are institutionalized and have legitimacy in Soga society. This results in many conflicts, particularly for chiefs, who are now pulled in the direction of one of the norms, now in the direction of the other.

Another way of explaining the relationship between ideal norms and real behavior is through the concept of anticipated behavior. Anticipations of deviance from the ideal come to be culturally standardized and help explain behavior patterns that seem contradictory and self-defeating. Elliot Liebow uses this concept to explain the failures in marital relationships among some poor black ghetto dwellers (1967). These men and women, he says, do believe in the ideal of a permanent, monogamous relationship. They get married with the same high hopes as everyone else in our culture. The women, however, based on their knowledge of the difficulty of life in the ghetto and the precariousness of jobs, *anticipate* that their husbands will not in fact be able to take care of them and their children. Therefore, at the first sign of difficulty they reject their mates in ways that make it difficult for the relationship to continue.

Ideal norms may also be unclear. This allows for a wide range of legitimate behaviors. In the United States, for example, an ideal norm is that one should be "a good mother" to her child. But this takes in a wide range of behavior, so patterns of mothering run from almost complete permissiveness to harsh discipline, and all are justified as being "for the good of the child."

Because culture is largely viewed as a limit on action, an individual's manipulation of the culture for personal ends has, until recently, been a neglected topic in cultural anthropology. All the ways in which behavioral norms do not mesh with ideal norms actually give a culture flexibility. They allow people to adjust behavior to changing circumstances. An example of manipulation of cultural norms for personal ends can be seen among upper middle-class women in India. One important Indian ideal is that women should be in the home and not "moving about" with their friends. Another cultural ideal is that women should spend a lot of time in religious activities. Modern Indian women use the second ideal to get around the first. By forming clubs whose activities are religious, they have an excuse to get out of the house that their elders cannot object to too strongly.

In our own society, we can easily see a similar flexibility in the gap between ideal and behavioral norms. The "little white lie" is a behavioral norm. It does not meet the ideal of "the truth, the whole truth, and nothing but the truth," but it is justified to spare the feelings of another person, or to hold on to information given in confidence, and so on. Although this gap between the ideal of total honesty and the necessity of "the little white lie" is functional under some circumstances, the Watergate scandal is a powerful reminder of what happens when ideal norms no longer have any bearing on actual behavior, and self-interest becomes the end that justifies any means.

CULTURAL INTEGRATION

A culture is not simply a list of norms, values, activities and objects. Cultural elements are interrelated to form a system. Although anthropological analysis may require that parts of a culture be studied separately, the idea of culture as "a complex whole," or system, is basic. One way of looking at **cultural integration** is in terms of the consistency of cultural themes or values. Most anthropologists agree that there is a tendency for a culture to be dominated by a particular value system or ideology, although most would also agree that no culture achieves complete integration. Cultures may have more than one dominant theme, and sometimes these themes (values, ethos) may be in conflict. According to Ruth Benedict, for example, the culture of the Plains Indians of North America was dominated by the theme of extravagant sensation-seeking and individualism. It took the forms of fasting and self-torture to seek supernatural visions through which a warrior acquired the power necessary for success in war. Other ethnographers pointed out, however, that there was a second theme in Plains culture, that of the "considerate peace chief" (Hoebel 1960). This theme emphasized gentleness, generosity, reasonableness, and wisdom, and called for self-restraint and consideration of others. These themes operated in different spheres of Plains life and provided a balance in the culture. It is clear that cultures can and do function with some disharmony and lack of integration, but this may be adaptive. A culture needs flexibility to respond to changes in the physical and social environment. On the other hand, too great a lack of integration in culture may impose intolerable stress on the individual.

The concept of cultural integration raises some interesting questions about American culture. Do we in fact have one theme that characterizes our culture? Or do different activities have different, even contradictory themes? Some anthropologists have pointed out the contradiction between our economic life, where the dominant theme is competition and the advance of the individual at the expense of others, and our family life, where the dominant theme would seem to be cooperation for the good of the *total* group. On the other hand, some anthropologists believe that all of American culture, and especially the family, is characterized by themes of deception, individual competition, and the

Fourth of July parades are an attempt to recapture an earlier era of United States history when ideals and dominant values appeared less ambiguous than they do today. (Ravinder Nanda)

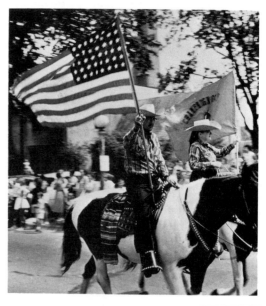

Adaptation is the way living populations relate to the environment so that they may survive and reproduce. Culture is the major way in which human populations relate to their environments. The most directly adaptive aspect of culture is the way in which the energy potential of the environment is transformed into food. The extent to which food-getting patterns are correlated with other aspects of the system is not agreed upon by anthropologists, although many would say that there is at least a tendency for such correlation: "Similar technologies applied to similar environments tend to produce similar arrangements of labor in production and distribution, and . . . these in turn call forth similar kinds of social groupings, which justify and coordinate their activities by means of similar systems of values and beliefs" (Harris, 1968:4). For example, the size of the effective social unit responds to the availability of food. Generally, agricultural populations have a higher density of population than hunters and gatherers. Since larger populations require more coordination of labor, agricultural societies tend to have more complex sociopolitical systems.

How the specific activities and institutions in which people are involved fit into the overall adaptive strategy of their society is based on the assumption that different types of food-getting patterns—hunting and gathering, pastoralism, horticulture, agriculture, and industrialization—make different demands on human beings and lead to the development of different kinds of family structure, political organization, religious beliefs and practices, and even patterns of personality (Cohen 1971).

An example of these functional interrelationships is the correlation presented in Chapter 2 between the nuclear family and hunting and gathering and industrial societies. Both types of strategies require geographical mobility, and the nuclear family allows for more mobility than the extended family. On the other hand, the *tendency* for functional integration may be just that; as we will see in Chapter 10, the extended family may be adaptive under certain conditions in contemporary urbanized society.

The view that culture is an adaptive system does not necessarily mean that every aspect of the system is adaptive. Some parts of a culture may be neutral, that is, they may contribute little or nothing to survival. Some parts may also be maladaptive, although it would seem that ultimately a maladaptive trait would be modified or die out altogether. Nor does the view of culture as an adaptive system mean that every system is the most efficient design for utilizing its environment. Existing sociocultural systems represent one possible solution out of a number of alternatives that might have been equally adaptive in the same environment.

The different ways in which parts of a sociocultural system contribute to the survival and reproductive success of a particular human community are not always apparent, as we saw in Harris' treatment of the adaptive value of the Hindu taboo on beef. If we keep in mind the fact that not every element of a culture can be explained in terms of its adaptive value, we will see how the perspective of culture as an adaptive system helps make sense of patterns that seem useless, odd, cruel, and irrational.

desire to control others in our own self-interest (Henry 1963). The opposition of values—equality and inequality, democracy and hierarchy, individualism and conformity—seems to appear as a theme in much of United States social, political, and economic history. Each new generation swings from an emphasis on one of these value opposites to the other.

CULTURE CHANGES

The view of culture as an adaptive system emphasizes stability rather than change. The technologically simpler societies traditionally studied by anthropologists have generally, it is true, been relatively stable. Their designs for living permitted relatively satisfactory adaptations to the sociophysical environment; changes occurred very slowly until the period of contact with the West. Archeologists have been able to document cultural patterns that exhibit stability over thousands of years both in their broad outlines and in some of their details.

And yet, we know that all cultures do change in response to the changing requirements of the environment. Some of the changes in a culture are not adaptive, and the archeological record is full of cultures that collapsed and disappeared. Still other kinds of changes lead sociocultural systems into more efficient stages of energy transformation and greater complexity. These major kinds of changes the anthropologist calls evolutionary changes. Regardless of whether we look at change with an evolutionary or a historical perspective, we know that because culture is a system, change in one aspect will lead to change in other aspects. In Chapter 15 we will look at some of the ways in which cultures change as they come into contact with the modern industrialized nations of the West. Here we will focus on the two major processes by which all cultures change, innovation and diffusion.

Innovation

An **innovation** is a variation on a preexisting cultural pattern that is then accepted or learned by other members of the society. Most innovations are slight modifications of already existing habits of thought and action. Although each individual innovation may be slight, however, the accumulated effects may be great over the long run. An innovation can be the result of deliberate experimentation, or it can come about by accident, as in the following case of style change in the pottery of the Pueblo Indians of North America.*

Pueblo Indian women had been making pottery for some fourteen hundred years, and the traditional color of Pueblo pottery was red. Around the turn of the century the making of pottery began to die out and an anthropologist named Kenneth Chapman decided to try to revive this traditional craft. Chapman chose to promote the work of a woman named Maria, who came from the village of San Ildefonso and was considered the best of the Pueblo potters. In the conservative tradition of Pueblo pottery making, Maria made only red pots. One day, by accident, two of Maria's pots turned black. When a Santa Fe storekeeper ran out of her red pots, she gave him two "spoiled" black ones, which sold very quickly. The white people to whom Maria's pots were sold had no tradition about the color of pottery. As long as the pots were smooth and well made, with a symmetrical design, they were satisfied.

* Based on Edward Hall, *The Silent Language*. Greenwich, Conn.: Fawcett, 1959.

An innovation is a variation on an established cultural practice. Pictured are storage jars from Morocco made in the traditional centuries old shape but using worn out rubber tires instead of clay. (Joan Gregg)

Since Maria understood how her accidental innovation had come about, she taught the technique to the rest of the potters in her village. The black pots had a market, so the other women soon followed Maria's example. Today the village of San Ildefonso is associated with black rather than red pottery. As a result of this success, the Pueblo craftspeople were more willing to experiment. They used other new pottery designs and finishes and even moved into the making of silver jewelry, which was not a traditional Pueblo craft at all.

An innovation means a slight modification of an existing cultural pattern; an **invention** is the combination of existing cultural elements into something altogether new. Although we are likely to think of inventions as primarily technological, invention is not limited to the material aspects of culture. New art forms and new ideas may all be considered inventions. All inventions involve human ingenuity and creativity, but even the genius is limited in what he/she can invent by the nature and complexity of the preexisting cultural pattern. Had Einstein been born into a society which had not developed the complex scientific understandings of Western civilization, he could never have "invented" the theory of relativity. Each "genius" in a culture builds on what has gone before and moves in the direction of expanding an existing tradition. Even Beethoven, Bach, and Mozart did not compose with the musical scale of India.

Because inventions depend on the recombination of previously existing cultural elements, the more elements already present in a culture, the more likely it is to produce even more inventions. This partly explains why change occurs much faster in technologically complex societies than in technologically simpler ones. This cumulative effect of change also applies to human

CULTURAL INTEGRATION AND CULTURE CHANGE

Because culture is a system, change in one aspect of culture will lead to change in other aspects, whether the initial change was introduced from within the society itself or through borrowing from another culture. Some cultures can handle more change from the outside than others. If a culture is tightly integrated, the introduction of even a seemingly small change can lead to a total breakdown. One example of this is the Yir Yiront of Australia.*

The Yir Yiront were an aboriginal hunting and fishing people who had not learned the use of metal. They had used stone axes until the introduction of steel axes by Western missionaries. The stone axes had been used in a variety of ways: for gathering firewood, making tools and weapons, gathering wild honey, and also for fashioning objects for religious purposes. The ax handles were made by men, and all normal men were competent to produce their own since it was not a difficult or complex task. The ax heads were obtained by trade through long-established relations with trading partners in other tribes. Although women and children used axes in a variety of tasks, the ax "belonged" to the man who made it, and a man's wife and children had to ask his permission to use it and return it quickly. A man had to ask permission to borrow an ax from an elder kinsman. Thus, the use of the stone ax helped define status relations among various members of the tribe. Women borrowed from men, the young borrowed from their elders. The missionaries, on the other hand, distributed the steel axes to younger men, women, and even children who won their favor. One significant result of this was the undermining of the status hierarchy of Yir Yiront society, as expressed in the subordination of women to men and younger people to older ones. Another result was the loss of interest in trading ax heads. Traditional trading relationships, which were an important integrating mechanism for Australian tribal society, also broke down and the festivities and communal visiting that accompanied trading lost value. The final result of the introduction of the steel ax was the almost total disintegration of Yir Yiront culture.

*Lauriston Sharp, "Steel Axes for Stone Age Australians," in Edward H. Spicer, ed., Human Problems in Technological Change. New York: Russell Sage Foundation, 1952.

culture as a whole. It took several million years for humans to change from hunters and gatherers to agricultural producers. After the first domestication of plants and animals about ten or twelve thousand years ago, it took about five or six thousand years for writing and cities to be invented. All the other technological knowledge, and the social complexity that came with that knowledge, has been learned in the past few thousand years and involves a rate of change unlike anything know earlier.

Diffusion

As we saw in Chapter 2, anthropologists have always been interested in discovering whether the similarities among different sociocultural systems were due to independent invention or to **diffusion,** the borrowing of cultural elements. Many anthropologists would agree that genuine independent invention accounts for only a small percentage of cultural change. The growth and development of human culture is primarily accounted for by the spread of the most important inventions from one or perhaps two centers of origin. Because diffusion is so important in cultural change, the rate of change is much slower in societies that are geographically isolated.

Diffusion, however, does not automatically result from contact. Borrowing takes place only if the borrowed element proves rewarding in some way. Furthermore, once accepted, a borrowed element may undergo many changes as it is worked into the preexisting cultural pattern. In the process called **stimulus diffusion,** only the general idea of an alien trait is borrowed, while the specific form is a local invention. An example of stimulus diffusion is the Cherokee syllabary, a writing system invented by Sequoyah, the famous Cherokee Indian chief. Although he was an illiterate man, Sequoyah came to the conclusion that the writing of the white men would be a useful skill for his own people. He invented a system that gave syllabic values to alphabet letters and typographical signs arbitrarily chosen and arranged from English and German type.

ANTHROPOLOGICAL APPROACHES TO CULTURE CHANGE

Anthropologists do not always agree on the ways to approach the study of culture change. In the historical approach, the focus is on the changes that occur in a particular society as a result of a particular, historical event—for example, the coming of the European missionaries to the Yir Yiront territory and the introduction of the steel ax. The evolutionary approach

Culture changes, but some cultures, because of their central location, change faster than others. Twenty-five hundred years of culture change is shown in this view of Athens, Greece.
(Ravinder Nanda)

looks for regularities in culture change that may indicate laws underlying the process or processes of cultural development. In Chapter 2, we discussed some evolutionary approaches to culture change.

Nor do anthropologists agree on what is the "prime mover" in cultural change. Does change originate in values and ideology, or in the material conditions of life, particularly subsistence economy and technology? Changes in technology, as we have just seen, have a major impact on the transformation of the social and cultural aspects of human life. Values and ideology can also be a source of changes in technology if people are motivated by new ways of thinking to find new ways of relating to the environment. Between the extreme views is a middle ground which holds that no single factor is of overriding importance in determining the organization and content of a given sociocultural system. In this view, culture change is a result of a cumulative feedback relationship between ecological stimuli, ideology, technology, and social relationships.

SUMMARY

1. Culture is learned—that is, it is transmitted socially, not genetically. The importance of learning in human adaptation is related to the long dependency of the human infant and the group life of our species.

2. Culture is shared behavior, but not all aspects of culture are shared equally within a society. Some are shared by all adults, others are the specialties of certain groups or social categories. In every culture a range of individual variation is permitted in any particular situation.

3. A subculture is a cultural pattern significantly different from that of the surrounding culture. The Amish are an example of a subculture in the United States.

4. Culture consists of both ideal and behavioral norms. Ideal norms are what people think they ought to do; behavioral norms are what people actually do. Both ideal and behavioral norms are patterned by culture.

5. The relation between ideal and behavioral norms is complex. In some cases they correspond; in other cases, the behavioral norms deviate from the ideal. Sometimes behavioral norms change, and this leads to a change in ideal norms. Sometimes ideal norms change first, leading to a change in behavioral norms.

6. Ambiguity or even conflict between ideal norms gives a culture flexibility; individuals can manipulate ideal norms for their own personal ends. But conflict between ideal norms can also put stress on the individual.

7. Culture is adaptive. In the general sense, this means that socially transmitted knowledge is the major adaptive mechanism of the human species. In the specific sense, it means that each culture is a design for living which enables a group of people to survive and reproduce themselves in a particular environment.

8. Culture tends to be integrated. The basic social institutions of a society tend to fit together, and the values underlying cultural patterns tend to be consistent. The integration of cul-

ture is a tendency; no culture is perfectly integrated.

9. Culture exhibits both stability and change. Because culture is a system, a change in one part of the culture leads to change and adjustment in other parts. The rate of change is different in different societies; it depends partly on geographical factors, level of technology, and cultural values regarding change.

10. Two important processes in cultural change are innovation and diffusion.

11. Diffusion is not an automatic process, and borrowed traits are integrated into preexisting cultural patterns. They are not adopted as is.

12. Anthropologists do not agree on whether ideology or technology is the most important element in change. A middle view holds that culture change is due to a complex interaction among the environment, ideology, and technology, acting so that changes in one area feed back and cause changes in the others.

SUGGESTED READINGS

Lee, Dorothy
  1959   *Freedom and Culture.* Englewood Cliffs, N.J.: Prentice-Hall. A provocative series of articles (that range from easily readable to difficult) dealing with the ideational aspects of culture.

Liebow, Elliot
  1967   *Tally's Corner.* Boston: Little, Brown. An ethnography of Negro street-corner men that highlights the contradictions between ideal and behavioral norms in American society.

Sahlins, Marshall D. and Service, Elman R.
  1973   *Evolution and Culture.* Ann Arbor: University of Michigan Press. A short but important statement of general and specific cultural evolutionary theory.

Shapiro, Harry, ed.
  1971   *Man, Culture, and Society.* London: Oxford University Press. (rev. edition.) A collection of articles on various aspects of culture, suitable for the beginning student.

Spradley, James P. and Rynkiewich, Michael A.
  1975   *The Nacirema.* Boston: Little, Brown. A book of readings on American culture.

I have on my table a violin string. It is free. I twist one end of it and it responds. It is free. But it is not free to do what a violin string is supposed to do—to produce music. So I take it, fix it in my violin and tighten it until it is taut. Only then is it free to be a violin string.

—Sir Rabindranath Tagore

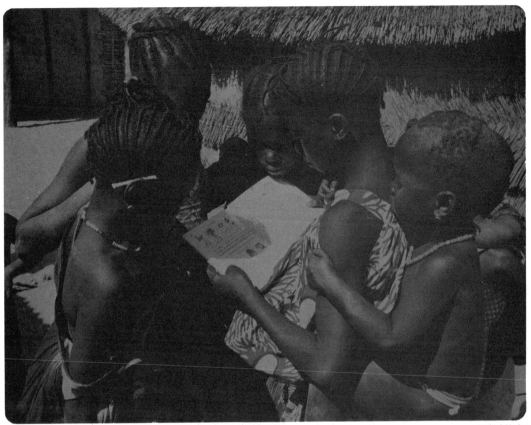

4
The Cultural Context of Human Behavior

Culture is necessary for the survival and existence of human beings as human beings. Practically everything humans perceive, know, think, value, feel, and do is learned through participation in a sociocultural system. The few well-documented cases on record of children relatively isolated from society in the early years of life bear out this statement.

One of these cases, that of the "wild boy of Aveyron" (Itard 1962) is of exceptional interest. In 1799, a boy of about 12 was captured in a forest in Aveyron, France. He was brought to Paris, where he attracted huge crowds who expected to see the "noble savage" of the romantic eighteenth-century philosophical vision. Instead, they found a boy whose

> . . . eyes were unsteady, expressionless, wandering vaguely from one object to another . . . so little trained by the sense of touch, they could never distinguish an object in relief from one in a picture. His . . . hearing was insensible to the loudest noises and to . . . music. His voice was reduced to a state of complete muteness and only a uniform gutteral sound escaped him . . . he was equally indifferent to the odor of perfume and to the fetid exhalation of the dirt with which his bed was filled . . . [his] touch was restricted to the mechanical grasping of an object . . . [he had a] tendency to trot and gallop . . . [and] an obstinate habit of smelling at anything given to him . . . he chewed like a rodent with a sudden action of the incisors . . . [and] showed no sensitivity to cold or heat and could seize hot coals from the fire without flinching or lay half naked upon the wet ground for hours in the wintertime. . . . He was

incapable of attention and spent his time apathetically rocking himself backwards and forwards like the animals in the zoo.*

This description of the "wild boy of Aveyron" is provided by Jean-Marc-Gaspard Itard, a young psychologist who undertook the education of the boy, whom he called Victor. He believed Victor's apparent subnormality was not due to incurable mental disease or idiocy, but to the lack of participation in normal human society. Itard's account of Victor's education makes fascinating reading. Beyond that, it emphasizes that the human potential can be realized only within the structure of human culture and through growing up in close contact with other human beings. Without the constraints imposed by a specific culture, we are not more free, but rather totally unfree, in that none of our human qualities and abilities can develop.

CULTURAL PATTERNING OF "REALITY"

The ways in which human beings perceive both the physical and social environment, what they believe to be true about the environment, and how they organize their responses to it are all patterned by culture. Culture is a "codification of reality," a system of meaning that transforms physical reality, what is *there*, into experienced reality. Dorothy Lee (1959), an anthropologist interested in the different ways peoples see themselves and their environments, describes her perception of reality as she looks out the window of her house: "I see

*Jean-Marc-Gaspard Itard, *The Wild Boy of Aveyron.* Translated by George and Muriel Humphrey. © 1962, Prentice-Hall, Inc., Englewood Cliffs, New Jersey. Reprinted by permission of the publisher.

trees, some of which I like to be there, and some of which I intend to cut down to keep them from encroaching further upon the small clearing I made for my house." She then describes the perception of the Dakota Black Elk Indian, who "saw trees as having rights to the land, equal to his own . . . standing peoples, in whom the winged ones built their lodges and reared their families."

According to Lee, the conceptual frameworks of different cultures provide different ways of perceiving the same physical reality. Lee believes that all culturally patterned views of reality may contain a different facet of the same truth. These culturally different conceptions of reality also shape our perception of the relationship we have with the natural environment. Thus, continues Lee, "the breaking of the soil in the agricultural process may be an act of violence, of personal aggression, of mastery, of exploitation, of self-fulfillment; or it may be an act of tender fostering, of involvement in the processes of the earth, of helping the land to bring forth in its due time; it may be an act of worship, and the field an altar." The individual may be seen as the center, the mover and master of nature, as in Western culture. Or he/she may be seen as in harmony with nature, simply actualizing the potential in both animals and inanimate things, as is true among many native American peoples.

Not only the perceptions of reality, but proving those perceptions to be "real" is culturally patterned. In many cultures, inner experience can be enough. In Western culture, validation consists of "proof," evidence that can hold up under repeated and objective investigations. The contrasts between these two systems is nicely illustrated in an exchange between Carlos Castaneda, a Western-trained anthropologist,

and Don Juan, a "sorcerer," or in his own words, a "man of power" among the Yaqui Indians of northern Mexico. Castaneda has been learning Don Juan's "power," which includes the ability to transform himself into various animals. One day Don Juan says that under his commands, Castaneda will be transformed into a crow. These are Castaneda's words about the experience:

I had no difficulty eliciting the corresponding sensation to each one of his commands. I had the perception of growing bird's legs, which were weak and wobbly at first. I felt a tail coming out of the back of my neck and wings out of my cheekbones. The wings were folded deeply. I felt them coming by degrees. The process was hard but not painful. Then I winked my head down to the size of a crow. But the most astonishing effect was accomplished by my bird's eyes. My bird's sight! When Don Juan directed me to grow a beak, I had an annoying sensation of lack of air. Then something bulged out and created a block in front of me . . . I remember I extended my wings and flew. I felt alone, cutting through the air, painfully moving straight ahead . . . the last scene I remembered was three silvery birds . . . I liked them. We flew together.*

A few days after this experience, Castaneda asks Don Juan "the unavoidable question: did I really become a crow?" And what we mean in Western culture by "really" is explained in Castaneda's next question: "I mean would anyone seeing me

* Carlos Castaneda, *The Teachings of Don Juan: a Yaqui Way of Knowledge*. Berkeley: University of California Press, 1968, pp. 122–124. Reprinted by permission.

have thought I was an ordinary crow?" Modern science, which is the core of the Western validation of reality, teaches us to distrust our inner experience as a source of knowledge. We frequently label people whose inner experiences seem "real" as abnormal, if those experiences do not match our own culturally patterned definitions of reality.

Cultural Patterning of Time

In his book *The Silent Language* (1959), the anthropologist Edward Hall presented the theory that perceptions of time and space are different in different cultures, and that these perceptions are culturally patterned. Hall called these dimensions of culture "out of awareness" because most people are not conscious of having learned them. In one sense, of course, many aspects of culture are out of awareness. Perceptions of time and space, however, are among the most ingrained of culturally patterned behaviors.

"Time is human; nature knows only change." Telling time is a strictly human invention. Although all cultures have some system of keeping time, in Western industrial societies time is kept track of in what seems to other peoples an almost ridiculous fashion. We calculate not only the seasons, but the years, months, weeks, days, hours, minutes, seconds, and even thousandths of a second. We are very concerned in the United States with being *on time;* we don't like to *waste time* by having to wait for someone who is late, and we like to *spend time* wisely by keeping busy. All this sounds very natural to a North American. In fact, we think, how could it be otherwise? It is difficult for us not to get irritated by the seeming carelessness about time in other cultures, where individuals frequently turn up an hour or more late for an appointment. But "being late" is at least within our cultural framework. How can we begin to enter the cultural world of the Sioux Indians, where there is no word for "late" or for

Among Zen Buddhists the inner experiencing of reality is achieved through meditation. (Sheldon Brody)

"waiting." The fact is, of course, we have not had to enter the Sioux culture, but the Sioux have had to enter ours! It is only when we participate in other cultures, on their terms, that we begin to see the cultural patterning of time.

North Americans have a sense of time that is oriented toward the future—not an infinite future, but the foreseeable future. We look back at the past only to measure how far we have come in the present, and look at the present as a stepping stone to future accomplishments. The Navajo, in contrast, look skeptically at the promise of benefits in even the foreseeable future. The future among Hindus is conceived of in terms of more than a lifetime; it extends infinitely through many births and rebirths.

Cultural Patterning of Space

Like time, space is organized somewhat differently according to different cultural patterns. Because North Americans are taught to perceive and react to the arrangement of objects, we think of space as "empty." The Japanese, however, are trained to give meaning to spaces. Their perception of shape and arrangement of what is to us emptiness appears in many aspects of Japanese life. There seems to be a similarity between culturally patterned perceptions of time and of space. Just as North Americans think of time as being "wasted" unless one is doing something, so we think of space as wasted if it is not filled up with objects.

The cultural patterning of space can be seen in the arrangements of urban space in different cultures. In the United States, most of our cities are laid out along a grid, with the axes generally north-south and east-west. Streets are numbered in order and buildings are numbered the same way.

This arrangement makes perfect sense to us. A city like Paris, which is laid out with the main streets radiating from centers, can be confusing for those who are used to the grid pattern. We tend to "get lost" easily, because walking a relatively short distance in the wrong direction leads us much farther from where we want to go than is true with a grid system. Hall suggests that the layout of space that is characteristic of French cities is only one aspect of the theme of centralization which permeates French culture. Paris is the center of France, French government and educational systems are highly centralized, and in French offices the most important person has the desk in the middle of the office.

Another aspect of cultural patterning of space has to do with the functions of spaces. In middle-class America, we have particular spaces for particular activities. Any intrusion of one activity into a space it was not designed for is immediately felt to be inappropriate. In Japan, this is not the case. Walls are movable, and rooms are used for one purpose during the day and another in the evening and at night. In India, there is yet another culturally patterned use of space. Space in India, both in public and in private places, is connected with concepts of superiority and inferiority. In Indian cities and villages, and even within the home, certain spaces are designated as polluted or inferior because of the activities that take place there and the kinds of people who use them. Spaces are segregated so that high caste and low caste, male and female, sacred and secular activities are kept apart. Archeological evidence uncovered in ancient Indian cities indicates that this pattern may be thousands of years old. It is remarkably persistent even in modern India, where Western influence is strong. Ruth Freed, for example, found this in her study of Chandigarh, a city in North India (1977).

Chandigarh is a modern city designed by the French architect Le Courbusier. Its apartments were built according to European concepts, and the Indians living there found certain aspects of the design inconsistent with their previous use of living space. Freed found that Indian families modified their apartments in a number of ways. Curtains were put up so that men's and women's spaces would be separate. The families also continued to eat in the kitchen, a traditional pattern, and the living room-dining room was used only when Western guests were present. Traditional village living takes place in an area surrounded by a wall. The courtyard gives privacy to each residence group. Chandigarh apartments were built with large windows, reflecting the European desire for light and sun. Many families pasted paper over these windows to re-create the privacy of the traditional courtyard. Freed suggests that the traditional Indian patterns of space use may represent an adaptation to a densely populated environment.

Anthropologists have proposed that culturally patterned perceptions of space may be adaptive in terms of the environment. In different cultures, people seem to need different amounts of what Hall calls "personal space." North Americans, for example, seem to require more distance between themselves and others in order to feel comfortable. People from the Arab countries and Latin America appear to want to stand closer to each other than is true for North Americans and peoples from Northern Europe. It is quite possible that these differences in the need for personal space are adapted to the different levels of population density in North America and Europe on the one hand, and in the Middle East and Latin America on the other. Whatever the reasons for the different experiences peoples have with space and time, these "out of awareness" cultural patterns are often a source of personal conflict and mutually negative stereotyping.

CULTURAL PATTERNING OF PERCEPTION AND COGNITION

Cognition refers to the ways in which human beings perceive, understand, and organize their responses to the environment. Interest in the relationships among culture, perception, and cognition has a long history in anthropology. Because they relied on the reports of travelers and missionaries, early scholars were mainly concerned with the *differences* in perception and thought between Europeans and the non-Western peoples they encountered. Some of these scholars attributed the differences to innate differences in mental processes. They characterized non-Western peoples as mentally deficient, childlike, incapable of abstract thinking, lacking ideas of causality, and unable to differentiate between reality and fantasy. By the turn of the twentieth century, however, anthropologists were arguing that there was a basic similarity in both mental and perceptual processes among all human groups.

It is generally taken for granted in modern cross-cultural research on perception and cognition that the uniformities outweigh whatever differences may be found. Given the common experiences with the physical world shared by all peoples, a strong case can be made that physically normal adults in every human society have the same fundamental perceptual abilities:

they can recognize familiar objects under varied conditions (object constancy), they have depth perception, and an ability to coordinate information from several sensory sources (intersensory integration) (Munroe and Munroe 1977:64). The most influential contemporary anthropologists and cross-cultural psychologists also hold that there is no evidence that different reasoning processes are characteristic of different cultures. That is, there is no evidence for a "primitive" mentality or logic.

As Michael Cole points out in his excellent survey of cross-cultural psychology, the thinking of Don Juan, the Yaqui sorcerer, seems quite different from our own style of thought. Yet in his interpersonal relations, Don Juan demonstrates problem-solving techniques "compelling enough" to greatly influence Castaneda (the anthropologist trained in Western scientific thinking) himself (Cole and Scribner 1974:169). Cole and the other contemporary anthropologists who believe basic thinking processes are the same among all humankind emphasize that all peoples employ logic, all are concerned with the relationship of cause and effect, and all classification systems are arrived at by the same processes of abstraction and generalization. It is the content of culture—values, beliefs, and ways of classifying the world—that differs among different human groups.

Culture and Perception

Research in anthropology and the new field of cross-cultural psychology has shown interesting differences in specific perceptual and cognitive abilities as well as basic similarities. One area of research has been on visual perception. Differences among cultures have been found for color differentiaion, susceptibility to optical illusions, and pictorial depth perception. It is possible that ability to differentiate color and susceptibility to an optical illusion have some physiological component. For example, the color-naming systems of cultures in tropical zones characteristically contain fewer names for different colors than in nontropical cultures. It may be that tropical cultures, which tend to be technologically simple, have no need for complex color-naming systems. Peoples of the tropics are also somewhat insensitive to blue color, however, and this may be the reason that names for these colors are not contained in their languages. A physiological component has also been suggested for the response to optical illusions (such as the one shown in Figure 4.1). The degree of pigmentation on the retina may affect ability to detect contours and thus susceptibility to illusions.

Figure 4.1 *The horizontal–vertical illusion. Although both lines are of the same size, the vertical line appears bigger to individuals susceptible to the illusion. Members of some cultures, such as the Arunta of Australia, appear to be extremely susceptible to this illusion; Westerners are moderately susceptible. It has been suggested that susceptibility to this illusion is related to the degree of open space characteristic of particular environments, such as the Australian desert in which the Arunta live.*

ECOLOGY, CULTURE, AND PERCEPTION

A comparison of two groups—the Temne, a horticultural tribe of Sierra Leone in Africa, and a group of Eskimo from Baffin Island who depend on hunting for their food supply—shows the influence of culture on perception. The Temne score relatively low on tests of spatial ability and differentiation. The Eskimo score extremely high, coming very close to a sample of Scottish subjects, which provided a Western population for comparison with these two non-Western groups. The explanation of these test scores is provided by comparing the cultural ecology of the Temne with that of the Eskimo.

The physical environment of the Temne is highly differentiated; it is full of colorful vegetation and is naturally structured. The Temne, as farmers, are not very mobile; they tend to "stay put" on their land. Given this particular ecological relationship, it is not necessary to develop spatial discrimination skills. The Eskimo are in a completely different position. Their physical environment consists of "endless, uniform, snowfields"; theirs is a highly undifferentiated environment. Furthermore, hunting requires the Eskimo to travel widely. In this situation, the Eskimo need spatial perceptual skills to find their way. They must be aware of minute details in the physical environment, and be able to locate themselves in relation to objects around them. These perceptual skills are obviously related to survival among the Eskimo.

The Temne and the Eskimo have very different child-rearing patterns. Temne parents try to enforce strict discipline through physical punishment, and there is an emphasis on conformity to adult authority. The Temne mother plays an extremely dominant role in raising the children, and a child is not encouraged to take on adult roles or responsibility. This kind of child-rearing is associated with a *field dependent* perceptual-cognitive style, one aspect of which is a less well developed ability in spatial awareness and visual discrimination. Among the Eskimo, on the other hand, punishment of children is generally avoided and the child is given a lot of freedom. Self-reliance, individualism, individual skill development, and curiosity and ingenuity are encouraged. This child-rearing pattern is correlated with a generally high degree of differentiation and leads to a *field independent* perceptual-cognitive style, which in turn is correlated with a high degree of spatial awareness and visual discrimination.

A cultural-ecological explanatic differences in susceptibility has also been developed. The Arunta of Australia, for example, are extremely susceptible to the illusion in Figure 4.1. The Arunta live in flat, open desert, and the individual sees great stretches of desert that, on the retina, would be projected as foreshortened planes, but that he would learn to interpret as lengthier planes extending away into

The differences between the two groups in their arts and crafts are also related to their different perceptual skills. The arts and crafts of the Eskimo are known for skill in design and execution. Those of the Temne are considered to be of relatively poor quality and tend to be produced by a few specialists in the society. A high quality of arts and crafts engaged in by the general population promotes the early learning of spatial manipulation and discrimination of detail and is positively related to spatial perceptual competence. In language, too, the contrast between the Temne and Eskimo shows the influence of culture on perception. The Temne language contains relatively few terms that express geometrical-spatial concepts, while the Eskimo language contains many (Berry 1974).

The relatively undifferentiated landscape of the snow-covered arctic is an important factor in the high degree of visual discrimination found among some Eskimo populations. (United Nations/Canadian Government Travel Bureau)

space. Shown Figure 4.1, a person from this environment would tend to perceive the vertical line as representing a plane extending along his line of vision and would therefore perceive it as longer than the horizontal line (Munroe 1977). Peoples who do not live in environments with a great deal of vast, open space are less susceptible to this illusion.

Performance on tests of spatial ability

(see Figure 4.2) also show great variation among cultures. Spatial ability means an ability to sort out the different components in an environment, to separate an element from its context, and to locate oneself accurately in relation to environmental features. A number of studies confirm the hypothesis that cultural patterning, particularly ecology and child-rearing practices, have an important impact on the development of spatial-perceptual abilities (Berry 1974).

Figure 4.3 illustrates the relationship between ecology, culture, socialization, and individual perceptual and cognitive skills.

In addition to increasing our understanding of the relationship between the ecological demands placed on a society, various aspects of culture, and the development of specific perceptual-cognitive abilities, this study has a more general relevance. When we see the tiny differences in test scores between the Scottish and Eskimo sample populations, as well as the significant differences between the scores of the traditional and more urbanized populations *within* each culture, racial factors cannot explain perceptual-cognitive variation. Furthermore, the differences in performance between the Eskimo and the Temne, as well as among other non-Western peoples who have been tested, would seem to finish once and for all any notion of a "primitive mentality."

Culture and Cognition

Cognitive competence, or intelligence, consists of many capacities, skills, and adaptive responses to the environment. In our own society, we see "intelligence" as a particular way of solving problems that involves the ability to abstract, analyze, and reintegrate data into new patterns. This analytic cognitive style is at one end of a continuum; a global cognitive style is at the other. On tests, an individual with the global cognitive style has more trouble separating the different elements in a pattern, taking them from their context, and recombining them in novel ways. Although the analytic cognitive style appears to develop with age, there is some empirical research that shows the important ways in which culture patterns cognitive skills and style (Witkin 1974). As the material on the Temne and the Eskimo indicates, different perceptual-cognitive skills appear to be adaptive in different ecological situations. One style is not superior to another, but rather is more suitable in different environments and life situations. The value

Figure 4.2 *Items from the Embedded Figures Test. The simple figure on the left is located in each of the other two figures. This test is one measure of spatial perception, and the results appear to differ among different cultures. From H. A. Witkin, "Individual differences in ease of embedded figures."* Journal of Personality, *Vol. XIX, Sept. 1950–June 1951, 1–15. Copyright 1951 by Duke University Press. Reprinted by permission.*

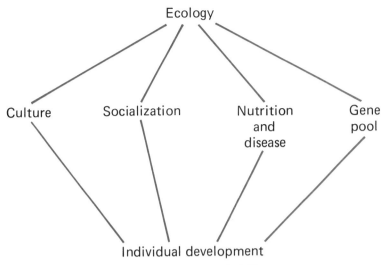

Figure 4.3 *Individual development in its relationship to ecological and other factors, both biological and cultural.* (Berry 1974)

of the *analytic* style in our own society has an obvious relationship to formal education, the specialized nature of industrial technology, and the rise of scientific thought as a way of understanding the world.

Cross-cultural research is only now beginning to shed some light on the relationship between many different cognitive skills and the cultural patterns and ecological settings in which they exist. It appears, for example, that child care patterns which encourage freedom and separation of the child from the family tend to be correlated with and are assumed in some way to produce a more analytic style. The high scores on Western intelligence tests for the Tiv, a people of Africa, emphasize the importance of a cultural explanation of intelligence as this applies to human populations. The Tiv, a nonliterate people, stand out in sub-Saharan Africa for their child-rearing patterns. Most other African peoples (like the Temne) teach respect for authority and obedience to elders. The Tiv put less pressure on obedience (vis-à-vis assertiveness) in children. Tiv children also stand out for the extent to which they have spontaneously and enthusiastically participated in intelligence testing experiences.

The mainstream of anthropology and cross-cultural psychology tries to show that understandings of the universe and of relationships within the universe are learned, and do not reflect any innate or biologically inherited differences in intelligence among human groups. No matter what the differences in the ways in which different peoples perform on "intelligence" tests, all human groups studied demonstrate the capacity to remember, generalize, operate with abstractions, form concepts, and reason logically.

Intelligence tests do *not* provide valid information on innate differences in mental capacities among human groups. They *do* predict well the academic success of different groups, which is what they are designed to do. Intelligence tests measure the specific ability to perceive relationships using abstract symbolic material: numbers, forms, spatial relationships, and word meanings. This is just one culturally patterned way of understanding the world. It is because the culture on which intelligence tests are based is the same as the cultural understandings required in the middle-class American school that the tests can predict academic success (Alland 1973:177).

Not only do standard intelligence tests measure just one "codification of reality," but they measure it in a context that is not equally meaningful for different groups in our society. For the middle-class child, who has some reason to believe that his/her performance on tests is related to success in later life, the motivation for taking them is obviously higher than for a child who believes his/her fate is sealed by race or ethnicity, no matter how well he/she may do on a test. The effect of motivation, sophistication in taking tests, and culturally different attitudes toward testing must all be taken into account in interpreting the intelligence test scores of different groups of people.

DOING WHAT COMES NATURALLY?

The importance of cultural patterning is not easy to understand, particularly in areas of action and emotional response that we assume to be "natural"—sex, eating, feeling, and expressing certain emotions and attitudes. Natural, in the case of every society, is natural according to its own beliefs and customs. In this next section, we examine some of the ways in which basic human behavior patterns and responses are influenced and shaped by culture.

Cultural Patterning of Food Habits

Every individual must eat to survive. But what people eat, when, and in what manner are all patterned by culture. No society regards everything in its environment that is edible and might provide nourishment as food. Certain edibles are ignored, others are tabooed. Food taboos may have such a hold on a society that just the thought of eating forbidden foods causes individuals to feel sick. A Hindu vegetarian would feel this way about meat, an American about eating dogs, and a Muslim about pork. Most Americans will shudder at eating insects, though this is a common practice in many parts of the world.

Cannibalism is probably the human food practice that arouses the most horror in our culture. Although in most societies in which cannibalism is practiced it occurs only under special conditions and in ritual contexts, there have been a few societies in which human flesh was simply another available source of animal protein. In societies in which cannibalism is strongly tabooed, however, the taboo is rarely overcome. Two famous cases of cannibalism in Western societies are that of the Donner Pass party, which got caught in a snowstorm in the winter of 1846–47 crossing the Sierra Nevada mountains, and the recent case of the South American soccer team whose plane crashed in the Andes. These two exceptions and the furor they generated prove the rule. Many individuals have been in equally desperate circumstances and have not resorted to eating the flesh of their dead companions.

Anthropologists have attempted to understand some seemingly irrational food habits in terms of their long-term adaptive significance. We have already mentioned the Hindu taboo on beef as an ecological adaptation. It is also possible that there is a biological component in the avoidance of certain foods. The Chinese aversion to milk may have to do with the fact that lactase, an enzyme that acts to digest the sugar lactose in milk, ceases to be produced in many Mongoloid populations after weaning has occurred. As a result, the milk sugar cannot be digested, and the use of milk and milk products frequently causes intestinal distress. But evidence supporting biological interpretations of food taboos is scarce. Given our knowledge at this point, it seems safe to say that it is primarily culture which channels hunger so that only some edible substances and not others can satisfy it.

Sexual Practices

If the cultural component in food habits is easily understood, that in sexual habits is not. Of all the kinds of human behavior, sexual activity is most likely to be viewed as "doing what comes naturally." But a cross-cultural perspective on sexual practices tells us that every aspect of human sexual activity is patterned by culture and influenced by learning.

Culture patterns the habitual responses of different peoples to different parts of the body. What is considered erotic in some cultures evokes indifference or disgust in others. Kissing, for example, is not practiced in many societies. The Tahitians have learned to kiss from the Europeans, but before this culture contact they began sexual intimacy by sniffing. The patterns of social and sexual preliminaries leading to sexual intercourse also differ among cultures. The Trobriand Islanders, as described by Malinowski, "inspect each other's hair for lice and eat them . . . to the natives a natural and pleasant occupation between two who are fond of each other" (1929). This may seem disgusting to us. To the Trobrianders, the European habit of boys and girls going out on a picnic with a knapsack of food was equally disgusting, although it is a perfectly acceptable custom for a Trobriand boy and girl to gather wild foods together as a preliminary to sexual activity.

Who is considered an appropriate sexual partner is also different around the world. Our own feeling about homosexual activity is not shared by all cultures. In some societies, a period of obligatory homosexual relationships is part of the training of every adolescent male, who as an adult is expected to, and apparently does, make a heterosexual marriage (van Baal 1966). In still other cultures, such as in parts of Tahiti, homosexual practices almost never occurred until they were introduced by the Europeans. In these cultures, homosexual activity is not considered particularly shameful or abnormal, as is largely true in the United States; rather, it is seen as an activity that does not make much sense if members of the opposite sex are around. The ages at which sexual response is believed to begin and end, the ways in which people make themselves attractive to the opposite sex, the importance of sexual activity in human life—all these are patterned and regulated by culture, and affect sexual response and behavior. Partly because anthropology grew up in an age in which sexuality was a forbidden topic, and partly because of the difficulty of observing sexual activity, ethnographic descriptions often ignore this

As economic opportunities for women change, so do conceptions of female sexuality.
(Jane Hoffer)

topic. What information we do have is enough to show the great contrasts in different societies. A comparison of just two cultures, the Irish of the island of Inis Beag, and the Polynesians of the island of Mangaia, who are at opposite ends of a continuum regarding sexual behavior, makes clear the role of culture in this area of life.

John Messenger describes Inis Beag as "one of the most sexually naive of the world's societies" (1971). Sex is never discussed at home when children are near, and practically no sexual instruction is given by parents to children. Adults express the belief that "after marriage nature takes its course." (As we shall see, "nature" takes a very different course in Inis Beag than it does in Polynesia!) Women are not expected to enjoy sexual relations; it is a "duty" to be endured, for to refuse to have intercourse is considered a mortal sin. There appears to be widespread ignorance in Inis Beag of the ability of females to reach a climax, which in any case is considered deviant behavior. Nudity is abhorred by the islanders, and there is no tradition of "dirty jokes." The main style of dancing allows little bodily contact among the participants, but even then, some girls refuse to dance because it means touching a boy. The separation of the sexes begins very early in Inis Beag and lasts into adulthood. Other cultural patterns related to sexual repression here are the virtual absence of sexual foreplay, the belief that sexual activity weakens a man, the absence of premarital sex, the high percentage of celibate males, and the extraordinarily late age of marriage. The differences in sexuality between men and women are expressed by a female informant as "Men can wait a long time before wanting 'it' but we [women] can wait a lot longer."

Although the belief that total sexual freedom exists in the South Sea islands is a Western myth, the island of Mangaia, as described by Donald Marshall (1971), presents a strong contrast to that of Inis Beag. In this Polynesian culture, sexual intercourse is one of the major interests of life. Although sex is not discussed at home, sexual information is transmitted to boys and girls at puberty by the elders of the group. For adolescent boys, a two-week period of formal instruction about the techniques of intercourse is followed by a culturally approved experience with a mature woman in the village. After this the boy is considered a man by himself and others. This is an interesting point of comparison with Inis Beag, where a man is considered a "lad" until he is about 40.

Sexual relations in Mangaia are carried out privately, but there is continual public reference to sexual activity. Sexual jokes, expressions, and references are not only common, but expected as part of the preliminaries to public meetings. This pattern of public verbal references to sex contrasts with the public separation of the sexes. Boys and girls should not be seen together in public, but practically every girl and boy has had intercourse before marriage. The act of sexual intercourse itself is the focus of sexual activity. What Westerners call sexual foreplay is generally engaged in by Mangaians after, not before, intercourse. In Mangaia both men and women are expected to take pleasure in the sexual act, and to reach a climax. Female frigidity, male celibacy, and homosexuality are practically unknown. So it is not simply that different societies hold different attitudes about sex, but that these attitudes pattern the sexual responsiveness of males and females in that society.

Like any other aspect of culture, beliefs about human sexuality and sexual practices are integrated into a pattern and functionally related to other aspects of the total sociocultural system. In the absence of artifical birth control, for example, beliefs and practices that limit heterosexual intercourse may be adaptive in contributing to population control.

Sex and Gender

Sex refers to the *biological* differences between male and female, particularly the visible differences in external genitalia and the related difference in the role each sex plays in the reproductive process. Gender refers to the *social* classification of masculine and feminine. Every society gives cultural recognition to the sexual division of the species into male and female, but cultures differ in terms of what they consider masculine and feminine. Some male-female differences in behavior appear to be very widespread, however (D'Andrade 1974). Males, for example, have been observed to be more likely to initiate activity than females in various cultures. Females have also been observed to be more altruistic—that is, offer to help others——than males.

An important study on the question of whether the characteristics defined as "feminine" in Western culture were universal was carried out by Margaret Mead in New Guinea (1963). Mead studied three different cultures and found that male and female roles and masculine and feminine temperament were patterned differently in each culture. Among the Arapesh, both men and women were expected to act in ways we in the United States consider "naturally" feminine. Both sexes were concerned with taking care of children and with nurturing generally. Neither sex was expected to be aggressive. In the second culture, the Mundugamor, both sexes were what we would call "masculine"—aggressive, violent, and with little interest in children. In the third society, the Tchambuli, the personalities of males and females were different from each other, but opposite to our own conceptions of masculine and feminine. Women had the major economic role, showed "common sense" and business shrewdness, and carried out the mundane tasks. Men were interested in esthetics. They spent much time decorating themselves and gossiping. They also had their feelings easily hurt and sulked a lot.

Mead's study showed that the whole repertoire of behavior, emotions, and interests which go into being masculine and feminine are patterned by culture. In the process of growing up, each child learns hundreds of culturally patterned details of behavior that become incorporated into its gender identity. In addition to all the direct instructions about being masculine or feminine that every culture imparts, culture unconsciously affects masculinity and femininity by providing different images, aspirations, and adult models for girls and boys. In assessing the idea that biology determines gender, anthropologists have pointed to the great variability in human societies regarding the behavior, temperaments, and roles of women and men. As always, the anthropologist attempts to deal with the question of the relation of biology to culture by looking outside our own Western traditions, for it is only in this way that we can grasp the variety in human life. What we see is that whatever biological dispositions may be characteristic of one sex or the other, these are responsive to a tremendously wide range of cultural patterning.

Cultural Patterning and Emotions

The range and quality of human emotions is potentially the same for all human groups. It is in the course of growing up in a particular culture that the range narrows and becomes shaped to a pattern. Fear, love, anger, hostility, shame, guilt, grief, joy, or indifference become channeled by culture so that they appear in different situations, against different objects and persons, or hardly appear at all. Each culture selects, elaborates, and emphasizes certain emotional possibilities and defines certain feelings about oneself, others, and the world as appropriate or not. This is communicated in direct and indirect ways. A boy who learns not to cry may have been told "crying is only for girls." He also is surrounded by males who do not cry. Both experiences help pattern his inner responses to situations.

Because human emotions have an "inner" reality, they are felt to be "natural." Drawing on our own experience, we consider it natural for a mother to love her child, for an individual to be jealous of another's success, for people to be sad when someone dies. The seeming naturalness of human emotions leads us to see them as causes for certain kinds of behavior. War is then explained by humankind's natural aggression, marriage is viewed as the result of love, motherhood as an expression of the maternal instinct, and free enterprise capitalism as the inevitable expression of a natural desire to get ahead in the world. In all this we have lost sight of the role of culture and its tremendous impact on the human psyche. We project emotions we have been trained to feel on peoples in other cultures. We consider our own emotional responses as "natural" and responses that differ from ours as "unnatural."

It becomes hard for us to understand cultures in which several women married to the same man are not jealous of each other, in which mothers neglect their children's health and permit them to die, or

The expression of emotions in body or facial movement is also of interest to anthropologists, particularly because such expressions are important ways of communicating. A basic issue here is whether there are universal ways of communicating. Evidence that there is a cross-cultural universality in the facial expressions used to convey happiness, surprise, fear, anger, disgust, and sadness, raises the issue of whether these expressions may have a biological basis (Ekman 1977). At the same time it is equally clear that culture and experience have a strong effect on the shaping of facial expression, just as they do on bodily movement. Some emotions, like contempt, seem to have culturally specific facial movements. In other cases, the importance of masking emotions will affect all facial movement in the presence of other people. Where people are taught to be polite and sensitive to the feelings of others, as in Japan, this will affect the facial movements used in the presence of others. In the same situation, Japanese smile more, for example, than Americans do.

The Cultural Patterning of Selfishness and Aggression

One of the characteristic responses of individuals in North American society is to "look out for number one." John and Beatrice Whiting (1973) studied this "egoistic" attitude in a number of different cultures. They contrasted egoistic behavior, in which the self was the primary beneficiary of interaction, with altruistic behavior, in which another person benefited more. Through carefully controlled observations and comparisons of children they found that in those cultures where women contributed importantly to the economy, and younger children were therefore depended on to help with

The Indians of the North American Plains allowed more variation in gender identity than is true in the United States. The "berdache" allowed men who felt they could not live up to the Plains warrior ideal to wear women's clothing and perform women's tasks. A male Crow Indian, "Finds-Them-and-Kills-Them" takes on the female role. (Courtesy of Museum of the American Indian, Heye Foundation)

even kill them. Every culture sets up expectations not only about how people are supposed to behave, but also about how they should feel in different situations. In our own culture we are taught that it is not good to "carry a grudge," to store up anger or hatred against a person who has hurt us. In cultures where the blood feud exists, an individual is not only allowed to feel the desire for revenge, but his/her very honor will depend on it. A man who does not avenge a hurt loses face for himself and his whole group of kin.

domestic chores, particularly taking care of a younger sibling, altruistic behavior was more frequent than egoistic behavior. It should not surprise us to discover that the culture rated highest on egoistic behavior was Orchard Town, U.S.A. In a later chapter, we will study more specifically the ways in which early socialization is related to the development of group-oriented versus individualistic kinds of behavior.

Related to the view in the United States that selfishness is part of "human nature" is the tendency to see aggression as an innate and "natural" human predisposition. The idea that the human species has an aggressive "instinct" most often comes up in connection with warfare. Given the frequency of war throughout human history, it would seem to make sense to believe that humankind has an aggressive, warlike nature. If we examine the matter carefully, however, it can be shown that this theory does not hold up. War is between societies, not between individuals. Many (perhaps most) of the individuals who fight in wars are not there because they are aggressive, but because their society insists they participate. Furthermore, the degree to which propaganda is used in modern warfare indicates that aggression must be evoked by culturally appropriate means against a culturally approved enemy.

It is true that human beings are among the very few animal groups not provided with a biological mechanism that inhibits killing a member of the same species. Humans thus have the potential for intraspecific lethal aggression, and there is no denying that it has frequently been used. Biological interpretations of human aggression are attractive to us because they seem to explain in a simple manner much of the behavior found in Western society. But this kind of explanation fails to take into account the importance of cultural patterning, which can be observed only by looking at the total variety of human cultures.

There are some cultures in which there is little or no organized aggression, and in which aggressive behavior by individuals is severely condemned and may almost be nonexistent. One such culture is that of the Semai of the Malay peninsula (Dentan 1968). The Semai are slash-and-burn agriculturalists who have only recently given up a dependence on a hunting and gathering existence. Under the pressure of the dominant Malays, the Semai have retreated to the hills and mountains of central Malaya. They consider themselves, and are considered by others, as a nonviolent people. They believe that anger is a bad thing, and the enthnographer observed that they rarely do get angry. Semai life is not without conflict, however, usually over the sexual favors of women. When an individual is offended by another, the Semai believe the offended person will become prone to an accident if he stays angry. Thus, one reason Semai do not want to become angry is that in their culture it is the angry man who gets hurt. If a man feels himself offended by another, he can ask for compensation for his distress. If the offender admits the offense, he will pay the compensation. If not, hostility simmers, leading at the very most to insults and the spreading of rumors. No murder has ever been recorded in Semai society.

The Semai are very gentle, even with animals. A man will not kill an animal he has raised himself, but exchanges it with someone in another village, knowing that it will be killed, but not wanting to do it himself.

Yet when the Semai joined the military during the 1950s in response to the Malayan government's attempt to put down Communist guerrilla activity, they were not only able to kill, but seemed to enjoy it. How can this be explained? The answer cannot be found in a human instinct for aggression. The Semai culture was built on non-aggression, and the same Semai who served in the army went back to their non-aggressive way of life. If aggression were an instinct, it could not be modified by changes in situations so rapidly.

The variability of the amount, expression, and direction of aggression within human societies testifies to the importance of cultural patterning. In societies in which warfare is a highly valued cultural pattern, males will be taught to be more aggressive than in those cultures in which warfare is absent. Warfare itself does not exist in all societies, and its presence and the form it takes is best explained in terms of ecology. Only under specific circumstances does the human potential for aggression become mobilized in the service of warfare. Human behavior is based on customs and values that develop only in the context of

The influence of genes on sex roles is a question being intensely discussed in contemporary anthropology. Is the self-sacrificing behavior human beings often show toward their close kin genetically determined or learned through participation in a sociocultural system? (United Nations)

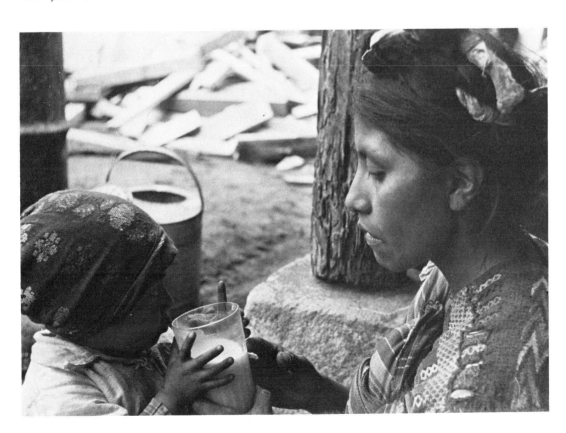

specific social and environmental conditions. Although culture is rooted in human biology, it frees humans from strictly biological controls over behavior to a degree far beyond that of any other animal. An understanding of the cultural context of human behavior—the ways in which specific patterns specify and provide the necessary context for the development of biologically based capacities—is critical to an understanding of what it means to be human.

SUMMARY

1. Human capacities and human behavior develop only within a human sociocultural system. Dramatic evidence of this is demonstrated by the nonhuman behavior of children brought up in relative isolation from other human beings.

2. Culture patterns the ways in which human beings perceive physical reality. Culture also patterns what people believe to be true about their universe.

3. Keeping track of time is a human invention. The passing of time, the sense of past and present, and the way time is used is different in different cultures.

4. Cultural patterning affects the way humans perceive and see relationships in space, the way in which spaces are used, and how much space people feel they need to be comfortable.

5. One of the basic principles of anthropology is that all human groups have the same capacity for intelligent behavior. Intelligence tests do not measure innate mental capacities of different human groups. Standardized intelligence tests given in the American school are constructed in terms of only one cultural system: that of the middle-class American.

6. Because of the tremendous variability in culture, it is difficult to say what human nature consists of. Every society tends to look at its own ways of behaving as not only right, but "natural." The difficulty in isolating the genetic bases of human behavior is that everything human beings do is patterned by the specific culture in which they live.

7. Food habits differ considerably among cultures. All humans must eat to live, but what and how people eat is patterned by culture. Food preferences and taboos that seem irrational may often have long-term adaptive significance in terms of efficient use of natural resources.

8. The great variety in human sexual behavior indicates that culture plays an important role in patterning and regulating sexual drives and responsiveness. In this sense, we may say that human sexual behavior is learned.

9. Male and female are biological categories. Masculine and feminine are cultural creations. By looking at cultures outside Western civilization, anthropologists try to understand the relationship between sex (male and female) and gender (masculine and feminine).

10. Body and facial movements are patterned by culture, although evidence from recent research also indicates

that some facial expressions may be universal.

11. Culture patterns not only the forms of outward behavior, but the inner life of the individual as well. How people feel, and what motivates them to act, are part of a conscious and unconscious teaching process that is culturally variable.

12. In the United States, we are taught to "look out for number one." The equation of individual self-preservation with "human nature" is contradicted by the ethnographic evidence from many non-Western societies.

13. Intraspecies aggression is a potential in the human species. Societies vary greatly, however, in the degree to which individuals act aggressively, and some societies have practically no physical aggression. Aggression is not a human instinct, but rather a possibility that is patterned differently in different cultures.

SUGGESTED READINGS

Alland, Alexander, Jr.
   1972 *The Human Imperative.* New York: Columbia University Press. A book that can easily be understood by the beginning anthropology student that persuasively demolishes the case for aggression as a human instinct.

Barash, David P.
   1977 *Sociobiology and Behavior.* New York: Elsevier. An introduction to sociobiological theory and research. The last chapter is devoted to the usefulness of sociobiology for understanding human behavior.

Bates, Marston
   1971 *Gluttons and Libertines: Human Problems of Being Natural.* New York: Random House. An entertaining and informative book by a natural scientist on such topics as food, sex, rebellion, and the pursuit of happiness.

Cole, M., and Scribner, S.
   1974 *Culture and Thought,* New York: Wiley. A summary of the important research in cross-cultural psychology, including a historical perspective on scientific interest in this issue.

Lane, Harlan
   1977 *The Wild Boy of Aveyron.* New York: Bantam. Based on original documents, this book about a "wild" child raises provocative questions about human nature.

Money, John, and Tucker, Patricia
   1975 *Sexual Signatures.* Boston: Little, Brown. A distinguished researcher in human sexuality discusses the biological and cultural components involved in being a man or a woman.

Oakley, Ann
   1972 *Sex, Gender and Society.* New York: Harper & Row. A well-researched book examining the biological and cultural sources of the differences between men and women.

Sahlins, Marshall
   1977 *The Use and Abuse of Biology: An Anthropological Critique of Sociobiology.* Ann Arbor: University of Michigan Press. A critical view of sociobiology from both an intellectual and political perspective by an important cultural anthropologist.

United Nations/Siceloff

2
Sociocultural Adaptations

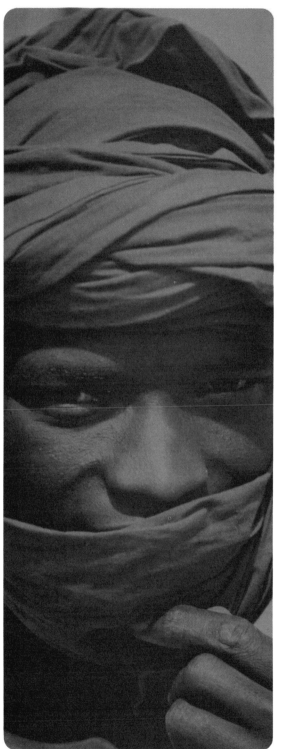

United Nations/Aid/Purcell

5
Language

All animals communicate. **Communication** is the act of transmitting information that influences the behavior of another organism. Interaction in all animal species depends on a consistent set of signals by which individuals convey information. These signals are channeled through one or several of the senses: visual, olfactory (smell), auditory (sound), or tactile (touch). Even among lower animals, the type of information communicated can be quite complex. One example is the dance of the honey bee. Through stereotyped and patterned movements, a scout bee conveys the direction and distance of a field of pollen-bearing flowers to the others. But although bees can "say" a lot about where flowers are, they cannot "say" much about anything else. Animals use sounds as well as movements to communicate, or share, information. Crows caw as a signal of danger, while crickets chirp when they are ready to mate. While all animal species exchange information related to the basic

79

requirements of survival, only human language, or speech, is capable of re-creating complex thought patterns and experiences in words. Without human language, human culture could not exist.

COMMUNICATION AND LANGUAGE

Primate Communication

Among higher animals, far greater amounts of information can be transmitted about many more subjects. Baboons in the wild, for example, constantly transmit information to each other. Lip-smacking, grunts, stares, poses, and screams are parts of the baboon communication system. One long-term study of rhesus monkeys revealed over 120 behavioral patterns that are used in communication.

Because chimpanzees are generally agreed to be humans' closest relations, their communication system is of great interest to social scientists. In the wild, chimpanzees, like other primates, exhibit a wide variety of communication behaviors. Chimpanzees use gestures and physical contact to express feelings. When they meet each other in the forest, "old friends" will kiss and hug, pat each other on the head, or rest a hand on the thigh of the other. Chimpanzees also play a great deal. Some anthropologists believe that play may have been one important way our prehuman ancestors developed the capacity for language. In addition to gestures, chimpanzees use calls to communicate. These calls are quite distinctive: a "waa" bark for danger, a series of soft moans for worry, a hooting to communicate excitement caused by the presence of an abundance of food, screams and squeals of fear. Each kind of call expresses a feeling

within the animal, is "understood" by other animals who hear it, and has effects on the behavior of others (Reynolds 1965). But a primate **call system** is not the same as human language. Although intonation can intensify the meaning of a call—for example, "danger," or "extreme danger"—a chimp can signal a danger only in its immediate presence. A second important limitation on primate communication is that parts of calls are not combined in new ways to generate new information: Each call has just one meaning.

Studies of chimpanzees brought up or trained by humans show that they are capable of a much more complex level of communication than they naturally display in the wild. Washoe was a 10-month-old chimpanzee raised in a completely human environment (Gardner and Gardner

Grooming is an important communication pattern among nonhuman primates. Here an adult female vervet monkey grooms another female, who nurses her infant. (David Klein)

1967). She spent all her waking hours in the company of a researcher who "talked" to her in the American Sign Language of the Deaf. Only part of this time was spent in language training. Washoe very quickly learned to respond to her human companion. She also learned to use sign language, and after learning about ten signs, she began spontaneously to produce combinations of signs. For example, she put "water" and "bird" together to make "duck." Recently other chimpanzees have been trained in symbolic communication. Their capacity for language is truly amazing; the chimps have demonstrated an ability to learn many different symbols, to combine symbols spontaneously, to conceptualize, to understand spoken English words, and to use signs in correct order. But although chimps can learn previously assigned symbolic values, there is no evidence that they can originate them. In spite of the fact that the vocal apparatus of the chimpanzee is quite similar to that of humans, chimpanzees have not developed human speech. This suggests that there are important differences between the brain of nonhuman primates and the human brain.

Human Language

Human language is a unique system of communication, distinct from any other animal communication system in three ways. In human language, a limited number of sounds (hardly any language uses over fifty) are combined to refer to thousands of different things and experiences. The association between a meaningful sequence of sounds and what they "stand for" is purely conventional in human language: The animal is no more a *dog* than it is a *chien* (French), a *perro* (Spanish) or a *kutta* (Hindi). Words "stand for"

things, and the symbol (the word) is not tied to the thing it stands for. It is this capacity to separate the vocal symbol from its referent that is absent in the call systems of nonhuman primates. It is this capacity to recombine sounds to create new meanings that makes human language such an efficient and effective communication system. If we had to use a different sound for every item of meaning, we would wind up with either a very small vocabulary, or an impossibly large number of sounds.

Not only is human language efficient, it is also infinitely *productive:* humans can combine words and sounds into new meaningful utterances they have never heard uttered. The English sentence below uses words in a combination none of us has probably ever heard before, and yet can be easily made and understood by any English-speaking person: "I don't know the man who took the spoon that Horace left on the table that was lying upside down in the upstairs hallway of the building that burned down last night" (Southworth 1974). Speakers of any human language can generate an almost infinite number of such sentences. This productive capacity of human languages makes them extremely flexible instruments for communication, capable of conveying all kinds of new information.

The third distinguishing characteristic of human language is its ability to convey information about something not in the immediate environment. We can describe things that happened in the past, will or may happen in the future, things which exist only in the mind, and things which are hypothetical (may not happen at all). This "displacement" characteristic of human languages allows us to think abstractly. Among other animals, communication is always about the present and the particular: a particular threatening object is in a particular place at this particular time. Human language generalizes; it categorizes some objects and events as similar and other objects and events as dissimilar. Humans can talk about a particular tree ("this tree I see in front of my house") and also about trees in general ("trees are standing people with rights to the land"). Language allows trees to be differentiated from bushes and bushes from flowers and flowers from grass. Hundreds of thousands of natural and manufactured objects have significance for human beings. Taking command of this incredibly complex world means classifying objects and events in an orderly way. Human language is the most effective means for doing exactly that. These qualities of human language—conventionality, productivity, and displacement—allow humans to make plans, to understand and correct mistakes, and to coordinate their activities. They also give our species a distinct advantage over other animals.

By translating experience into language, humans build up a storehouse of knowledge that can be transmitted to new members of the group. Although some of the things humans teach each other could be learned without language, teaching through language is more efficient and adaptive than relying on the slower and often clumsy process of imitation used by other animals. Furthermore, some human behavior patterns, such as religion, law, and science, would not be possible without the symbolizing capacity of human language. It is through this capacity for accumulating experience and passing it on by teaching others in the social group that human culture has developed.

Although at one time even many anthropologists and linguists believed contemporary human languages could be classified into "primitive" and "civilized," less complex and more complex, inferior and superior, we know today that this is not so. Every human language is a well-defined system of sounds, finite in number, and combined to form words, phrases, and sentences according to definite rules. Although the vocabulary of each language reflects what is important in terms of a particular physical and sociocultural environment, every language has a vocabulary adequate to deal with that environment. Vocabulary can be expanded in any language, and new words added as cultural change requires. All human languages have the capacity to categorize phenomena in the natural environment; the capacity for abstract thought is a property of all human languages. No language limits its references to the concrete or individual phenomena, and thus no language as a system of communication can be considered less developed than any other. Nor does any human language reflect a limited mental capacity on the part of its speakers. Languages *do* differ in the specific ways in which they categorize the environment, and these affect perception and thinking. We will take up this aspect of language and its relationship to culture later.

The Origins and Development of Human Language

Like all other aspects of cultural and biological evolution, the development of human speech was a long, gradual process. The question for the anthropologist is not when exactly human speech was "invented," but rather what pressures were at work on our remote ancestors that eventually led to the development of human speech (Hockett and Ascher 1964). As our human ancestors moved out of the forest into the open environment of the grasslands, they adopted a bipedal or upright position. This led to better vision, increased mobility of the hand, and increasing complexity of the brain. All of these developments were adaptive in an open environment, both for finding food and for protection against predators. These abilities are also involved in making tools. In his book, *The Emergence of Man* (1972) John Pfeiffer suggests that it was our ancestors' use of tools which made language an especially useful adaptation. At this time, several million years ago, the call system of our ancestors was probably not too different from that of modern chimpanzees—that is, it was triggered by immediate events. It was perhaps in play that new activities and new calls related to these activities developed. Evolutionary pressure increased the fitness of individuals who could "reconstruct the past in their minds, and express their images vocally, and conceive new sequences of actions to serve as the basis for future plans." The multiplication of new experiences, especially the coordination between individuals needed for hunting and conveying information to those who remained behind, required more elaborate communication than was possible with a call system. Through a shift of attention from whole calls to parts of calls, a vocal alphabet might develop. With population increases, larger settlements, group cooperation for large-scale hunting, and greater social organization, there was extra pressure for the development of grammatical rules. With each successive phase of human evolution, the world became steadily more complex and required complicated mechanisms to deal with it. It was in this context that human language developed.

Acquiring Language

The fact that linguistic symbols are nearly all arbitrary—that is, conventions by which certain sounds are attached to certain objects and events—emphasizes the social aspect of language. In this sense, language is a part of culture. An individual learns a language only by interaction with other human beings who speak that language. An individual from any human population, if taken at birth and brought up in a different society than that to which the parents belong, will grow up speaking the language of the group in which he or she is raised. The normal physical and mental apparatus of human beings everywhere allows them to learn any language with equal ease.

If you are wondering what language a human being would speak if he or she was not taught any particular language, the answer is *none.* In one attempt to determine this, the Egyptian pharaoh Psammetichus ordered two infants reared where they could hear no human voices. He assumed they would "naturally" talk in the language of their ancestors. To his ears, their babbling sounded like Phrygian, which he concluded was the original human language. King James IV of Scotland tried a similar experiment, and claimed that the two infants spoke Hebrew. This, not surprisingly, coincided with the theory of biblical scholars at that time who claimed that Adam and Eve spoke in Hebrew. Because experiments involving isolating human beings at birth are morally unacceptable today, cases of children brought up in isolation, such as Victor, the "wild child" of Aveyron, have always been of great interest to the scientific community. In Victor's case, Dr. Itard's training did result in showing that Victor could hear and understand much of what he heard. But although Victor lived in human society until he was 40, he never learned to speak. His case suggests that there may be a critical period of language development in the human animal. It seems that if speech is not learned at a certain age, the capacity to learn it at all is seriously impaired.

Recent studies of how children learn language indicate that human beings may have an innate (inborn) predisposition or mechanism for learning language patterns or rules. Children actually take the initiative in learning language. By six months, the babbling of the infant gives way to consonant and vowel sequences and repetitive patterns. It is apparent that each child "discovers" language on his own, though this can be done only in the context of a particular social group speaking a particular language. Most adults do not know the rules of the languages they speak, certainly not well enough to teach them to children. What happens is that the child is surrounded by a flow of sounds, words, and intonations. A normal child not only imitates these, but takes the initiative in forming combinations of words he or she may have never heard before, but that are consistent with the rules of the language. Even when the child does not understand the meaning of what he says, he can speak grammatically, using the different parts of speech in correct relation to each other. This understanding of how children learn language has led to an increased interest in the biological basis of human language.

The human brain appears to be uniquely constructed for the development of language. Not only are the visual and auditory areas directly connected to each other, but both areas are directly connected to the area concerned with touch. Thus, human children are able to make the association between the visible image,

the feel of an object, and the sound pattern, or word, used to designate it, even though the word itself is an arbitrary symbol.

STRUCTURAL VARIATION IN LANGUAGE

Every language has a structure, an internal logic and a particular relationship between its parts. The structure of any language consists of three subsystems: a **phonemic system** (a system of sounds), **syntax** (the relationship between forms and the rules for combining forms), and **semantics** (a system that relates forms to meaning). Descriptive linguistics, a subfield of linguistics that studies the structure of a given language at a particular point in time, is the basis of historical linguistics, which studies the change in the structure of a language over time, and comparative linguistics, which seeks to understand the relationship between different languages based on a comparison of their structures. One of the interests of descriptive anthropological linguistics is to record the structure of as many different human languages as possible. The first thing a descriptive linguist does in studying a language is to record the sounds and regular combinations of sounds in that language. These sounds are usually written in the International Phonetic Alphabet. The IPA was developed to represent all the sounds used in the different languages of the world and allows the linguist to record in writing sounds that are not used in his or her own language. When the linguist figures out how a particular sound is made, that sound can be represented phonetically with an IPA symbol. Let us look now in more detail at these subsystems of language structure.

The anthropological linguist is greatly aided by the tape recorder in recording the many sounds of human speech that are part of the phonemic structure of a language. (Raymond Kennedy)

Phonemics

A phone is a sound. All languages use only a limited number of sounds out of the vast range of sounds that can be made by the human vocal apparatus. Sounds used in one language may be absent in other languages. English for example, does not make use of the "click" sound of the language of the African Bushman or many of the tonal sounds of Chinese. Furthermore, combinations of sounds are used in different ways in different languages. For example, an English speaker can easily pronounce the "ng" sound in "thing" at the end of an utterance, but not at the beginning; yet this sound is used in the initial position in Swazi, a language of Africa.

Not every sound used in a language conveys meaning. The smallest sound unit in a language which distinguishes meaning is called a **phoneme.** An example will make clear what we mean by a phoneme. The sound /d/ in the English word "day" and /ð/ as in the English word "they" are phonemes. Their significance is shown by the fact that the words "day" and "they" have different meanings, and this meaning is carried by the initial consonant: /d/ as contrasted to /ð/. Spanish also uses these sounds. But in Spanish the sounds /d/ and /ð/ do not have significance; that is, they are not phonemes. They are used in different contexts: /d/ at the beginning of words and /ð/ when the sound appears in the middle of a word. Thus, they do not create a difference in meaning between utterances. A person who says *nada* using the sound in *dia* will still be understood to be saying "nothing," although people may think the accent is "wrong" or "foreign."

Most languages utilize only about thirty phonemes in their structure. By an unconscious process, the native speaker of a language not only learns to make the sounds used in a particular language, but also to differentiate between those sounds which are significant (phonemes) and those sounds which are not. The ordinary person does not consciously think about the phonemic pattern of his or her language. It is only when trying to learn another language, or hearing a foreigner speak our own language, that we become aware of the variation in sounds and phonemes.

Grammar: Morphology and Syntax

A **morpheme** is the smallest unit of a language that has a meaning. In English, -s, as in "dogs," means plural; un- means negative, as in "undo"; -er means "one who does," as in "teacher." Because -s, un-, and -er do not occur by themselves, but only in association with another unit of meaning, they are called *bound* morphemes. A morpheme, such as the word "giraffe," is called a *free* morpheme because it can stand alone. A word is the smallest part of a sentence that can be said alone and still retain its meaning. Some words consist of only one morpheme. "Giraffe" is an example of a single-morpheme word. "Teacher" has two morphemes, teach and -er. "Undoes" has three morphemes: un-, do, and -s.

Languages differ in the extent to which their words tend to contain only one, several, or many morphemes. In Chinese, most words have only one morpheme. English, like Chinese, has many single-morpheme words—"dog," "house," "car"—but also many words that contain more than one morpheme—plural words such as "dogs," "houses," "cars"; and words for one who does—"worker," "teacher," "gambler." English also has words with three morphemes: "Teachers" consists of the morphemes teach, -er, and -s. English also has words with four morphemes: "undesirables." The four are un-, desire, -able (a suffix turning a stem word into an adjective), and -s. English might then fall midway on a continuum between Chinese, with its mainly single-morpheme words, and languages like Navajo or Eskimo, which have many words with eight or ten morphemes.

Morphemes combine with other morphemes to make up complex words, phrases, and sentences. The combination of morphemes in any language is fixed by rules. One part of descriptive grammar has to do with formulating the particular rules in a language by which morphemes are arranged to make words. One of the rules of English grammar is that the morpheme for plural, -s, follows the element it is pluralizing. In other languages, the pluralizing morpheme may come before the element it pluralizes. Things are not quite that easy, however. The plural of "dog" is made by adding -s, but the plural of "child" is not made by adding -s. A grammar therefore not only specifies the general rules of morpheme combination, but also exceptions to the rules and the rules for different classes of exceptions.

Syntax is the part of grammar that has to do with the arrangement of words to form phrases and sentences. Languages differ in their syntactic structures. In English, word order is important to convey meaning. The syntax of the English language gives a different meaning to these two sentences: "the dog bit the man," and "the man bit the dog." In German, the subject and object of a sentence are indicated by word endings rather than word order. In attempting to understand the syntactic structure of a language, the descriptive linguist establishes the different form classes, or parts of speech, for that language. All languages have a word class of nouns, but different languages have different subclasses of nouns. In the Romance languages (Spanish, French, and Italian), as well as in many others, nouns are divided into masculine, feminine, and neuter subclasses. This gender classification applies to verbs, indefinite and definite articles, and adjectives, all of which must agree with the gender classification of the noun. Other languages make class distinctions we do not use in English; for example, Papago, a native American language, classifies the features of their world into "living things" and "growing things." Living things includes all animated objects, such as people and animals, while growing things refers to all inanimate objects, such as plants.

All linguists agree that the grammatical categories of one language cannot be used to describe another language. Languages differ in the numbers and kinds of grammatical categories they have and how these categories are indicated. Thus, the information which in English would be expressed as "the dog bit the man" would be "dog bite man" in Chinese. In China, the tense of the verb need not be indicated, as it must be in English, although it can be brought in by using a time word such as "now" or "yesterday." In Chinook, an Indian language spoken in the American Northwest, conveying the same information would require the speaker to use morphemes indicating the following: "singular-feminine-subject-dog singular-masculine-object-man singular-feminine-subject-singular-masculine-object-directive-bite instantaneous-past." The rules of grammar in different languages not only require different information to be included in a sentence, but also differ in the ways they do this.

Although grammatical rules carry meaning, the grammar of a sentence can be understood independent of its meaning. To use a now classic example (Chomsky 1965), consider the following sentences:

"Colorless green ideas sleep furiously."
"Furiously sleep ideas green colorless."

Both sentences are meaningless in English. But the first is easily recognized as grammatical by an English speaker, while the second is both meaningless and ungrammatical. The first sentence has the parts of speech in English in their proper relation to each other; the second sentence does not.

Transformational Grammar

Traditional descriptive grammars formulate the rules of a language by breaking down sentences into constituents (parts of speech) and analyzing the relationships these parts of speech have to each other and to the sentence as a whole. But this kind of descriptive grammar cannot account for all the features of a language. Traditional descriptive grammars cannot, for example, account for the ambiguity of certain sentences. The sentence "they are flying planes" (Allen 1971) can be understood to have two meanings: ". . . those specks on the horizon are planes flying in the air," and ". . . my friends are flying planes."

A traditional descriptive grammar that understands sentences by breaking them up into their elements and stops there will not be able to show that the sentence ". . . they are flying planes" has two different meanings. Nor can traditional descriptive grammars account for the differences we feel between the following two sentences: (1) "The picture was painted by a new technique," and (2) "The picture was painted by a real artist." A traditional grammar would have to represent the structure of these sentences in the same way.

Because of these and other limitations in traditional descriptive grammars, a new approach to understanding language called **transformational generative grammar** was developed by Noam Chomsky in the 1950s. Instead of focusing on the parts of speech in a sentence and their relationship to one another, transformational grammar focuses on the relationship between levels of language structure. According to transformational grammar, languages have two levels, deep structure and surface structure. The deep structure of a language is revealed in basic or kernel sentences. These kernels are simple, declarative, affirmative, active sentences: "John loves Mary." They can be transformed by a set of rules into a variety of surface structures. For example, the rule for transforming the positive into the negative would lead to this surface structure: "John does not love Mary." The rule for transforming the declarative into the interrogative would lead to "Does John love Mary?" and so forth. Not all sentences which seem similar—that is, have similar surface structures—have the same deep structure. The two sentences "The picture was painted by a new technique" and "The picture was painted by a real artist" can be shown to have different deep structures and dif-

Where the population of a nation speaks two mutually unintelligible dialects, as in the People's Republic of China, a common written language is an important means of communication and an instrument of forging national unity. (Bernhard Krauss)

ferent transformational histories. The first is derived by a double transformation from "John painted the picture by a new technique." The second is the passive of "A real artist painted the picture." Transformational grammar can also account for the surface ambiguity in the sentence "They are flying planes" by showing that the two meanings are generated by different deep structures and can be represented differently at this level.

The excitement created by transformational grammar can be better understood in the context of the goals of linguistic theory. A grammar is an account of the competence, or implicit knowledge, of a speaker of a language. It describes and attempts to account for the ability of a speaker to understand a sentence in the native language and to produce an appropriate sentence on a given occasion. Ideally, the competence of a speaker-hearer can be expressed as a system of rules that relate signals to their meanings. The problem for the grammarian is to discover and make explicit the system of rules the speaker-hearer knows only implicitly. For the linguist, however, the correct statement of the grammatical principles of a language is of interest primarily for what it tells about the more general question of the nature of universal grammar. One universal grammar is primarily of interest for the information it provides concerning innate intellectual structure. The aim of linguistic theory is to understand the nature of mental processes, the ways in which sentences are produced and understood, and the ways in which linguistic competence is acquired. The success with which transformational grammar accounts for linguistic competence has opened up new vistas in the science of linguistics and in our understanding of the workings of the human mind.

Vocabulary

A **vocabulary** is the total stock of words in a language. The relation between culture and language is perhaps most clearly seen in vocabulary. In industrial society, the vocabulary will contain many words reflecting technological complexity and specialization. In a technologically simpler society, the vocabulary will be different. The vocabulary of all cultures is elaborated in the direction of what is most important in that culture. The Subanum of the Philippines, a relatively simple agricultural society, have 132 separate words for the diagnosis of disease (Conklin 1969).

This same society possesses over a thousand words for the plants in that environment. The Eskimo have many different words for snow; snow falling on the ground (*aput*); falling snow (*gana*), drifting snow (*piqsirpog*), and so on. This elaboration of Eskimo vocabulary has an obvious relationship to the importance of weather conditions for survival.

Because vocabulary reflects the way people with a certain culture perceive their environment, anthropologists use vocabulary as a clue to understanding experience and reality in different cultures. Through vocabulary, anthropologists attempt to get a "native's" view of the world not influenced by the anthropologist's own classification system. This perspective has long been used in studying the vocabulary for kinship. In English, for example, the word "brother-in-law" lumps together my sister's husband, my husband's brother, and the husbands of all my husband's sisters. In Hindi, a language of northern India, there are separate terms for my sister's husband (*behnoi*), my husband's elder brother (*jait*), my husband's younger brother (*deva*), and my husband's sisters' husbands (*nandoya*). Kinship vocabulary is a good clue to the nature of the most significant family relations in a culture. The single term brother-in-law in English reflects the similarity of a woman's behavior toward all the men in those different kinship statuses. The variety of words in Hindi reflects the fact that each of these categories of people are treated differently.

Anthropologists also attempt to discover the criteria for applying a particular label to an aspect of the physical or social environment in order to understand how a culturally specific area of meaning is divided into parts and how these parts are related to each other. One kind of relationship is that of exclusion, or contrast. Thus, going back to our example of kinship, English terminology contrasts "brother-in-law" with "sister-in-law" by the criterion of sex. "Brother" is contrasted with "brother-in-law" by the criterion of blood versus affinal relationship (relation through marriage). But both "brother" and "brother-in-law" are included in "relatives," a more general category that contains people related both by blood and marriage. The category of relatives contrasts with the category of close nonrelatives—"friends"—and this category contrasts with unknown people or "strangers."

LANGUAGE AND CULTURE

We have just seen how language, especially in its vocabulary, reflects cultural emphases, and the ways in which cultures divide up their physical and social environment. But language does more than just reflect culture; it is the way in which the individual is introduced to the order of the physical and social environment. Language, therefore, would seem to have a major impact on the way an individual perceives and conceptualizes the world. This importance and special role of language was made clear by Edward Sapir (1949), who wrote:

Human beings do not live in the objective world alone . . . but are very much at the mercy of the particular language which has become the medium of expression for their society . . . the fact . . . is that the "real world" is to a large extent unconsciously built up on the language habits of the group. No two languages are ever sufficiently similar to be considered as representing the same social reality. The worlds in which different societies live are distinct worlds, not merely the same world with different labels attached.

If my language has only one term—brother-in-law—that is applied to my sister's husband, my husband's brothers, and my husband's sisters' husbands, I am led by my language to perceive all these relatives in a similar way. Vocabulary, through what it groups together under one label and what it differentiates with different labels, is one way in which language shapes our perception of the world.

Anthropologists have long been interested in the ways in which grammatical categories influence the perception of reality. Both Sapir and a student of his, Benjamin Whorf, investigated the ways in which different peoples "see" the universe through the medium of their languages. The **Whorf-Sapir hypothesis,** as it has come to be called, asks these two questions: Are concepts of time, space, and matter given in substantially the same form by experience to all people or are they in part conditioned by the structure of particular languages? Are there correspondences between linguistic patterns and cultural and behavioral norms? Most anthropologists would probably give a qualified "Yes" to both questions, although we have little actual research to document these answers.

Harry Hoijer (1964) applied the Whorf—Sapir hypothesis to the Navajo, an Indian tribe in Arizona. He demonstrated that many aspects of Navajo grammar (for example, the conjugation of active verbs, the reporting of actions and events, and the framing of substantive concepts) emphasize movement and specify the nature, direction, and status of such movement in considerable detail. Where English would say, "one dresses," "one is young," "he is carrying a round object," Navajo would say "one moves into clothing," "one moves about newly," and "he moves along handling a round object." The Navajo language conceives of the universe being in motion; position is defined as a withdrawal from motion. Where English would say "on," Navajo would say "at rest." Parallels to this linguistic conception of the universe in motion are found in many aspects of Navajo culture. In Navajo mythology, for example, gods and culture heroes restlessly move from one place to another, seeking by their motion to perfect the universe.

Although some correspondences between grammatical categories and cultural themes or world views have been demonstrated, linguistic determinism is not an absolute or established fact. For example, the necessity to distinguish gender (male/female) in the Romance languages does not correspond to the relative importance of gender in these cultures when compared, for example, to its importance in Chinese and Polynesian cultures, neither of which has gender classes in its language. And the lack of gender classes in English does not correspond to any fact of culturally perceived equality between male and female. This illustrates one of the many difficulties in accepting the Whorfian hypothesis and illustrates why it is not totally accepted by anthropologists.

THE ETHNOGRAPHY OF COMMUNICATION

Anthropological linguistics has mainly been interested in languages as systems of knowledge independent of the ways in which people actually speak. The relatively new field of **sociolinguistics** focuses on speech performance: the actual encounters that involve verbal (and also accompanying nonverbal) communication between human beings. Where traditional anthropological linguistics assumes a homogeneous speech community, sociolinguistics is interested in variations in language use as these can be observed by the ethnographer. Finally, where the anthropological linguist usually works with one informant and attempts to elicit the ideal pattern of a language, the sociolinguist observes verbal behavior among different individuals and groups in society.

The sociolinguist attempts to identify, describe, and understand the cultural patterning of different speech events within a speech community (society or subsociety). For example, a political speech has different purposes and is limited by different norms from those for a political discussion among friends. The norms regarding political speeches will be different in different cultures: Who can participate as speaker and audience, the appropriate topics for such a speech, what kinds of cultural themes can be used, where such speeches can take place, the relation between the speaker and hearer in this context, the language used for political speeches in a multilingual community, and so forth. Sociolinguists are interested in the ways speech varies depending on an individual's position in a social structure or social relationship. In some cultures, different speech forms are used depending on whether the speaker and hearer are intimate friends, acquaintances on equal footing with each other, or of distinctly different social statuses. In French, German, and Spanish, among other languages, there are formal and informal terms of address that are lacking in English. Parents in these cultures will use the informal term to address their children, but children will use the formal term to their parents. In

Hindi, the status of a husband is much higher than that of a wife. A wife will never address her husband by his name (certainly not in public), but will use a roundabout expression that would translate into English something like "I am speaking to you, sir."

It is also clear that in socially stratified societies, speech norms are different in different social classes. Elites and working class people not only have a different vocabulary, but they pronounce words differently. Where variation in pronunciation exists, one form will be considered proper, or the "prestige" form, and another will be associated with lower

Sociolinguists are interested in the study of speech performance: how people actually speak and what choices they make in different social situations. (Serena Nanda)

socioeconomic status. Individuals may be aware of these two forms and vary their pronunciation in different contexts. Some people who use the "lower" form in casual speech will switch to the prestige form in more careful speech. For example, William Labov (1972) studied the pronunciation of certain vowels used in ordinary speech in New York City. He found that pronunciation of these vowels (characteristic of a "New York accent") varied with socioeconomic class, ethnicity, and age of the speaker. The degree of speech variation also correlated with social class. The lowest class of people did not vary their speech much from casual talk to careful speech. Upper-middle-class people, whose pronunciation normally falls midway between the extreme correct form and the extreme stigmatized form, also showed little variation. The most extreme variations was exhibited by the lower middle class, who used the stigmatized forms in casual speech, but the correct form in careful speech.

This study might be interpreted as demonstrating that those on the bottom do not vary their pronunciation because they have little hope of moving up socially; those at the top do not vary their pronunciation because they are relatively secure in their social position, and those in the middle (lower middle class) vary their pronunciation most because they are "social climbers," and therefore most sensitive to behaving in "correct" ways. But in any case, Labov's study makes clear what many of us know but do not like to admit: We do judge a person's social status by the way he/she speaks. The function of speech is not limited to communicating information. What we say and how we say it is also a way of telling people where we are socially—or perhaps, where we want to be.

In many new nations or speech communities, more than one language is known and used by the ordinary person. Sociolinguists are interested in the different contexts in which one or the other language would be used. In India, for example, where many upper-middle-class people are fluent in English, the native language is used at home among family, even if all the people present speak excellent English. The language a person chooses to use can be a way of solidifying ethnic or familial identity, or of distancing oneself from another person or group.

Nonverbal Communication

Ethnographers are also interested in nonverbal communication. In Chapter 4, we noted the work of Edward Hall on space and time. Think of some of the ways in which, to quote Hall, "time talks" and

"space speaks." In our culture, what are we saying to a person when we show up for an appointment 40 minutes late? Are we saying something different if we show up 10 minutes early? Is a Latin American who shows up late for an appointment saying the same thing?

Part of a nonverbal communication pattern is how close we stand to another person, whether we face them directly or stand at an angle, whether our arms are folded in front of us or hanging down at our sides. All cultures use nonverbal gestures to communicate. Some of these gestures are conscious; some are unconscious. What people say with their facial expressions is a powerful form of communication. Among the Tuareg, a tribal people of North Africa, where men are veiled, the position of the veil is an important part of nonverbal communication (Murphy 1964). A Tuareg man will only lower his veil among intimates and persons of lower social status. When he is engaged in an encounter in which he does not wish to commit himself to a particular course of action, he will wear the veil very high on the bridge of his nose, so that the other party can read as little as possible from his facial expression. In our culture, as in many cultures, the eyes are considered an important clue to what a person is feeling and thinking. This explains why some individuals wear dark glasses in situations where the glasses are not required as protection from the sun. By hiding the eyes, an individual attemps to control the flow of communication, and through this, the entire encounter. Because nonverbal communication is more ambiguous than verbal communication, it leaves the "speaker" with more options. To "say it with flowers" does not involve the same degree of commitment as "saying it with words."

LANGUAGE CHANGE

Language, like other parts of culture, shows both stability and change. The first step in studying language change is to identify it. Historical linguists study different stages of a language in order to identify the kinds of changes that have taken place. The fact that language does change can easily be seen in the differences between the Old English and Modern English versions of the Lord's Prayer:

Fæder ūre þū þe eart on heofonum, sī þīn nama ʒehālʒod. Tōbecume þīn rīce. Geweorþe þīn willa on eorþan swā swā on heofonum. Ūrne ʒedæʒhwāmlī- can hlāf syle ūs tō dæʒ. And forʒyf ūs ūre ʒyltas, swā swā wē forʒyfaþ ūrum ʒyltendum. And ne ʒelæd þū ūs on costnunʒe, ac ālȳs ūs of yfele.

Our Father, which art in heaven, hallowed be thy name. Thy kingdom come, Thy will be done, in earth as it is in heaven. Give us this day our daily bread. And forgive us our trespasses, as we forgive them that trespass against us. And lead us not into temptation, but deliver us from evil. (Lehnert 1960)

Historical linguistics can be applied to phonology, morphology, or vocabulary. With regard to phonology, linguists have been able to discover certain regularities in the ways in which sounds change. These regularities are called **phonetic laws.** An example of a phonetic law is the change from the accented vowel $\bar{a}$ in Old English to the vowel [ow] in Modern English. This phonetic law is illustrated in the following examples (Sturtevant 1947:65):

Old English	Modern English
bān	bone
bāt	boat
fām	foam
mān	moan
stān	stone
rād	road

This is an example of internal change. Language change can also come about through borrowing. When the Apache borrowed certain words—*loca, rico*—from the Spanish, a new phonemic occurrence was introduced, that of "l" and "r" in initial position, which was not part of the Apache phonemic pattern.

The vocabulary of a language also undergoes both internal and external changes. Words change their meanings, and new words are added. Sometimes, as cultures come into contact, cultural items are borrowed and the original name for the item is kept. Pajama is an item of clothing borrowed from India, and we have kept the original Indian word, incorporating it into the English vocabulary. Sometimes new items are referred to by a new combination of words already part of a language. When the Apache adopted corn, which was introduced by the Spanish, they referred to it using the words for "food" and "enemy" in their own language. Some native American groups, upon seeing their first horses (introduced by the Spanish), called them "ten dogs." Americans refer to their automobiles in terms of "horsepower." In New York City, the Spanish language spoken by Puerto Ricans has incorporated many English nouns that are given Spanish noun endings, thus creating new words; for example, *los ratones* (the rats), *el rufo* (the roof), *la factoria* (the factory), *la norsa* (nurse), *la mapa* (mop).

Historical linguists use the data on internal linguistic change to discover the relationships between different languages. If two languages appear related, what is the nature of the relationship? Are the similarities due to historical contact between cultures and resultant borrowing? Or are similarities between certain languages a result of their being derived from the same ancestral language? In other words, do similar languages have a historical or a generic relationship?

When the similarities appear too numerous, too regular, and too basic to be accounted for by borrowing, a generic relationship is assumed. Comparative linguists attempt to work out the relationships between generically related languages. By comparing the basic vocabularies (the words most resistant to change) of the descendant languages, comparative linguists attempt to reconstruct certain features of the ancestral or protolanguage. The list below shows the words in Sanskrit, Greek, Latin, and Gothic on which the reconstruction of the numbers one to ten in the original proto-Indo-European language are based (Sturtevant 1947)*:

The rate at which basic vocabulary is retained from an original language is assumed to be 80 percent per thousand years. Thus, by computing the percentage of shared basic vocabulary words between two languages, an estimate can be made about how long ago the two separated out from an original ancestral language. For example, if language A and language B share 50 percent of their basic vocabulary, it is estimated that they diverged from a common language, C, about 500 years ago:

Comparative linguistics has been successful in documenting the relationships between many languages and grouping them into language families. Although this has been done in greatest detail for Indo-European languages, the technique has also been applied to non-European languages. Thus, comparative linguistics is an important way of tracing cultural and historical processes. Through reconstruction

Sanskrit	Greek	Latin	Gothic	Proto-Indo-European
	oinē 'ace'	ūnus	ains	oinos
duā, dvā	dyō, dōdeca	duo	twa	duō, dwō
trayas	treis	trēs	þreis	treyes
catvāras	tettares	quattuor	fidwor	kwetwōres
panca	pente	quīnque	fimf	penkwe
sat	hex	sex	saihs	seks
sapta	hepta	septem	sibun	septm
astau	octō	octō	ahtau	oktōu
nava	ennea	novem	niun	newn
daśa	deca	decem	taihun	dekm

*Edgar H. Sturtevant, *An Introduction to Linguistic Science,* 1947. Reprinted with permission of Yale University Press.

of a protolanguage, comparative linguistics can also tell us something about the culture of the people who spoke that language. For example, because the basic vocabulary of proto-Indo-European contains words for trees and animals that existed in northern Europe, this may have been the home of the original Indo-Europeans.

Traditional linguists have mainly been concerned with internal language change. Sociolinguists are interested in language history, or the study of historical events that affect language change. Some of the contemporary problems here have to do with the impact of industrialization, acculturation, social stratification, and national politics, as these relate to changes in language structure and language use. Sociolinguists are also interested in the social factors within a society that affect changes in both structure and language use. As Labov showed in his study, sound change not only follows phonetic laws; it is also affected by the pattern of social stratification in a society since different social classes adopt a sound change at different times.

SUMMARY

1. All animals communicate. Although nonhuman primates have a complex communication system, they lack the features of true human language: conventionality, productivity, and displacement.

2. Conventionality means that human languages use a limited number of sounds in combination to make an infinite number of meaningful utterances.

3. Productivity means that humans can produce and understand an infinite number of utterances they have never said or heard before.

4. Displacement refers to the ability of human languages to describe things and experiences not immediately present in the environment.

5. Human speech is adaptive: it is efficient and flexible. It allows humans to think, to plan, to coordinate activities, to store up knowledge, and to teach others. The complexity of culture depends on human ability to communicate through speech.

6. All human languages display the same capabilities of conventionality, productivity, and displacement. There are no primitive languages.

7. A child takes the initiative in learning language and learns to speak grammatically without being taught grammatical rules. This suggests that human beings have precultural or innate language-learning capacity. This potential for speech will only be realized, however, through interaction with other human beings speaking a human language.

8. All languages have structure. The three subsystems of a language are a sound system, a grammar, and a vocabulary. Phonemes are minimal sound units that carry meaning; syntax is the combination of morphemes used to produce meaningful utterances; vocabulary links words to their meanings.

9. The grammatical categories of a language are the vehicles by which people think. Grammar and vocabulary

structure perception of the environment. The ways in which different cultures perceive reality through the grammatical categories of their language may show relationships to other aspects of that culture.

10. A language is not the same as speech. A language is a system of knowledge independent of the way it is used; speech is what people actually do when they communicate with each other. Sociolinguists are interested in speech behavior as it is culturally patterned and varies according to social factors.

11. Language changes. Historical linguists are interested in internal linguistic change. Comparative linguists attempt to discover which languages are generically related. Sociolinguists are interested in the historical and social factors in language change.

SUGGESTED READINGS

Burling, Robbins
   1970 *Man's Many Voices.* New York: Holt, Rinehart and Winston. An excellent introduction to all aspects of language including topics not usually covered in introductory texts, such as Black English and word games.

Farb, Peter
   1974 *Word Play: What Happens When People Talk.* New York: Knopf. As is usual with this author, this book is comprehensive, entertaining, and interesting for the nonspecialist.

Gumperz, John J. and Hymes, Dell, eds.
   1972 *Directions in Sociolinguistics.* New York: Holt, Rinehart and Winston. A compilation of interesting articles from a number of different cultures on a variety of kinds of speech performances.

Southworth, F. C., and Daswani, C. J.
   1974 *Foundations of Linguistics.* New York: Free Press. This is a good complete introduction to the study of language written in a straightforward, clear manner.

Stross, Brian
   1976 *The Origin and Evolution of Language.* Dubuque: William C. Brown. A highly readable book that includes discussion of what the fossil record suggests about the evolution of human speech.

United Nations/Anthony Fisher

6
Learning Culture

Human infants become adults only by growing up in a human society. More than any other species, human beings are dependent on others for survival and growth. The human infant cannot survive without the care of other people. It cannot get food, it cannot move around, it cannot cling, it cannot force an adult to respond to its needs. The human's period of helplessness and dependency on others is the longest in the animal world. It is the price *Homo sapiens* pays for its big brain and its enormous potential for learning. And it is during the long period of infancy that cultural patterning has its strongest effect. The infant simply has no choice about learning to respond in culturally patterned ways. Thus, the infant grows up into a child and later into an adult not simply as a human, but as a particular kind of human: a Kwakiutl, or a Trobriand Islander, a Briton, Eskimo, or Tahitian. **Enculturation** is the term anthropologists use to refer to the ways in which human infants and children learn to be adult members of their society.

BIOLOGY, SOCIALIZATION, AND CULTURE

In spite of its helplessness, the human infant is not simply an "empty slate" on which culture writes its pattern, or a lump of clay on which culture impresses its own shape. As we have seen in the chapter on language, human beings have a biologically based disposition to learn human behavior. The human infant and child actively participates in culture. Human brains and nervous systems are organized to promote social interaction with others, learning, and adaptation to the requirements of a particular sociocultural system. In addition to the biological characteristics of the species, each human individual has a unique genetic inheritance as well, which it brings to the socialization process. Becoming a human being, therefore, is the result of a complex interaction between universal human capacities and culturally variable child-rearing practices, individual heredity, and the common experiences patterned by culture.

Anthropologists are not in complete agreement about what exactly these innate human capacities and potentialities are. We know that infants have not only physical needs but emotional ones as well. Studies of infants in a variety of situations have demonstrated that "tender loving care" is a prerequisite for healthy emotional development (Spitz 1975). This need also exists among nonhuman primates. Experimental studies demonstrate that infant monkeys who are deprived of the company of their mothers do not develop in the same way as other monkeys. They play less; they are less curious, more hostile, and sexually clumsy. Male monkeys raised apart from their mothers show little interest in female monkeys as adults. Female monkeys raised apart from their mothers show little interest in their own babies (Harlow 1962).

All human beings also pass through a similar sequence of developmental stages, each characterized by an increase in the capacity to deal with the physical and social environment. At each stage physical, mental, and psychological potentialities unfold, given at least a minimum of encouragement. Physically, the infant increases in muscular coordination; from an immobile creature barely able to focus the movement of eyes and limbs, it begins to be able to lift its head, focus its eyes, sit up, creep on all fours, stand, and then walk by itself. Mentally, it increases its capacity to differentiate and classify objects and people in the environment. Its curiosity increases. Human infants will, if given a chance, take an active role in trying new ways of behaving and exploring the world around them. Psychologically, the infant increasingly develops a sense of itself and others. As the infant grows, it learns to modify its demands so that it will meet with success in its social environment. The infant becomes increasingly able to distinguish what actions will bring gratification, and what actions will be met with no response or negative response from others. Cultural variability in child-rearing must be seen against the background of universals that grow out of the biological characteristics of the human organism: the needs for physical gratification and for emotional contact with others, and stages of developmental capacities. Thus, socialization must be seen against the different stages of the life cycle.

Every system of cultural transmission takes into account these different stages of life, although the definition of the stages may vary from culture to culture. Infants are treated differently from children, children reach puberty and eventually become adults; adults are distinguished as middle-aged and old. With each of these status changes, different roles are assumed and different kinds of cultural transmission take place. Although in anthropology we have traditionally emphasized early socialization rather than the transmission of culture in later life, we are now paying greater attention to learning in adulthood and among the old.

Not only do societies transmit culture in terms of life stages, but not all people in a society are given the same social conditioning. Status differences and the roles, or behavior patterns associated with them must be considered in investigating the way culture is transmitted. In societies where social ranking and differentiation is important, what one learns may be largely a function of one's position in the social hierarchy. At the very least, every society treats males and females differently.

SEX ROLE SOCIALIZATION

This process of sex role socialization frequently begins at infancy or shortly thereafter. The ways in which this is done and its effects on behavior and personality are always of interest to anthropologists. Two important processes associated with sex role learning are imitation and internalization through identification with a same-sex role model. In child's play, for example, girls most frequently imitate the domestic activities of their mothers and boys of their fathers, or elder males and females who stand in this relation to them. This imitation is subtly encouraged along the lines of sex even when it is not a consequence of direct teaching. Girls and boys are both discouraged from imitating activities culturally considered appropriate for the opposite sex, and rewarded for the imitating activities considered culturally appropriate for their own sex. The internalization of gender identification— that is, the inner conceptualization of self as being masculine or feminine—is tied up with the playing out of these sex-related activities.

Part of the controversy in the study of sex role socialization is the extent to which the differences that have been found to be related to sex are based on biology (Draper 1974). Since learning begins at birth, untangling the complex interaction between biology and culture becomes extremely difficult. When adult expectations of children become stereotyped according to sex role, it may be this expectation, even more than possible biological differences, that explains the differentiation in male-female behavior and personality.

The complex way in which biology and culture may interact to produce differences in male-female behavior is illustrated by the findings that girls seem to have greater verbal ability and boys greater spatial ability. It is generally agreed that girls have a better and earlier ability to acquire language than do boys and that they are more sensitive to social cues than boys. Boys, on the other hand, are almost universally shown to have superior spatial ability. If we assume that these abilities have some biological basis, we can also assume that they would be incorporated into parents' expectations of children. They would expect little girls to talk more and respond to others and might talk more with them. They would allow, reward, or even initiate activities in which boys can explore their environment. Subtle but persistent interactions with others based on the initial biological differences

Sex role socialization often involves the informal participation of children in the appropriate economic roles of their sex. Here, small boys in Fez, Morocco, hold the golden threads that their tailor fathers are using to make embroidered djellabahs, the local garment. (United Nations)

may play a large role in explaining some sex-role-related patterns in adults—for example, the greater success girls have in school (which rewards verbal ability and social sensitivity) and the superior performance of males on tests of spatial ability.

But the evidence is not clear. In practically all societies, small boys are allowed to roam farther from their home than small girls. This is both consistent with, and may be a cause of, the superior spatial abilities of males. Yet studies of exceptional girls in one East African society who were allowed to roam farther from home than was typically the case showed they matched their male counterparts on tests of spatial ability. Such findings put us back to a position in which sex role socialization appears to be best understood in terms of both biological and cultural components

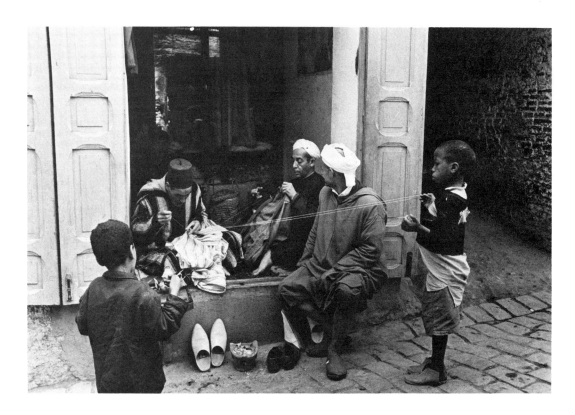

interacting in complex ways. One useful model for understanding this process may be that socialization practices act back upon and intensify possible biological predispositions that are different in males and females.

PERSONALITY, CULTURE, AND EARLY SOCIALIZATION

Child-rearing practices in all cultures are designed to produce adults who will be able to function effectively in that culture. In order to be able to do this, adults must learn certain skills, norms, and values; they must learn the cultural *content*. But the transmission of culture involves more than cultural content; in the socialization process, children learn more than just skills and knowledge. The transmission of culture involves patterning a child's attitudes and values as well as its outward behavior. The shaping of values and personality, or the inner life of the child, often does not take place consciously. Through unconscious, although culturally patterned, interaction with others, the growing individual learns to respond to the world in culturally selected ways. From the vast potential of emotional responses, cultures select out some that are considered appropriate. Through the details of its experiences with others, the child learns to pattern its emotional responses in culturally approved ways.

Culture as Communication

The covert aspect of socialization calls attention to culture as a communication process. From this point of view, what is important in cultural transmission is not so much what children are taught or not taught, or what they do or do not do, but the ways in which things happen to them and the attitudes of the people around them with whom they are interacting (Schwartz 1976).

The subtle ways in which personality is shaped through unconscious cultural patterning is illustrated in a study of Japanese and American mothers and infants carried out by William Caudhill and his associates (1973). In an earlier study, Caudhill noted that Japanese adults were much more accepting of each other's dependency needs than were Americans, for whom the emphasis was on independence. Caudhill hoped to throw some light on this difference in adult personality by studying the relationships between mothers and infants in Japan as compared to those in the United States.

He found that the actual time infants spent in various activities, such as sleeping and feeding, were the same in both cultures. Japanese and American mothers also spent almost the same amounts of time feeding, diapering, and dressing their infants. American infants, however, spent more of their waking time in an active manner—playing with toys and with their hands. Japanese infants were more passive when awake. In order to check whether this difference might have a genetic basis, Caudhill tested matched samples of Japanese-American infants, those who genetically were Japanese but whose parents and grandparents had been born and lived in the United States. The Japanese-American infants turned out to be significantly like the American infants and unlike the Japanese sample.

Caudhill then turned his attention to the "style" of caretaking in an attempt to account for the difference between the Japanese and American infant behavior. American mothers encouraged their infants to be active and vocally responsive, whereas the Japanese mother acted to soothe and quiet the baby. The American mother, for example, spends more of the baby's waking time looking at, positioning the body of, and chatting with her infant. The Japanese mother does more carrying, rocking, and lulling. Caudhill relates these and other differences in caretaking style to a basic difference in psychological attitude between Japanese and American mothers. American mothers see the baby as a separate person who should learn to think and do for itself. Encouraging vocalization is one way in which the American mother "teaches" her infant to express its needs. Japanese mothers, on the other hand, have a much closer attachment to their infants. A Japanese mother feels she knows what her infant needs; there is no need for it to "express" itself. This is consistent not only with the lesser vocalization of the Japanese baby, but also with the greater physical contact between the Japanese baby and its mother. Thus, the dependency of Japanese and the independence of Americans, differences that show up in the adult personality, seem to come under cultural direction as early as three to four months of age.

PERSONALITY IN ADAPTATION

The idea that personality develops as an adaptation to the basic food getting pattern of a society is not new in anthropology but has recently attracted increasing attention. One important anthropological project examining the interrelation between food getting, social structure, child rearing

and personality, is the study of six cultures carried out by Beatrice Whiting and her associates (1963). Briefly, this project developed the thesis that maintenance systems which include basic economy and aspects of social structure, such as residence, sets the parameters for child rearing practices. These, in turn, shape adult personality, which in turn is reflected in other cultural elements such as religious beliefs and folklore (see Fig. 6.1, p. 104).

SOCIALIZATION IN LATER LIFE

Learning one's culture is a process that continues after infancy and early childhood, although most social scientists agree that the earliest years are crucial. In looking at later socialization, anthropologists have been interested in a number of different aspects of the transmission of culture. One is the relationship between early enculturation and later enculturation. As the child grows up and moves into new and adult roles, is what it has learned in childhood useful for those roles? Is there, in other words, cultural continuity in socialization?

Cultural Continuity and Discontinuity

Ruth Benedict (1938) characterized American culture as containing major discontinuities between what is expected of children and what is expected of adults. Children in our culture are not expected to be responsible: They are supposed to play, not work. Few children in America have the opportunity to contribute in any meaningful way to the basic tasks of society. Children take on responsibility only when they become

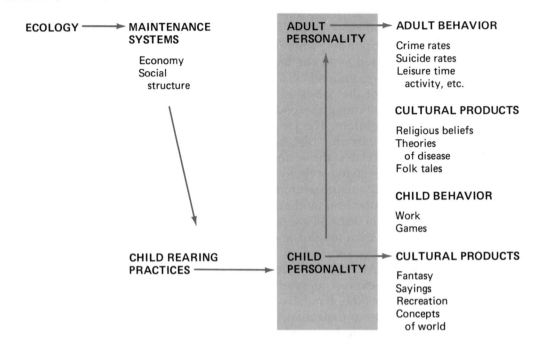

Figure 6.1 *A theory of the relationship of personality to culture based on the following process:* ecology *determines* maintenance system, *which includes basic economy and elements of social structure. For example, climate and soil determine the nature of crops grown in an agricultural society and whether or not herding is present. The way in which people get food determines in part the arrangement of people in space and household composition. This in turn sets the parameters for* child-rearing practices. *Different child-rearing practices lead to differences in the* personality of children *and also differences in* adult personality. *These personality dimensions will in turn be reflected in* cultural products *such as religion and folklore. From* Six Cultures: Studies of Child Rearing. *Edited by Beatrice Whiting. John Wiley & Sons, Inc., 1969. Reprinted with permission.*

adults. A second major discontinuity is that children are required to be submissive, but as adults are expected to be dominant. This is especially true for males, sons must obey their fathers, but as fathers they must dominate their sons. A third major discontinuity has to do with sex. As children, Americans are not allowed to engage in sexual behavior, and for many people just the thought of childhood sexuality is repellent. As adults, however, especially as men and women marry, sex is considered to be a normal, even valued, activity.

In great contrast to the discontinuities experienced by the individual learning to participate in American culture is the continuity of socialization among many native American societies. The Cheyenne, a Plains Indian tribe, exhibit a great degree of continuity in their culture. Cheyenne children are not treated as a different order of people from adults. They are regarded as smaller and not yet fully competent adults, although by American standards the competence of Cheyenne children is quite astounding. The play of small

(continues on p. 111)

CHILD-REARING AND PERSONALITY IN VILLAGE INDIA*

One of the cultures studied in the six culture project was that of the Rajput caste in the village of Khalapur in northern India. Two basic principles that organize Indian society are caste and family. The castes, which are groups traditionally associated with particular occupations, are ranked as superior or inferior. Although castes change their position in the hierarchy, an individual cannot move from one caste to another. An individual's social mobility or social status is dependent on the caste into which he or she is born. A person is also a member of a family group. In northern India, the family is generally patriarchal, patrilineal, and patrilocal. This means that the males have the power, inheritance is through the male line, and the wife goes to live in her husband's home after marriage. Family and caste are the most important arenas of social, religious, and economic activity. The group, not the individual, is the center of culture and society. An individual will rarely be called upon to act independently, and setting himself against the group involves the great risk of being left without the social networks on which success in India depends.

Child-rearing practices in Khalapur must be understood in terms of the socially restricted lives of Indian villagers. These practices are directed, both consciously and unconsciously, toward training the child to function effectively within the social framework of family, caste, and village. Three aspects of child-rearing practices related to this are training in emotional unresponsiveness, training in controlling aggression and assertiveness, and the lack of training in self-reliance.

The Rajput caste claims descent from the ancient warrior kings of India. Today, however, they are mostly farmers. Rajput dwellings in the village of Khalapur include separate quarters for males and females, which is a typical Indian spatial configuration. The women's quarters are within an enclosed courtyard. Rajput women practice purdah: they wear a veil in front of all male strangers and any men in their husband's family who are older than their husbands. The life of Rajput women and small children is largely lived within the confines of the courtyard. The men have their own quarters, where they spend most of their time; they socialize, eat, and frequently sleep apart from the women.

Training in emotional unresponsiveness begins at birth. Although Rajput infants will be picked up and attended to when they are hungry or fussing, for the most part they are left in their cots,

---

*John T. Hitchcock and Leigh Minturn, "The Rajputs of Khalapur" in *Six Cultures: Studies of Child Rearing,* Beatric Whiting, ed. © 1963. John Wiley & Sons. Reprinted by permission of the publisher.

wrapped up in blankets both to keep off insects and to avoid the evil eye. Except for anxieties about a baby's health, it is not the center of attention. A baby receives attention mainly when it cries. At that time someone will try to distract it, but when it becomes quiet the interaction will stop. Adult interaction with babies is generally aimed at producing a cessation of response, rather than stimulation of it. Infants and children of all ages are not shown off to others for fear, parents say, that they will attract the evil eye. Children are also not praised by their parents, who fear this will "spoil" them and make them disobedient.

The Rajput child spends its first two years as a passive observer of courtyard life. It is never left alone, yet neither is it the center of interest. Rajput mothers do not tease or frustrate their children, but neither are they very emotionally responsive toward them. Unresponsiveness is itself a message; the child learns that moodiness will not be tolerated. Few demands are put on Rajput children; they are not pressured or even encouraged to become self-reliant. Weaning, which generally occurs without trouble, takes place at 2 to 3 years; but if the mother does not become pregnant, a child may be nursed into its sixth year. Elimination is also no problem. Babies are not diapered, and when the baby is being held by someone it is simply held away from the body when it urinates. The mother will try to anticipate bowel movements and hold the baby over a trash pile outside the courtyard at the appropriate time. When a child can walk, it is led outside the courtyard to urinate or defecate; since this is done in public by adults, the child can easily imitate the proper behavior.

In many ways Rajput children are discouraged from doing things on their own and encouraged to seek aid from others. Babies, for example, are not encouraged to crawl. They learn to walk when they are ready, and mothers say they see no reason to rush this. When a baby can walk alone, it wanders about the courtyard, or may be taken by an older child to the men's house. Village women do little to guide a child's behavior by explaining or reasoning with it. There is also little direct instruction to small children. A child is not considered trainable until it can talk; no demands are made on children to modify their behavior until they can walk and say a few words. Small children learn the skills, customs, and values of the group through observation and imitation. In the first five years of life, the child moves very gradually from observer to participant in village and family life.

The preschool child plays most of the time. Although some of this child's play involves imitating adult activities, such as farming and cooking, children are not encouraged in any way to participate in adult activities. The chores a child is given are mainly directed to helping the mother, who is confined to the courtyard. Thus, children may go to the store, or carry water, or deliver messages to the men's house. There is little feeling that a child should be given chores on principle in order to train it in responsibility. Because a daughter goes to live with her husband's family after marriage and because she will have to work so hard in her husband's house under the eyes of a dominating mother-in-law, she is considered "a guest in her own house" and is given even less to do than a boy.

Rajput children take little initiative in solving problems by themselves, but are taught instead who they can depend on for help in the web of social relations of kin group, caste, and village. Children follow the adult pattern of giving aid only when asked and often only if it is insistently demanded. Although chores increase somewhat as the child gets older, it is not a Rajput custom to require children to work if adults can do it. Children are not praised for their work, and a child's inept attempt to do an adult job is belittled. Thus, children are reluctant to undertake what they cannot do well.

This lack of responsibility is consistent with the pattern of values in a caste society. In the Indian caste system, menial and manual work is considered not only degrading socially but ritually polluting. Many Rajputs are quite wealthy and employ servants to do the menial tasks which in other cultures might be assigned to children. Finally, as a caste of warriors, Rajputs have contempt for farming, although that is how they earn their livelihood. A Rajput family that can afford it will hire laborers to do the farm work. Even if a Rajput man does his own farming, he passes on a negative attitude about this work to his sons.

The third aspect of child-rearing in Khalapur related to the requirements of Indian social organization is that aggression and assertiveness are inhibited in small children. There is some ambivalence here. The caste system and the family system require an individual to be submissive to those above, but dominant with those below. Also, as a warrior caste, there is an aggressive image that Rajput males feel they ought to maintain. The lack of consistency in training children to control aggression reflects this. On the one hand, mothers *say* a child ought to be passive, submissive, and restrained in the presence of others. Fighting among children is discouraged. Most of the mothers never give the child advice to "fight" or even to "fight back," and several were shocked that the anthropologist would even consider giving such advice to a child. On the other hand, the mothers allow a certain aggression against themselves, especially on the part of sons. Males learn pretty early that women have a low status in the village and family and can thus be abused, at least verbally. Men are more willing than women to teach a child to be aggressive. Although they believe a child should not start a fight, fathers in Khalapur do admit telling their children to fight back. This aggressiveness is reinforced by the traditional storytelling and drama of Hindu mythology, in which the bravery of the Rajput warriors is an important feature.

Rajput child-rearing thus emphasizes emotional unresponsiveness, represses individuality, and teaches children to know whom to ask for aid, rather than to solve their problems themselves. They are not encouraged to be outwardly aggressive, but they do learn to be dominant with their social inferiors. Child-rearing practices in Khalapur make sense in terms of the social structures of a caste hierarchy, limited geographical and social mobility, and living in an extended family in which group harmony rather than individual assertiveness is a basic requirement.

The ritual of the birthday party teaches children in the United States to place importance on the self and encourages individualism.
(Serena Nanda)

IDEOLOGY, COMMUNAL CHILD-REARING, AND PERSONALITY ON THE ISRAELI KIBBUTZ

The *kibbutz* is a collective agricultural settlement in the state of Israel. The kibbutz was created by European Jews who wanted to create a community built on social justice and the economic principles of "from each according to his ability and to each according to his needs." Private property would be done away with; the community rather than the family would be the most important group. Women who had been limited to a secondary role in the traditional East European nuclear family would have a new chance to become full human beings, equal with men, working alongside them and not limited to the private domestic sphere of family life. Although the pattern of communal child-rearing originally started out as an expedient to allow women to work, it has since developed into an important part of kibbutz ideology. There is a great deal of variation in the degree to which communal child-rearing is considered essential to the kibbutz way of life; the description above is not characteristic of all *kibbutzim* (Spiro 1958).

An infant born on the *kibbutz* is placed in an infants' house as soon as the mother returns from the hospital; the infant remains there for six months. During that time, several infants are cared for by a woman specially trained as an infant nurse. The infant is regularly visited by its mother and usually breast fed. This is done at the same time by all the mothers of infants sharing an infant house. Feeding is thus a social experience for the infants as well as the mothers. It is also a time of close emotional contact between each individual mother and her infant. In the first six months, the mother also comes to put her infant to bed. Fathers also visit the infant regularly. When the infant reaches the age of 6 months, the parents may take it to their own room during the day for an hour or so, but the infant must return to the nursery to sleep.

Around the age of 1, a group of about five babies moves into the toddlers' house. These children will stay together until the age of 4. Ideally, they will have the same nurse with them for the whole time they are in the toddlers' house, although sometimes, there may be more than one nurse throughout their stay. When the children are 3 years old, a nursery teacher is added to, or occasionally replaces, the nurse. In the toddlers' house the mothers do not come to feed the child. This is done by the nurse: As soon as the children can manage it, they eat with the whole group, feeding themselves under the nurse's supervision. Children are frequently left in playpens with other children while the nurse is cleaning or attending to a particular child. Toilet training begins at around 2 years. All the toddlers are put on the potty together, and the peer group is now a major helping agent.

The children's parents visit them daily, several times a day. The parents' visit is always a positive experience; the parents are in no way responsible for disciplining or training the child. They praise their child for whatever it has accomplished and devote themselves to the child's needs. All toys in the toddlers' house are communally owned, although the child may also have its own toys in its parent's house, which it visits daily.

At the age of 4, the toddler group merges with another toddler group, and about ten to sixteen children move into the kindergarten house. This group will stay together for the rest of childhood, up until adolescence. The nurse or nursery teacher from each group accompanies her group into its new residence, giving some continuity of caretakers. But the peer group now becomes the main factor of continuity in the child's life, and the major agent of enculturation. The peer group does everything together: eating, playing, bathing, studying, and sleeping. The group is made up of boys and girls, and the communal life, including toilet training, bathing, and sexual play, is encouraged as a way of preventing the guilt and shame associated with sexuality in traditional Jewish life and culture.

Studies of personalities of *kibbutz* children seem to indicate that communal child-rearing has accomplished many of its aims. The children raised in this way feel themselves to be "children of the *kibbutz*" and are regarded as such by adults. They feel they belong not to individual families, but to the whole community, and most particularly to the peer group with which they were raised. Even as adolescents, when growing sexuality might seem to threaten this solidarity, group values are strong enough to prevent any conflict. In spite of the sexual permissiveness of *kibbutz* life, adolescents do not appear to have any sexual interest in each other. Group activities are the norm, and exclusive dating is actively discouraged by the peer group.

There is little serious pathology, deviance, or delinquency on the *kibbutz*. Studies of the outcomes of communal child-rearing thus seem to show that children can grow up emotionally healthy and productive without an exclusive emotional involvement with a mothering figure.

children centers on imitation of and real participation and responsibility in adult tasks. Both boys and girls learn to ride horses almost as soon as they can walk. This skill is related to the importance of the horse in traditional Cheyenne culture, in which buffalo were hunted on horseback. By the time they are 6, little boys are riding bareback and using the lasso. By 8, boys are helping to herd the horses in the camp. As soon as they can use them, boys get small but good-quality bows and arrows. Little girls who are just toddlers help their mothers carry wood and water. Boys and girls learn these activities in play, in which the routine of family life is imitated. Girls play "mother" to the smallest children; boys imitate the male roles of hunter and warrior, and even the rituals of self-torture that are part of Cheyenne religious ceremonies.

Control of aggression is an important value among the Cheyenne, and aggression rarely occurs within the group of adults. A chief rules not by force and dominance, but by intelligence, justice, and consideration for others. The needs of the group are more important than the need of the individual. The Cheyenne learn this lesson at an early age. Infants who cry are not physically punished but they will be removed from the camp and their baskets hung in the bushes until they stop. This is an early lesson in learning that one cannot force one's will on others by self-display. Aggression and lack of control of one's emotions does not bring rewards for either children or adults; rather, they result in social isolation.

The repression of sexuality is another lesson traditionally learned early in childhood and carried through adult life. A Cheyenne girl is considered unchaste if a boy even touches her genitals or breasts,

and she cannot enter into a respectable marriage. From the time of her first menses, a girl puts on a "chastity belt" of rope and rawhide which she takes off only at marriage, and in fact may continue to wear even during marriage when her husband is away fighting or hunting. Males are also taught to control their sexual impulses. They cannot even think of courtship or marriage until they have been in a war party. Sexual control continues to be an ideal even in marriage. The Cheyenne ideal is to space children ten to twelve years apart. A couple who takes a vow to refrain from sexual relations for this period after the birth of a child is highly respected in the camp.

Although Cheyenne childhood seems to require a great deal of discipline, responsibility, and competence, these demands are consistent with the demands on adults. There is no discontinuity between Cheyenne childhood, adolescence, and adulthood. The transition to adult status is very easy, being a continuum of what was learned in childhood. For a boy, the public recognition of this status comes with his first participation as hunter and warrior, which occurs at about the age of 12. This is a real and important event, and his achievement is publicly rewarded by his parents' praise and a feast given in his honor. As Hoebel (1960), the ethnographer of the Cheyenne says: "Cheyenne youths have little reason to be rebels without a cause. They slip easily into manhood, knowing their contributions are immediately wanted, valued and ostentatiously rewarded."

Initiation Rites

It has been suggested by a number of anthropologists that there is more discontinuity in socialization for males than for females (Chodorow 1974). For boys to become men frequently requires an assertion of independence that involves a rejection of feminine qualities and identifications. For girls, the transition to adult status is more of a continuation of their early life, which is organized around and involved with the family, primary and personal relationships, and caring for others. The need for boys to break away from female identifications and female dependency may be one explanation of the frequency of male **initiation rites** in many societies around the world. From this perspective, male initiation rites may be seen as bridging the gap where discontinuities exist between early childhood socialization and the requirements of an adult masculine role. Thus, John Whiting (1967) and his associates have shown that male initiation rites are more likely to occur in cultures where there is a strong identification of the boy with his mother and hostility toward the father. This may grow out of sleeping arrangements in which children sleep with the mother apart from the father. In these cases, says Whiting, male initiation rites are necessary to ensure the development of an adequate male role.

In many societies, a boy between the ages of 5 to 12 must undergo an initiation, after which he is publicly recognized as a man. This "rite of passage" is frequently lengthy, dramatic, and painful, and often involves circumcision. During this initiation, a boy may also be taught tribal lore as well as more practical elements of culture. From this perspective, some anthropologists have seen initiation rites primarily in terms of their educational functions. They are the equivalent of the formal schooling received by children in our own society. Still another explanation offered for male

initiation rites is that of dramatizing the values of society in a context outside the intimacy of the home (Hart 1967). By taking the child out of the home, the initiation rite emphasizes the importance of citizenship—the fact that an individual must be responsible to the whole society, and that society as well as the family has an interest in him. A fourth function suggested for male initiation rites is that of explicitly affirming and maintaining the solidarity of the male bond in society and the importance of male organization to social life. Still other interpretations have focused on the symbolism of the rites themselves. Bruno Bettelheim (1962), a psychoanalyst who studied rites that involve circumcision, suggests that they are symbolic of the male envy of the female power of bearing children. The bloodletting associated with the rites is an attempt to imitate and thus participate in these life-creating powers at a symbolic level.

The Marginal Status of Adolescents

Anthropologists have looked at later socialization in terms of the ways in which adolescents, who are in a marginal status, become fully incorporated into their culture. Where cultural continuity is present, as among the Cheyenne, youth are not marginal. There is a gradually increasing social participation from childhood through adulthood. In many societies where there is discontinuity, where a youth must change in order to become an adult, dramatic rituals of initiation ensure that this change is made. In other societies, like our own, there is a discontinuity but no ritual. Young men, particularly, are left on their own to "initiate themselves." This

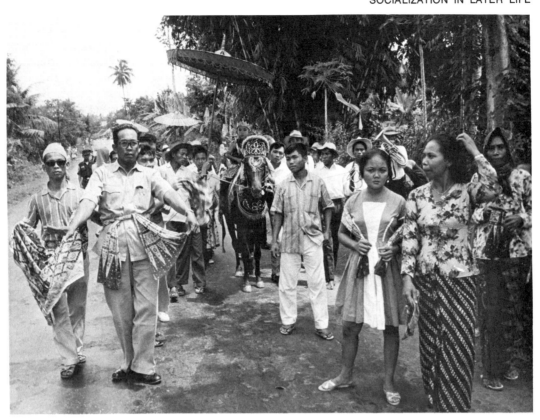

Male initiation rites are a common feature in the world's cultures and mark the transition from childhood to adulthood. On the eve of his circumcision ceremony, a boy rides a horse accompanied by dancers and musicians in a village in Indonesia. (United Nations)

may lead to the formation of youth gangs, or to various other informal peer-group activities in which peers socialize each other into the male role. This behavior is frequently rebellious and contrary to society's values, but not always. Among the Xhosa of South Africa, youth groups engage in activities that dramatize the male role, provide an arena for physical and sexual activity, and yet are in full accord with the adult values and roles of the culture (Mayer and Mayer 1970). Here again we are back to the two-faced coin of enculturation: On the one hand, each child must grow up and in doing so achieve the competence and psychological growth necessary for healthy human functioning. On the other hand, each culture must find a way of transmitting its values and knowledge to the growing child and youth so that the basic culture will be continued. As we have seen, and will continue to see in later chapters, there is great variability in the ways in which this is done. Many cultures seem far more successful than our own in providing cultural continuity, and yet allowing the needs of different stages of development to be met within the cultural structure.

BECOMING A SOCIAL PERSON: MALE INITIATION AMONG THE KAGURU*

The Kaguru, a matrilineal tribe living in East Africa (see Fig. 6.2) have initiation rites for both boys and girls. The Kaguru view initiation as necessary in order to convert irresponsible, immature minors into morally responsible adults. Kaguru male initiation includes both the circumcision and moral instructions. Kaguru initiates learn how they will be expected to conduct themselves as adults. The physical distress of initiation makes the difference between the old life of the child and the new life of the adult more dramatic and leads to a greater acceptance of a new code of behavior.

Ideally a group of boys is initiated together, both to increase the prestige of the ceremony and to divide the costs, and because it is felt that the boys will bear the pain of circumcision and learn better if they are in a group. The most important persons in charge of putting the boy through initiation are his father and his mother's brother, who plays an important role in all matrilineal societies. A professional circumcisor is hired for the operation. He is chosen for his skill in cutting and the effectiveness of his medicines, which protect the boy from both physical and supernatural dangers.

The themes of danger and vulnerability are dominant in the ritual. On the announced day, the boys, some senior male kin, and the circumcisor are led into the bush. The boys are stripped of their clothing and shaved of all body and head hair. This symbolizes the separation from their previous statuses. The boys are told they may die from the circumcision. The boy's elder kinsmen hold him down in a sitting position while he is circumcised. It is considered admirable not to flinch or cry out, but those who do so are not condemned. The cutting is accompanied by songs and ritual. The foreskin is cut off, removing the "low, dirty," femininelike part of the boy. The bloodied objects are buried secretly. The boys are led to a shed to rest and be fed by elders. During the healing time, they are considered to be helpless, like babies.

Each day food is brought to them by the men, who sing a song telling of their pity for the wounded boys. The boys learn songs and riddles, many of which are related to the teaching of proper sexual behavior and knowledge. These songs also have a deeper meaning related to basic Kaguru values. Here is one example: "Child, don't go out early in the morning or you will meet a rhinoceros with its horn slashing and exposing red flesh." The hidden meaning here is that a youth should not to enter his parents'

* Based on *The Kaguru: A Matrilineal People of East Africa*, by Thomas O. Beidelman. New York: Holt, Rinehart and Winston, 1971.

house too early in the morning or he may see them having sexual relations. Any hint of sexuality is considered shameful among Kaguru parents and children. The horror of such conduct is expressed by allusion to the rhino (a fierce wild animal), to redness, which is the color of blood, fire, danger, and death, and the slashing, which reflects the aggressiveness with which sexuality is viewed among the Kaguru.

When the boys recover physically, each day they are allowed to go farther back into the camp. The boys are told that if they reveal the secrets of initiation, they will be devoured by wild beasts. During this time, the kin of the boys are also on their best behavior, because their actions may supernaturally endanger the boy's life. When the boys have fully recovered, they are sent out into the forest to perform some task. Everything in the initiation camp is then burned or buried. When the boys return, they are told the elders have swallowed everything. After staying up all that night, the youths, singing to show they have "conquered" the bush, are led out of the camp the next morning by their friends and kinsmen. After a feast and dance, the boys will be considered fully initiated. During this feast, the boys are blessed and given new names associated with certain kinsmen, both living and dead. The youth is now considered a full social person. He may engage in an adult sex life, court girls, and consider marriage. He will require a full funeral when he dies and become a true ancestral ghost.

Figure 6.2 *The location of the Kaguru in the modern African nation of Tanzania.*

SOCIALIZATION AND FORMAL EDUCATION

Although few anthropologists have devoted their attention to the school as an agent of socialization, Jules Henry has been particularly concerned with the kind of learning that goes on in American schools. Henry points out that the school not only formally instructs children in the skills they will need to participate in a highly industrialized society, but also transmits some basic cultural values without the students or the teacher being aware of what is going on. In the following incident, "At the Blackboard," Henry observes that competition as a social value is covertly learned along with the overt content of mathematics:*

Boris had trouble reducing "$^{12}/_{16}$" to the lowest terms and could only get as far as "$^6/_8$." The teacher asked him quietly if that was as far as he could reduce it. She suggested that "he think." Much heaving up and down and waving of hands by the other children, all frantic to correct him. Boris pretty unhappy, probably mentally paralyzed. The teacher, quiet, patient, ignores the others and concentrates with look and voice on Boris. She says, "Is there a bigger number than two you can divide into the two parts of the fraction?" After a minute or two, she becomes more urgent, but there is no response from Boris. She then turns to the class and says, "Well, who can tell Boris what the number is?" A forest of hands appears, and the teacher calls Peggy. Peggy says four may be divided into the numerator and denominator.

*Jules Henry, Culture Against Man. New York: Random House, Inc., 1963, p. 295. Reprinted by permission.

Henry goes on to say: "Boris' failure has made it possible for Peggy to succeed, his depression is the price of her exhilaration; his misery the occasion for her rejoicing." Whether Boris has learned math is questionable. Perhaps Boris' "nightmare at the blackboard" was a lesson for him in controlling himself so that "he would not fly shrieking from the room under the enormous public pressure." Boris has learned the fear of failure which, according to Henry, is one of the things a child must learn in order to get along in the competitive society of the United States.

As formal schooling has been introduced into many cultures through contact with the West, more anthropologists are turning to the role of the school in socialization. Many of these studies address the problems that occur when Western-style middle-class schools and education are imposed on traditional kin-based, non-Western communities. The education in typical Western schools is based on a particular kind of cognitive style: the ability to see abstract relationships which are mediated largely through language. The school atmosphere encourages an active mode of learning, solving problems on one's own, and a situation in which the teacher is involved in an impersonal and impartial role of instructing. Teaching style, educational context, and cognitive skills appear to conflict with traditional informal socialization in non-Western cultures. Here, learning takes place in the context of life, teaching is largely by example, verbal instruction plays a minimum role, and many of the problems are posed in terms that require a single solution to a particular case, rather than the ability to generalize. Although numerous studies have shown that with special training children from such traditional learning contexts can develop other cognitive skills and

CULTURE CONFLICT AND FORMAL EDUCATION

In a monograph called *The New Mathematics and an Old Culture* (1967), John Gay and Michael Cole present this "culture conflict" as it exists for the Kpelle of Liberia, in West Africa. Traditionally, Kpelle learning is based on the unquestioned acceptance of authority and rote learning. For the Kpelle, the "world remains a mystery to be accepted on authority, not a complex pattern of comprehensible regularities." The Kpelle child does not look for patterns in visual stimuli or in words, nor does he think of numbers, measurements, and time in terms of laws and regularities. Among the Kpelle, for example, objects are counted and can be put into sets, but there are no words for independent abstract numerals in their language. Numerals must always be used to modify a noun or pronoun, as in "two of this and two of this make four of them." The abstraction "two and two make four" is not a normal part of Kpelle thinking, and presents an obvious source of difficulty when multiplication is taught to Kpelle children through rote memorization of the multiplication table.

Although Kpelle learning is functional for traditional Kpelle culture and consistent with the highest Kpelle values of conserving the past and learning to conform to traditional norms, it inhibits learning the scientific culture of the West which is transmitted through the school. The Kpelle schools try to teach new concepts through old methods. Children are taught Western mathematics, which requires a problem-solving approach, through the old methods of rote learning and imitation. Gay and Cole suggest that teachers must try to break through this authority structure, using material and analogies from the child's daily life and putting them in a framework that will make Western education comprehensible and meaningful. Western culture is impinging on Kpelle life at a very fast pace, and the school is one of the most important agents of Western culture. It is the teacher's task to help the Kpelle child cross the bridge from the old to the new. The teacher must make the classroom a living example of the scientific method, drawing from the child and from the strengths and concepts in Kpelle culture.

perform well on Western "intelligence" tests, as a rule there is conflict between the two systems, and many children from traditional cultures do not do well in school.

Cross-cultural studies of schoolchildren demonstrate the relationship between culture, cognition, and school performance. A recent long-term study that compares personality traits and school performance between children in Mexico and the United States (Holtzman et al. 1975) obtained significant cross-cultural differences for all the cognitive measures, nearly all the cognitive-perceptual style variables, and most of the personality and attitudinal measures. The authors see these differences as hinging on the active coping style of American children versus the passive coping style of the Mexican children, and on the emphasis in American culture on intellectual curiosity and independent thinking, in contrast to the Mexican emphasis on interpersonal relationships. These two important cultural differences correspond to differences in the home life of Mexican and American children. Mexican families were less likely to have intellectually stimulating reading material in the home. Only rarely did Mexican parents read regularly to the preschool child, whereas American parents read on a regular basis to their children. Most Mexican children were unable to read, count, or write before entering school. American children could, a point in which their parents took great pride.

The mother's education in the Mexican families was significantly lower than in the matched American sample. The typical number of children in the Mexican family was almost twice that in the American family. So the Mexican mother has to devote more time and energy to managing the house and has less time to stimulate the child's intellectual interests. The presence of other relatives in the Mexican household also discourages the pursuit of solitary intellectual activities.

The different modes of formal education in the two cultures intensifies the differences in Mexican and American culture. The Mexican emphasis on rote learning and lots of homework encourages a passive learning style that does not lead to independent thinking. This contrasts with the more active learning style characteristic of American schools. The passive coping style characteristic of Mexican culture affects children's attitudes toward testing. A Mexican child is willing to cooperate on a test, but will seldom take the initiative in the testing situation. The American middle-class child, on the other hand, sees testing as a challenge to be mastered, an opportunity to show how much he or she can do.

These cultural differences are modified by social class. A study using tests similar to those used above but carried out among upper-class Mexican families with children enrolled in an American school in Mexico City shows that most of the cognitive differences between the Mexican and American children disappear. Social class and type of shooling are clearly interrelated, and together account for differences in group scores on intelligence tests, success in school, and chances for higher-status professional and managerial positions in the society.

Some anthropologists who have studied public schools among lower-class and minority group populations in the United States have found in them the same conflict of cultures that occurs when formal schooling is introduced into traditional contexts—and the same failures. In describing a school in Harlem, a black ghetto in New York City, Gerry Rosenfeld (1971) calls attention to the cultural differences between the black, lower-class students and the white, middle-class teachers, to the different conceptual frameworks that organize life in the school and outside it, to the low expectations teachers have for students, and to the subsequent failure of the children in school. Rosenfeld sees the teacher in the ghetto school as a transmitter of a different culture. He or she is an agent of socialization similar to the "outsider" who teaches in a "native" school: largely alienated, even hostile, and ignorant of the culture of the students being taught. Until the teacher learns to understand the cultural context and the life of the student, and to get involved with the student as an individual, student performance in such schools will continue to be poor. A common result of the imposition of an alien and irrelevant system of education is that children do not learn what they are supposed to learn; rather, they learn a set of evasive strategies that subvert the intended goals of the teacher and become in themselves the child's primary adaptation to the schoolroom.

It is problems like these in the United States that are directing more anthropological attention to the socialization process as it occurs in both traditional contexts and in the formal context of the school. It is an interest consistent with the anthropological focus on cognitive styles and the ways in which such styles are related to larger cultural patterns and to social-class differences in stratified societies.

SUMMARY

1. Developing into a normal functioning adult is the result of the complex interaction between universal human capacities and culturally variable child-rearing practices. Enculturation is the culturally specific ways in which human infants are reared to become functioning members of a particular sociocultural system.

2. Adequate mother-child interaction is necessary for adquate human development, both physical and emotional, and also appears to be of great importance among nonhuman primates.

3. Enculturation proceeds differently for males and females almost from birth. Both overt teaching and covert communication patterns and role modeling are the most important factors leading to sex role differentiation among adult males and females in a particular culture.

4. The enculturation process not only transmits the skills and knowledge of a culture, but also shapes the values, attitudes, and personality of the growing child. The expectation is that people who have grown up with culturally patterned experiences will have similar personality tendencies.

5. An important theory confirmed by much recent research is that personality develops as an adaptation to the requirements of the basic subsistence pattern of a culture. This point is illustrated by examples from Khalapur, India, and the Israeli *kibbutz.*

6. The major factor that shapes the conforming and dependent personality of the Indian village child is the pattern of joint family living and the need for familial harmony. The cooperative style of the peer-centered Israeli *kibbutz* leads to a group-oriented personality. This is consistent with the collective economic ideology on which the *kibbutz* is built.

7. Enculturation continues past childhood; even adolescents and adults learn new roles and activities. In some traditional cultures, there appears to be greater continuity of enculturation than in our own; adults do not have to unlearn attitudes or skills they have learned as children. The Cheyenne are an example of a culture with major continuities in enculturation.

8. Anthropologists have suggested that males may experience more discontinuities in enculturation than females, as the dependent male child must make the transition to an independent and assertive male role. In many cultures, male initiation rites help the individual make this transition from boy to man. An ex-

ample of such a rite, which suggests some of its symbolic qualities, is that of the Kaguru of East Africa.

9. Where cultural continuity is lacking, and there are no male initiation rites, young men may "initiate themselves," as exemplified in the American youth gang and informal adolescent peer group.

10. Although in traditional societies enculturation is largely an informal process, in complex, highly technical societies formal education (school) plays an increasingly important role. Schools teach not only the formal problem-solving thought processes necessary for competence as an adult, but also indirectly com- municate the American values of competitiveness and individualism.

11. Western education has not always been successful in traditional cultural contexts, where other values and learning contexts conflict with those presented in school. Children from lower-class homes, where cultural values and content may not support or reinforce the school culture, may also not achieve success in school and are likely to score less well on various tests of ability than children from middle-class homes. This is demonstrated by a cross-cultural study comparing the United States and Mexico, and by studies of ghetto schools in the United States.

SUGGESTED READINGS

Barnouw, V.
   1973   *Culture and Personality.* Homewood, Ill.: Dorsey. A survey, suitable for the beginning student, on the relationship between culture and personality.

Edgerton, Robert B.
   1971   *The Individual in Adaptation: A Study of Four East African Peoples.* Berkeley: University of California Press. Compares the personalities of four different cultures and the farmer and herder divisions within each group.

Mead, Margaret
   1961   *Coming of Age in Samoa.* New York: Dell (orig. 1928). The classic study of adolescence in a society where the transition from childhood to adulthood is much less turbulent than in our own.

Munroe, R. L., and Munroe, R. H.
   1977   *Cross-Cultural Human Development.* New York: Aronson. A survey of cross-cultural research on such aspects of human development as physical growth, cognition, sex role, and aggression, including a more intensive look at three different cultures—the Gusii of Africa, the Trobriand Islanders, and the Ainu of Japan.

Whiting, Beatrice, and Whiting, J. W.
   1974   *Children of Six Cultures: A Psycho-Cultural Analysis.* Cambridge, Mass.: Harvard University Press. The most recent analysis of the comparative data on child-rearing gathered as part of the six-culture study referred to in the text.

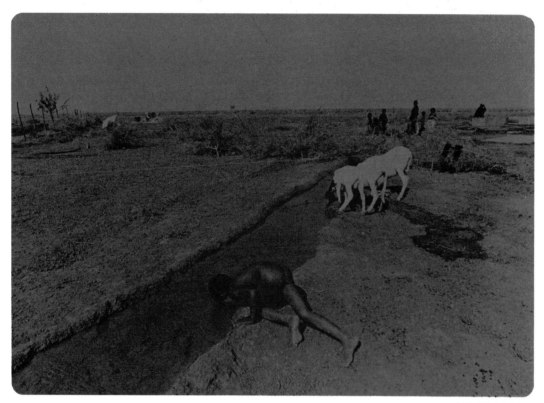

7
Getting Food

Anthropologists view a human population and its environment as an interacting ecosystem. The environment, or surroundings, of a human population includes both a physical and a social aspect. In its physical aspect, the environment is climate, soil quality, existing plant and animal life, and the presence of vital resources such as water, vitamins, and proteins. In considering the capacity of various environments to support human life, both the quantity and the quality of natural resources must be taken into account. Most environmental zones permit a diversity of food-getting strategies. Some environmental zones are harsher than others and more limiting in the types of cultural adaptations they support. The productivity of any particular zone, however, must be considered in connection with the type of technology used to exploit it.

THE ENVIRONMENT AND CULTURAL DIVERSITY

In considering the effect of environment on culture, including subsistence patterns (food getting), we may say that the environment places limits and provides possibilities, but does not determine culture. Each environment always offers some alternatives, and even within culture areas, variation always exists.

The level of technology is the deciding factor in the utilization of a particular environment. In the Midwest of the United States, for example, the complex technology of the industrial age has permitted an adaptive pattern of intensive mechanized agriculture. This area today supports millions of people. In aboriginal America, it supported a much smaller population of hunters and gatherers. In the same way, a desert area that can support very little human life without irrigation can be made to bloom and support much larger populations through intensive agriculture pattern of adaptation. In explaining the particular subsistence pattern of a society, many factors must be taken into account: the nature of the broad environmental zone, variation within the zone, seasonal changes, social groups in the environment, level of technology, cultural history and diffusion, and cultural configurations and values.

Environmental Zones and Food-Getting Systems

The earth contains six major environmental zones, each of which has a particular climate, soil composition, and plant and animal life (Figure 7.1). The major area of the earth's surface (26 percent) is covered by grasslands, sometimes called steppes, prairies, or savannas. These areas, which can support hunters and gatherers and also populations dependent on herding animals, are inhabited by 10 percent of the world's population. Where complex machine technologies exist, these areas can be made enormously productive for agriculture. Desert regions or dry areas make up 18 percent of the earth's land but contain only 6 percent of its population. Desert areas do not all conform to the popular image of sand dunes and the complete absence of water. Many deserts are covered by brush, and in some areas oases, or fertile concentrations of soil, exist and support small agricultural settlements. With a simple technology, deserts can support hunters and gatherers. With extensive irrigation, some areas can support intensive agriculture and relatively dense populations. The arctic and subarctic zones cover 16 percent of the earth, but as we would

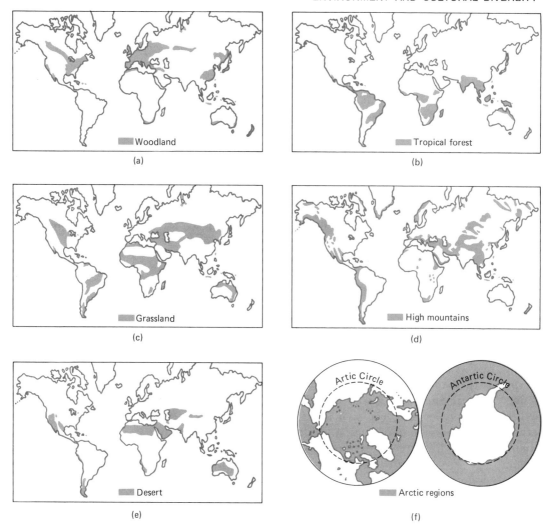

Figure 7.1 *Six major regions of the world shown in order of decreasing population.*

expect, only a tiny fraction of the earth's population—less than half of 1 percent—who live mainly by hunting, herding, and trapping.

Almost three-fourths of the world's population lives in the two remaining major environmental zones. The tropical forest zone, with abundant rainfall and luxuriant vegetation, takes up 10 percent of the earth's land mass but supports 28 percent of its population. The typical pattern of subsistence in these areas is extensive agriculture (sometimes called horticulture). The most hospitable environmental zone for contemporary human populations is the temperate forests. Today, 43 percent of the world's population lives in these zones. Again, we can see how technology must be taken into account in understanding population distribution. It is only with iron tools that the hardwood trees in these temperate forests could be cut down and the fertile soil used for agriculture. Without iron tools, the trees presented an insurmountable difficulty. Mountains, which vary in climate and other characteristics according to their elevation, occupy 12 percent of earth's land surface and are inhabited by 7 percent of its population, engaged primarily in pastoralism and extensive agriculture.

Sometimes a number of societies make similar adaptations to a particular ecological zone, and through diffusion come to develop similar cultural patterns. Where this happens, anthropologists speak of a **culture area.** Although the concept of a culture area has its uses in explaining certain developments, culture areas also contain cultural variation. Among the American Plains Indians, for example, there were important differences in values and configurations among the different tribes, in spite of the basic similarity in the subsistence pattern. Similar cultural variation exists among the Eskimo, who have in general made similar adaptive responses to their relatively limiting natural environment.

Seasonal Variation and Cultural Response

Due to climatic variation, food resources vary in availability and abundance at different times of the year in any particular local environment. Many aspects of a food production system will reflect this seasonal variation. Among the Hanunoo of the Philippines, who are horticulturalists, there is an impressive system of intercropping, planting different crops at different times of the year when the weather was most favorable for each, and harvesting them in turn, so that one harvest season does not interfere with an-

other. Rice, the main crop, is planted in June and harvested in October; in between a short-season maize crop is planted and harvested. Between October and May, several dry-season crops such as beans, sugar cane, and potatoes are also grown (Conklin 1969). Hunters and gatherers are, of course, also sensitive to seasonal change because it affects the availability and abundance of game and wild food. Game migrates with the changing seasons, and the size and social organization of hunting groups adjust to this seasonal migration, as we will see for the Copper Eskimo later in this chapter.

Long-Run Variations in the Environment

Sociocultural systems also develop in response to variations that are unpredictable over the short run, such as drought, floods, or diseases which affect animals, but that are a persistent part of the environment over the long run. Subsistence patterns most directly reflect adaptation to long-run environmental uncertainty. Food habits and preferences, for example, can be adapted to a wide variety of resources, rather than limited to those which are not so readily available. Australian aboriginal peoples have a very simple technology, but they utilize an enormous variety of plant and animal foods in their environment—kangaroos, opossum, mice, wild dog, whale, frog, turkey, birds, lizards, snakes, bird and lizard eggs, fish, roots, fruit, nuts, seeds, flowers—and are thus unlikely to be severely affected if some of these foods become unavailable.

A group can also structure its diet so that although it uses a wide variety of resources, it also has one that is dependable—that is, in constant abundant supply. The Bushmen of the Kalahari, for example, although they know the plants and animals in their seemingly hostile environment well and do use this knowledge to give their diet variety when possible, can always fall back on the protein-rich nuts of the mongongo tree. These nuts are abundant, easily stored, and little affected by environmental variation (Lee 1968).

In addition to various kinds of subsistence strategies designed to increase a group's survival in a particular environment, adaptation to the environment is also affected by regulation of population. In cultures where the level of technology affords only a limited exploitation of the environment, and where safe and reliable methods of artificial contraception are unknown, abortion and infanticide are used to limit population growth. Other culturally determined practices and beliefs also result in limiting population. Late weaning and postpartum taboos on sexual intercourse, for example, regulate population by spacing births. Sometimes methods of increasing a group's survival seem harsh to us, but they are necessary because of extreme food shortages. Among the Eskimo, for example, old people were left on the ice to be exposed to a sure death in particularly hard years when food was scarce. Sometimes an old person suggested this course of action him- or herself. These suicides or "mercy killings" indicate not a lack of concern for human life, but rather a commitment to the survival of the group.

In addition to these more obvious ways of adapting to environmental uncertainty, a society can establish trade relations with other groups and thus expand its resource base. This, for example, is always necessary for pastoral groups who do not also do a little farming themselves. Furthermore, some of the ways in which sociocultural systems adapt to long-run environmental uncertainty may not be a part of the cultural consciousness, as we saw earlier in Harris' explanation of the Hindu

taboo on beef. Frequently, the role such beliefs and practices play in regulating population or increasing the rational utilization of the environment may only be understood through anthropological analysis.

Although increasing technological efficiency is an obvious way of increasing control over the environment, the enormous diversity of sociocultural systems is evidence that technologically simpler societies have been able to make satisfactory adaptations even without modern science. Although nonliterate peoples may not express it in the technical terminology of modern science, they have a much wider knowledge of their environment than they have generally been given credit for. Harold Conklin, who studied the horticulturalist Yagaw Hanunoo of the Philippines, found, for example, that they had forty linguistic categories referring to soil quality and mineral content. They understood what causes soil erosion, and had developed techniques to conserve the soil. The Hanunoo distinguish over 1,500 types of plants in their environment and cultivate over 400 in fields and gardens, frequently experimenting with new types. In this sense, their knowledge exceeds that of modern scientific botany, in which plants are grouped into species by more gross criteria than those used by the Hanunoo. The Hanunoo also recognize over 450 animal types in their environment. These people clearly understand the connection between human food-getting activities and their impact on the environment, and utilize this knowledge in an efficient way to exploit various food resources. Similarly, even where the technology for hunting and agriculture among nonliterate peoples seems primitive compared to our own machine technology, in fact these groups have developed quite adequate strategies for fulfilling their needs. They make up for the lack of sophisticated technology by human skill, such as in observing the habits of various animals and in stalking them.

The Social Environment and Food-Getting Strategies

Cultural patterns, including how people get their food, are adjusted to the presence of different groups in the environment. Some peoples who originally inhabited a larger area, like the Semai of Malaysia, have recently been pushed back by other groups into marginal areas and have had to change their subsistence patterns. The Pygmies of the Ituri forest in northeastern Zaire have adapted to the tropical forest as hunters and gatherers, but almost all the Pygmy bands are closely associated with their non-Pygmy neighbors, who are agriculturalists. These other people fear the forest and will not enter it. This has allowed the Pygmies to exploit the forest, while at the same time making use of their more culturally sophisticated agricultural neighbors, with whom they trade and sometimes live with for parts of the year (Turnbull 1961). Human groups (like other animal communities) tend to engage in specialized adaptations to the environ-

With the introduction of the horse by the Spanish, hunting bison on the American Plains became a more productive strategy than agriculture. This drawing, by Bear's Heart, was made in 1875. One hundred years later the American bison are virtually extinct. (Courtesy of Museum of the American Indian, Heye Foundation)

ment which, over time, become integrated in their cultural systems and an important part of their identity. A specialized adaptation to a local environment by a particular group is called its **niche.** Frederick Barth describes a pattern of social interaction in Pakistan in which three different ethnic groups, the Kohistanis, the Pathans, and the Gujars, who live within the same mountainous area, each have a different niche (Barth 1956). They are able to live peacefully because each group exploits a different aspect of the environment. The Pathans are farmers, utilizing the valley regions for raising wheat, corn, and rice. The Kohistanis live in the colder mountainous regions, herding sheep, goats, cattle, and water buffalo, and raising millet and corn. The Gujars are full-time herders and utilize marginal areas not used by the Kohistanis. The Gujars provide milk and meat products to the Pathan farmers and also work as agricultural laborers during the busy seasons. Such patterns of specialized and noncompetitive interactions among different cultures in a local environment are found in many parts of the world and seem especially characteristic of pastoral peoples.

The Influence of Culture on Environment

The relationship between the environment and culture is not a one-way street. Although, as we have just suggested, the environment affects culture, culture also affects the environment. The ways in which people get food and the ways in which they live all have an impact on nature. On the one hand, technology and knowledge can transform deserts into gardens. On the other hand, as we know all too well today, the presence of human populations can have a devastating impact on nature. In industrial societies, factories and au-

tomobiles have contributed to polluting the air we breathe. Different methods of getting a living, whether hunting, trapping animals, cultivation, or keeping herds of livestock, all affect animal and plant life, quantity of natural resources, the soil cover, and the soil itself. The management of resources is clearly a pressing problem in the world today. One of the contributions of ecologically oriented anthropologists is to show that a wide variety of food-procurement strategies make good ecological sense and that what may at first appear to be a more efficient exploitation of a particular environment may turn out to raise as many problems as it solves.

MAJOR TYPES OF FOOD-GETTING PATTERNS

There are five basic patterns of utilizing the environment to support human populations (Cohen 1971): hunting and gathering, pastoralism, extensive agriculture, intensive agriculture, and industrialization. Although it is useful to describe basic types, there is a great deal of diversity within each type. Furthermore, any particular society will normally have one dominant way of utilizing the environment, but most actually use a combination of patterns in filling their needs. Each type of adaptation has a characteristic level of productivity (yield per person per unit of land) and efficiency (yield per person per hour labor invested), though situations vary depending on the particular ecological interaction. Each type of food-getting pattern also seems to have some social correlates (accompanying forms of social organization) and dominant values, though again, many anthropologists are more interested in examining specific cultural adaptations to a particular local environment rather than formulating cultural typologies.

Hunting and Gathering

Hunting and gathering or **foraging** relies on food that is naturally available in the environment. Included in this strategy is the hunting of large and small game animals, fishing, and the collecting of various plant foods. Hunting and gathering does not involve the production of food, either directly by planting, or indirectly by controlling the reproduction of animals, or keeping domestic animals for consumption of their meat or milk.

In the past, hunting and gathering occurred in more diverse environments than is true today. For 99 percent of humankind's existence life was supported by a hunting and gathering existence. Today, only about 30,000 of the world's people live by this strategy. Most contemporary hunters and gatherers occupy marginal areas, having been pushed back by culturally dominant or militarily superior agricultural peoples (see Figure 7.2).

Anthropologists are particularly interested in contemporary hunters and gatherers because this pattern was such an important part of early human history. The sexual division of labor (males hunting, females collecting food), the sharing of food in the group, and the development of language all came into existence as correlates of the hunting and gathering way of life. But although contemporary hunters and gatherers can be expected to give us important clues to understanding the early life of humans, these groups do not in any way represent a way of life unchanged from the past. It too has changed and is in fact rapidly disappearing as a way of human life.

Hunting and gathering strategies vary in their productivity. Although it is true that some hunters and gatherers have faced starvation, the marginal existence of contemporary hunters and gatherers may be due to recent effects of culture contact. But even here, some foraging groups make out rather well, thanks to their ingenious technology and their wide knowledge of the environment. Lee points out that the Bushman actually have a more secure existence than their Herero neighbors, who are agriculturalists and cattle herders. Because the Herero rely completely on water and pasturage for their cattle, they leave themselves open to starvation in years of drought. The Plains Indians also did well with a hunting strategy, especially after the introduction of the horse by the Spaniards in the sixteenth century. Some Plains groups, such as the Cheyenne, gave up an agricultural life for the more productive hunting of bison. But in general, hunting and gathering supports fewer people per unit of land than other food-getting strategies. Among the Bushmen, 44 people are supported per 100 square miles of land, but this figure is somewhat higher than is generally true for hunting peoples today.

Hunting technology is simple, but not crude, and ingenious methods are used to hunt a wide range of different animals. Because hunting is a prestige activity, it is only recently that much attention has been given to the collecting of vegetable foods. For many foraging groups, vegetable foods make up a substantial part of the group's diet (up to 80 percent), and it is this rather than hunting that makes foraging a relatively secure way of life. Foraging thus tends to be a generalized pattern of adaptation that utilizes many different aspects of the natural environment for subsistence. The Copper Eskimo described below represent a specialized hunting adaptation to a relatively harsh and limiting environment.

Contrary to stereotypes, hunting and

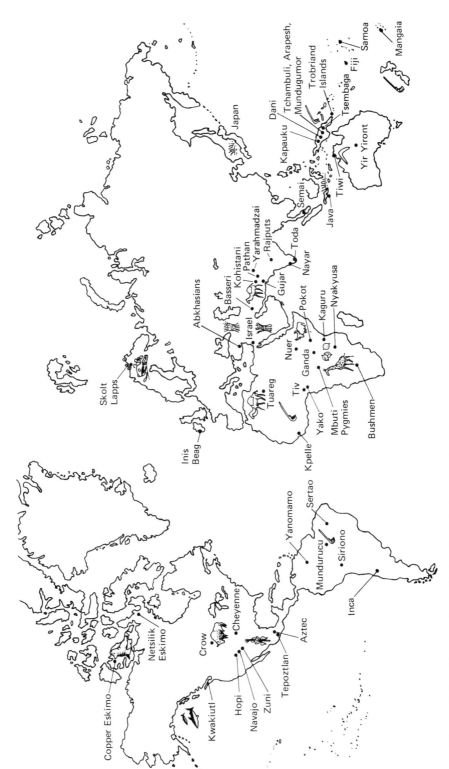

Figure 7.2 *This map shows the location of the major human groups discussed in the text. The accompanying symbols indicate the group's major food-getting strategy.*

THE COPPER ESKIMO OF THE CANADIAN ARCTIC: A SPECIALIZED HUNTING ADAPTATION*

The Copper Eskimo, so called because of their use of native copper tools, have lived as hunters in this extreme climate for over a thousand years. (see Figure 7.3). The tundra habitat in which they live contains some trees, moss, grass and flowers, but many areas are virtual wasteland. The climate is variable, with a long, cold winter and a short, cool summer. From around September to June, the water areas become sheets of ice. The main land animal hunted was the caribou, which provided both meat and skin used in clothing. Fish, hare, and fowl were important supplements to the diet. Plant life was scarce and berries were eaten only during a brief season. When a caribou was killed, the first thing eaten was the half-digested reindeer moss that remained in its stomach. The seal was the most important sea animal hunted, providing a major source of food for people and dogs, fat for fuel, and skins for summer clothing.

The Copper Eskimo culture was adapted to a seasonal cycle in response to the availability of different animals at different times of the year. From late May to November, the Eskimo fished and hunted caribou, often driving them into lakes and harpooning them from kayaks. During November and early December, they lived on stores of dried and frozen caribou meat and fish, while the women sewed winter clothing. In December they moved to the sea ice for the winter seal hunting season. Snow houses were built in from the coast, and a radius of about five miles (considered a convenient walking distance from camp!) was exploited for sealing.

In the winter, seals live in the water under the ice. They make breathing holes by scratching with their flippers on the new ice, and have the ability to breathe up through quite a lot of snow. Each seal makes many holes during a winter and may use any one of these. The hunter finds the holes with the aid of specially trained dogs. The method of winter sealing is called "he waits," for that is what a hunter must do. He settles down on a block of ice and waits for an indicator to move, showing the presence of a seal. He may wait for hours, or even days. Many men are needed for a successful breathing hole sealing, so the Copper Eskimo winter populations ranged from about 50 to 200 people, with the average group about 100. In spring, the group disperses into smaller units in response to the lesser requirements of caribou

*David Damas "The Copper Eskimo" in *Hunters and Gatherers Today*, M. G. Bicchieri, ed. New York: Holt, Rinehart and Winston, Inc., 1972, pp. 3–50.

Figure 7.3 *The location of the Copper Eskimo.*

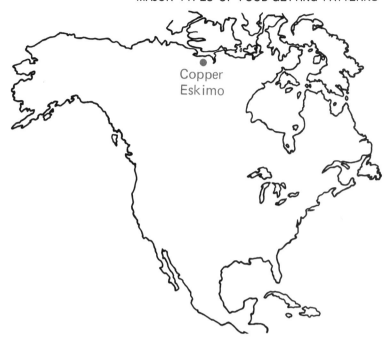

hunting. Caribou are usually scattered into small herds, easily hunted by a few men. Fish were the most important source of food in the spring. They were widely available over the area in numerous lakes, and so did not require communal effort to catch.

The routine just described was altered somewhat by the introduction of new technology by the whites. By 1925, rifles, traps, and fishnets substantially influenced the Eskimo food-getting pattern. Using rifles to hunt caribou led to a lengthened caribou season and a correspondingly shorter sealing season. More Eskimo stayed inland, not only hunting caribou, but also trapping and setting nets in lakes and streams to catch fish. Other aspects of the economy also changed. With the rifle, the kayak hunting of caribou ended and the kayak fell into disuse. Large caribou drives also became less frequent. With a rifle, one man could succeed at long-range caribou hunting, which then became a much more individual pursuit.

The market for fox furs among whites led to the trapping of foxes. Trapping drew the Eskimo into the marketing system of the outside world, providing them not only with goods that increased the exploitation of the environment, but also with food,

The ways in which human populations adapt to their environments through different food-getting strategies is an important factor in cultural variation. The Eskimo are an example of a specialized hunting adaptation. Here two Eskimo women from Coppermine set fishnets under the ice.
(Courtesy of The American Museum of Natural History)

tobacco, tea, canvas tents, and clothing. With the establishment of fox traps, dog team travel became more important, since mobility was needed to set and watch traps. Where previously a typical family had owned two dogs, many might now own five or six, and the dogs might actually consume more meat than a man's family.

By the mid-1950s, the decline in caribou due to hunting with rifles led to further changes in Eskimo life. Some Copper Eskimo poulations shifted to areas where seals could be hunted year-round, and fishing also became more important. In other areas, the decline of the caribou led to an increased amount of time spent in breathing hole sealing, a reversion to the aboriginal pattern. Still other Copper Eskimo populations moved to areas where they could be employed by the government, which had established DEWline radar installations in the Arctic. Trading posts were established and also attracted permanent settlement. Handicrafts and tourism contribute to the present Eskimo economy, and when necessary, the Canadian government provides welfare payments and airlifts of food.

gathering is not a particularly difficult and inefficient way of life in terms of the number of hours required to obtain an adequate food supply. Marshal Sahlins (1972) has called hunters and gatherers "the original affluent society." James Woodburn (1968), who studied the Hadza of Tanzania, estimated that they spend less time and energy obtaining their subsistence and appear to be better off nutritionally than neighboring agricultural tribes. Lee estimated that an adult Bushman spends an average of two and a half six-hour days per week in subsistence activities, and a woman can gather enough in one day to feed her family for three days.

There appear to be some typical social correlates of the hunting way of life. Hunters are generally **nomadic,** with their movements following the availability of game and wild plants. A typical form of social organization among hunters is the small camp made up of kinsmen, coming together when seasonal conditions permit. Recent investigation has shown that the typical hunting band is much more flexible in its membership than was previously believed. Among the Blackfeet bison hunters of the North American Plains, even strangers would be included in the camp. With the notable exception of the fishing and foraging societies of the Northwest Coast of North America, there tends to be little occupational specialization in foraging societies and few differences in power and authority. There is ordinarily a division of labor by age and sex; women collect plant foods, and men hunt. Women in these societies also make clothing and contribute in other important ways to the economy, such as by carrying and processing food. There tends to be a higher degree of sexual equality in such societies than in other ways of life—for example, pastoralism or horticulture.

Pastoralism

Pastoralism primarily involves the care of domesticated herd animals. It is a specialized adaptation to an environment which, because of hilly terrain, dry climate, or unsuitable soil, is not sufficiently productive to support a large human population through agriculture. It can support native vegetation sufficient for animals if they are allowed to range over a large area. The main animals herded by pastoralists are cattle, sheep, goats, yaks, or camels, all of which produce both meat and milk. Because the herd animals found in the New World were not of a variety that could be domesticated (with the exception of the llama in Peru), pastoralism did not develop as a New World way of life. The major areas of pastoralism are thus found in East Africa (cattle), North Africa (camels), Southwest Asia (sheep and goats), and the sub-Arctic (caribou and reindeer).

Two characteristic patterns of pastoralism are **transhumance** and **nomadism.** In transhumance, herd animals are moved regularly throughout the year to different areas as pastures become available at different altitudes or in different climatic zones. Generally, the males take the animals to the different pastures, while the women and children and some men remain at a village site. In a nomadic form of pastoralism, the whole population—men, women, and children—move with the herds throughout the year. There is no permanent village.

Pastoralism by itself cannot support a human population; food grains are needed as a supplement to the diet. Therefore, pastoralism is either practiced along with cultivation, or trading relations are maintained with cultivators from whom food grains are obtained. In terms of social organization, in most pastoral groups, a

THE YARAHMADZAI OF BALUCHISTAN: A PASTORAL ADAPTATION*

The Yarahmadzai are a patrilineal tribe of some several thousand people, living in the area of southeastern Iran known as Baluchistan. (see Figure 7.4). The total tribal territory is about 3,600 square miles. The plateau on which the Yarahmadzai live is at 5,000 feet and is cut by high mountains. The winters are cold and the summers hot. Some years there is no rain at all, and the maximum tends to be about 6 inches a year, most of which falls in the winter. The main natural vegetation is grass, although some areas are completely barren. The area is bounded to the east by a vast desert that contains almost no vegetation.

In winter (December, January, February) each local community of the tribe has a traditional camping area on the plateau consisting of about five to twenty tents. The herds of goats and sheep are taken out together by shepherds, and camels are herded separately by camel boys. At this time there is practically no vegetation for the animals to eat, and they exist primarily on the accumulated fat of the previous spring. During the winter months, the entire Yarahmadzai area is barren, so there is no point in moving. Their strategy is to "sit tight," protect the animals as best they can, and compensate for the lack of pasturage by feeding the camels with roots, the goats and sheep with grain, and the lambs and kids with dates, processed date pits, and grain. As this is the rainy season, water is normally available. Since no food is produced, the community depends on stores from the previous year.

In spring (March, April, May), grass begins to appear and plants to bud. Because of the variability of the rain and winter runoff water from the mountains, the availability of pasture varies from year to year within the territory. Thus, the community does not know beforehand where it will go. After spending quite a bit of time gathering information about where the pasture is good, the camp packs up and migrates. In the period observed by Philip Salzman, his camp moved seven times, covering distances of 5 to 25 miles. As even pasturage in a good area is quickly exhausted, all the camps are rather constantly moving from place to place.

In the first part of summer (June and July), the pasturage begins to dry up. Currently, the Iranian government has introduced some irrigation technology into the area, and many of the tribesmen migrate to these areas to harvest grain. The livestock grazes on stubble and fertilizes the ground with droppings. From March to July, the animals give enough milk both for their young and for heavy consumption by the people. Milk is consumed in many

* Philip C. Salzman, "Multi-Resource Nomadism in Iranian Baluchistan." In William Irons and Neville Dyson-Hudson, eds., *Perspectives on Nomandism.* Leiden: E. J. Brill, 1972, pp. 61–69. Reprinted by permission.

Figure 7.4 *The location of the Yarahmadzai.*

different forms and preserved as dried milk solids and butter. The butter is sold or exchanged for other products, mostly grain.

In late summer and early autumn (August, September, October), the Yarahmadzai migrate to the lowland desert, leaving their winter tents, goats, and sheep on the plateau in the care of young boys. The group makes an eight-day migration to the groves of date palms. During this time, they live in mud huts, harvesting and eating dates and preparing a number of food products for the return journey. Dates, date preserves, and date pits are all needed for consumption in the winter; salt, which is gathered from salt wastes, is consumed year-round; and palm leaves are woven into ropes for tying and packing tents and baggage. The date palms are easily cultivated: A river drains into the desert basin, creating a sandy soil with a 5-foot water table into which the date palms sink their roots. Because of the heat, wind, and lack of rain, however, it is not possible for sheep and goats to live there, even for a short time.

In November, the group migrates back to the plateau; those tribesmen who are also cultivators plant grain at this time, and women go off to work for cash in nearby towns. This labor is a substitute source of subsistence for the extensive livestock raiding of an earlier era, which has since been stamped out by the government. Pastoralism, date cultivation, and additional sources of subsistence are all necessary to an economy that exists in such a marginal and unproductive environment.

These Masai herdsmen of East Africa engage in transhumant pastoralism in which men take the cattle to different areas as pasture becomes available in different climatic zones while the women and children remain at the village. (United Nations/Ida/Pickerelli)

woman joins her husband after marriage and herds are transmitted from fathers to sons. Recent studies have shown a great diversity in pastoral adaptations, and the very flexibility that has allowed pastoral groups to survive in marginal environments makes this strategy difficult to categorize. Because pastoralism always includes either cultivation or trade, this also leads to rather important variability among pastoralists. Many pastoralists have also been drawn into a market economy, and this too is an important part of contemporary pastoralist adaptations. Pastoralism, like hunting, depends on an extensive knowledge of the natural environment. Like hunting, it is also a nomadic adaptation, and the movement patterns of pastoralist groups are of central importance in understanding their culture.

Extensive Agriculture

Extensive agriculture, sometimes called **horticulture,** involves the production of plants using a simple, nonmechanized technology. An important defining characteristic of extensive agriculture is that cultivated fields will not be used permanently, year after year, but will remain fallow for some time after being cultivated. This is one of the important contrasts between an extensive and an intensive agricultural strategy. Horticulturalists plant and harvest with simple tools, such as hoes or digging stocks, and do not use draft animals, irrigation techniques, or plows. Extensive agriculture has a relatively lower yield per acre compared to intensive agriculture and does not use as much human labor as other forms of farming. Extensive agriculturalists grow enough food in their fields or gardens to support the local group, but do not produce surpluses that could involve the group in a wider market system with nonagricultural populations. Population densities among horticultural peoples are generally low, usually not exceeding 150 persons per square mile (McNetting 1977). There is great variation in horticultural productivity, however. In the highlands of New Guinea, intensive cultivation of the sweet potato supports populations of up to 500 per square mile.

Although extensive agriculture may be practiced in dry lands, such as among the Hopi Indians, who live in southwest Arizona and cultivate maize, beans, and squash, it is typically a tropical forest adaptation. As such it is found mainly in Southeast Asia, sub-Saharan Africa, some Pacific Islands, and the Amazon Basin in South America. In these environments, a form of cultivation called **swidden** or **slash and burn** is practiced. In slash and burn agriculture, a field is cleared by felling the trees and burning the brush. The burned vegetation is allowed to remain on the soil, which prevents its drying out from the sun. The resulting bed of ash acts as a fertilizer, returning nutrients to the soil. Fields are used only for several years (one to five) and then allowed to lie fallow for a number of years (up to twenty), so that the forest cover can be rebuilt and fertility restored. Swidden cultivators require as much as five to six times fallow land as that under cultivation. Swidden agriculture can have a deteriorating effect on the environment if fields are cultivated before they have lain fallow long enough to recover their forest growth. Eventually the soil will deteriorate, the forest will not grow back, and the tree cover will be replaced by grasses. It is this irreversible ecological deterioration that has caused swidden agriculture to be considered both inefficient and destructive by Western observers.

Recent anthropological investigation has shown, however, that swidden cultivation is not an uninformed, casual, and careless food-getting strategy. Swidden cultivators often have well-developed techniques of clearing, firing, fertilizing the soil, and crop rotation. The Kofyar, a people of the Jos plateau in Africa, for example, have an impressive system of stepped terraces that are constructed to deepen the soil, stabilize sloping ground, and prevent runoff and erosion. Among the Tsembaga of New Guinea, planting of several crops is carefully ordered; sweet potato leaves cover the soil at ground level, taro leaves project over this mat, hibiscus and sugarcane stand still higher, and banana trees spread out above the rest. This ordering results in a garden that has maximum leaf exposure to sunlight, protects the soil, discourages insects, and provides a variety of foods as insurance if one kind of crop fails (Rappoport 1971).

Although some swidden cultivators depend primarily on one crop, many more cultivate several. Because plants grown by swidden cultivators do not provide all the necessary proteins for human health, however, horticulturalists may also hunt and fish, or raise some domestic animals. In New Guinea, for example, domestic pigs are an important source of protein; the Hopi raise sheep; and the Kofyar keep goats, chickens, sheep, and cows.

Because swidden cultivation requires shifting of fields, it has been assumed that

**THE DANI:
NEW GUINEA
HORTICULTURALISTS***

The Dani live in the central mountains of West New Guinea, above the tropical jungles of the coast (see Figure 7.5). Because of the altitude, rainfall is evenly distributed throughout the year and temperature variation is slight. In the tropical forest there are a few wild animals. Although a few wild foods are collected from the forests and fields, these do not play an important role in the Dani diet. Basically, the Dani rely on the products from their gardens and on their domesticated pigs for subsistence. Like many other highland New Guinea peoples, the main item of the Dani diet is the sweet potato. Other cultivated plants which are eaten are taro, banana, ginger, sugar cane, and greens. For ordinary meals, sweet potatoes are merely cooked and eaten; ceremonial meals consist of steamed vegetables and pork.

The Dani cultivate three kinds of gardens: great ditched fields on the valley floor, hill slope gardens, and small garden plots behind the houses in their compounds. The bulk of the sweet potato crop is grown on the valley floor. In these gardens, a typical swidden round of activities takes place: The fields are cleared of brush and trees which have grown since the last planting, and the cleared vegetation is burned. The sod is then turned with digging sticks, which are the only agricultural implements among the Dani. Sweet potatoes are planted with vine cuttings from other gardens and spread with the fertile mud that comes from the cleared ditches. A few months later the gardens are weeded, and about seven months later the harvesting begins. When the plot is exhausted, pigs are allowed to root over the field. Fields lie fallow anywhere from one year to twenty. Since there is no seasonal growing period in the valley, sweet potatoes are harvested year-round. Each household maintains several garden plots that are kept at different stages of growth. During the harvesting time for any one plot, enough potatoes are harvested to feed the family for the following day. The valley fields, in contrast to those on the slopes, are cultivated intensively, normally not allowing a chance for heavy vegetation to grow up. The ditching and use of the mud as cover supplies the necessary refertilization of valley gardens.

A more extensive slash and burn cultivation is practiced on the slopes. Here sugar cane, taro, cucumber, and yam are more common than sweet potato. In the village gardens the Dani plant tobacco, banana, and a few vegetables. Banana plants grown in

* Karl Heider, *The Dugum Dani*. Chicago: Aldine, 1970.

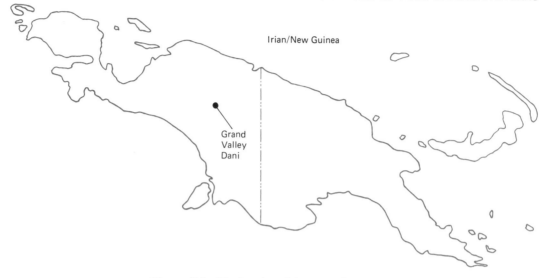

Figure 7.5 *The location of the Dani of New Guinea.*

the compound are partly used for food, but also have other uses; the trees shade houses, the leaves are used as wrappers for food, and the outer stem can be made soft enough to use for binding. Pigs provide an essential source of protein. Most men have from one to twenty pigs. Every day the pigs must be taken from their stalls to root in the nearby forest or in fallow gardens. Herding is quite tedious, and means a lot of responsibility. Pigs also play an important role in Dani culture because they are used for exchange and eaten on ceremonial occasions.

The basic division of labor among the Dani is according to sex. Usually men do the heavy work, women the light work. Men fight, build houses, and clear fields and gardens; women plant, weed, harvest, cook, and make salt. Children frequently herd the pigs. In their basic economy, the Dani are pretty self-sufficient. They provide their own food, shelter, and clothing from materials found or grown in the area. Except for ax and adze blades, which are needed for felling trees and butchering pigs, the subsistence economy of the Dani is self-contained, and small residential groups are economically independent. It is in the requirement of the ceremonial economy that each Dani group is dependent on a broad trade network.

Horticultural peoples supplement their diets by a number of different means. Fishing with a bow and arrow in Papua New Guinea. (Courtesy of Office of Information, Port Moresby, Papua New Guinea)

horticulturalists shift residences as well. This is not necessarily the case; some swidden cultivators do occupy villages permanently or at least on a long-term basis. In horticultural populations there is a typical division of labor by sex. The men do the clearing, burning, planting, weeding, and fencing; women harvest, carry plant foods back to the village, and transform raw food into cooked or processed edibles. Where hunting is practiced, it is a male task, although either men or women may fish. Females may help plant, weed, and harvest. They also care for pigs, where these are raised.

There is great variety in social systems among horticulturalists. The basic unit is most frequently a group of people who believe they are descended from a common ancestor. This descent group most frequently reckons descent through males, but societies in which descent is reckoned through females occur in greater proportion among horticultural peoples than in any other type of society. This may be related to the important role of women in the cultivation of plants and cooperative domestic activities.

In spite of the generally low population densities, the size of horticultural villages may be quite large, ranging from 100 people to up to 1,000. It appears that small, low-density village societies are more egalitarian than those with larger populations and higher density, although generally it can be said that horticulturalists have more formalized group leadership than hunters and gatherers. These societies also frequently engage in warfare, which may be a way of regulating population size and density.

Intensive Agriculture

This form of food production is characterized by the use of the plow, draft animals, and more effective techniques of water and soil control than among horticulturalists. In **intensive agriculture** the same piece of land is cultivated permanently and needs no fallow period. Plows are more efficient in loosening the soil than are digging sticks or hoes. By turning the soil, nutrients are lifted to the surface. Plowing requires a much more thorough clearing of land, but also allows land to be used year after year. Irrigation is another important pattern in intensive agriculture. Although some horticulturalists do practice some simple methods of water conservation and control, intensive agriculture in dry areas can only be carried out with sophisticated irrigation techniques. In hilly areas, intensive agriculture requires some form of terracing in order to prevent crops and good soil from being washed down the hillside. Pre-industrial intensive agriculture also utilizes techniques of natural fertilization, selective breeding of livestock and crops, and crop rotation, all of which increase productivity. Where horticulturalists have to increase the land under cultivation in order to support a larger population, intensive agriculture can support population increases by more intensified use of the same piece of land.

Many more people can be supported per acre of land with intensive agriculture. A comparison of extensive and intensive agriculture in Mexico demonstrated, for example, that with irrigation, which permits two crops a year, a given amount of land can support almost fourteen times as many families as the same area exploited by slash and burn techniques. A dramatic example of the differences in productivity of slash and burn versus intensive agriculture is offered by the island nation of Indonesia. Java, which makes up only 9 percent of the Indonesian land area, supports over two-thirds of the Indonesian population. The "outer islands," which make up almost 90 percent of the land area and support about a third of its population, are mainly exploited by swidden agriculture. In Java, intensive wet rice cultivation using elaborate irrigation terraces supports an average of about 480 people per square kilometer. Some of the more crowded parts of the island have population densities of up to 1,000 per square mile. This contrasts sharply with the maximum population density of swidden areas, which has been estimated at about 50 persons per kilometer (Geertz 1963).

The greater productivity of intensive agriculture results not only from more sophisticated technology, but also from greater use of labor. Intensive agriculturalists must work long and hard to make the land productive. In terraced agriculture, for example, ditches must be dug and kept clean, sluices constructed and repaired, and terraces leveled and diked. It has been estimated that growing rice under a swidden system requires 241 worker days per yearly crop, while wet rice cultivation requires 292 worker days a year. Intensive agriculture also requires more capital investment than horticulture. In horticultural societies, the only necessary tool may be a simple digging stick. In intensive agriculture, apart from the cost of human labor, plows have to be bought, and draft animals raised and cared for. Although intensive agriculturalists may have more control over food production, they are also more vulnerable to the environment. By depending on the intensive cultivation of one or two crops, they can face disaster in case of a crop failure. Draft animals may be struck by disease, again affecting the cultivator's ability to produce.

Intensive cultivation is generally associated with stable village life and other complex forms of social organization. With the development of intensive agriculture and population increase, we see the rise of cities, an increase in occupational specialization, social stratification arising from great differences in wealth, political centralization, and the development of the state. Cultivators who form part of complex state organizations are called **peasants.**

Although peasants produce mainly for subsistence of the household, they are distinguished from other kinds of cultivators by their participation in larger social and political entities, such as the state. Where horticulturalists produce for the subsistence of the local group and own the land

Intensive rice farming can be enormously productive but is backbreaking work. The greater productivity of intensive agriculture results from more sophisticated technology, such as irrigation, and from intensification of labor. Below, women plant rice outside Jogjakarta, Indonesia. (United Nations)

they use for cultivation, peasants have little control over their land, and produce to support non-producing populations. The characteristic of a peasant economy is that part of its agricultural production is commandeered by a politically dominant and non-food-producing class. The peasant must pay for access to land either in cash, a percentage of the harvest, the donation of agricultural labor to the landowner, or tribute to the state. Because modern peasants are required to maintain their own seeds, tools, and animals, they must participate in market economies over which they have no control. In this way also, they are distinguished from horticulturalists and from farmers in industrial societies. Farmers in the United States, for example, have control over their land and other means of production, and produce for a

TEPOZTLAN: A PEASANT VILLAGE IN MEXICO*

Tepoztlan is a village of 4,500 people located 60 miles south of Mexico City (see Figure 7.6). The peasants of Tepoztlan basically grow corn, which when ground and made into flat cakes called *tortillas*, is the mainstay of the traditional diet. The land around the village is rocky, steep, and forested; little is available for agriculture. Although 90 percent of the villagers engage in agriculture, this by itself cannot support the population. Most Tepoztlecans seek out other sources of income, many of them working at a variety of jobs during the year. There are two methods of cultivation in Tepoztlan, slash and burn hoe culture, and plow culture.

Although the ideal in Tepoztlan is to own land privately, 64 percent of the families own no land at all. Those that do generally own very small plots. Around Tepoztlan, only 15 percent of the land area is cultivatable by plow and oxen and about 10 percent by hoe culture. Hoe culture is practiced on communally owned land, and plow culture on privately owned land. Plow culture requires relatively little time and labor, but considerable capital. Hoe culture is carried out by families; plow culture depends to a greater extent on hired labor.

The basic tools of production in plow culture are the plow, the machete, the hoe, and the ax. Both steel and wooden plows are used. The work cycle of plow culture consists of preparing the land, planting, cultivating, and harvesting. In August, during the rainy season, new land is broken in preparation for planting the following year. This is done with the steel plow. One man with a single team of oxen can plow on the average about two-fifths of an acre a day. If time permits, the new fields are plowed up twice. Planting usually begins in early June, after the beginning of the rains. The finest ears of corn, which have been set aside after the January harvest, are saved for seed. The corn is then placed in the fields to rot, and the fields cultivated two or three times at twenty-day intervals. After the third cultivation, about mid-August, planting is finished. The corn ripens in September. Between late September and November, when there is little work in the fields, the villagers look after their animals, cut wood, and do various home maintenance tasks. In early November, the harvest begins. The leaves are stripped at this time, and the corn is picked in early December. Each family, sometimes with the aid of hired

*Oscar Lewis, *Tepoztlan, Village in Mexico*. New York: Holt, Rinehart and Winston, 1960.

Figure 7.6 *The location of the Mexican village of Tepoztlan.*

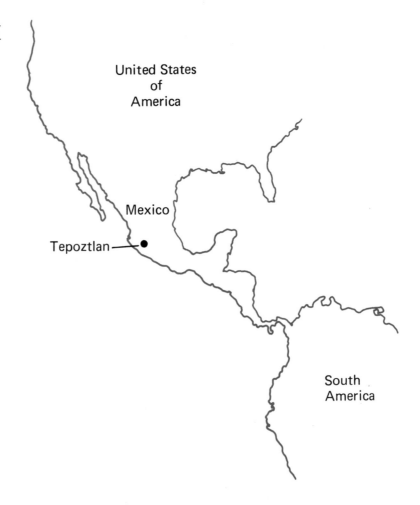

United States
of
America

Mexico

Tepoztlan——

South
America

laborers, harvests its own field. By early January, most fields are harvested and the corn is placed, unshelled, in storage bins. The women may shell what they need for daily consumption or small-scale trade. Around April or May, the men do the large-scale shelling, using a native volcanic rock or dry corncobs tied together over which the corn is rubbed. The shelled corn is stored in sacks.

In this particular area, hoe cultivation has a greater yield than plow cultivation. It is much more exhausting work, however, and also has less status than plow cultivation. Because of the capital investment required by intensive agriculture, many Tepoztlecans have engaged in hoe culture. As a short-run adaptation this makes sense, but the amount of land needed makes it a poor long-run strategy for the village, whose population is increasing.

Tepoztlan has relatively little livestock, and most of it is of poor quality. Climate and topography are not conducive to raising high-quality cattle or sheep. The main care given to animals by those families who have them is to guard against their being stolen. Horses, donkeys, and mules are owned for work, and riding a horse is considered a luxury. About 40 percent of the village families own hogs. Most of the animals used for food are slaughtered in the village itself. Milk is sold locally by about a dozen families. Most is converted into cheese, which is also sold in the village market. One of the most important sources of income for poor families is the production of charcoal, a part-time activity carried on in conjunction with farming. Another important home industry is rope making, and fibers are obtained from the local maguey plants. Many women raise chickens, turkeys, and pigs; others grow fruit, vegetables, and flowers to supplement the family income. In order to earn extra cash, Tepoztlecans also engage in such nonagricultural occupations as teaching, baking, masonry, storekeeping, butchering, barbering, and carpentry. This trend toward nonagricultural work has accelerated in the last thirty-five years. Although the economy of Tepoztlan is essentially a household economy, where the primary motive for production is subsistence of the family, the village depends on trade with nearby regions for many necessities, such as salt, sugar, rice, and chili. From urban centers it obtains cloth, agricultural implements, sewing machines, lamps, kerosene, guns, medicines, and other goods.

Like most peasant villages, Tepoztlan has undergone some important changes in the last thirty years. One of the most interesting ones is the result of the *bracero* movement. *Braceros* are temporary agricultural workers in the United States. In 1948 there were less than thirty *braceros* in Tepoztlan. By 1957, over six hundred men in a village population of some 4,500 had worked as *braceros*. Before the *bracero* movement, there was a shortage of agricultural land; but with so many young men going to the United States, many fields in Tepoztlan now lie idle. The *braceros* can earn more in a few months of labor in the United States than they could in almost two years in the village. This is just one of the important ways in which the economy of Tepotztlan is tied to the outside world, a pattern increasingly significant for peasant economies everywhere.

market in order to maximize personal profit. As Eric Wolf says (1966), "The American farmer runs a business; the peasant runs a household."

THE EMERGENCE OF VARIOUS FOOD-GETTING STRATEGIES

For most of human life on earth, people have exploited the environment through hunting and gathering. With the increasing improvement of tools during the last several hundred thousand years, hunters and gatherers were able to spread out into many different parts of the world, exploit many different kinds of environments, and develop many different cultural systems. About 25,000 years ago, humans arrived in Australia and the New World. Population increased in both the Old and New Worlds, even with relatively simple foraging technologies, but this strategy set certain limits on population densities and consequently on the complexity of social organization.

About 10,000 years ago, human groups began to domesticate plants and animals in the Old World. About 4,000 years later, similar developments took place in the New World. At one time anthropologists talked about the transition from a foraging to a food-producing strategy as a "revolution." Increasingly, archeological evidence is demonstrating that this transition was not "revolutionary" but gradual, although it was revolutionary in the new possibilities it opened up for cultural development. The earliest evidence of plant cultivation and the domestication of animals comes from Southwest Asia. It has been suggested that food production developed gradually out of a broad-spectrum foraging economy, and resulted from experimentation with different forms of wild plants in new habitats. The domestication

of animals similarly involved a gradual change in the relationship between humans and the wild sheep, goat, ox, and pig that they hunted (Flannery 1973).

Although archeologists have been able to show that village life is not synonomous with the domestication of plants and animals, increased populations could be supported, and sedentary village life became widespread with the advent of food production. With the increased population pressure, more intensive means of agriculture were developed, and where this occurred human labor had to be more closely coordinated and controlled. In conjunction with these developments state societies developed in the Near East, in Southwest Asia, in China, and also in Mexico and Peru.

Why intensive agriculture did not arise elsewhere, and why, in fact, some populations, such as the Australians, never made the transition from foraging to food production, has to be discussed in terms of the specific relationship between human populations and their environments. In some cases, such as in the Arctic, intensive agriculture could not develop. In other cases, such as in the fertile valleys of California, aboriginal foraging was so productive there was little pressure to make the transition to food production. Even in contemporary horticultural or pastoral societies, where methods of intensive agriculture are known, the transition to this adaptation is by no means inevitable. In some cases, other strategies may involve less risk, and therefore may be more adaptive over the long run. Ideology may also play a role, as different strategies become closely tied up with group identity. This seems to be true for many pastoral peoples, who despise their cultivating neighbors. For many hunting peoples, such as the Mbuti Pygmies, their whole culture and ideology are intimately associated with exploitation of the forest in which they live. In some cases, the transition to intensive cultivation is not made because it appears to require too much effort.

The history of humankind as a whole has moved in the direction of developing ways of exploiting the environment that are more efficient, can support greater population densities, and require more complex systems of sociocultural integration. With industrialization, which involves the use of machines rather than human or animal energy, we have seen incredible increases in productivity and efficiency.

From a typical preindustrial system, where 80 to 100 percent of the population must be actively involved in food production, we have moved to a situation in industrialized nations where 10 percent or less of the population can produce food for the other 90 percent. But industrialization, like other systems of adaptation, also raise problems. Industrialization has enormous potential for production and enormous potential for destruction as well. Only time will tell if new cultural forms and values will emerge to allow us to control technology to the advantage of the entire human race.

SUMMARY

1. Basic to the success and survival of every culture are the development of technology and knowledge for getting food in a particular environment.

2. Social organization, beliefs and values, religious ritual, and regulation of population growth also contribute to adaptation to the physical environment.

3. Different physical environments present different problems, opportunities, and limitations to human populations. Therefore, the physical environment influences, although it does not determine, culture. There are always at least a few cultural alternatives possible in any environment. The level of technology is the determining factor in the utilization of any particular physical environment.

4. The subsistence (food-getting) pattern of a society develops in response to seasonal variation in the environment, and environmental variations over the long run, such as drought, flood, or animal diseases.

5. Subsistence patterns are adjusted to the presence of different groups in the environment, as well as to physical factors such as climate, soil quality, and availability of water.

6. The environment influences culture, but culture also affects the environment. Through different patterns of exploitation, human societies affect the environmental zones in which they live.

7. Four major patterns of exploiting the environment to support human populations are described in this chapter: hunting and gathering, pastoralism, extensive agriculture (horticulture), and intensive agriculture.

8. Hunting and gathering, which relies on food naturally available in the environment, was the major food-getting pattern for 99 percent of the time humans have been on earth.

This way of life is rapidly disappearing, although even today it provides a more than adequate living for those groups who practice it.

9. The Copper Eskimo of the Canadian Arctic represent a specialized hunting-gathering adaptation: unlike other foraging societies, they do not have a large component of vegetable food in their diet.

10. Pastoralism involves the care of domesticated herd animals, which alone cannot provide the necessary ingredients for an adequate human diet. Supplementary food grains are required, and therefore pastoralism is either found along with cultivation, or involves trading relations with food cultivators.

11. The Yarahmadzai of Baluchistan are an example of a group that is predominantly pastoralist, but also utilizes a variety of other means of obtaining food: wage labor, date cultivation, and trade.

12. Extensive agriculture (horticulture) refers to food cultivation using a simple, nonmechanized technology. Fields are not used permanently, but allowed to lie fallow after several years of productivity. Horticulture is typically a tropical forest adaptation and requires the cutting and burning of jungle to clear fields for cultivation.

13. The Dani of New Guinea are horticulturalists, and like others in New Guinea also have domesticated pigs that provide needed animal protein. Other horticultural groups do some hunting or fishing to provide the protein supplement necessary for human survival.

14. Intensive agriculture refers to the subsistence pattern of food cultivation where both land and labor are intensively used, and a more complex technology involves plows, irrigation techniques, or mechanization. This food-getting pattern supports the largest population densities, and is thus associated with sedentary village life and the rise of the state.

15. Peasants are cultivators who produce mainly for the subsistence of their households, but who participate in the larger political entity called the state. Tepotzlan, a village in Mexico, has the typical characteristics of a peasant village: although agriculture is the main source of subsistence, there is also a well-developed market, participation in the larger cash economy of the state, wage labor, and some occupational specialization. Unlike farmers in the United States, peasant cultivators have little control over the land they work.

16. With a hunting and gathering strategy, humankind spread throughout the earth. About 10,000 years ago, through a gradual process, the domestication of animals and plants occurred in the Old World and some 4,000 years later in the New World. Populations increased, village life developed, and human labor required more control and coordination, leading to the rise of the state.

17. As a whole, humankind has moved in the direction of using more complex technology, increasing its numbers, and developing more complex sociocultural systems. With the rise of industrialization, many old problems have been solved and many new ones created.

SUGGESTED READINGS

Bicchieri, M. G., ed.

1972   *Hunters and Gatherers Today: A Socioeconomic Study of Eleven Such Cultures in the Twentieth Century.* New York: Holt, Rinehart and Winston. A good book for the introductory student. The articles cover a variety of geographical areas and include the ways in which such societies have changed through contact.

Forde, Daryll

1952   *Habitat, Economy and Society.* New York: Dutton. An introduction to the ethnography and human geography of 16 non-European peoples. The important aspects of economy and society are highlighted for each group.

Freuchen, Peter

1961   *Book of the Eskimos.* Greenwich, Conn.: Fawcett. A captivating account of the Eskimos of Greenland by an explorer who lived among them for many years.

Struever, S., ed.

1971   *Prehistoric Agriculture.* Garden City, N.Y.: Natural History Press. Explanations of the rise of agriculture and its consequences in various parts of the world.

Turnbull, Colin

1972   *The Mountain People.* New York: Simon and Schuster. A fascinating, shocking, and controversial ethnography about what happens to human relations in an African culture where people are starving.

Vayda, Andrew P.

1969   *Environment and Cultural Behavior.* Garden City, N.Y.: Natural History Press. An excellent reader edited by a leading cultural ecologist. Includes ecological perspectives on the traditional anthropological topics of religion, the potlatch, shifting agriculture, and family systems.

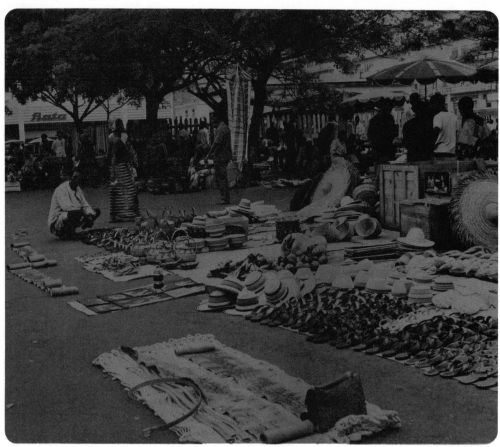

United Nations

8
Economics

Every society produces, distributes, and consumes (uses) goods and services. Every society therefore has an economy, a system for managing these processes. Its people also display certain economic behaviors—certain motivations and choices in the production, distribution, and consumption of those goods and services. We will look first at the study of economic behavior and then at economic systems before looking in detail at various patterns of production and distribution.

ANTHROPOLOGISTS STUDY ECONOMICS

Economic Behavior

Formal economics, which is a way of looking at human behavior, developed in the context of the Western industrial market economy. The basic assumption of formal economics is that human material wants are unlimited, but the means for achieving these wants are not. All people must therefore make choices about how to use time, energy, and capital in order to achieve desired ends. A further assumption of formal economics is that people **economize,** that is, make choices among alternative courses of action in a rational manner. Here rational means choosing a course of action that will maximize the individual's well-being and profit.

Economizing is seen as the key to understanding both the production and consumption of goods. Will a business firm cut down or expand its production? Will it purchase a new machine or hire more laborers? Where will it locate its plant? Will it manufacture shoes or gloves? How much will be spent on advertising its product? All these decisions are assumed to be rational—that is, based on the desire to max-

imize profit. Individuals are also assumed to act rationally, to allocate scarce resources in ways that increase their individual material well-being. How does one allocate one's income, which is limited, among an unlimited number of desires? Will an individual save to buy a new car, send the children to college, fix the roof on the house, take a vacation, or buy a spouse a gift? Or will he/she save it all? Will leisure time be spent playing with the children, getting a second job, or going back to school to get a degree in order to improve one's economic chances in the future?

The definition of economics as the study of economizing made sense in the kind of society in which formal economics developed. Is formal economic theory equally useful in the study of primitive and peasant societies? How much of the behavior in these societies can be understood in terms of maximizing one's individual material well-being? The data from anthropology show that although in every society people make choices in terms of means and ends, these choices are governed by values different from those in our own society.

Marshall Sahlins (1972) has questioned the whole idea of using the concept of scarcity in relation to hunting and gathering societies. He calls them the "original affluent societies" not because they are rich, but because what they desire is limited, and their technology is more than enough to meet their needs. According to Sahlins, the assumption that human needs are unlimited and resources are scarce is fundamental to capitalism, under which production units are motivated by profit. It is by no means a condition of all human societies; economizing is not a universal human value. Sahlins says: "We should entertain the . . . possibility that hunters are in business for their health, a finite objective, and that the bow and arrow are adequate to

Bushmen women filling egg shells with water. Among the Bushmen, women play an important role in the economy, but both men and women spend much of their time socializing. (Courtesy of the American Museum of Natural History)

that end." This point of view helps explain some behavior that appears puzzling—for example, "the inclination of hunters to consume at once all stocks on hand, as if they had it made." It also helps explain the economically nonproductive use of leisure time characteristic of many hunting societies.

Among the Hadza of Tanzania, for example, food is obtained without great effort. The Hadza live in an area with an abundance of animals and vegetable food. The Hadza man spends much of his time gambling, and there is no attempt to use leisure time to increase wealth. Surrounded by cultivators, the Hadza have, until recently, refused to give up their hunting way of life because it "would require too much work." Such behavior

seems irrational or "lazy" only if we assume that people have unlimited desires for more than they already possess (Woodburn 1968).

Enjoyable use of leisure time is only one of the ends toward which human effort may be expended. Increasing social status or respect is another value toward which individuals may direct their energies. In our own society, prestige is primarily tied up with increased consumption and display of goods and services by the individual. Within the value systems of other societies, individuals also make choices based on the desire to be respected by others. But prestige is associated not with individual display, but rather with generosity and the giving away of goods to others. Those who have much more than others may be considered stingy, and lose rather than gain prestige. "Conspicuous consumers" and stingy individuals become objects of envy and even subject to accusations of witchcraft. In our own society, although we expect to help relatives or close friends who are "down on their luck," we frequently do this only reluctantly, and often break off social relations with others who continually borrow. In other societies, social relations have priority over economic ones. Friends, relatives, and neighbors are expected to and do help each other out in times of need with little conscious thought of being paid back.

One allocation of resources in traditional societies that often seems excessive to Westerners is the investment in expensive ceremonial or ritual occasions that appear to have no direct material benefit to the individual, and may even cause a family to go into debt. Although we in the United States also engage in this kind of "uneconomic" behavior, such as spending far more on a wedding than we can "rationally" afford, it is difficult for us to understand such behavior in societies where the material standard of living is below what we consider minimal.

In nonindustrial societies, few aspects of behavior are strictly economic. Most economic activity in such societies is viewed by the people themselves as having social, ceremonial, or moral ends. The anthropological study of economics, called **substantive economics,** must therefore encompass an understanding of the relation of means to ends that goes beyond the maximization of individual material interest. Individuals everywhere make rational choices on the basis of self-interest. But although individuals do the "economizing," culture and society, values and social structures, provide the framework within which these choices are made. Anthropology makes an important contribution to the study of human behavior by demonstrating that rationality has different meanings for different societies. This understanding is of real practical value as nonindustrial societies begin programs of modernization and economic development. People who have never participated in a market economy will not necessarily see its value. Sudden changes in the economy can have unexpected consequences unless planners and administrators are aware of differences in values.

Economic Systems

An economic system is the part of a sociocultural system that deals with the production, distribution, and consumption or use of goods and services within a particular society. Economics deals partly with things, with the tools used to produce goods and the goods themselves. More important, it deals with the relationship of things to people and with people to each other in the process of producing, distributing, and consuming goods. Anthropologists are interested in understanding the relationship between the economy and the rest of a culture. One aspect of this interrelationship is that culture defines or shapes the ends sought by individuals and the means of achieving those ends. Society and economy are interdependent in other ways. The ways in which production is organized have consequences for the institution of the family and for the political system. Conversely, different types of political organization also have consequences for the modes of production and distribution of goods. How does a particular level of technological complexity affect the organization of work? How do the processes of production, distribution, and consumption relate to the formation of social classes or the absence of social differentiation? What is the consequence of different economic systems for economic growth and social change?

In primitive and peasant societies, it is often difficult to separate the economic system from the rest of culture. Economics is embedded in the total social process and cultural pattern. Few groups are organized solely for the purpose of production. Rather, production is carried out by groups such as families, larger kinship groups, or local communities. Productive units in traditional societies have many purposes; their economic activities are only one aspect of what they do. The distribution or exchange of goods is also embedded in relationships that have primarily social and political purposes, as is consumption. Under these conditions, in order to study the economics of a society, the anthropologist must build a model of a particular system from many activities that are not just economic in that culture.

PRODUCTION

In order to produce, people must have access to basic resources—land, water, and the materials from which tools are made. Every society has norms or rules that regu-

late access to and control over these resources as well as labor. After looking at the allocation of land, the basic resource of survival, we will turn to the organization or production—the composition of work groups and the division of labor in society. We will then look at capital—goods that are not directly consumed but used to produce other goods.

Allocation of Natural Resources: Land

Access to and control over land is basic to every productive system. In our own society, most land is privately owned. It belongs to an individual by right of sale, and the individual who owns it has the right to keep others off and dispose of it as he or she wishes. This system of private ownership is not generally found among hunters and gatherers, horticulturalists, and pastoralists. In these societies, rights to use the land are vested in groups rather than in individuals. An individual acquires the right to use a piece of land by virtue of

In peasant societies economics is embedded in the total social structure, and production is often carried out by families. (Serena Nanda)

belonging by birth to the group in whom the right to use the land is vested. But even the group that has rights to use the land may not dispose of it at will: Land is "inalienable" and may not be sold. With this type of land "ownership," no individual is deprived of access to basic resources, since every person belongs to a group within the society. Control over land, therefore, is not a means by which one group can exploit another or develop permanent control over other groups. Where rights to land do not include the right to keep others out, we may not really speak of land "ownership" at all. Let us look at what this means in four types of societies: hunters and gatherers, pastoralists, horticulturalists, and intensive agriculturalists.

Hunters and Gatherers. The requirements of a hunting and gathering way of life mean that a group of people must spread out over extensive areas of land. The division of land into exclusively defended and privately owned areas would make little sense since animals roam freely. The adaptive value of flexible boundaries is directly related to foraging strategies because ranges can be adjusted to a change in the availability of resources in a particular area. Since everyone knows where food is located, there is little concern that one or another group will gain exclusive access to basic resources. Thus, although certain areas are customarily used by particular groups within the society, these areas by no means *belong* to that group.

Among the Bushmen of the Kalahari, for example, camps are located near waterholes. The traditional area exploited by a local group is measured by one day's round trip walk (about 12 miles from the camp) in all directions. Thus, each camp has a core area of about 6 miles surrounding each waterhole. By fanning out from

the waterhole, camp members gain access to food resources within about 100 square miles. Points beyond this are rarely utilized. Although camps may be moved five or six times a year, they are not moved far. Sometimes the move is only a few hundred yards; the farthest move is about 10 or 12 miles (Lee 1968).

Hunters and gatherers require freedom of movement not only as a condition of success in their search for food, but also as a way of dealing with social conflict. Hunting bands are kept small in order to exploit the environment successfully. In such small groups, conflict must be kept to a minimum. When arguments break out, individuals can move to other groups without fear that they are cutting themselves off from access to vital resources. If land were individually or even communally "owned" and defended against outsiders, the freedom of movement in hunting societies would be severely limited.

The adaptiveness of flexible relations to the land for hunting groups seems to be demonstrated by recent studies of nonhuman primates in the wild. Gorilla groups, for example, appear to inhabit and use ranges that overlap considerably and do not have exclusive territories which they defend. Chimpanzees also appear to constantly change group membership and even different baboon groups have been observed to come into close daily contact without fighting over territories. Contrary to such popular theories as Robert Ardrey's "territorial imperative", anthropological research on both nonhuman primates and contemporary hunters and gatherers shows no evidence of a human instinct to occupy and defend a geographical area (Alland 1972).

Pastoralists. Among pastoralists access to grassland and water is gained through membership in corporate kin groups, but livestock is owned and managed by individual heads of households. Pastoral tribes have traditionally defined access to pasture and migration routes by arrangements with local authorities who have control over these areas. Within pastoralist camps, all members share equal access to pastures. It is this access rather than ownership that is important. Among contemporary pastoralists, access to land for grazing livestock is frequently established by contracts with the landowners of villages through which the pastoralists move in their migrations. These contracts which must be renewed every year, specify the rent for the pasture, the borders of the area, and the date by which the area must be vacated.

Horticulturalists. In horticultural societies, land tends to be communally owned by an extended kin group although rights to *use* a piece of land may be given to households or even individuals. The users of the land may not sell it or otherwise transfer it, however, because ultimately the land belongs to the larger community. Individual ownership of land does not make sense with a slash and burn horticultural strategy. Usually plenty of good land is available, and an individual has little use for land that was once farmed but now lies fallow. Once the land goes out of production, the claims to it gradually fade away, although fruit trees that have been planted may remain in private possession (McNetting 1977).

Among horticulturalists, the designated elders or officials of the group usually allocate plots to the members of the group or the heads of households. What is important in horticultural societies, therefore, is not exclusive title to land, but rather the work involved in clearing and cultivating.

The rights to cleared and productive land and to the products of that land are vested in those who work it, most often the domestic group or household. Because it is possible that the user of the land may die while the land is still productive, some system of inheritance of use rights is usually provided for. Cultivated plots in horticultural societies may be exclusively used and even defended against trespassers, but this system does not deprive anyone of the land necessary for subsistence.

Where population densities are low and/or great areas of land are available for cultivation, land use and group ownership is not a problem in horticultural societies. But when specific geographical conditions limit the amount of available land or population pressure increases, land shortages do occur. Sometimes this is dealt with by the development of warfare, which serves to redistribute populations. Sometimes it is taken care of by the development of more efficient technology. As technology advances and the material base of a society expands, notions of private property develop. It is therefore in systems of intensive agriculture that private ownership of land becomes important.

Intensive Agriculturalists. Under intensive agriculture, the material and labor investment in land becomes substantial. As land remains continually and indefinitely in production, it can feed more people than those who work it. It can support nonagricultural specialists and a class of landowners. Private or family ownership of rigidly defined fields becomes an economic asset of great value in a society that permits the landowner, not the cultivator, to claim the surplus. That person can then enjoy leisure and command the services of craftsmen. Intensive agriculture therefore tends to be associated with individual land ownership, with the leasing or renting of property, with a political organization characterized by a ruling landowning class, and with occupational specialization. Under such conditions, a peasantry emerges. Peasants, you may remember from Chapter 7, are agriculturalists who must pay rent on the land they work. Part of what they produce is thus taken by a ruling class.

Individual ownership of land may grow out of population pressures that produce land scarcity and lead to intensified methods of agriculture. Under these conditions, communal control of land creates conflict as people begin to grumble about their share. Those who have improved the land are unwilling to see the investment of their labor revert to a family pool. This may be particularly true when cash crops such as coffee are concerned, since these require long-term care and yield harvests over many years. Individuals thus become tied to particular plots of land. In a study of land use and rights in the New Guinea highlands, it was found that individual ownership of land was correlated with high population density and intensive agriculture. Individual rights to land (though within the framework of "group territory") occurred where plots of land were in permanent use or had a short fallow period (less than six years) and where trees and shrubs had been planted by the owner.

The Organization of Labor

In primitive and peasant economies, the basic unit of production is not a group organized solely around economic functions. Most often the household or some extended kin group carries out production as part of its many activities. These groups produce goods mainly for their own use. Their goals are often social or religious, rather than strictly economic. Labor is not a commodity bought and sold in the market, but rather one aspect of a role that derives its primary meaning and reward from membership in a social group such as the family. Work, therefore, is not a "job"; it is an aspect of social participation (Lee 1959). This pattern is very different from that in industrial societies, where the basic unit of production is the business firm, which is organized only for economic purposes. A firm does not produce goods for the use of its members; the items it produces are sold for profit. Under this system, labor becomes a commodity, bought and sold on the market just like milk and shoes. Work is carried out in an impersonal setting, and the rewards of work are primarily economic.

But the important difference between the business firm and the household is not the motivations of the actors: Households as well as firms are guided by the desire to maximize, and households also look for profit when they are involved in cash transactions. The point is that the structure of the household as a producing unit limits economic growth because in fact, households have other functions, such as social and ritual functions, as well as economic ones. Households are also restricted because they can draw labor from only a small group. Nor can a household liquidate if it makes poor choices in the allocation of its resources. Furthermore, it may use resources in economically unproductive ways for ceremonial or social goals (Nash 1967). The business firm, in contrast, is geared toward economic growth and can make its decisions solely on an economic basis. Even when they are not geared solely to the profit of the individual owner (as is the case, for example, in the Soviet Union), firms are always looking for technological innovation and expansion of productivity. In economies where households are the producing units, then, there can be little expansion, and innovation is not a by-product of economic activity. What this means is that large-scale production and the mass distribution systems with which we are familiar tend not to develop where economic systems are made up of households.

Division of Labor by Sex. The sexual division of labor is a universal characteristic of human society. In every society, some tasks are considered appropriate only for women and others only for men. The most obvious basis for the division of labor between men and women is that only women can bear and nurse children. Child care is thus a universal female role, with a biological foundation in the physical differences between men and women. Since it is women who get pregnant and nurse, this tends to make them less mobile than men, which may account for the fact that hunting large animals and warfare (in nonindustrial societies) is almost an exclusively male occupation.

The extent to which biological sex differences are an explanation for sex role differentiation is a matter of dispute among anthropologists. Ernestine Friedl (1975), among others, points out that the care of small children can be shared by others—older children, neighbors, relatives, old men and women not engaged in food production, and even fathers. Friedl suggests that the division of labor in society is not an inevitable result of the fact that women bear and care for children, but rather that the number of children a woman has is adapted to the division of labor in society and the role women play in getting food. Cultural norms with respect to family size and systems of child care may be arranged to conform with women's pro-

ductive work, rather than the norms of work being an adaptation to pregnancy and child care. Most anthropologists emphasize the tremendous variation in the sex-related division of labor, and look for explanations in the environment, food-getting strategy, and level of sociopolitical complexity of the particular society.

In foraging societies where hunting is done by one or a few individuals, it is always the men who hunt large animals. In most foraging societies, women collect plant foods near the base camp, although among the Hadza and also among the Paliyans of India (Gardner 1966), each man collects most of his plant food himself, and women do the same for themselves and their children. Where hunting is a communal activity, as among the Mbuti Pygmies, women and men from several families collectively drive the animals into some central area, although men do the actual killing. In some societies, men and women also work together gathering nuts or fishing in streams.

In horticultural societies, there is a greater variety in the sexual division of labor, although here too there appears to be a male monopoly—that of clearing the land. Ernestine Friedl (1975) suggests that men are assigned this task for several reasons. Not only is felling trees and cutting underbrush heavy work, but new land is often on the frontiers of other groups and may require warfare (a male activity) in order to gain access to it. Furthermore, game is more available in uncleared land, and among horticulturalists hunting is a male activity. Planting, weeding, harvesting, and carrying produce may be assigned to men or women. The most common pattern among horticulturalists is for men to clear the land, and both men and women to cultivate. In some cases women are responsible for cultivating the basic staples,

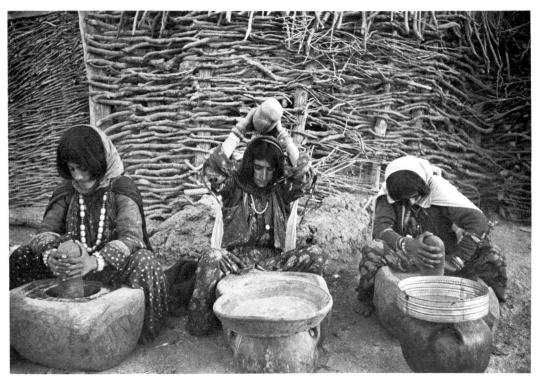

In addition to the processing of daily food, young Kurdish women take care of the water supply and cattle and look after the chickens and turkeys. (United Nations)

while men raise only the prestige crops used in exchange. In Highland New Guinea, for example, women raise sweet potatoes, which are the main food for humans as well as pigs, while men raise sugar, taro, and bananas, which are used only in exchange. A common pattern in West Africa is that both men and women cultivate staples and prestige crops, while women raise additional staples which they use for trade.

A relatively rare pattern of sex specialization in food production exists among the Yanomamo of the Amazon basin in South America. Here the men clear and cultivate, with the women giving only minor assis-

tance. Men also hunt and gather honey. Women gather wild plants and both sexes fish, but most of the food supply comes from the gardens cultivated by the men. One explanation of this pattern is that the Yanomamo are constantly engaged in warfare and raiding other villages for their women. This makes it quite dangerous for women to work unprotected in the forest. Among the Hopi Indians of Arizona also, men cultivate the staple crops—corn, beans, and squash—with simple irrigation techniques, while the women raise a few vegetables in small gardens near the village.

Wherever hunting and deep sea fishing occur among horticulturalists, these activities are done by men, although women may collect small fish from streams and kill small animals. Where domesticated animals are raised, whether the work falls to men or women seems to depend on the kinds of animals. If pigs are domesticated, as in New Guinea, women usually feed and care for them (though men exchange them); this may be because pigs root in the vicinity of the home and can more easily be taken care of by women with small children. Sheep, goats, and cattle, which graze at some distance from the home, are usually herded by men or boys.

Carrying food home from the fields is practically always part of a woman's role; a man may or may not also do this. The major daily work of cooking and processing food, which is a difficult task when it involves grinding grains and pounding root crops, is women's work everywhere, although the preparation of food for ceremonies is often the task of men.

Sex role specialization in craft activities varies except for metalworking, which is always a male task and perhaps developed out of the making of metal weapons for hunting and war. Weaving is done by women in the American Southwest, but by men in Africa. In Europe, India, and Central Africa, men are the potters, but in West Africa and the Americas, women are the potters. Making bark cloth is a male task in Africa but a female task in Southeast Asia. Baskets are usually made by women if they are for domestic use, but by men when they are sold.

Division by Age. The division of labor by age is also universal. In our own society, childhood is prolonged and young people do not generally engage in productive activities. In other societies, even very small children actually contribute to community life. At the other end of the spectrum, the elderly in our society are often forcibly retired from the workforce when they are still in good health. In the United States,

where an honest day's work is an important part of an individual's self-image and the most important connection to the larger social whole, this forced disengagement of the aged from productive tasks can lead to isolation, loneliness, and diminished feelings of self-worth (Clark 1973). In many traditional societies by contrast, the older person continues to make an important contribution to economic life. An outstanding example of this kind of society is the Abkhasians, a people famous for their longevity, who live in an area between the Black Sea and the Caucasus mountains in the Soviet Union. The Abkhasians were once herders but now live and work on collective farms. Almost everyone in the community works regularly. "Retirement" is unknown. After the age of 80, and more so after the age of 90, the workload decreases, but work does not stop. Men who have been shepherds will no longer follow the herds up into the mountains but instead may tend farm animals. Old men will cease plowing and lifting heavy loads but will continue weeding. Women of advanced age will no longer work in the fields, but they continue to do housework, feed chickens, and knit. One study of twenty-eight people over the age of 100 years showed they worked an average of four hours a day (Benet 1976).

The Abkhasians are an exceptional people. But even in traditional societies where such health and vitality do not exist, older persons often contribute to society by taking on the roles of ritual specialists and guardians of cultural traditions, and agents of enculturation. In societies without writing, older people who know and remember are valuable members of society, respected and socially involved even past the time of strictly economic productivity.

Specialization in Complex Societies. Nonindustrial societies have relatively simple technologies. Although many of their tools and techniques are ingenious and fit the requirements of the environment, toolmaking does not require skills beyond those that can be learned as part of an informal socialization process. The work involved in making the tools of production can be done by every normal adult and requires no machines or scarce materials. Because there are no specialized operations, there is little need for specialization of labor. Almost everyone can do every job.

In nonindustrial societies, all adult men and women are actively engaged in the quest for food. The few specialists—for example, religious practitioners—are usually part-time specialists, and also engage in food production. The characteristic division of labor is not by job but by age and sex. This contrasts with our own society, in which production is highly specialized.

In addition to the division of labor by sex and age which is found in all societies, complex societies are characterized by a great variety of occupational roles and productive specializations. In the caste system in India, for example, only people belonging to certain hereditary kinship groups are allowed to perform certain services or produce certain kinds of goods. Literally thousands of specialized activities—washing clothes, drumming at festivals, presiding over religious ceremonies, making pots, painting pictures—are the traditional specialty of various castes within a village, or even of villages as a whole.

The division of labor in society becomes more specialized and complex as population increases and agricultural production

intensifies. Industrialization as an adaptive strategy requires the most specialized and complex division of labor and only a small proportion of the population is directly involved in producing food. We all know how complicated mass production techniques and service delivery systems are in our own society, and we are familiar with how specialized jobs have become. Although specialization of production undoubtedly has advantages in terms of efficiency and the ability to produce large quantities of goods, we must also consider what price may have to be paid in terms of other, nonmaterial human values.

Capital

Capital is goods used to produce other goods. Where money exists, capital includes the money used to purchase these goods. In the small-scale economies we have been describing, capital goods are limited. Among hunting peoples, weapons used in the hunt are capital goods. Among fishing societies, they include water craft and elaborate trapping and netting devices that require great investment of time and labor. In agricultural societies, the tools of cultivation and storage facilities are part of capital. In pastoral societies, the main form of capital is livestock. Animals not only produce goods that are directly consumed, such as milk, but are also kept to produce other animals, and used in exchange. Capital goods in primitive and peasant societies are normally owned individually, except for those that are too costly for one individual to buy. In peasant societies, for example, cooperatives may be set up for the purchase of such things as tractors. In every society some time and energy must be invested in the maintenance of capital goods. Storage facilities must be built and maintained, tools must be made and re-

Dugout canoes are an important form of capital among the horticultural Paramacca Maroons of Surinam, who also fish in lakes. A man gets his matrilineal kinsmen to help him and he helps them in turn. (John Lenoir)

placed and repaired, animals must be fed and taken care of.

An important point of contrast in economic systems is the extent to which the members of a society have access to capital goods. Differential access to important capital goods develops with more complex political forms, as well as with more complex and specialized technology. In hunting and horticultural societies, where technology is simple and tools are made by hand, every normal adult has access to capital. No one is deprived of the means of producing food or manufactured items. In politically and technologically more complex societies such as some chiefdoms or states, access to the means of production falls into the hands of a ruling class. Ownership of the means of production may be limited to a small group, whose members thereby gain power over others and control their labor. (We will discuss this relationship between access to the means of production and political power more fully in Chapter 11.) Capitalist societies are those in which, among other things, capital is invested for profit, rather than used simply for the subsistence needs of the group. Because capitalism is associated with market economies and money, we will discuss it in the next section on distribution.

DISTRIBUTION: SYSTEMS OF EXCHANGE

In all societies, goods and services are exchanged. There are three main ways in which this exchange occurs: reciprocity, redistribution, and the market. Each system appears to be predominantly associated with a particular kind of political and social organization, although more than one kind of exchange system frequently exists in any particular society (Polyani 1944). Where there is more than one system, each will normally be used for the exchange of different kinds of goods and services. Let us look first at reciprocity.

Reciprocity

The mutual give and take among persons of equal status, which is actually a continuum of forms of exchange, is called **reciprocity.** Three types of reciprocity are distinguished from one another by the degree of social distance between the exchanging partners. Generalized reciprocity, which is usually carried out among close kin, has the highest degree of moral obligation. Balanced reciprocity is characteristic of the relationship between friends, or members of different tribes in a peaceable relationship with each other. Negative reciprocity refers to exchanges between strangers or peoples hostile to each other (Sahlins 1972).

Generalized Reciprocity. **Generalized reciprocity** involves a distribution of goods where no account is kept of what is given and no immediate or specific return is expected. Such transactions are ideally altruistic—that is, without any thought of economic or other self-interest. Assistance is given and if possible and necessary, returned. In our own society we are familiar with generalized reciprocity as it exists between parents and children. Parents are constantly giving things and providing services to their children "out of love," or at least out of a sense of responsibility. What would we think of a parent who kept an account of what a child "cost" and then expected the child to repay this amount? What parents do generally expect is perhaps some gratitude, love, respect, and the child's happiness.

Generalized reciprocity involving food is an important social mechanism among hunting and gathering peoples. In these societies, a hunter, or group of hunters, will distribute meat among the kin group or camp. Each person or family gets either an equal share, or a share dependent on their kinship relationship to the hunter. Dentan (1968) describes this system among the Semai of Malaya:

> After several days of fruitless hunting, a Semai man kills a large pig. He lugs it back to the settlement. Everyone gathers around. Two other men

meticulously divide the pig into portions sufficient to feed two adults each (children are not supposed to eat pork). As nearly as possible each portion contains exactly the same amount of meat, fat, liver, and innards as every other portion. The adult men take the leaf wrapped portions home to redistribute them among the members of the house group.

Similar systems are used by the Bushmen of the Kalahari and the Eskimo.

An American might wonder "What does the hunter get out of it?" "Aren't some people always in the position of providing and others always receiving?" These are really related questions. It is true that the hunter does not gain more from his kill than anyone else in terms of the amount of food he consumes. Still, he is bound by culturally prescribed rules of "generosity" to share. In these small societies, where the good opinion of others is really necessary for survival, the desire not to be thought stingy is a strong motivation to share and to do one's share. Since all men in the society are bound by the same rules, in the long run the system will provide everyone with an opportunity to give and receive. Generalized reciprocity also has important adaptive functions. One hunter and his family probably could not consume the meat from a large animal at one sitting. Without techniques for storing and preserving food, the meat would go to waste if it was not distributed among groups larger than the family.

Balanced Reciprocity. **Balanced reciprocity** involves a clear obligation to return, within a specified time limit, goods of nearly equal value. The fact that balanced reciprocity is most often called "gift giving" obscures its economic importance in societies where it is the dominant form of exchange. We are familiar with balanced reciprocity when we give gifts at weddings or birthdays, or exchange invitations or buy a round of drinks for friends. In these exchanges, it is always the "spirit" of the gift and the social relationship between the givers that is verbalized as important. The economic aspect of the exchange is repressed. We also know, however, that an unreciprocated gift or a return gift of very different value will evoke negative comment. Similarly, accepting an invitation involves the obligation to offer a similar invitation in the future.

The social obligation to give, to accept and to return, is at the heart of balanced reciprocity. A refusal to receive and a failure to return the gift is taken as a withdrawal from a social relationship. Because a gift that is accepted puts the receiver under an obligation to the giver, most people like to "pay off" the debt by making a return gift. In balanced reciprocity, however, the payoff does not have to be immediate. In fact, an attempt to return the gift immediately is an indication of unwillingness to be obligated, and therefore also an indication that a trusting social relationship is neither present nor desired (Mauss 1954).

Balanced reciprocity is often characteristic of trading relations among non-Western peoples without market economies. Such trade, which is frequently carried out over long distances and between different tribes or villages, is often in the hands of trading partners, men who have a long-standing social relationship with each other. Social rules between trading partners permit trade with others not related by kinship where no authority, such as the state, exists for protection.

The most famous anthropological study of this type of trading is that of the Kula ring, described by Malinowski in his ethnography of the Trobriand Islands (1961). The *Kula* is an extensive, intertribal trade among a ring of islands (Figure 8.1). Two kinds of articles are prominent in this trade, each type moving in a different direction. *Soulava*, long necklaces of red shell, move clockwise. *Mwali*, bracelets of white shell, move counterclockwise. As each of these articles travels around the islands, it meets, and is exchanged for, an article of the other type. Every detail of the transaction is fixed by tradition. In every village on the participating islands, some of the men take part in the Kula. These men receive the necklaces or bracelets from their trading partners, hold them for a while, and then pass them on. No man keeps any article in his possession permanently. These trading partnerships are permanent, lifelong affairs.

For the Trobriander, as Malinowski describes it, the satisfactions of the Kula trade were tied up with the prestige and sentiment associated with holding the Kula valuables. But the Kula exchange may also be viewed as a mechanism of social integration. Through the trading partnerships, the groups that participate are socially bound to one another. Malinowski also noted that "associated with it [trade of Kula valuables] and done under its cover, we find a great number of secondary activities and features. Thus, side by side with the ritual exchange of armbands and necklaces, the natives carry on ordinary trade, bartering from one island to another a great number of utilities, often unprocurable in the district to which they are imported, and indispensable there." This suggests that the Kula trade has important economic functions that have been obscured by the people's emphasis on the trading of Kula valuables. It is clear that

Figure 8.1 *The Kula ring. This map shows the islands participating in the Kula exchange and the directional movement of the ritual exchange of necklaces* (soulava) *and armshells* (mwali).

the functions of such exchanges are not necessarily recognized by the people who participate in them, and who are motivated by more personal considerations.

The importance of trade and balanced reciprocity in establishing alliances is clearly demonstrated among the Yanomamo. Yanomamo society is characterized by hostile relations between different villages. Villages are always looking for alliances, yet at the same time their pride forbids them from openly seeking ties with others. Trading is a good way to begin building up friendly relationships between

villages. Each Yanomamo village has one or more products in which it specializes. These include dogs, hallucinogenic drugs, arrows, cotton yarn, baskets, pots, and lately, steel tools. Napolean Chagnon, the Yanomamo ethnographer, says this specialization cannot be explained by the distribution of natural resources; each village is capable of producing all these things itself. Chagnon explains economic specialization and the "need" to trade among Yanomamo villages as an adaptation to the need for forming alliances. In other words, trade is an adaptation to the sociopolitical environment rather than to the physical one. Trade here functions as a "social catalyst," the "starting mechanism" through which mutually suspicious villages can be brought together over time. These contacts eventually lead to feasting, the exchange of women in marriage, and somewhat stable military alliances (1977).

The role of the reciprocal exchange of goods and services in producing social integration is clearly illustrated by the caste system in village India. Here, a number of different groups, or **castes,** each having its own occupational specialty and ranked social position, are interlocked in a complex system of exchange of goods and services. Traditionally, high-caste landowning families are provided goods and services by various lower castes such as carpenters, potters, blacksmiths, water carriers, leatherworkers (who remove dead cattle from the fields), barbers, and washermen. The Brahmin, or priestly caste, who have very high status, also perform services for landowning families, officiating at various life-cycle ceremonies and on other religious occasions. In return, the landowning families pay serving-caste families with grain, clothing, sugar, fodder for animals,

and animal products like butter and milk. The landowning castes may also give the serving castes small amounts of cash, free rent, or the use of tools. Serving caste families may be linked with landowning families over several generations.

The serving castes also exchange goods and services among themselves. Thus, with its norms of reciprocity, the caste system provides benefits to both the high-caste landowning families and the serving castes. Landowners get a steady supply of workers and can maintain a high-status life style; they need not perform menial and ritually polluting work. The serving castes, in turn, are assured economic security. This description, however, is a somewhat idealized one; many anthropologists have argued that the benefits of the system are much greater for the high castes than the low castes, and that social integration in the Indian village is due as much to physical coercion and the absence of alternatives for the lower castes as it is to the integrating force of reciprocity.

In India, the caste system is an important means of regulating the exchange of goods and services. Barbering, for example, is an activity traditionally performed in exchange for grain and clothes, rather than cash. (Serena Nanda)

Negative Reciprocity **Negative reciprocity** is the "unsociable extreme" in exchange between equals. It is conducted for the purpose of material advantage, and is based on the desire to get something for nothing (gambling, theft, cheating) or to get the better of a bargain (barter or haggling). Negative reciprocity is either an impersonal or an unfriendly transaction. As such, it is generally carried out with those who stand in the position of "outsiders" to each other. Both in our own society and in primitive and peasant society, outsiders, however they may be defined, are considered "fair game." In a large, complex society, where economic dealings are mainly carried out among strangers, abstract principles of morality develop that should apply to everyone. Tribal and peasant societies are more likely to distinguish between the insider, whom it is morally wrong to cheat, and the outsider, from whom every advantage may be gained. Among the aboriginal Navajo, for example, the rules vary with the situation; to deceive when trading with foreign tribes is a morally accepted practice. Even witchcraft techniques are considered acceptable in trading with members of foreign tribes. Among pastoralists, negative reciprocity in the form of theft of livestock was an important way in which animals changed hands. For the Plains Indians, who hunted buffalo on horseback, horse raids were an important aspect of the economy.

Redistribution

In **redistribution,** goods are collected or contributed from members of a group and then given out to the group in a new pattern. Redistribution thus involves a "social center" where goods come together and from which they are distributed. There are many contexts in which redistribution is the mode of exchange. In household food sharing, pooled resources are reallocated among family members. In state societies, redistribution is achieved through taxation, an obligatory payment on the part of the people in return for which various services are provided by a government.

Redistribution is especially important as a mechanism of exchange in societies where political organization includes chiefs or "big men." These act as "social centers" to which goods and food are contributed by the population, and from which these are redistributed back to the people through communal feasting. These feasts, which are sponsored by a chief or "big man," sustain his political power and raise his prestige. At the same time, they also reaffirm the values and solidarity of the society. The **potlatch** of the Kwakiutl Indians of the Northwest Coast of North America is one example of redistribution in action. In Kwakiutl society, social ranking was a consuming interest. Every time a chief wanted to demonstrate his prestige in relation to other chiefs, he would have to give a potlatch. Potlatches were public occasions (which were held to celebrate births, deaths, marriages, and a youth's coming of age). The host of a potlatch would invite other families as his guests, and the number of guests present revealed the wealth and prestige of the host. The host would publicly trace his line of descent and claim the right to certain symbolic privileges, such as ownership of a particular song or dance. Each of these claims was accompanied by feasting and the display and giving away of large quantities of food and manufactured goods, such as blankets, carved wooden boxes, boats, fish oil, and flour. When there was a competitive potlatch, that is, when two men competed for the same symbolic privilege, one of the rivals might ostentatiously destroy great quanities of property—canoes, blankets, and, in former times, even slaves—in order to show how great he was and how little his possessions meant to him (Rohner and Rohner 1970). Competitive feasts are not always characterized by the boasting and extremes of the Kwakiutl. This feature of potlatching is now believed by anthropologists to have been intensified when the Kwakiutl began to participate in the cash economy of the Canadians. The outside source of income resulted in the "inflation" of potlatching and the "wastefulness" of the destruction of goods described by informants to anthropologists in the late nineteenth and early twentieth centuries. Apparently, traditional potlatches were similar to the feasts that still exist in various parts of New Guinea and the islands of the Pacific.

In Ponape, a Micronesian island, for example, the competitive production and display of food at community feasts is not done with boasting, but with modesty. The prestige foods in Ponapean feasts are yams and breadfruit, contributed by the guests, and pigs and *kava* (an intoxicating beverage) contributed by the hosts. Those who bring yams and breadfruit are very modest about their display. A man who is considered "number one" in terms of the size and quality of the foods he brings will always protest that someone else's products are better than his own (Bascom 1970).

The earlier attention anthropologists gave to boasting and rivalry and to the motivations of the individual actors in these competitive giveaways obscures some of their ecologically adaptive functions and their economic importance as mechanisms of redistribution. Prestige economies, like those described for the Kwakiutl and the Ponapeans serve as a way of pushing people to produce more than they can immediately consume. It is a way of provid-

Pig feasts, at which great quantities of meat and other goods are distributed by a host to his guests, are an important mechanism of redistribution among horticultural peoples of New Guinea. (Courtesy of Office of Information, Port Moresby, Papua New Guinea)

ing reserves that can be used in times of shortage and is particularly necessary where food preservation techniques are not well developed. Systems of feasting also provide a way for food surpluses to be distributed among villages that are not in equally good environments. In lean years, such communities could accept the invitations of chiefs from other villages and receive food in return for the diminished status involved in receiving rather than giving. When things got better, the recipients could become hosts, distributing food and goods to others who needed it, and thus regain some of their lost prestige.

Market Exchange

The predominant feature of **market exchange** is that goods and services are bought and sold at a money price determined by the impersonal forces of supply and demand. Unlike reciprocity and redistribution, in which the social and political roles of those who exchange are important, a market exchange is impersonal and occurs no matter what the social position of the participants. Market exchange is thus the most purely "economic" mode of exchange, the one in which participants are interested only in maximizing material gain. In a society integrated by the market, social or political goals are less important than economic goals. Organization around strictly economic purposes and activities is a dominant feature of social life.

Market exchange is based on the existence of **all-purpose money;** that is, a medium of exchange that is used to purchase a wide range of goods and services, and that is a standard of value for stating prices. This feature distinguishes true market systems from societies in which money exists, but in which only certain kinds of goods and services are exchanged for money. Societies with market economies must also be distinguished from those in which reciprocity or redistribution are the primary integrating mechanisms, but where marketplaces also exist for the exchange of certain kinds of goods. These societies, which are found in New Guinea and West Africa, may be said to have "peripheral" markets; the important means of production, land, and labor are not exchanged through the mechanism of the market (Dalton 1967).

In systems of market exchange, labor is a commodity; people work for wages that are regulated, like other commodities, by supply and demand. Where, in addition to this feature, we find the private ownership of land and capital goods, and the investment of capital for profit (either in production or through interest on loans), we may talk of a **capitalist society.** A true capitalist society can exist only in connection with the state as a political system, because a powerful central authority is necessary to enforce the contracts on which market exchanges are based. Because the private ownership of basic resources results in denying some people access to these resources, permanently differentiated economic and social classes are also an important feature of a capitalist society. True capitalism is a late development in the history of humankind and in its purest form is best illustrated by the industrial nations of nineteenth-century Europe and the United States.

Leveling Mechanisms

Leveling mechanisms are practices, values, or forms of social organization that result in evening out the distribution of wealth. Leveling mechanisms force accumulated resources or capital to be used in ways that do not result in significant or permanent economic differences. They ensure that social goals take precedence over economic ones and thus result in socially stable, though economically static, social systems.

Leveling mechanisms have many different forms. Obligatory generosity as a basis of prestige and political power prevents the formation of social classes. Another leveling device is redistribution through feasting. Manning Nash describes a number of different leveling mechanisms that operate in the village of Amatenango, in the Chiapis district of Mexico (1967). One is the organization of production by households. As mentioned earlier,

(continues on p. 173)

PRIMITIVE CAPITALISTS: THE KAPAUKU*

Some technologically primitive societies, however, seem to contain many of the features of capitalist society. The Kapauku of western New Guinea (Figure 8.2), described by Leopold Pospisil (1963) are a good example. The Kapauku are basically horticulturalists. The sweet potato, their main staple, is grown to feed both people and pigs. The breeding and trading of pigs is the major source of prestige and political leadership. Kapauku technology is quite simple, but the economy has many features of capitalism. Its economy rests on the use of money: Both cowrie shell and two types of necklaces function as common media of exchange and the common measure of value. The exchange of all kinds of goods—food, domesticated animals, crops, land, and artifacts—is made through purchase. Money is also used for payment for labor in cultivation, for medical and ritual services, and for fines for misconduct. Cowrie shell money comes in various "denominations," and like modern money is easily portable. Cowrie shell is obtained through trade with coastal communities, which is sometimes a difficult enterprise. The value of cowrie shell is fixed by its scarcity and is relatively stable. Market prices for different commodities are thus also relatively stable, and an "ideal" or "fair" price is established by tradition for different goods and services. However, supply and demand can alter the price in any particular situation. Prices may also be affected by the relationship between the trading partners or the social status of the buyer. Prices are usually lower between close relatives, for example. Prices may also be lowered if the buyer is a rich man or a political leader, either in the hope of future favors or as gratitude for past ones. In this respect, the Kapauku market systems differs from a true market economy, where—theoretically at least—the price is the same for everyone.

Although buying and selling occurs among the Kapauku on a daily basis, most business is transacted on ceremonial occasions, particularly that of the pig feast. Hundreds of animals are killed and the meat distributed through sales, loans, and repayment of debts. In addition, the trading of other products, such as native tobacco, bowstrings, salt, bows and arrows, chickens, net bags, and axes also takes place. The pig feasts are an important institution of interregional trade as well as ceremonial and social functions.

Although practically everything is exchanged among the Kapauku through buying and selling, most of these exchanges take place within local kin groups. This is another difference between the

*Leopold Pospisil, *The Kapauku Papuans of West New Guinea*. New York: Holt, Rinehart and Winston, 1963.

Figure 8.2 *The location of the Kapauku of New Guinea.*

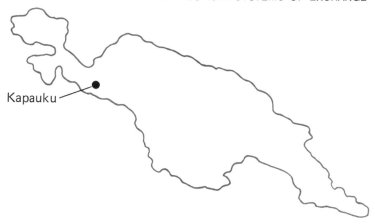

Kapauku

Kapauku economy and a true market system. In their buying and selling, however, the Kapauku are strictly profit motivated. Domesticated animals are bought for money and raised for breeding and profit, rather than for domestic consumption. Artifacts are also produced for sale. The extension of credit is an important way in which money is redistributed in Kapauku society, although no interest is usually charged on loans. The borrower may promise to pay a few extra cowrie shells for the favor of being lent money, but if he chooses not to do this later, there is no cause for legal complaint. Such a person, will, however, lose prestige and be regarded as untrustworthy. People will hesitate to lend money to him in the future.

Individualism, which is a major characteristic of capitalist societies, also has a prominent place in Kapauku life and culture. Every item in the society is individually owned; common ownership is unknown. The Kapauku claim that two men cannot own a plot of land together because they would steal from each other's crops, and each would avoid as much work as he could get away with. Money, movable property, houses, canoes, and land thus have only one owner. Even tracts of virgin forest belong to an individual. There is no family, lineage, or village property. When cooperative efforts are needed to build large structures for the benefit of the whole community, such as a drainage ditch, specific individuals own segments of the property and take care of the upkeep of their segment only. If a structure collapses or has to be taken apart, the individuals who built it come to claim the logs that went into the building. Wives and husbands also possess property individually, as do male children who are old enough to work a piece of land. Nor do people like to work cooperatively: A garden plot will be divided into individual sections, and even co-wives do not work together.

Also unlike many horticultural peoples, the Kapauku do not share their food on a communal basis. Individuals own the food they produce and act as hosts to the rest of the household. If a man has been treated to a meal in his own house by one of his co-residents, he must reciprocate by acting as host in turn. Even husbands and wives commonly exchange food rather than share it. Husbands provide pork, game, sugarcane and bananas; wives return these "gifts" by supplying sweet potatoes, which they cultivate.

Although the Kapauku sound like capitalists in many ways, there are two important differences between their economy and society and our own. The first is that although land is individually owned, in practice it is a kinship unit which controls a "territory." Since there is "mutual affection and a strong sense of unity" within a territory, no one appears to be denied access to the means of subsistence. Furthermore, although "grown men are expected to have gardens of their own" and the ethnographer found only two exceptions, the men without gardens helped their brothers and received part of the garden produce. Furthermore, an old man cannot validly sell his land without the consent of his sons. If he tries to, his heirs can repossess the land by giving the purchase price back to the buyer. Although property can be disposed of by the will of a dying man, no sons, brothers, fathers, or nephews can be deprived of their share of the land under any circumstances. Because of the importance of land in providing basic subsistence, this hedging of "individual ownership" is an important difference between Kapauku capitalism and our own economic system.

A second important difference is that Kapauku capitalism does not result in the establishment of permanently differentiated social classes. Kapauku wealth is displayed by generosity; a man who has much may lavishly distribute food or be generous in extending credit in order to keep up his reputation as a leader. Because pig breeding and trading is an activity many different people can engage in, the status system is constantly in flux. New men are constantly "coming up" and a rich headman may lose his position to a younger, more successful man. Wealth is therefore tied up with power only temporarily. The culturally prescribed obligation of a "big man" to be generous if he wishes to retain his influence acts to keep wealth fairly evenly distributed among the Kapauku.

economic expansion and accumulation of wealth is limited where households, rather than business firms, are the productive units. Another factor in Amatenango is that inheritance is bilateral; all a man's children share equally in his estate. This makes it difficult for large estates to persist over generations. Furthermore, a number of different village offices must be assumed by men in the village. This prevents their holders from working all the time, and the responsibilities of the offices take up some of a family's extra resources. A man must serve in twelve such offices before he can "retire" from public life, so the cost continues throughout adulthood. In addition to these twelve offices, there is the *alferez*, a ritual position filled by a younger man. Part of the requirement of this office is the sponsoring of a community feast, which involves paying for the food and liquor and also renting the costumes. Men are selected for this prestigious office by their ability to pay, and it is an enormous drain on the economic resources of a household. Should a family in Amatenango manage to accumulate more than its neighbors, village sanctions of gossip and accusations of witchcraft come into play. A man who is thought to be a witch is likely to be killed. Such accusations are most often leveled at those who are rich but not generous and who refuse to accept the communal obligations of taking office. Thus, through the interplay of social and economic forces, through the value system of the community, and through informal but powerful systems of control, economic differences are minized and the stability of the society as a whole is ensured.

SUMMARY

1. Formal economics, which focuses on action that maximizes the individual's well-being and profit (economizing) has limited application in economic systems where the production, distribution, and consumption of goods is part of other aspects of culture and society. A major task of the anthropologist studying non-Western and traditional societies is to build a model of the economic system extracted from activities and norms that are not solely economic from the people's point of view.

2. Access to and control over land is basic to every productive system. Among hunters and gatherers, there are few exclusive rights to land; among horticulturalists, land is controlled by the kin group. It is mainly with the rise of intensive agriculture that land becomes subject to private ownership by individuals. Generally speaking, the more the investment of labor and technology and the less land available, the more likely private ownership will be.

3. In tribal and peasant economies, the basic unit of production is a kin group. Resources are produced and used mainly by this group, and production often has social and religious rather than strictly economic ends. This provides an important contrast with Western societies, where the basic unit of production is the business firm, whose interests are almost solely economic.

4. There is little specialization of labor in tribal and peasant societies, com-

pared to the high degree of occupational specialization in industrial societies. Two universal bases of occupational specialization are sex and age.

5. The sexual division of labor has some universal aspects: hunting, fighting and clearing the land among horticulturalists is done by men. Women are predominantly responsible for children, and gather crops and do the daily processing of food for domestic use. Beyond this, the sexual division of labor is highly variable; a man's job in one society may easily be a woman's job in another.

6. Capital, goods used to produce other goods, is limited in small-scale economies. In noncapitalist societies, most members have equal access to capital goods, and no one group is deprived of the ability to produce.

7. In all societies, goods and services are exchanged in some way. Three systems of exchange are reciprocity, redistribution, and the market. Reciprocity exists in all societies, but is the characteristic system of exchange in band and tribal societies. Redistribution is the characteristic mechanism of integration and exchange in chiefdoms, and the market system predominates in industrial societies. Systems of exchange function to integrate various elements of a society; they have a social as well as an economic function.

8. Leveling mechanisms are norms and activities that result in an evening out of wealth among a population. The many different kinds of leveling mechanisms—obligatory generosity, witchcraft accusations, gossip, religious obligations to give—all work to force accumulated resources to be used in ways that do not result in significant or permanent economic differences among individuals and groups within a society.

SUGGESTED READINGS

Dalton, George, ed.
1967 *Tribal and Peasant Economies.* Garden City, N.Y.: The Natural History Press. A reader suitable for an introduction to economic systems. Contains many of the most important articles in the field of economic anthropology.

LeClair, E. J., Jr., and Schneider, H. D., eds.
1968 *Economic Anthropology: Readings in Theory and Analysis.* New York: Holt, Rinehart and Winston. A collection of readings organized around substantive economic theory. Shows the ways in which economics is embedded in society and culture.

Malinowski, Bronislaw
1961 *Argonauts of the Western Pacific.* New York: E. P. Dutton (orig. 1922). The classic on the Kula exchange by an outstanding anthropological fieldworker.

Mauss, Marcel
1954 *The Gift.* New York: Macmillan. The classic on reciprocity in tribal societies.

Rohner, Ronald P., and Rohner, Evelyn C.
1970 *The Kwakiutl: Indians of British Columbia.* New York: Holt, Rinehart and Winston. An ethnographic monograph including much information on the ceremonial behavior of the potlatch, showing its many social and economic functions.

9
Social Ranking and Stratification

One important difference in the way societies are organized is the degree to which individuals within the society have equal access to prestige, power, and the resources necessary to sustain life. Although it is clear that not all human beings are equally endowed with talents, appearance, and skill, not all societies formally recognize this inequality. In approaching this aspect of social organization, anthropologists have distinguished three basic types of societies: egalitarian societies, rank societies, and stratified societies. Each of these three principles of social organization is tied up with economic and political organization. As we have seen, the economies of egalitarian societies are primarily organized through reciprocity, those of rank societies through redistribution, and those of stratified societies through market exchange. Similarly, as we will see in

United Nations/Ray Witlin

Chapter 12, egalitarian societies have little specialization of political roles; rank societies are characterized by chiefs as the ruling powers; and stratified societies are correlated with a particular kind of political organization known as the state. Although for some purposes economics, social status systems, and politics can be separated, they are in fact all interrelated.

EGALITARIAN SOCIETIES

In **egalitarian societies,** no individual or group has more access to resources, power, or prestige than any other. This does not mean that in such societies all members have equal prestige. In addition to age and sex differences, individual differences in skill at a variety of tasks will always be recognized. Some individuals are better hunters; others are regarded as more skilled at a craft; others are singled out for their healing ability; still others are acknowledged as knowing more or speaking in a more expressive manner than the ordinary person. In an egalitarian society, however, no individual, no matter how high or low in esteem in the group, is denied the right to make a living, or is subject to the control or exploitation of others. Furthermore, whatever prestige an individual gains on the basis of ability is not transferable to his or her heirs or relatives. There is no fixed number of positions that are ranked and for which individuals must compete. The prestige attached to being a good hunter, for example, will go to as many good hunters as there are in the group.

Hunting and gathering societies are characteristically egalitarian: the lack of land ownership; the relatively low technological level, which inhibits storing up large quantities of food; the need for mobility, which inhibits the accumulation of material goods; and the obligation to share food prevents any permanent and unequal distribution of wealth. The activity of hunting and foraging itself does not require a permanent leader, and food-getting activities are often carried out individually, or in groups in which individuals are organized as equal, cooperating members. Even when hunting societies have a headman, this position carries no real power or economic advantage and is not inherited or inheritable. But not all foraging societies are equally egalitarian. Among some Eskimo groups, for example, differences in wealth did develop. In groups where whaling was important, a successful whaler accumulated more wealth than others and often distributed it in such a way as to control the less successful men. The fishing groups along the Northwest Coast of America were not egalitarian at all, and in fact exhibited a higher degree of ranking than many horticultural societies.

RANK SOCIETIES

In **rank societies,** there are formal differences in prestige, but no important restrictions on access to basic resources. There is an inherited position of chief, and his prestige is linked to the redistribution of goods, frequently in the form of competitive feasts and religious ceremonies. But although chiefs in such societies may have great prestige and certain privileges, they do not accumulate food and goods for their own use. Their basic standard of living does not differ from that of the ordinary members of the society. Rank societies have not only the high-prestige position of chief, but also ranking of kin groups. Kin groups closest to the chief genealogically have the most prestige, and in some rank societies order of birth is important as a criterion of social status.

Rank societies are mainly found among cultivators and herders, though simple ranking also exists among some hunting groups. The Siriono of eastern Bolivia, for example, have a simple ranking system (Holmberg 1969). In spite of its simple technology, this impoverished society does have the office of chief, which is generally passed on from father to son. But the Siriono chief has few privileges: the main ones are that only he is allowed more than one wife, and his family occupies the center of the communal dwelling in which the Siriono extended families live. As chief he is entitled to be called *ererekwa*, but this title is also used by women generally to refer to their husbands. Since the chief is usually a better hunter than the others, he uses his position to distribute meat and build up obligations from others. Because chiefs "know more about things and are able to do them better than anyone else," they are given more respect than the average man. Some prestige is gained among the Siriono by being a close relation to the chief, but an individual's position depends much more on ability to provide food than on any other factor.

The most complex ranking systems are found in Polynesia and among the Indian societies of the Northwest Coast of America. These societies consisted of a series of individual positions, all ranked in order; no two individuals were precisely equal. Among the Nootka, rights to manage all economic resources, such as fishing, hunting, and gathering grounds, are held by individuals, although a relative cannot be prevented from using them. Inheritance of these rights pass only through the line of the eldest sons. The same is true for the office of chief. The line that goes through lesser sons is ranked lower than that of eldest sons, and these differences in rank are typically expressed in terms of wealth. This wealth consists only partly of important economic resources; it was also symbolic, as in the right to use special names, perform certain ceremonial functions, sponsor potlatches, and wear certain items of clothing and decoration. Only chiefs, for example, were allowed to wear abalone shell jewelry and sea-otter fur on their robes. The right of directing the use of economic resources supported the symbolic ranking system. As manager, a chief of a kin group would receive resources that formally acknowledged his rank—the first of the salmon catch, the best parts of sea mammals that had been killed, blankets and furs. It was from this source that a chief could sponsor a potlatch at which most of these goods would be given away.

A similar ranking system existed in Tahiti, although that society could be divided into the Ari'i, who were the immediate families of the chiefs of the most important lineages in the larger districts; the Ra'atira, who were the heads of less important lineages and their families, and the Manahune, which included the remainder of the population. Social rank in Tahiti had an economic, political, and religious aspect. *Mana,* a spiritual power, was possessed by all individuals, but in different degrees depending on rank. The Ari'i had the most mana because they were closest to the ancestral gods from which mana comes. An elaborate body of taboos separated those with more mana from those with less and also regulated social relations between individuals in the three ranks. Higher-ranked persons could not eat with those of lower rank; and because men had higher rank than women and children, they could not eat together. The highest-ranking Ari'i was so sacred that anything he touched became poison for those below him. Thus, in some Polynesian islands the highest chief was kept completely away from other people, and even used a special vocabulary no one else was allowed to use.

Rank societies, then, are organized by kinship. Rank is based on position (birth order and genealogical closeness to the chief) within the kinship system, and membership in the kinship group entitles each individual to access to basic resources. No one group of people is exploited in order to maintain a ruling class exempt from food production. Even in ranked societies where slaves existed, they were actually individuals attached to. wealthier families

In rank societies the Chief is a source of supernatural power. Here a chief on the island of Ponape, Micronesia, is being served kava, a ceremonial drink. The server's head is turned away as no one may look directly at the Chief. (Raymond Kennedy)

and not an exploited class on which the economy depended. In these ways rank societies are distinguished from societies with social stratification, which will be discussed in the next chapter.

STRATIFIED SOCIETIES

A **stratified society** has formal, permanent social and economic inequality. Some individuals and groups (over and above those defined by age and sex) are denied access to the basic resources necessary for survival and well-being. Stratified societies have relatively permanent and wide differences between groups in terms of standard of living, security, prestige, political power, and life chances. These major dimensions of social stratification are usually analyzed in terms of power, wealth, and prestige. Anthropologists are interested in the relationships between and among these dimensions within a society, and also

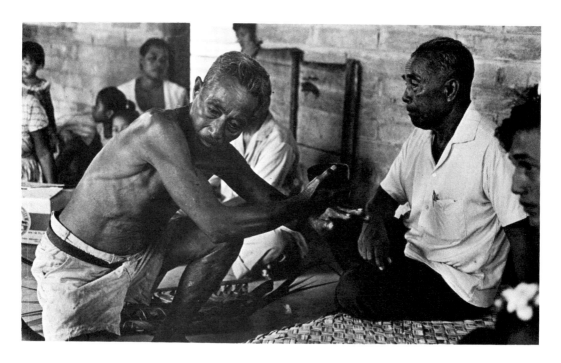

in comparing stratification systems in different cultures.

One important distinction that is made in comparing systems of social stratification is whether they are based on ascription or achievement. In a stratification system in which ascription is important, an individual's **status,** or position in the system, is mainly determined by birth. **Ascribed statuses** are those social positions to which an individual is born. Sex, race, and ethnic group are examples of ascribed statuses in American society. Kinship group and caste membership are other examples of ascribed statuses. In a stratification system based on achievement, an individual's position is largely determined by his or her own efforts. **Achieved statuses** are those an individual chooses or achieves on his or her own. Wife, doctor, criminal, and artist are examples of achieved statuses in the United States. In simpler societies most statuses are ascribed, although in some of them individual achievement plays an important role, and there are many opportunities for moving up in society through a combination of skill and hard work.

Although different systems of social stratification can be described as based primarily on ascription (closed systems) or achievement (open systems), most societies contain both. Anthropologists are interested in the many different kinds of statuses, both ascribed and achieved, and the ways in which individuals are chosen to fill social positions.

Power, Wealth, and Prestige

Power is the ability to produce intended effects on oneself, on other human beings, and on things. Power thus means the ability to make and carry out decisions affecting one's own life, to control the behavior of other human beings, and to transform objects or resources. Power used with the consent of the members of a society is called **authority** and is legitimate. Power may also be illegitimate, exercised without the approval of society. The powerful individuals or groups in a society are best able to act on their perceptions of where their self-interest lies. In stratified societies, this frequently means at the expense of the goals of other individuals and groups. From an anthropological standpoint, our interest is in knowing who has the power in a society, through what channels it is exercised, and what its sources are. As one example, we might compare power in the United States as it rests with corporation presidents, elected public officials, movie stars, or the heads of organized crime families. From a cross-cultural perspective, we might compare the sources and management of power of an American president, a Bantu chief, and the head of the Communist Party in the Soviet Union.

Wealth as an aspect of social stratification is the accumulation of material resources, or access to the means of producing these resources. Many social scientists believe wealth is the most important aspect of social stratification and the foundation on which the other dimensions, such as power and prestige, rest. For Karl Marx and those who follow his thinking, the basic principle of social organization is the system by which resources are produced and allocated to provide for the satisfaction of basic human needs. Marx differentiated between two main strata in society: the capitalists, who own the means of production, and the workers, who are employed by others. According to Marx, it is this relationship to the means of production that is important in determining not only how much power and prestige one has, but also one's chances to survive. One

This San Blas Cuna woman of Panama wears gold jewelry that represents the wealth of her family. Although there are differences in wealth and prestige in rank societies, no individual or group is denied access to basic resources. (United Nations/Jerry Frank)

does not need a Marxist perspective to see the obvious ways in which wealth can translate into power: rich men are more likely to run for political office and win than others, and the wealthy capitalist can influence government in ways that are in his/her own self-interest.

Prestige, or social honor, is a third dimension of social stratification. Complex societies, which are occupationally specialized, contain a number of different positions that are ranked high or low in relation to each other. Occupations are ranked somewhat differently in different societies. We will see, when we look at the Hindu caste system, that one criterion for ranking occupations in India has to do with the level of ritual purity or pollution. Although this exact concept does not exist in

the United States, we do have the idea of a "dirty job" ranked lower than jobs that are not dirty. Generally speaking, white-collar occupations, which imply work in offices, carry more prestige than blue-collar occupations, which imply working with one's hands. As socioeconomic conditions change, the value system that supports a particular system of prestige will also change. Different occupations may gain or lose prestige. In ancient China, for example, the intellectual had high status; in modern China, an attempt is being made to raise the prestige of the worker, and the intellectual is regarded as a parasite.

The prestige given different occupations is related to the power inherent in such occupations, the income derived from them, and their importance to the society, among other factors. Although amount of income earned is a basis for prestige in American society, the ways in which that income is earned and wealth is accumulated also have to be taken into account. People who earn their incomes illegally, generally speaking, have less prestige in the community than those whose incomes are legally earned. Who do you think has more prestige in our society—a baseball player who signs a $2 million contract, a heart surgeon who earns $200,000 a year, or the head of an illegal gambling syndicate whose profit runs to millions? On the other hand, money eventually buys high social position, at least in our society. Sending one's children to the best schools, buying a home in the best neighborhood, joining the right clubs, and so on, give individuals the chance to interact socially with others in high social positions. All these opportunities cost money. The social status of a family can thus improve dramatically over just a few generations. Some families now prominent in United States political life, for example, made their fortunes in ways that today would be considered deviant or illegal.

The question of whether prestige or money is more important as a basis for protecting one's self-interest has long been argued by social scientists. Two opposing views on this question are those of Karl Marx and Max Weber, a German sociologist of the late nineteenth century. Where Marx saw people as conscious of themselves as a group mainly in terms of similar economic interests, Weber believed that people may value prestige and the symbolic aspects of status even more than money. Weber further argued that political action can be motivated by a group's desire to defend its social position as well as, or even in opposition to, its economic self-interest. For example, poor whites in the American South may refuse to join poor blacks in working for improvement of their common economic position because they are more interested in maintaining the status differences based on color.

SOCIAL CLASS

The two basic forms of social stratification are class and caste. In a **class system,** the different strata (classes) are not sharply separated from one another, but form a continuum. **Social mobility** (movement from one class to another) is possible. An individual born into one social class can, through various means (education, marriage, good or bad luck, hard work) move into another.

Social Class in America

The United States is said to have a relatively open class system; one's position depends largely on achieved statuses such as occupation, education, and life style, and there is a relatively good chance for upward mobility. The open class system of our society is part of our mythology and is based on the democratic principle of equality and opportunity for all. Many people in the United States find it difficult to accept the evidence that this equality has not yet been fully realized, and that, in fact, social class is an important aspect of social organization in our nation. Many studies have shown that social class membership does appear to correlate with various attitudinal, behavioral, and life style factors, testifying to the reality of social classes.

Although social scientists agree that class is important in the United States, they do not agree on the exact nature of our class system, nor on how to go about studying it. Earlier studies of social class, some of which have been carried out by anthropologists, have mainly been carried out in small cities and towns, whose social organization may be more typical of the American past than its future. One study of social class in a sprawling metropolitan area was that carried out by Harold Hodges (1963)* in the San Francisco Peninsula area of California. Hodges' study points up a social class system that includes six basic divisions.

1. *Lower-lower class.* This stratum, which accounts for about 20 percent of the population, includes unskilled blue-collar workers who are frequently unemployed. Members of this class tend to be school dropouts who marry and have children at an early age. They

* Harold M. Hodges, Jr. "Peninsula People: Social Stratification in a Metropolitan Complex," in Harold M. Hodges, and W. Warren Kallenbach, eds., *Education and Society.* Columbus, Ohio: Charles E. Merrill, 1963.

live in slum areas, are heavily in debt, and buy most of their household goods on time. Although the people of this class subscribe to many middle-class American goals, such as material well being, technological progress and upward mobility, they admit they have no control over their lives and tend to be pessimistic about their futures. They believe in traditional domestic roles for women and value obedience in children. Their leisure time is spent reading magazines, watching television, and (for the men) going to bars. They are mainly Catholics or belong to fundamental Protestant sects. They are looked down upon by everyone in the community and know it.

2. *Upper-lower class.* Thse people are about 30 percent of the population. They are semiskilled or skilled blue-collar workers and have higher incomes and steadier jobs than the lower-lower class. They have either finished or almost finished high school. The men hunt, fish, and watch sports in their leisure time. The members of this class are very concerned with raising their social position in life and in "keeping up with the Joneses." Although the "he-man" self-image is very important to the males of this class, they are more likely to help their wives with domestic chores than husbands in any other class category. Members of this class belong to trade unions, vote Democratic, and support liberal legislation on economic matters.

3. *Lower-middle class.* These also are about 30 percent of the population and include salespeople, clerks, and owners of small businesses. They are

an important market for the mass media, as they are typically high school graduates with good incomes. They tend to live in suburban tract houses. Politically and economically they are conservatives. They tend to be patriotric and religious and committed to the "Protestant Ethic" of hard work. Although they give lip service to the ideals of thrift and frugality, they, more than any other class, tend to spend above their means. For all their hard work and old-fashioned morality, however, they feel neglected and alienated in contemporary American society and are sometimes referred to in the media as the "silent majority" or the "forgotten Americans."

4. *Upper-middle class.* This group includes 10 to 15 percent of the population and is made up of professionals, semi-professionals, independent businesspeople, and corporate employees in middle management. The members of this class usually have attended college a year or two beyond the B.A. degree. They are the pacesetters of American society in style of clothing, furnishings, and behavior. They are democratic, tolerant, and optimistic about human nature and their own lives. They are also competitive and upwardly mobile, preparing their children as best as they can educationally so that they can compete economically and socially. From this class come the joiners; they join professional societies and are active in politics. The upper-middle class spends its leisure time reading, listening to music, going to museums and to the theater. They may have a religious affiliation, but

for them religion is primarily a social obligation. This class has the lowest rate of broken marriages. Another characteristic of this class is their high geographical mobility.

5. *Upper-middle, newly rich.* This class includes only a fraction of the population. They are in various statuses that are marginal to the main class system, such as movie star and international celebrity, but they are very rich. People in this class seek admittance into the higher class, but will have to wait a couple of generations. These are the people who attract attention for their showy life style and the display of their possessions, which symbolize their wealth.

6. *Upper-upper class.* This group, only 1 to 2 percent of the population, has everything: power, prestige, and the right family background. They are in the Social Register and trace their ancestors back to the *Mayflower*. This class does not display its wealth in obvious ways, but entertains lavishly and often. Its members have attended the best schools and colleges. Tradition is important, and they are more authoritarian than the upper-middle class. Their occupations tend to be those of banker, stockbroker, architect, and physician.

This description of social class will not fit every region and local community in the United States. But in general outline, it does coincide with many earlier studies of social stratification in "typical" American communities, such as the Lynds' (1937) study of a midwestern city they called Middletown, and Lloyd Warner's (1963) study of a New England town he called Yankee City.

As we can see from Hodges' study, social class is more than an economic phenomenon. A social class is also a **subculture;** its members share similar life experiences, occupational roles, values, educational backgrounds, associational affiliation, leisure time activities, buying habits, and political views. Beyond being linked by these shared traits, members of a social class tend to associate more with one another than with persons in other classes. Studies of social stratification in many societies show that informal social interaction such as visiting most frequently involves members of the same class. Thus, the life style and interactional dimensions of social class reinforce one another. Through interaction based on common residence and schooling, for example, individuals learn the life style of their social class. Since life style is an important part of sociability, people with similar life styles tend to associate with one another.

Social Class and Life Chances

Some social scientists argue that an approach to social stratification which emphasizes life style, cultural patterns, and prestige, as Hodges' study does, obscures important economic and power differences in American society. Another way to look at social class that brings economic factors and power into sharper focus is to examine the differences in life chances among social classes. **Life chances** refer to an individual's opportunity to fulfill or fail to fulfill his or her potential in society. An individual's life chances include the chance of survival, opportunities to obtain an education that will help maximize intellectual and creative potential, opportunities to participate in associations and cultural life, and opportunities to live in comfort and security.

Some characteristics defined as part of the "culture of poverty" are mother-centered families, low income, large numbers of children, low educational levels, and a lack of participation in political institutions. The culture of poverty is an adaptation to the marginal position of the poor in stratified societies, as for example, Mexico. (Bernhard Krauss)

An individual's life chances are linked to his or her position in the stratification system. Although the American myth of equality includes the belief that "anyone can become president," the relationship between life chances and social mobility does not uphold this idea. Social mobility is also a life chance that depends on where one already is in the class system. Individuals born into positions of wealth, high status, and power strive to maintain those positions, and because of their high social class frequently have the means to keep others from achieving mobility. People born into the middle class have a better chance of improving their life chances than people born into a poor class. The very poor, and those who belong to minority groups that are discriminated against in our culture, have lower life chances than the middle class. Low social position not only tends to negate one's own life chances, but also those of one's children. Poverty tends to perpetuate itself through generations, calling into question the openness of the American class system.

CASTE

In contrast to class systems, which are based primarily on achieved statuses, a caste system is based on birth. An individual belongs to the caste of his or her

(continues on p. 189)

THE CULTURE OF POVERTY

The self-perpetuating nature of poverty has attracted the interest of both social scientists and policymakers. A number of anthropologists, notably Oscar Lewis, argue that poverty is not just an economic condition, but a way of life that tends to perpetuate itself by failing to provide its members with the values and skills necessary to be successful in the larger society. According to Lewis (1966), the **culture of poverty** is an adaptation of the poor to their marginal position in stratified, capitalistic societies. Some of the characteristics of this "culture" are lack of participation in the cultural and social institutions of the larger society, chronic shortage of cash and the absence of savings, low levels of education, mistrust of government and fear of the police, early experience with sex, consensual marriages and a high rate of children born out of wedlock, and families centered around the mother, with fathers weak or absent.

The matrifocal or mother-centered family, in which there is no economically productive husband and father, has been one of the main points of the culture of poverty debate. The term "matrifocal" became popular with the publication of the Moynihan Report, written in 1965 by the then assistant secretary of labor, Daniel Moynihan. In it he attempted to demonstrate that the matrifocal family was the "cause" of the high incidence of crime and social disorganization in lower-class black communities. The report held that the matrifocal family is disorganized and "pathological" and is unable properly to socialize or control its children. Individuals brought up in this kind of family are said to develop strong feelings of inadequacy, have poorly developed egos, be fatalistic about the future, and live for the moment, rather than being able to defer gratification for the sake of future rewards and achievement. These personality traits appear to be internalized by the age of 6 or 7 and inhibit the ability of these individuals to take advantage of opportunities to improve their position when and if these become available. These traits thus account for the continuation of poverty over generations as well as for the criminal and pathological behavior that is the result of improper and inadequate socialization.

Lewis' concept of the culture of poverty appears to place much of the blame for the conditions in which the poor live on the poor themselves. Critics of the concept say it obscures the role of social, political, and economic forces in the larger society that create and maintain a class of poor people, and that need to be changed if the poor are going to change their lives. Among these critics is

Charles Valentine, an anthropologist who has studied a poor community in the United States. Valentine offers an alternative interpretation of the behavior patterns of the poor in America. He suggests that whatever is distinctive about social life at the lowest economic levels of society is determined primarily by the socioeconomic and political structure of the larger society. According to Valentine, the poor have the same values and desire the same things as other people, but the constraints of poverty do not allow them to realize the values and behave in the same way as the middle class. The mother-centered family, for example, may be viewed as an adaptation to economic conditions that prevent adult males from obtaining decent jobs. Males prevented from having adequate access to jobs are unable to carry out the economic aspects of the roles of husband and father. Furthermore, the system of welfare does not allow for child support if an able-bodied man is living in the household. Among lower-class black populations, both the greater availability of work for females as compared to males and the economic independence from males provided by welfare allotments gives women an extra economic value that leads to their becoming the center and power in the household.

In addition, recent research has indicated that the picture of the matrifocal family presented by the Moynihan Report does not give a full picture of lower-class black family life. Carol Stack, for example, in a book called *All Our Kin* (1974) shows that the basis of familial structure and cooperation in these communities is not the nuclear family, but an extended cluster of relatives related chiefly through children, but also through marriage and friendship. These people carry out the whole range of domestic and child-care functions. This domestic network spreads over several kin-based households formed around women and based on the role of women in child care, but men also play important roles. They contribute to the networks of both the mothers of their children and their own mothers. The shifting of residences and "elastic boundaries" of households is an adaptation to the crises and calamities that are always part of life among the poor.

Critics of the culture of poverty concept hold that the lack of motivation of poor children in school is based on a realistic perception of the fact that where jobs are not available, doing well in school means nothing. Fear and mistrust of government, including the police, is based on the reality of government neglect and police brutality. The inability to defer gratification is based on the fact that the future offers very little. *Tally's Corner*, a study of the world of black street-corner men in the inner city of Washington, D.C., written by Elliot Liebow (1967) gives an interpretation of unemployment among lower-class black males that contradicts the popular explanation of "laziness." Liebow showed that it is not unwillingness to work that explains high male unemployment but rather a combination of the exploitation of these men when they do find work, the lack of self-esteem that stops them from taking work opportunities, and the culture of the street-corner group, which gives emotional support only for failure.

In the United States a man is "worth" what he is paid. The self-worth of the street-corner man is constantly under attack because he cannot often get work, and because much of the work he is offered is low paying, psychologically unrewarding, physically difficult, and intermittent. Those who hire the street-corner man often justify the low wages they pay on the grounds that these men steal from them, and thus the material rewards of the job are actually much higher than the stated salary. But it is in terms of salary that an American man measures his self-worth. What is stolen from the job does not count in society's terms, and it also leaves the worker vulnerable to the wishes of an employer who might want to fire him or exploit him in other ways. The poor, black, inner-city male is seen by himself as a failure; in this he reflects society's view of him as a failure because of his marginal work role. The street-corner society is participated in by men who are all failures; success pulls the man out of the only group from which he has received psychological support. The dependency of the poor black family on welfare further undermines the male's self-esteem and the stability of the family. Thus, the entire social structure, cultural values, male-female relations, and the psychological components of dependency have to be viewed as an integrated whole if poor people are to become self-supporting.

Valentine suggests that by focusing on the weak, dependent personality which is said to be created by the culture of poverty, the strength and vitality of the many poor people who manage to survive under the worst conditions have been overlooked. For Valentine and other critics of the culture of poverty concept, values and psychology are not the heart of the issue. Rather, these are rationalizations for a society that discriminates against the poor and that has failed to provide the kinds of employment necessary to give all its citizens a reasonable standard of living.

parents, and cannot move from one caste to another. In a class system, individuals from different classes may marry (and marriage is one route to upward social mobility). In a caste system, an individual can marry only within the caste. Caste, in other words, is hereditary and **endogamous.** The castes, however many there are, are ranked in relation to each other and are usually associated with a particular occupation. A **caste system,** then, consists of a ranked and culturally distinct number of interdependent endogamous groups. Unlike class systems, in which no clear boundaries exist between the different classes, a caste system has definite boundaries between castes. Many of the social rules in a caste system are directed toward maintaining social distance between castes.

Some anthropologists (Dumont 1970) define caste only as it exists in India, where it is firmly embedded in the Hindu religion. Others view caste as a system of stratification that is found in a number of societies outside India, for example Japan and parts of Africa. A cross-cultural definition of caste has also been applied to the relations between whites and blacks in the United States, particularly in the South until very recently. The castelike aspects of this social system include membership based on birth (one is born white or black and remains in that category for life), marriage within the caste, cultural distinctiveness of the two groups, traditional occupations each group could enter or was prohibited from entering, and a rank order in which white was superior. Many of the norms of behavior in the old South revolved around keeping "blacks in their

Apartheid, or separateness, is the official state policy of the Republic of South Africa, and illustrates the extremes to which stratification may lead. Here, workers in the Elsies River Plant of the Chrysler Corporation must leave their work by segregated exits. (United Nations)

place," and preventing blacks and whites from mixing except under certain conditions. Like a caste system anywhere, this system had a full-fledged mythology associated with it, an attempt to "explain" and justify the inferior position of the lower caste. Ultimately, this system, like other caste systems, was maintained by physical force, which came into the open whenever the status quo was threatened. In writing of the South in the 1930s, John Dollard, (1937) in his *Caste and Class in a Southern Town,* demonstrated that although social classes existed within the two castes, a castelike line was drawn between blacks and whites. No matter how high a position a black reached, he or she could not cross the caste barrier. In a comparison of caste in India and the United States, Gerald Berreman (1959) demonstrated convincingly that not only did castelike features operate in the United States, but classlike features operated in the Indian caste system.

The Caste System in India

The unique elements of the Indian caste system are its complexity, its relation to Hindu religious beliefs and rituals, and the degree to which the castes (or more properly subcastes) are cohesive and self-regulating groups. The Hindu belief about the division of society is that there are four caste categories called *varna.* The *varna* are ranked according to their ritual purity, which in turn is based on their traditional occupations. The Brahmins, who are ranked highest, are priests and scholars, the Kshatriyas or warrior caste are second, the Vaisha or merchants are ranked third, and the shudras, or menial workers and artisans, are ranked fourth. Below these four *varna* is a fifth group, called the untouchables. The untouchable castes, who perform the polluting work of cleaning latrines or working with leather, are considered so ritually impure that just their mere touch contaminates the purity of the higher castes. An individual's birth into one of these *varna* is said to be a reward or punishment for the quality of his or her actions in a previous life.

Many traditional rules of behavior in India are designed to maintain the boundaries between castes. Members of different castes do not eat with each other, and a higher-caste person will not accept most kinds of food or drink from a lower-caste person. Untouchable castes are segregated in their own part of the village, and are not allowed to drink water out of the same wells as higher castes. Before recent laws establishing legal equality, marriage and sexual relations between castes was forbidden. Each caste has distinguishing cultural features, and the higher castes more nearly approximate Hindu religious ideals in their behavior. This includes vegetarianism, a taboo on alcohol, and the prohibition of remarriage for widows. Only high castes are allowed to perform certain rituals, such as the tying of the sacred thread on young boys, which symbolizes a second birth. Brahmin priests would not minister to the religious needs of the untouchables and lower castes, and untouchables were not allowed to enter village temples.

As we saw in Chapter 8, caste in India is tied up with the exchange of goods and services within the village. Families of various artisan and serving castes traditionally performed necessary services for families of landowning castes, and in return received food from them. This client-patron, or *jajmani,* relationship was often carried on over several generations between the same families. Thus, the different castes formed an interdependent, organic whole at the village level.

The Dynamics of Caste

Idealized views of the caste system, which emphasized its stability, were obtained by anthropologists mainly from high-caste Hindus. New studies of caste in rural and urban areas reveal a dynamism that earlier studies overlooked. Lower and middle-ranked castes frequently do not accept their position and use a number of different strategies to rearrange their rank. Efforts by untouchable castes to change their rank often brings a violent reaction from the higher castes, who want to preserve their own prestige, wealth, and power.

Social mobility in the caste system is a group rather than an individual effort. A caste that has achieved a certain amount of economic success might try to raise its prestige by adopting the customs of a higher-caste group and claiming a new rank for itself. An upwardly mobile caste attempts through its caste council to change the behavior of its members, getting them to conform to high-caste behavior patterns. A lower caste might also, as part of its strategy, invent a myth for itself showing that originally it came from one of the higher-ranked *varna*.

With the achievement of Indian independence in 1948 and the creation of a democratic constitution, caste in India has both weakened and gained strength. The Indian government, in an attempt to make up for past discrimination and suffering, has reserved special jobs and places in the universities for members of untouchable and lower castes. The advantages to be gained by claiming membership in one of these castes may therefore be substantial, and a number of caste associations have grown up to help members use these new opportunities. Discrimination against untouchables was also outlawed, although as we have seen with race relations in the United States this is difficult to enforce at the local level. The vote has been extended to all castes, and low castes now have a potential for political power through elected representation. These factors have somewhat altered the strategies of upward mobility for some low castes.

Owen Lynch (1969) has described these changes in strategy for the Camars, an untouchable caste of leatherworkers in the city of Agra. Camars have traditionally been shoemakers, and due to the increased demand for shoes both in India and abroad, some of them have become fairly wealthy. Changes in the economic conditions of the Camars, as well as political circumstances, have stimulated them to try to raise their position in the caste system. They have claimed to be Kshatriyas, and in an effort to get this claim accepted by the higher castes, they outlawed the eating of beef and buffalo and adopted some high-caste rituals, such as the tying of the sacred thread. These efforts, however, were not successful. Under the leadership of an untouchable, Dr. B. R. Ambedkar, who was educated in England and the United States, the Camars are now trying a different strategy, that of conversion to Buddhism. Unlike their earlier attempts to raise their status within the caste system, this move is an attempt to improve their position by putting themselves outside the caste system altogether. At the same time, they wish to retain their status as a special caste in order to be eligible for the benefits of affirmative action undertaken by the Indian government.

The Camars of Agra offer a good example of the dynamics of caste, and how it is both weakened and perpetuated in modern India. The study also invites comparison with similar efforts by other groups in other societies—for example, among blacks in the United States.

Although Indian castes are ranked on the basis of prestige rather than wealth, the gains of high-caste position are not just symbolic. The higher castes also benefit materially from their higher status, and are in a better position to exercise political power in their own self-interest. The lower castes appear to accept their low position without question, but their conformity actually hinges a great deal on their awareness that economic sanctions and physical force will ultimately be used against them if they dare to try and break out of their low place. Members of the upper castes, whether in India or the United States have long used the rationalization that the lower strata of their society are "happy where they are." That this is not the case is clear from the protest movement by the poor and oppressed in both India and the United States.

PERSPECTIVES ON SOCIAL STRATIFICATION

Social stratification results from the unequal distribution of goods and services within a society. The basic question here, who gets what and why, depends on cultural values, the organization of production, and the access different individuals and groups within a society have to societal goals. Social scientists approach the understanding of social stratification from two major theoretical perspectives: functionalism and conflict theory.

Functionalism stresses the integrative functions of social stratification and the contribution such systems make to social order, stability, and social functioning. Functionalists hold that the existence of every complex society depends on the regular performance of specific tasks which require special training and intelligence. If the most intelligent, talented, and best-trained individuals are to perform these tasks, they must be motivated by a system of rewards. An assumption is made here that if you pay a surgeon the same thing as a sanitation worker, no one would be a surgeon since it takes long years of training and involves enormous responsibilities. Thus, a major function of social stratification is that it provides a system of rewards, both material and symbolic, so that all the necessary jobs in society will be filled. From a functionalist perspective, social stratification also contributes to the social order by integrating different groups who have common economic and political interests when kinship no longer plays an important integrating role. A system of social stratification is seen here as inhibiting social conflict between individuals and groups; social inequality is the price of social stability.

Critics of functionalism point out that societies do not always reward individuals who fulfill the most essential roles. Such vital roles as nurse and schoolteacher, for example, do not carry material or symbolic rewards equal to those of a baseball player or television personality in our own society. Furthermore, a stratification system prevents many intelligent and talented people who are members of low-prestige and powerless groups from gaining access to the training and opportunities that lead to the more highly rewarded occupations and positions in society.

Conflict theory holds that the natural condition of society is change and conflict, not order and stability. From this perspective, social stratification results from the constant struggle for scarce goods and services that takes place in all complex societies. Stratification exists because those who have acquired power, wealth, and prestige exercise their power to keep what they have. This is accomplished not only by the threat of force or the use of force, but also by social values and beliefs that justify the present system of inequality in the minds of those in the lower social positions. According to conflict theorists, stratification not only results from but *generates* conflict, because the interests of the different social classes are opposed. They tend to view conflict and change in a more positive light than functional theorists, since they see progress which results from conflict as better for a society than maintaining the status quo. Thus, conflict theory is useful in calling attention to conflict and change as universal aspects of human life and society. In examining a social phenomenon, such as class and caste, for example, we can look at them from two perspectives: (1) How do such systems contribute to social integration and social order? (2) How do they reflect conflict and stimulate social change?

SUMMARY

1. Social ranking is an important feature of variation in social organization. Anthropologists have identified three types of ranking systems: egalitarian, ranking, and stratified. Egalitarian systems, which are found among hunters and gatherers, give every individual and group in society equal access to basic resources, power and prestige.

2. Rank societies, or chiefdoms, recognize differences in prestige among individuals and groups, but no one is denied access to the resources necessary for survival. Like egalitarian societies, rank societies are still organized along kinship lines. The ruling family maintains its position largely through the distribution of goods and food throughout the entire society, rather than through force.

3. In stratified societies, social, political, and economic inequality is institutionalized and maintained through a combination of internalized controls, political power, and force. Kinship ties between the upper and lower strata are no longer recognized, and there is a wide gap between them in standard of living. Some of the productive efforts of the lower strata go to support the life style of the upper strata, who control the basic resources but are themselves exempt from food production.

4. The three major dimensions of social stratification are power, wealth, and prestige. Power refers to the ability to control people and things, wealth to accumulation of economic resources, and prestige to the way in which an individual is socially evaluated by others. The particular value system of a culture determines the ways in which power, wealth, and prestige interact to determine where a person will be placed in the stratification system.

5. Two major types of stratification systems are class and caste. In a class system, social position is largely

achieved, though it is also determined partly by the class into which a person is born. People may move between social classes, which form a continuum from bottom to top. Roughly six social classes have been distinguished in the United States.

6. Social classes may be viewed as subcultures, each characterized by a particular life style. The identification of a culture of poverty has been used by some anthropologists to explain the perpetuation of poverty over several generations. Critics of this concept point out that it is not the culture of poverty that makes people poor, but rather that poor people are excluded from access to the political and economic resources with which they could improve their position.

7. In a caste system, social position is ascribed (based on birth). Boundaries between castes are sharp, and there is no intermarriage. The Indian caste system is the most complex, and is based on Hindu ideas of ritual purity and pollution. Aspects of a caste system are also said to exist in the relations between blacks and whites in the traditional social system of the southern part of the United States.

8. Social stratification can be viewed as functional for the social order, because it motivates people to undertake all the jobs necessary for the society to survive. Social stratification can also cause conflict, however; different social strata, with opposing interests, can clash with each other over goals and resources.

SUGGESTED READINGS

Drucker, Peter
   1967   *To Make My Name Good*. Berkeley: University of California Press. Another perspective on the Kwakiutl of the Northwest Coast of America and their ranking system.

Gould, Harold
   1971   *Class and Caste: A Comparative View*. Modular Publications 11. Reading, Mass.: Addison-Wesley. A brief and useful overview of forms of social stratification.

Mills, C. Wright
   1956   *The Power Elite*. New York: Oxford University Press. A well-known conflict theorist puts forth his view that power in the United States is in the hands of top corporate, military, and government leaders.

Turnbull, Colin
   1961   *The Forest People*. New York: Simon and Schuster. An ethnography of the egalitarian Pygmies of the Ituri Forest in Africa.

Warner, Lloyd W.
   1963   *Yankee City*. abridged edition. New Haven, Conn.: Yale University Press. A readable and interesting work on social class in a New England city.

Wiser, William and Wiser, Charlotte
   1971   *Behind Mud Walls, 1930–1960*. Berkeley: University of California Press. A classic description of an Indian village showing the workings of the jajmani system, with a sequel showing changes up until 1970.

Dittman/Foxx

10
Marriage, Family, and Domestic Groups

Every human society must solve three basic problems: the regulation of sexual access between males and females, the division of labor between males and females, and the need to assign responsibility for child care. The need to regular sexual access stems from the continuous receptivity of the human female to sexual activity. The human male also has the potential to be sexually aroused continually, rather than just at certain times of the year. Sexual competition could therefore be a source of serious conflict in society if it were not regulated and channeled into relatively stable relationships that are given social approval. These relationships need not be permanent, and theoretically some system other than marriage could have developed. But in the absence of effective contraception, and with the near certainty that children would be born from such relationships, a relatively permanent union between a male and female that involves responsibility for children as well as economic exchange would seem to be more adaptive than other alternatives. In any case, the near universality of marriage indicates that it is the most adaptive solution to these human problems.

MARRIAGE AND THE FAMILY: FUNCTIONS

Earlier we pointed out that differences in strength and mobility between males and females lead to some universal differences in economic roles in hunting and horticultural societies. Marriage is the way most societies arrange for the products and services of men and women to be exchanged. We have also mentioned the necessity for the intense care of human infants and the prolonged care of children. A relatively permanent relationship between an adult male and an adult female provides a structure (the family) in which the male can provide food and protection and the female can nurse and provide the intense interaction needed for the healthy development of the human child. Marriage is a way of assigning responsibility for this care. Still another function of marriage which is important in accounting for its near universality in human societies is that marriage links different families and kin groups. In doing so it leads to cooperation among groups of people larger than the primary husband-wife pair, and this would appear to be of great advantage for the survival of the species.

Marriage refers to the customs, rules, and obligations that establish a special relationship between a sexually cohabiting adult male and female, between them and any children they produce, and between the kin groups of husband and wife. Although marriage and the formation of families rests on the biological complementarity of male and female and on the biological process of reproduction, both marriage and family are cultural patterns. As such, they differ in form and functions among human societies. In our own society, the marriage tie is the most important in the formation of the family, but this is not true everywhere. In many societies, the most important family bond is between blood relations rather than husband and wife. In some, it is the blood tie between generations (father and children or mother and children) that is the most important. In matrilineal societies, the tie between brother and sister is the most important. We must be careful, therefore, not to think of the family only in terms of the form it takes in our own society.

From a cross-cultural perspective, it appears that the most basic tie in society is between mother and child. The provisioning and protective male role *may* be played by the husband of the mother, but it may also be played by her brother. Even where marriage is an important emotional relationship, as on the Israeli *kibbutz,* the division of labor and the care of children may not be in the hands of the married couple but in the hands of the community as a whole. Anthropologists are coming to the conclusion that the most useful way to approach the study of marriage and the family is not to establish definitions that will apply to every known group, but rather to look at the different ways in which the basic needs of sexual regulation, infant care, the division of labor, and the establishment of rights and obligations are legitimized in different societies.

MARRIAGE RULES

Incest Taboos

Every society has rules about mating. In all societies there are some prohibitions on mating between persons in certain relationships or from certain social groups. The most universal prohibition is that on mating among certain kinds of kin: mother-son, father-daughter, and sister-brother. The taboos on mating between kin always extend beyond this immediate family group, however; in our own society, the taboo extends to the children of our parents' siblings (in our kinship terminology called first cousins), while in other societies individuals are not allowed to mate with others who may be related up to the fifth generation. These prohibitions on mating (that is, sexual relations) between relatives or persons classified as relatives are called **incest taboos.**

Since sexual access is one of the most important rights conferred by marriage, in-

cest taboos effectively prohibit marriage as well as mating among certain kin. The outstanding exception to the almost universal taboo on mating and marriage among members of the nuclear family are those cases of brother-sister marriage among royalty in ancient Egypt and in traditional Hawaiian society. Incest taboos have always been of interest to anthropologists, who have attempted to explain their origin and persistence in human society, particularly as they apply to primary (or nuclear) family relationships. Many theories have been advanced, and we will look here at four major ones.

Imbreeding Avoidance. The inbreeding avoidance theory holds that mating between close kin produces deficient, weak children and is genetically harmful to the species. The incest taboo is therefore adaptive because it limits inbreeding. This theory, proposed in the late nineteenth century, was later rejected for a number of decades on the grounds that inbreeding could produce advantages as well as disadvantages for the group, by bringing out recessive genes of both a superior and an inferior character. Recent work in population genetics has given more weight to the older view that inbreeding *is* usually harmful to a human population. The proportion of negative recessive traits to adaptive recessive ones is very high, and in the human animal inbreeding has definite disadvantages. Furthermore, these disadvantages are far more likely to appear as a result of the mating of primary relatives (mother-son, father-daughter, sister-brother) than of other relatives, even first cousins. It would seem, then, that the biological adaptiveness of the incest taboo as it applies to the nuclear family must be considered in explaining both its origins and its persistence.

The question raised here, of course, is how prescientific peoples could understand the connection between close inbreeding and the biological disadvantages that result. But the adaptive results of the incest taboo need not have been consciously recognized in order to persist; rather, groups that had such a taboo would have had more surviving children than groups without the taboo. This reproductive advantage would eventually account for its universality as groups without the taboo died out.

Familiarity Breeds Avoidance. The familiarity breeds avoidance theory holds that the incest taboo is just a formal prohibition for a natural aversion to sexual relations between people who have grown up together. There are two sources of evidence that such an aversion may develop. Some studies of the Israeli *kibbutz* show that children "who sit on the potty together" have little sexual interest in one another. Studies of *kibbutz* marriages tend to show that mates are almost never chosen from the peer group. Most frequently they are chosen from another *kibbutz* altogether, in spite of the fact that the *kibbutz* does not discourage marriage between members. *Kibbutz* members themselves attribute this lack of sexual interest in their peers to the fact of their having grown up together (Talmon 1964).

Marriage in Bolivia. Among the functions of marriage is the regulation of sexual access between males and females, setting up an exchange of goods and services between males and females, and assigning responsibility for the care of infant children. (United Nations/Rothstein)

A study of marriage in Taiwan by Arthur Wolf (1968) makes a similar point. Some Taiwanese practice a form of marriage in which a girl from a poor family may be given away or sold as an infant to a family with a son, with the expectation that she will be his wife. She is brought up with the son as his playmate, and at the proper time they marry. Wolf found that these "daughter-in-law-raised-from-childhood" marriages are much less successful than other marriages. There are more sexual difficulties, fewer children, and a higher rate of extramarital affairs.

Although the evidence from the *kibbutz* and Taiwan may show that familiarity can lead to sexual avoidance, the familiarity breeds avoidance theory does not explain why a formal and strongly sanctioned taboo had to arise to prevent what was a natural aversion anyway. Furthermore, as a theory, it is contradicted by evidence which shows that in fact incest does occur in many different parts of the world. The actual occurrence of incest raises questions about whether familiarity does breed sexual aversion. Some anthropologists (and some psychoanalysts) have suggested the very opposite.

Preventing Disruption. Malinowski and Freud believed that the desire for sexual relations within the family is very strong. They suggested that the most important function of the incest taboo is in preventing disruption within the nuclear family. Malinowski argued that as children grow into adolescence, it would be natural for them to attempt to satisfy their developing sexual urges within the group of people emotionally close to them—that is, within the family. If this were to happen, conflict would occur and the role relationships within the family would be disrupted; fathers and sons and mothers and daughters would compete. This would hinder the family in carrying out the transmission of cultural values in a harmonious and effective way. According to this theory, the incest taboo arose to repress the attempt to satisfy sexual desires within the family and to direct such desires outward.

This theory appears to make quite a bit of sense; unregulated sexual competition within the family would undoubtedly be disruptive. However, an alternative to the incest taboo would be the regulation of sexual competition among the family members, as in fact does happen in a few societies in which father and son, mother and daughter, and brothers and sisters do share the same sexual partners. Furthermore, although Malinowski's theory suggests why the incest taboo exists between parents and children, it does not explain the prohibition of sexual relations between brothers and sisters. Regulating sexual activity within the family might solve the problem of disruption through sexual rivalry, but it would not solve the genetic problem. Only the familial incest taboo has both advantages: it prevents disruptions of the family over sexual competition, and promotes outbreeding and genetic variability.

Forming Wider Alliances. Another theory, proposed most recently by Claude Levi-Strauss (1969), stresses the importance of cooperation among groups larger than the nuclear family. The incest taboo forces people to marry outside the family, thus joining families together into a larger social community. This has undoubtedly contributed to the success of the human species. The alliance theory does not account for the origin of the incest taboo, but alliance between nuclear families certainly seems to be adaptive and can account for the persistence of the familial incest taboo and its extension to groups other than the nuclear family.

In summary, then, it does appear that the familial incest taboo has a number of advantages for the human species. In other animal species, incest is frequently prevented by expelling junior members from family groups as they reach sexual maturity. Because humans take so long to mature, the familial incest taboo seems to be the most efficient and effective means of promoting both genetic variability, familial harmony, and community cooperation. These advantages can explain the spread and persistence of the taboo, if not its origins (Aberle 1963).

Exogamy and Alliance

Exogamy specifies that an individual must marry outside particular groups. Because of the association of sex and marriage, prohibitions on incest produce an almost universal rule of exogamy within the primary family group of parents and children and between brothers and sisters. In every society, exogamous rules also apply to some group larger than the nuclear family. Most often **lineages** and **clans,** which are descent groups based on a blood relationship, are exogamous.

The advantages of exogamy are similar to those proposed for the incest taboo. In addition to reducing conflict over sex within the cooperating group, such as the hunting band, exogamy leads to alliances between different families and groups. Alliance between groups larger than the primary family is of great adaptive significance for humans. Such alliances may have economic, political, or religious components; indeed, these intergroup rights and obligations are among the most important kinds of relationships established by marriage. Thus, the biblical text from Genesis "Then will we give our daughters unto you, and we will take your daughters to us, and we will dwell with you and we will become one people" illustrates what must have seemed to be a clear alternative to primitive and ancient peoples—that between marrying out (of the family or local group) or being killed out. Early hunting and gathering bands undoubtedly exchanged women in order to live in peace with each other and to extend the social ties of cooperation.

One outstanding feature of marriage arrangements among contemporary hunters and gatherers is a system of exchange and alliance between groups who exchange wives. These alliances are important among peoples who must move around to take advantage of the availability of a food supply. Different groups take turns visiting and playing host to each other, and this intergroup sociability is made easier by exchanging wives. One consequence of exchanging women is that each hunting-gathering camp becomes dependent on others for a supply of wives and is allied with others through the bonds that result from marriage. This system contributes to the maintenance of peaceful relations among groups that move around, camp with each other, and exploit overlapping territories. It does not entirely eliminate intergroup aggression, but it probably helps keep it down to a manageable level.

The benefits of exogamy were very clear to the mountain-dwelling Arapesh with whom Margaret Mead (1963:92) worked. Their attitude about marriage was summed up in the following saying:

Your own mother
Your own sister
Your own pigs
Your own yams that you have piled up,
You may not eat.
Other people's mothers,
Other people's sisters,
Other people's pigs,
Other people's yams that they have piled up,
You may eat.

Just as hoarding one's own food and not sharing or exchanging with the community is unthinkable for the Arapesh, so is keeping the women of one's group to oneself. In many societies, the very mention of incest is often accompanied by protestations of horror. For the Arapesh, incest simply does not make sense. In answer to Mead's question about incest, an Arapesh informant answered: "No, we don't sleep with our sisters. We give our sisters to other men and other men give us their sisters." When asked about a man marrying his sisters, the Arapesh answer was, "What, you would like to marry your sister. What is the matter with you. Don't you want a brother-in-law? Don't you realize that if you marry another man's sister and another man marries your sister, you will have at least two brothers-in-law, while if you marry your own sister you will have none? With whom will you hunt, with whom will you garden, with whom will you visit?"

In peasant societies, rules of exogamy may apply to the village as well. In northern India, a man must take a wife from outside his village. Through exogamy, the Indian village becomes a center in a kin-

Pictured here is a kin group among the Bushmen. A characteristic feature of marriage among contemporary hunters and gatherers is a system of alliances among bands who exchange wives. This allows maximum flexibility among peoples who must move frequently to obtain food. (Courtesy of the American Museum of Natural History)

ship network that spreads over hundreds of villages. Because the wives in a typical Indian village may come from many different villages, the Indian village has a "cosmopolitan" character. This also affects the quality of family life in northern India. As we have seen in Khalapur, "peace at any price" is an important value in a household where brothers' wives are strangers to one another. The potential for conflict among sisters-in-law shapes child-rearing and personality and helps explain many rules of conduct in the North Indian family.

Village exogamy is not characteristic of all peasant societies. In Mexico, for example, women tend to marry within, rather than outside, the village. In the village of Tepoztlan, studied by Oscar Lewis, over 90 percent of marriages take place within the village, and 42 percent within the same neighborhood. This gives the Mexican village a more cohesive sense of community compared to the Indian village, where the caste that cuts across villages, rather than the village community, is the most important unit of identification.

Other Kinds of Marriage Rules

Endogamy. **Endogamy,** the opposite of exogamy, refers to marriage within one's own group, however that group may be defined. In order to keep the privileges and wealth of the group intact, blood relations may be encouraged or required to marry. This helps explain endogamy among royalty. In India, the caste is an endogamous group. An individual must marry someone within the caste, or within the specific section of the caste to which he or she belongs. Although American society does not have specific named groups within which one must marry, so-called racial groups and social classes tend to be endogamous. In the past, in some states racial endogamy was enforced by law. In the case of social classes, opportunity, cultural norms, and similarity of life style all contribute to maintaining endogamy. It may be as easy to love a rich person as a poor one, but it is a lot harder to meet one unless you are rich yourself.

Preferential Marriage Rules. In addition to rules about whom one may *not* marry and the group within which one *must* marry, some societies have rules about the groups or categories of relatives from which marriage partners are drawn. One of the most common is that an individual (ego) should marry a cross cousin. **Cross cousins** are people related through siblings of the opposite sex at the parental generation—that is, the child of either the mother's brother or the father's sister. In the United States, we do not distinguish our cross cousins from our **parallel cousins,** children of siblings of the same sex at the parental generation—that is, of one's mother's sister or one's father's brother. Both relations are generally excluded from the categories of people from which a mate is selected.

Preferential cross-cousin marriage is related to the organization of kinship units larger than the nuclear family. Where descent groups are **unilineal**—that is, formed by either the mother's or the father's side exclusively—parallel cousins will be members of ego's own kinship group, but cross cousins will not. Since unilineal kinship groups are usually exogamous, a person is prohibited from marrying parallel cousins (who are frequently called and treated as "brothers" and "sisters"), but will be allowed, or even required, to marry cross cousins, who are outside the kinship group. Preferred cross-cousin marriage reinforces ties between kin groups established in the preceding generation. In this sense, the adaptive value of preferential cross-cousin marriage is the same as exogamy: the establishing of alliances between groups. But where exogamy establishes alliances between a number of different groups, preferential marriage rules intensify the relationship between a limited number of groups generation after generation.

A few societies practice preferred parallel-cousin marriage. Among the Muslim Arabs of North Africa, the preference is for an individual to marry the son or daughter of the father's brother. Muslim Arab has a rule of **patrilineal descent;** descent and inheritance is in the male line. Parallel-cousin marriage may serve to prevent the fragmentation of family property because economic resources can be kept within the family. A result of parallel-cousin marriage is to reinforce the solidarity of brothers. On the other hand, by socially isolating groups of brothers parallel-cousin marriage adds to factional disputes and disunity within the larger social system.

The Levirate and the Sororate. The **levirate** is the custom whereby a man marries the widow of his dead brother. In some cases, the children born to this union are considered children of the deceased man. Among the Nuer, a pastoral people of Africa, a form called "ghost marriage" exists: A man can marry a woman "to the name of" a brother who had died childless. The offspring of this union would be designated as children of the deceased. Where the **sororate** exists, the husband of a barren woman marries her sister, and at least some of these children are considered that of the first wife. The term is more commonly used to refer to the custom whereby when a wife dies, her kin group supplies a sister as a wife for the widower.

The existence of the levirate and sororate attests to the importance of marriage as an alliance between two groups rather than between individuals, as is the case in our own society. Through such customs as the levirate, the sororate, and widow inheritance, not only are group alliances maintained, but the marriage contract can be fulfilled even in the event of death. Since marriage involves an exchange of rights and obligations, the family of the wife can be assured that she will be cared for even if her husband dies. This is only fair if she has fulfilled her part of the marriage contract by providing domestic services and bearing children.

But what if there is no one of the right relationship for an individual to marry? Or what if, as in the case of the levirate or sororate, the preferred marriage partner is already married? The point to note here is that there are often kin who are classified as equals for the purpose of marriage and who can be chosen as marriage partners. For example, if a man is supposed to marry his father's sister's daughter, the daughters of all women classified as his father's sisters, whether or not they are biologically in this relationship to the man in question, will be eligible as marriage partners.

Number of Spouses

All societies have rules about how many spouses an individual may have at one time. **Monogamy** permits only one man to be married to one woman at any given time. Monogamy is the rule in our own society, although it is by no means the most frequent rule in the world's cultures. Given the increasing divorce rate and sub-

sequent remarriage in the United States, perhaps the term "serial monogamy" most accurately describes the pattern in our own society. In this pattern, a man or woman has one marriage partner at a time, but because of the relatively easy divorce laws, will not necessarily remain with that partner for life.

Polygamy is plural marriage. It includes **polygyny,** which is the marriage of one man to several women, and **polyandry,** which is the marriage of one woman to several men. Most societies in the world permit (and prefer) plural marriage. In a world sample of 554 societies, polygyny was favored in 415; monogamy, in 135; and polyandry, in only 4 (Murdock 1949). Thus, about 75 percent of the world's societies prefer plural marriage. This does not mean, however, that most people in these societies actually have more than one spouse. Even where polygyny is preferred, the ratio of males to females may be such that few men will be able to have more than one wife, if all men are to have at least one. Furthermore, where men must exchange wealth for wives, many men will not be able to afford more than one wife and will therefore have to settle for monogamy.

In our own society, marriage is so closely tied to sexual and emotional exclusivity that it is hard for us to understand how polygynous marriages could exist without conflict and jealousy. The American reader must keep in mind, however, that sexual jealousy among women might not be a problem in societies which do not idealize romantic love and exclusive sexual rights in marriage. In some societies, in fact, sexual intercourse plays a very small role in the marriage relationship. Karl Heider (1970) reports that for the Dani of New Guinea, there is a period of about four to six years of sexual abstinence after

(continues on p. 208)

POLYGYNY: THE TIWI OF NORTH AUSTRALIA*

Polygyny as a cultural ideal is related to different factors in different societies. Where women are economically important, polygyny can increase a man's wealth and therefore his social position. Also, since one of the most important functions of marriage is to ally different groups with each other, having several wives from different groups within the society serves to extend an individual's alliances. Thus, chiefs, headmen, or leaders of states may have wives from many different clans or villages. This provides leaders with increased economic resources that may then be redistributed among the people, and also binds the different groups to the leader through marriage. Polygyny thus has important economic and political functions in some societies.

A society in which polygyny serves all these purposes is the Tiwi of Australia, who are hunters and gatherers (Figure 10.1). Among the Tiwi, as in most human groups, the male-female ratio is about equal, except that in the older age groups women tend to predominate, since they tend to live longer than men. Because the Tiwi require that every single woman must be married but do not require this of men, plural marriage is not only the cultural ideal, but actually a reality for many Tiwi males.

A Tiwi male has the right to betroth his infant daughter to whomever he chooses (within the limits of the kinship system). In choosing a future son-in-law, men looked for their own best economic and social advantage. Hart says: "In Tiwi society daughters were an asset to their fathers and they [the fathers] invested these assets in their own welfare." A Tiwi father bestowed his daughter on a peer who was already a friend or an ally, or someone he wished to become a friend or ally. Or he might bestow his daughter on a man who had already bestowed a daughter on him. If he was looking for "old age insurance," a father might choose a man much younger than himself who showed signs of being a good hunter and fighter and who seemed likely to rise in influence. When the older man could no longer hunt, his son-in-law would still be young enough to provide him with food.

In all these cases, the future husband would be a great deal older than his young wife. The men on whom infant "wives" were bestowed tended to be in their forties or fifties or perhaps in their late twenties or thirties. As happens in our own society, where "money comes to money," a younger man who looked good to

*C. W. M. Hart and Arnold R. Pilling, *The Tiwi of North Australia*. New York: Holt, Rinehart and Winston, 1960.

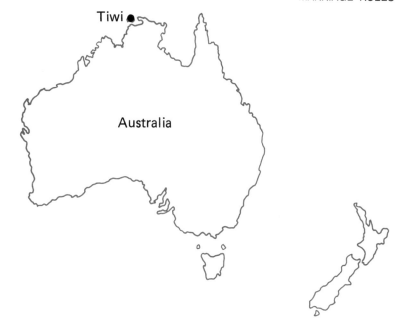

Figure 10.1 *The location of the Tiwi.*

one girl's father would also be an attraction for other fathers. A man who was a "good catch" might have no wives living with him until his late twenties or thirties. Then, as his betrothed wives came of age (around 14), he would quickly acquire two or three. As these wives began to have children, he in turn could become an "investor": by betrothing his daughters to other men, he could acquire still more wives for himself.

In this system many younger men, especially those who were not promising hunters, wound up with few or even no wives. These men could acquire wives by marrying older women who had been widowed. Older men who had outlived their contemporaries could marry widows, as could younger men who were not sufficiently attractive to acquire wives by bestowal of other men's daughters. Among the Tiwi, being an important, influential man required having a great many wives.

The large, multiple-wife household among the Tiwi can be regarded as an adaptation to the conditions of their existence. The Tiwi lived in an environment in which there was an ample supply of game and fish and an abundance of vegetable foods. Although kangaroo, lizards, fish, turtle, and geese were hunted by the men, it was the vegetable foods gathered by the women that provided the staple of everyday meals. The major problem in the Tiwi environment was not the shortage of food, but rather the collecting of the food that was abundantly available. We can see how useful Tiwi wives were. The more wives a man had, the more food could be collected. A Tiwi man readily admitted: "If I had only one or two wives I would starve; with ten or twelve wives they can all go out collecting and at least two or three are likely to bring back something at the end of the day so we all can eat."

Because of the importance of food collecting, old wives were needed as well as young ones. An older woman knew the environment and was experienced in finding food. Younger wives served as apprentices and reinforcements for older wives. For this reason, every man who could tried to marry an older woman first. Hart found that households in which a man had only one or two wives, especially if both were young, had a much lower standard of living.

POLYANDRY: THE TODA OF SOUTH INDIA

Polyandry occurs primarily in parts of Tibet, Nepal, and India. Although the system may be an adaptation to a shortage of females in a society (this has been suggested for the Toda of southern India and the Pahari Hindus of the Himalayan foothills), in two of these societies, the Toda and the Tibetan, it is the practice of female infanticide that creates a shortage of women. In a society where men must be away from home for long periods of time, polyandry provides a woman with more than one husband to take care of her. In Tibet, polyandry appears to be related to the shortage of land. If several men marry one woman, this keeps down the number of children a man has to support. If brothers marry the same women, land can be kept within the family rather than fragmented over the generations.

The Toda of southern India (Figure 10.2) are a classic case of fraternal polyandry. The Toda female marries one male and at the same time becomes the wife of his brothers. If other brothers are born after the original marriage, they will also share in the marital rights. Sexual access to the wife appears to rotate rather equally, and there is little reported friction or jealousy. When all the brothers live with their wife in one hut, a brother who is with the wife will place his cloak and staff outside as a warning to others.

Figure 10.2 *The location of the Nayar and the Toda of India.*

When a wife becomes pregnant, determining the biological father is not considered necessary. Rather, a ceremony called "giving the bow," held in the woman's seventh month, assigns the child a legal or social father. This man makes a ceremonial bow and arrow from twigs and grass and presents these to the wife in front of his relatives. Usually the eldest brother performs this ceremony, and then all subsequent children are considered his. After two or three children are born, another brother will usually "give the bow." Occasionally a woman will marry several men who are not biological brothers. When these men live in different villages, the wife will live in the village of each husband for a month. The men arrange among themselves who will "give the bow" when she becomes pregnant. Since the practice of female infanticide has largely ceased among the Toda, the male-female ratio has evened out. Due to this, as well as the influence of Christian missionaries, the Toda today are largely monogamous (Queen and Hahenstein, 1974).

the birth of a child. Although polygamous men may have sexual intercourse during this time with any one of their wives other than the new mother, many men appear to prefer to stay with the wife who has just given birth and forgo sexual activity. Given Heider's view that the taboo on extramarital intercourse appears to be generally taken seriously, the Dani are a good example of a culture in which interest in sex, even as an aspect of married life, is much lower than in our own. Like people of other cultures in New Guinea, most married Dani men normally sleep in the men's house, sometimes visiting their wives at night.

Even where a low level of sexual interest is not typical in a society, other kinds of mechanisms exist to minimize potential conflict between co-wives. Sororal polygyny, where a man marries women who are sisters, is one such mechanism. Women who have grown up together may be more willing to cooperate and can get along better than women who are strangers to each other. Also, co-wives usually live in separate dwellings. A husband who wants to avoid conflict will attempt to distribute his economic resources and sexual attentions fairly evenly among his wives so there will be no accusations of favoritism. Where women's work is hard and monotonous, co-wives provide company for one another.

CHOOSING A MATE

As we have indicated, in most societies marriage is important because it links the kin groups of the married couple. This group interest in marriage frequently overrides any interest the individuals getting married have in each other, and accounts for the practice of arranged marriages. In our own society, where marriage is primarily an affair of individuals and where the married couple tends to make a new home apart from the parents, families have less interest in who their children marry and certainly less control over marriage than is the case elsewhere. Although choice is not quite as free in practice as American ideals would lead us to believe, theoretically any individual is quite free to choose a mate. Furthermore, since sexual compatibility and emotional needs are considered so important in the United States, mates are chosen on the basis of personal qualities largely having to do with physical attractiveness and that whole complex of feelings we call romantic love. Ideally, economic considerations are subordinated to the ideal of marrying for love.

In societies where the personal satisfactions of the married couple are subordinate to the needs and interests of the larger group, choosing a mate is much less of an individual, haphazard affair. The kin groups of both bride and groom have a strong vested interest in seeing that both parties fulfill their obligations, and therefore have much more control over marriage arrangements, including the choice of a spouse for their children. An important consideration in arranging a marriage is family reputation. In Muslim societies, for example, the honor of a family is a primary consideration in its reputation. This honor is upheld both by men and women, and an individual who is disgraced brings disgrace on the family. This honor is expressed differently by men and women. For men, honor is a public matter involving bravery, piety, and hospitality; it may be lost, but it may also be regained. The honor of women involves one major consideration, sexual chastity. Once this is lost it cannot be regained. If a woman's loss of virginity becomes known, no one of the appropriate group will want to marry her.

Therefore, the family, to the extent that this is possible (and this differes among different social classes), zealously guards daughters, isolating them behind the veil or restricting their movements outside the household. This concern for female sexual chastity is prominent in societies where the children belong to the kin group of the father or where inheritance follows the male line, making the paternity of the child of paramount importance. Only if a woman is a virgin at marriage, and is thereafter restricted in her movements and contacts with men, can a man be sure the child she is carrying is his own.

In societies with elaborate social hierarchies, such as in India, the family's social status is also important. A marriage will typically be arranged from within the same section of the same caste, although it is the ideal that the family of the boy have somewhat higher social status than the family of the girl. This is related to the degree of control the groom's family wishes to have over the bride. In this patrilineal society, the bride's family must ritually defer and accept a subordinate status to the family of the groom. This is psychologically easier if the social position of the bride's family is a little lower than that of the groom's family. If the bride is expected to move in with her husband's family after marriage, again as is the case in India, this also shapes the personal qualities considered desirable in a potential marriage partner. Domestic abilities are considered very important—but even more important is the willingness of the girl to be obedient to her elders. A girl

In some patrilineal societies, especially among Islamic peoples, great emphasis is put on guaranteeing a husband's control over his wife's sexuality. In order to ensure her honor and that of her family, Moslem women wear a fully protective veil when out in public. (Serena Nanda)

who shows signs of having an independent or complaining nature is viewed as a potential source of trouble by her future in-laws.

Where marriages are arranged, go-betweens are frequently used. A go-between or marriage broker has more information about a wider network of families than any one family can have. Furthermore, by using a go-between neither the family of the bride or that of the groom will lose face if its offer is rejected by the other party. Although the arranged marriage system tends to become less rigid as societies urbanize and industrialize, it still remains true that in most societies, families and larger kin groups have much more control over marriage and the choice of a spouse than in the United States.

TRANSFER OF RIGHTS AND EXCHANGES AT MARRIAGE

The essence of marriage is that it is a publicly accepted relationship which involves the transfer of certain rights and obligations among the participating parties. These rights primarily involve sexual access of husband and wife to each other, rights of the husband over any children born to the wife, obligations of children born to the union to be cared for by one or both parents, and rights of husband and wife to the economic services of the other. Marriage may also give the families or kin groups of the bride and groom certain rights in each other for goods or services. These "relationships of affinity" may be symbolically expressed, as in India, where the family of the wife owes certain forms of deferential behavior to the family of the husband. This is true for all kin. Any person "from the girl's side" will be expected

to behave in a ritually respectful manner to a person "from the boy's side."

The transfer of rights in marriage is often accompanied by an exchange of goods and services. Sometimes this exchange may be simply "presents"—that is, items customarily given as a way of "winning and preserving the goodwill of those with the power to transfer marital rights," though not necessary to complete the transfer. In other cases, the exchange of goods and services is essential for the transfer of marital rights to take place. If such an exchange is not completed, the rights in marriage can be forfeited.

Three kinds of exchanges made in connection with marriage are bridewealth, dowry, and bride service. **Bridewealth** (or **bride price**) refers to goods presented by the groom's kin to the kin of the bride. **Dowry,** a rather rare practice found in India and at one time customary in Europe, is a presentation of goods by the bride's kin to the family of the groom. **Bride service** refers to the practice whereby a young husband must work for a specified period of time for his wife's family in exchange for his marital rights. This practice tends to be customary in societies where accumulating material goods for an exchange at marriage might be quite difficult, and is found among some foraging societies. Among the !Kung Bushmen, for example, a man may work for his wife's family for as long as fifteen years, or until the birth of the third child.

The most common form of exchange of wealth is bridewealth. A major function of the payment of bridewealth is the legitimation of marriage (Ogbu 1978). This is confirmed by the fact that in societies where bridewealth is customary, an individual can claim compensation only for the violation of conjugal rights if the bridewealth has been paid. Furthermore, bridewealth paid at marriage is returned (subject to specified conditions) if a marriage is terminated. Another function of bridewealth which has been emphasized by anthropologists is that it entitles the husband to domestic and sexual rights over his wife. Although this is true, marriage confers rights on the wife as well as the husband. By establishing marriage as legal—that is, recognized and supported by public sanctions—bridewealth allows wives to hold their husbands accountable for violations of conjugal rights, as well as the other way around. A third function traditionally ascribed to the payment of bridewealth is that it serves to stabilize marriage.

It is true that the exchange of goods at marriage does indicate the importance of marriage as a social, rather than an individual affair, and would seem to give the family of the groom a vested interested in keeping the couple together. A recent examination of cross-cultural data, however, shows that marriage may be stable for reasons other than the payment of bridewealth, and that the bridewealth payment itself does not mean that divorce will not occur. Finally, the idea that bridewealth is a payment for the loss of the woman to her husband's family is not fully supported by the cross-cultural data either. In some societies, for example, bridewealth is customary even though the husband goes to live with his wife's family or the husband assists his wife's family economically, especially as they get older. This recent reexamination of the conditions under which bridewealth is customary has also led to the reopening of the question of the relationship between bridewealth and women's status. The long-held assumption by colonial administrators, missionaries, and even anthropologists that the payment of bridewealth resulted in a lower status for women can be questioned. Ogbu (1978) argues that such

payment enhances rather than diminishes the status of women, by enabling both husband and wife to acquire reciprocal rights to each other. The low status of women in parts of Africa where bridewealth is customary has nothing to do with the use of bridewealth in the legitimation of marriage.

Whatever the exact nature of the exchange of goods and/or services in marriage, the transfer of rights in marriage is a "public" affair, almost always surrounded by ritual and ceremony. These ceremonies are a way of bearing witness to the lawfulness of the transaction. It is these ceremonies, publicly witnessed and acknowledged, that distinguish marriage from other kinds of unions which resemble it. "Living together," for example, may have

One function of bride price is as a payment for the economic services of women. In many parts of West Africa, however, women are allowed to keep control over products that they raise for the market. (United Nations)

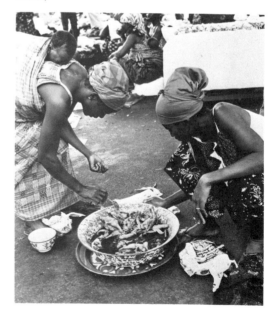

some of the same emotional functions for the two individuals, but it does not involve obligatory economic exchanges or establish relationships between the individual and his/her spouse's kin.

DEFINING MARRIAGE

In a few societies, sexual rights, economic responsibilities, or socialization of children are not derived from relationships in marriage, but are part of the rights and responsibilities of groups other than those formed by husband-wife and parent-child. We have seen that on the Israeli *kibbutz*, for example, it is the community that socializes children and it is the community that is economically responsible for them. Nor do husbands and wives exchange goods and services. On the *kibbutz*, the community, not the family, is the basic economic unit, both for production and consumption.

The data on the Nayar indicate that any universal definition of marriage would have to be very general indeed to cover all the known variations. Anthropologists are not so interested in such a definition as they once were. More important than establishing a definition to cover all known cases is looking at the kinds of rights that are transferred through marriage in dif-

---

THE NAYAR OF SOUTH INDIA

The classic case presenting problems to anthropologists attempting to reach a universal definition of marriage are the Nayar of South India (Figure 10.2, p. 207). They are a landowning caste who live in the state of Kerala. The Nayar "family" was not formed through marriage, but consisted rather of male and female kin descended from a female ancestor. This household group, called the *taravad*, typically contained brothers and sisters, a woman's daughter and granddaughters, and their children. *Taravad* property was held jointly in the name of the oldest surviving male. This type of family was related to the system of Nayar marriage.

Traditionally there were two kinds of marriage among the Nayar, the *tali*-tying ceremony and the *sambandham* relationship. Every Nayar girl had to undergo the *tali*-tying ceremony before she reached puberty; this rite marked a girl's transition to womanhood. The man with whom a girl tied the *tali* had no further rights in her nor did she have any obligations to him (except that at his death she performed certain rituals). After this ceremony, however, a girl could enter into *sambandham* unions with a number of different men of the proper caste with whom she would have children. The *taravad*, however, retained rights over a Nayar woman's procreative powers and authority over her children. Even so, for a child to have full birth rights in the *taravad*, a father had to be acknowledged. Any one of the men with whom the women had had a *sambandham* union could acknowledge paternity by bearing certain expenses associated with the birth of the child. Where paternity was doubtful, an assembly of neighbors would attempt to coerce the current "visiting husband" to make the payments. If no man of the appropriate caste would take on the role of father, the women and child were expelled from the *taravad* and from the caste, because it was assumed that the women was having relationships with a lower-caste man. This was considered polluting not only for the woman, but for the entire *taravad*.

In the Nayar system, then, a woman had several "husbands" (*sambandham* unions), but the responsibility and care of children were in the hands of a group of brothers and sisters (the *taravad*). From the point of view of the polyandrous woman and her *taravad*, polyandry enhanced both individual and group prestige. Polyandry also gave the Nayar woman access to men who were in many different occupations, and their services could then be accessible to the *taravad*. The Nayar marriage and family system were well suited to the traditional Nayar occupation of soldiering. Without permanent responsibilities and permanent attachments to wife and children, a young Nayar man was free to pursue a military career. The agricultural land owned by the Nayar *taravad* was worked by lower-caste landless serfs and managed by an older male, an economic system that also freed younger Nayar men from the necessity of living in the *taravad* (Mencher 1965).

---

ferent societies, and the kinds of families and domestic groups marriage creates. Our interest in the Nayar, then, focuses not on whether they have marriage or not, but on the way in which sexual access to women, economic responsibility, and rights over children are legitimized in Nayar society.

THE FAMILY

Two basic types of families identified by anthropologists are the elementary or nuclear family and the extended family. Nuclear families are organized around the conjugal tie—that is, the relationship between husband and wife. The extended family is based on consanguineal or blood relations extending over three or more generations.

The Nuclear Family

The **nuclear family** consists of a married couple and their children. This type of family may exist as a relatively isolated and independent unit, as it does in our society, or it may be embedded within larger kinship units. The claim of some anthropologists (Murdock 1949) that the nuclear family is a universal social institution has been disputed on the basis of some exceptional cases, such as that of the Nayar and the Israeli *kibbutz*. The independent nuclear family is the ideal in only a small percentage of the world's societies, primarily among hunters and gatherers and in modern industrialized nations, both of which require a high degree of mobility.

In our own society, the nuclear family ideally has its own residence, away from the parents of either husband or wife. Because the married couple forms a separate domestic and economic unit, the involvement of parents or other kin in mate selection is marginal. Larger kin groups are not expected to exercise control over or interfere in the affairs of the nuclear family. Although there are some ideals about the different roles that should be played by husband and wife with regard to economic support, sexual activity, and child care, these roles are not rigidly defined. Failure to carry out familial roles may result in dissolution of the nuclear family, but since larger kin groups are not involved in the transfer of rights and obligations in marriage, the dissolution primarily affects only the family members. The nuclear family may also be dissolved by the death of one of the spouses.

In our society today, many functions formerly belonging to the nuclear family have been taken over by other groups. At one time the family in Europe and the United States was a productive unit, and this is still true of some farm families. The typical American family, however, has largely lost this function; economically, its most important function is a unit of consumption. Once leisure activities and recreation were also carried out primarily within the family group; today, the peer group plays a much more important role in leisure activities and in inculcating values. The state has also, through various kinds of social security programs, undermined the importance of caring for the aged or sick person as a family function. Socialization of children, too, takes place in important ways outside the family, in school and through the mass media.

In contrast to this picture of the declining functions of the nuclear family in our own society is the increased expectation that the family will satisfy our needs for affection and intimacy. Critics of the nuclear family in the United States feel that this burden is too much for the family to bear. In an age in which personal happiness has become a primary cultural value, it is perhaps beyond the capacity of any one social group. The alienation experienced by many Americans indicates that families often do not carry out their "affective" functions very well (Bronfenbrenner 1974).

The nuclear family is adapted in many ways to the requirements of industrial society. Where jobs do not depend on family connections, and where geographical mobility may be required for obtaining employment and success in a chosen career, a small, flexible unit like the independent nuclear family has its advantages. This type of family also seems to be adaptive to the requirements of a hunting and gathering life, since more than three-fourths of foraging societies have this type of family unit. In such societies, however, the nuclear family is not nearly as independent or isolated as in our own society; the family unit almost always camps with the kin of the husband or the wife.

Composite or **compound families** are aggregates of nuclear families linked by a common spouse. A polygynous household, consisting of one man with several wives and their respective children, would constitute a compound family. In this case, each wife and her children will normally occupy a separate residence. The dynamics of compound families are quite different from the dynamics of a family that consists of one husband, one wife, and their children, all of whom occupy a common residence. In the compound family, for example, the tie between a mother and her children is particularly strong, and the relations between the children of different mothers by the same father is different in a number of ways from the relationship between full siblings in the typical Euro-American nuclear family. Furthermore, in analyzing the dynamics of the compound family, the interaction between co-wives must be taken into account, as well as the different kinds of behavior patterns that emerge when a man is husband to several women rather than just one.

Is the Nuclear Family Universal?: Social organization on the Israeli *kibbutz* raises the question of whether the nuclear family is in fact a universal social institution. On the *kibbutz,* socialization of children is carried out by the community as a whole. The basic economic unit, both for production and consumption, is also the whole community rather than a family. Nor does the *kibbutz* family eat together. Eating is a communal activity, both for adults in the communal dining room and for children who eat with their peers in the children's residence. Nevertheless, the nuclear family is a recognizable unit in kibbutz life (Spiro 1958). Affective ties are stronger between men and women who are married to each other than with other *kibbutz* comrades. The child's affective ties to its own parents are also of a different and more intense quality than its ties to other caretakers. Furthermore, although the *kibbutz* rather than the family provides the basic necessities of life, small luxuries and extras are provided within the nuclear family.

The examples of the Nayar and the *kibbutz* suggest that rigid definitions of family types are not the most useful way of understanding the family as it exists in specific cultural contexts. It is more useful to examine the different components of the nuclear family "complex" and investigate how these various rights, obligations, activities, and functions are actually distributed in different societies.

The Extended Family

The **extended,** or **consanguineal family** consists of two or more lineally related kinfolk of the same sex and their spouses and offspring, occupying a single household or homestead and under the authority of a household head. An extended family is not just a collection of nuclear families. In the extended family system the ties of lineality—that is, the blood ties between the generations—are more important than the ties of marriage. In more than half of the world's societies, the extended family is the ideal.

Extended families may be organized around males or females. A patrilineal extended family (such as the Rajputs of Khalapur, India, described in Chapter 6), is organized around a man, his sons, and the sons' wives and children. A matrilineal family is organized around a woman and her daughters and the daughters' husbands and children. The Nayar represent the extreme of the consanguineal family, for the conjugal tie is for most purposes completely absent. Most extended family systems do give some recognition to the nuclear family. Thus, among the Rajputs of Khalapur, women are considered responsible for caring for their own children, and the conjugal tie is clearly recognized, if only as a potential source of trouble for the larger family group.

The Patrilineal Extended Family. A society in which the extended family was the ideal was premodern China. In China, lineal descendants from father to son to grandson are the backbone of family organization. The family continues through time as a permanent social entity. As older members are lost through death, new ones are added through birth. As in India, marriage in China is viewed more as acquiring a daughter-in-law than taking a wife. It is arranged by the parents, and the new couple live with the husband's family. Again, as in India, the obedient relationship of the son to his father and the loyalty and solidarity of brothers is given more importance than the ties between husband and wife. In fact, in both societies the public demonstration of affection between a married couple is severely criticized. In both systems it is anticipated and feared that a man's feeling for his wife will interfere with his carrying out responsibilities to his own blood kin.

In these cultures, a good wife is one who is a good daughter-in-law. She must work hard, under the eye of her mother-in-law and her husband's elder brothers' wives. With the birth of a son, a woman gains more acceptance in the household. As the years go by, if she has been patient and played her role well, the relationship between husband and wife develops into one of companionship and a more equal division of power. As her sons grow up, the wife achieves even more power in the household as she begins to arrange for their marriages. When several sons are married, a woman may be the dominant person in the household, even ordering her husband about, as his economic power, and consequently his authority, wanes.

The Matrilineal Extended Family. Extended matrilineal families are found among the Hopi, a Western Pueblo native American group who live in the Southwest. The Hopi household revolves around a central and continuing core of women. When women marry, their husbands come into the household and have important economic functions, though they do not participate in its ritual. Husbands are peripheral, with divided residences

and loyalties. When crises arise, the father is often blamed and treated as an outsider.

The father's obligations to his sons are primarily economic. He prepares them to make a living by teaching them to farm and herd sheep, and he may go into partnership with them in herding activities. When a son marries, a father will frequently present him with a portion of the flock and a small piece of land. The economic support a son receives from his father is returned in the father's old age; a son supports his father and takes the responsibility for his funeral rites. In return for this service, the son will receive a larger share of his father's personal property than his brothers. The father's role is more that of friend and teacher, and the father-son relationship is characterized by affection and little punishment. A father's relationship to his daughter is generally affectionate but not close, and he has few specific duties in regard to her upbringing.

The mother-daughter relationship is an exceedingly close one based on blood ties, common activities, and lifelong residence together. A mother is responsible for both the economic and the ritual training of her daughters. The daughter behaves with respect, obedience, and affection to her mother and normally will continue to live with her mother and her mother's sisters after marriage. A mother also has a close relationship with her son. He belongs to her lineage and will keep much of his personal and ritual property in her home. A son shows a respect for his mother as head of the household and consults her on all important questions. The strongest and most permanent tie in Hopi society is between sisters. The foundation of the household group is the relation of sisters to one another and to their mother. The children of sisters are raised together; if one sister dies, another looks after her children. Sisters cooperate in all domestic tasks. There are usually few quarrels, and when they occur they are settled by the mother's brother or their own brothers.

As in all matrilineal societies, the mother's brother's relation to his sister's sons is a very important one. As head of his sister's lineage and household, his position is one of authority and control; he is the chief disciplinarian and has the primary responsibility for transmitting the ritual heritage of the lineage and clan, which occupies the highest place in Hopi values. He usually selects the most capable nephew as his successor and trains him in the duties of whatever ceremonial position he may hold. A nephew is frequently afraid of his maternal uncle, in contrast to the affectionate relationship with his father. A mother's brother plays an important role at the time of his nephews' and nieces' weddings and is consulted in the choice of a spouse. It is he who instructs his nephew in the proper behavior toward his new relatives and who formally welcomes his niece's husband into the household.

The Advantages of the Extended Family. The extended family is clearly adaptive under certain kinds of economic and social conditions. Murdock's survey indicated that the extended family prevails in all types of predominantly cultivating societies. The main advantages of this type of family are economic; the extended family can provide a larger number of workers than the nuclear family. This is useful both for food production and for producing and marketing handicrafts, which are generally more well developed among cultivators than foragers. Furthermore, in stable agricultural societies, ownership of land becomes important; it is a source of pride, prestige, and power. The family becomes

attached to the land, knows how to work it, and becomes reluctant to divide it. A system in which land is divided into small parcels through inheritance becomes relatively unproductive. The extended family is a way of keeping land intact, which provides additional security for individuals in times of crisis. This relationship between land and family type is supported by evidence from India which shows that the higher castes, who own more land and other property, are more likely to have extended families than the lower castes.

There are also the values of companionship in the extended family as daily activities are carried out jointly by a number of kin working together. A further advantage is that the extended family provides not only economic support, but also a sense of participation and dignity for the older person, who lives out his or her last years surrounded by respectful and affectionate kin. This contrasts with the independent nuclear family, in which the presumed advantages of privacy and personal autonomy are paid for as people grow old and are regarded as a burden and a nuisance if they join the household of one of their children.

Although it may be generally true that old people fare better in societies with extended family systems, the life of individuals past their prime is not always enviable, even in these societies. When sons begin to raise families of their own, extended families frequently split into parts. As the father loses his productive abilities, he is slowly divested of his former status and power. In a Fijian society studied by Sahlins (1957), the people say: "His time is up"—and an old man literally waits to die. Although the Fijian ideal is that an old father should be properly cared for by his brothers and sons, "actually he sinks into a

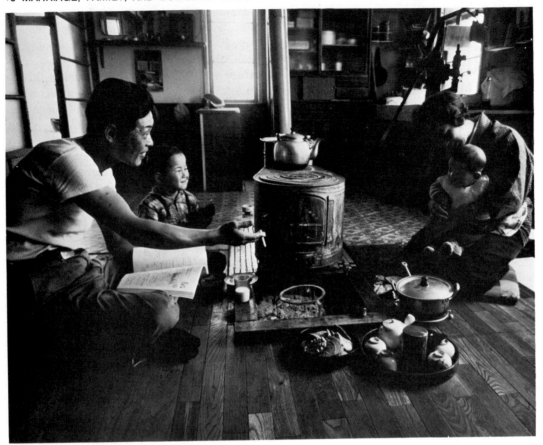

With increasing industrialization, there appears to be a shift to nuclear family households in many societies, such as Japan, although the ideal of the extended family remains strong. (United Nations)

pitiable position. In the old days, he might even be killed. Today he is barely kept alive, his counsel is never sought and he is more often considered silly then wise."

Because the independent nuclear family appears to be adapted to a modern industrialized society, many social scientists have predicted that the extended family will be modified in the direction of the independent nuclear family as modernization and industrialization spread. The corollary of this assumption is that while the extended family has advantages among cultivators or economically marginal populations, these advantages become liabilities with urbanization and industrialization. Milton Singer (1968), an anthropologist who has studied the families of industrial leaders in the city of Madras, India, says no. He points out that the patrilineal joint family as it exists in India is a flexible institution. The principles of mutual obligation of extended kin, joint ownership of property, and an authority structure in which the male household head takes responsibility for making decisions after consultation with junior members can easily be, and have been, successfully transferred to the management of modern corporations.

DOMESTIC GROUPS AND POSTMARITAL RESIDENCE RULES

A **domestic group,** or household is not the same as a family. Although domestic groups most often contain related members, nonkin may also be part of the domestic group. On the other hand, members of a family may be spread over several domestic groups, or households. The composition of domestic groups is affected by the rules a society has about where a newly married couple will live. **Neolocal residence** exists when it is the norm for a married couple to establish an independent domestic unit. Only 5 percent of the world's societies are neolocal. Neolocal residence is the ideal in our own society. It is related to the high degree of mobility required in an industrial system, and to a value system that makes romantic love, the emotional bond between husband and wife, privacy, and independence primary.

Most societies have a rule of **patrilocal residence.** A woman lives with her husband's kin after marriage, either in the same household or in a nearby dwelling or compound. In societies with a **matrilocal residence** rule, the husband lives with the wife's kin after marriage. If a couple has the choice of living with either the wife's or the husband's family, the pattern is one of **bilocal residence.** A fifth and rare residence pattern is called **avunculocal residence.** In this case, the married couple is expected to live with the husband's mother's brother.

In attempting to explain why a society would have a particular kind of residence rule, anthropologists have generally em-phasized economic factors. It has been suggested that where men must work cooperatively, such as in societies dependent on big-game hunting or intensive agriculture, there will be a patrilocal rule of residence. Matrilocality would appear to be adaptive in horticultural societies, where women have an important role in the economy. The cross-cultural data do not prove this reasoning to be entirely correct. Although it is true that most matrilocal societies do practice horticulture, this is also the case for the majority of patrilocal societies.

The importance of male cooperation in warfare is suggested as another reason for a patrilocal rule of residence (Ember and Ember 1971). Where fighting between lineages or villages is common, it is useful for men who will fight together to live together. Otherwise they might wind up having to make the choice between defending their wife's local group, the one with whom they live, against the families with whom they grew up. Where warfare takes place between societies, rather than within them, and where men must leave their homes to fight, cooperation among women is very important. Since common residence promotes cooperation, matrilocal residence is a functional norm where males engage in warfare that extends beyond local groups.

Residence rules are ideal or preferred norms of behavior; actual behavior is frequently different. The choices couples make about where to live after marriage depend on many individual situational factors, although they are likely to be guided by the ideal norms of the society. Because kinship ideology (to be discussed in the next chapter) is derived from both norms and actual patterns of postmarital residence, residence rules, as well as the actual choices made by individuals, are important in the social organization of a society.

SUMMARY

1. Three major functions of marriage and the family are regulating sexual access between males and females, arranging for the exchange of services between males and females, and assigning responsibility for child care.

2. Although marriage and family are rooted in the biological complementarity of male and female and the biological process of reproduction, they are cultural patterns and differ in different human societies.

3. Incest taboos are prohibitions on mating between relatives or persons classified as relatives. Some theories that attempt to account for the universality of such taboos are that the taboos limit inbreeding, that they reflect the natural aversion to sexual relations between close kin, that they prevent disruption within the family, and that they force people to marry out of their immediate families, thus joining people into a larger social community.

4. Exogamy is a rule that requires people to marry outside a particular group. This rule is adaptive in forging alliances between families within a society

5. Endogamy is a rule requiring marriage *within* a specified group. One of its functions is to keep wealth within the group or to maintain the so-called purity of the blood line.

6. All societies have rules about the number of spouses allowed a man or woman. Most of the world's societies allow some form of plural marriage (polygyny or polyandry), whereas our own society has a rule of monogamy (one spouse only).

7. Marriage, which is a publicly sanctioned relationship, most often is legitimated by the exchange of goods between the kin of the bride and the kin of the groom. The most common form of exchange is bridewealth, where the kin of the groom gives various kinds of goods to the kin of the bride.

8. There are two basic types of families. The nuclear family is organized around the tie between husband and wife (the conjugal tie); the extended family is organized around blood ties extending over several generations.

9. The nuclear family, which is predominantly found in contemporary industrial and foraging societies, appears to be adaptive where geographical mobility is important. The extended family predominates among cultivators because it provides a larger number of workers than the nuclear family, and is also a means by which landholdings can be kept intact over generations.

10. A domestic group is a household; it usually, but not necessarily, contains members of a family. The composition of domestic groups is shaped by the postmarital residence rules of a society.

11. The most widespread rule of residence is patrilocality, by which the wife goes to live with her husband's family. Matrilocality, by which the husband goes to live with his wife's family, is found primarily in horticultural societies. Neolocality, by which the married couple live independently, is found in a relatively small number of societies, including that of the United States.

SUGGESTED READINGS

Bohannan, P., and Middleton, J., eds.
1968   *Marriage, Family and Residence.* Garden City, N.Y.: The Natural History Press. This reader includes articles on incest, marriage, family, and domestic groups from a wide variety of cultures.

Briggs, Jean L.
1970   *Never in Anger: A Portrait of an Eskimo Family.* Cambridge, Mass.: Harvard University Press. An intimate account of an Eskimo family and its relation to the author.

Fox, Robin
1967   *Kinship and Marriage.* New York: Penguin Books. A clear and readable introduction to social organization.

Leibowitz, Lila
1978   *Females, Males, Families: A Biosocial Approach.* North Scituate, Mass.: Duxbury Press. An interesting book based on lectures for an introductory course on the family, including a survey of sex and nurturing among nonhuman primates.

Stack, Carol.
1975   *All Our Kin: Strategies for Survival in a Black Community.* New York: Harper & Row. A view of the black, lower-class kin group that emphasizes the adaptive nature of extended domestic networks.

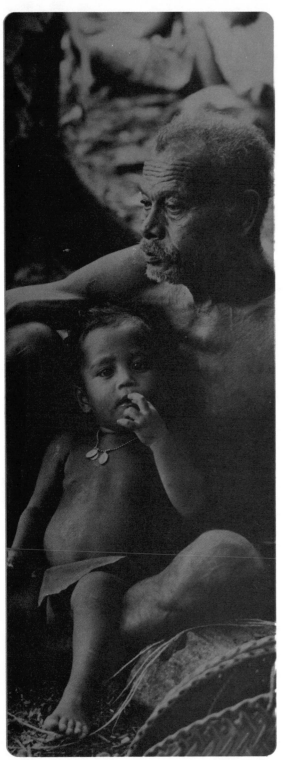

United Nations

11
Kinship and Association

Human beings are social animals, and our pattern of group living has undoubted value for our survival as a species. One way of looking at social organization is to look at the different groups that are found in a society. In societies traditionally studied by anthropologists, kinship is the most important social bond. Kin relations are the basis of group formation; relationships between individuals are mainly governed by kinship norms; and the extension of kinship ties is the main way of allying groups to each other and incorporating strangers into a group. The importance of kinship in most of the world's cultures provides an important contrast with our own society, in which other principles of social organization, such as work, citizenship, and common economic and political interests operate to structure behavior and act as the basis on which groups are formed. This does not mean that kinship is insignificant in modern industrialized society. The nuclear family is, after all, a kin group and a core social institution in the United States. Larger groupings of relatives also become important on various ceremonial occasions. Even in the United States, a person claiming a kin relation is regarded differently from someone who is not a relative.

KINSHIP

Kinship includes relationships through blood and relationships through marriage. In every society, the formation of groups and the regulation of behavior depends to some extent on socially recognized ties of kinship. A **kinship system** refers to the totality of relationships based on blood and marriage that links individuals in a web of rights and obligations, to the kinds of groups formed in a society on the basis of kinship, and to the system of terms used to classify different kin (kinship terminology). It is because there is an interrelationship between the formation of kinship groups, the development of kinship ideology, the behavior of different kin toward each other, and the kinship terminology of a society that anthropologists refer to kinship as a system.

Although a kinship system always rests on some kind of biological relationship, kinship systems are cultural phenomena. The ways in which a society classifies kin is cultural, and may or may not be based on a scientifically accurate assessment of biological ties. The term for "father" for example, may refer to the actual biological father (*genitor*) of a child, or it may refer to a man who takes on the responsibility for the child's upbringing and/or is socially recognized as the father (*pater*). In the Trobriand Islands, for example, the biological role of the male in reproduction is not given cultural recognition, and fatherhood is established by marriage; the "father" is the mother's husband. As we saw for the Toda, biological paternity is irrelevant; fatherhood is established by the performance of a ritual. In this and other similar cases, social fatherhood is what counts. Because kinship systems are cultural creations, there is a wide variety of ways in which both consanguineal (blood) and affinal (marriage) relatives are classified in different societies. There are also differences in the kinds of social groups formed by kinship, and in the ways in which kin are expected to behave toward one another.

Culturally defined ties of kinship have two basic functions that are necessary for the continuation of society. First, kinship serves to provide continuity between generations. In all societies children must be cared for and educated so that they may become functioning members of their society. With the possible exception of the *kibbutz* and other contemporary attempts at collective child-rearing on communes of unrelated people, it is a kinship unit that is fundamentally responsible for socialization. Furthermore, a society must also provide for the orderly transmission of property and social position between generations. In most human societies, inheritance (the transfer of property) and succession (the transfer of social position) takes place within kin groups.

Second, kinship defines a universe of others on whom an individual may depend for aid in a variety of ways. The minimal group of importance in mutual aid is the

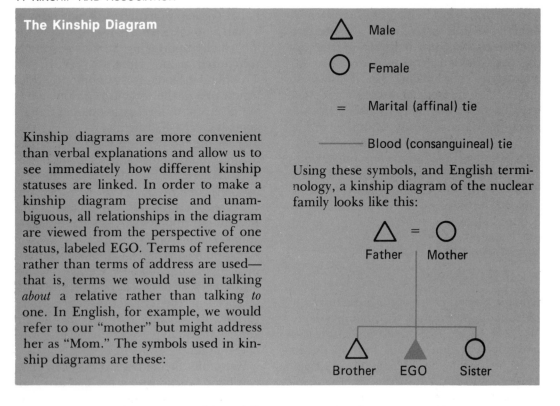

The Kinship Diagram

△ Male

○ Female

= Marital (affinal) tie

――――― Blood (consanguineal) tie

Kinship diagrams are more convenient than verbal explanations and allow us to see immediately how different kinship statuses are linked. In order to make a kinship diagram precise and unambiguous, all relationships in the diagram are viewed from the perspective of one status, labeled EGO. Terms of reference rather than terms of address are used—that is, terms we would use in talking *about* a relative rather than talking *to* one. In English, for example, we would refer to our "mother" but might address her as "Mom." The symbols used in kinship diagrams are these:

Using these symbols, and English terminology, a kinship diagram of the nuclear family looks like this:

△ = ○
Father Mother

△ ▲ ○
Brother EGO Sister

domestic group of a woman and her children and an adult male. In most societies, however, kin groups that include relatives beyond this minimum are very important. It is undoubtedly the adaptiveness of social groups larger than the elementary family that accounts for the fact that expanded kin groups are found in so many human societies.

RULES OF DESCENT AND THE FORMATION OF DESCENT GROUPS

In anthropological terminology, **descent** refers to the culturally established affiliation with one or both parents. In many societies, descent is an important basis of social group formation. In one sense, of course, the nuclear family is a descent group, but here we use **descent group** to mean those groups of consanguineal kin who are lineal descendants of a common ancestor extending beyond two generations. Where descent groups are found, they have important functions in the organization of domestic life, the socialization of children, the use and transfer of property and political and ritual offices, the carrying out of religious ritual, the settlement of disputes, and political organization and warfare.

Two basic types of descent rules or kinship ideology operate in society. In a system with a rule of **unilineal descent,** descent group membership is based on links through either the paternal or the maternal line, but not both. Two types of unilineal descent rules are **patrilineal descent** and **matrilineal descent.** In societies with patrilineal descent, an individual belongs to the descent group of his or her father. In societies with matrilineal descent, an individual belongs to the descent group of the mother. (There are some exceptions, as in societies with double descent, which will be described later.)

In societies with a system of **bilateral descent,** both maternal and paternal lines are used as the basis for reckoning descent and for establishing the rights and obligations of kinship. Bilateral kinship systems are found in relatively few societies throughout the world, although they are characteristic of Western European culture and of the United States.

Unilineal Descent

The frequency of unilineal descent in the world's cultures is due to two major advantages: (1) Unilineal rules result in the formation of descent groups that can perpetuate themselves over time, even though their membership changes (like modern corporations). Corporate descent groups are permanent units and have an existence over and above the individuals who are members at any given time. Old members die and new ones are admitted through birth, but the integrity of the corporate group as a group persists. Such groups (like lineages) may own property and manage resources, just like a modern corporation). (2) Such rules provide unambiguous group membership for every individual in the society. In short, where descent is traced through only one line, group membership is both easily and clearly defined. By knowing the descent group to which he or she belongs and the descent group of others, an individual's rights of ownership, social duties, and social roles are clear. He or she can also easily relate to a large number of known and unknown persons in the society.

Although systems of unilineal descent share certain basic similarities throughout the world, they do not operate exactly the same way in every society. In addition, actual behavior in any society does not correspond exactly to the rules as they are defined in the kinship ideology. Systems of descent and kinship are basically a means by which a society relates to its environment and circumstances. As situations and conditions change, the rules of kinship, like other ideal norms, will be bent and manipulated so that a group may be successful in its environment. The accepted departures from the norm which exist in every society give unilineal systems a flexibility they would otherwise lack, a flexibility necessary for human adaptation. We will look now at some of the different types of unilineal descent groups.

Types of Unilineal Descent Groups. A **lineage** is a group of kin whose members trace descent from a common ancestor and who can actually demonstrate those genealogical links among themselves. Lineages formed by descent through the male line are called **patrilineages.** Lineages formed by descent through the female line are called **matrilineages.** Lineages may vary in size from one consisting of a male or female, their children, and their children's children, to one consisting of more than three generations. Where lineages own land collectively and where the members are held responsible for one another's behavior, the lineage is considered a corporate group. In some societies the lineage functions as a corporate group; in other societies it does not.

A **clan** generally refers to unilineal kinship group whose members believe themselves to be descended from a common ancestor, but who cannot trace this relationship genealogically. Sometimes the presumed common ancestor may be a mythological figure, and sometimes no specific ancestor will be known or named. Clans are frequently named and may have a **totem**—that is, some feature of the natural environment with which it is closely identified and toward which the clan members must behave in a special way.

Clans and lineages have different functions in different societies. The lineage is frequently a local residential or domestic group, and its members therefore cooperate on a daily basis. The lineage is also important in regulating marriage; in most societies, an individual must marry outside his or her lineage, or the lineage of either parent. Clans are not generally residential units, but tend to spread out over many villages. Clans therefore often have political and religious functions, rather than primarily domestic and economic ones.

One of the most important functions of a clan is to regulate marriage. In most societies, clans are exogamous. The prohibition on marriage within the clan strengthens its unilineal character. If a person married within the clan, his or her children would find it difficult to make sharp distinctions between maternal and paternal relatives. Lowie (1948:237) says of the Crow Indians of North America, among whom clans are very important, that in case of marriage within the clan, "a Crow . . . loses his bearings and perplexes his tribesmen. For he owes specific obligations to his father's relatives and others to his mother's, who are now hopelessly confounded. The sons of his father's clan ought to be censors; but now the very same persons are his joking relatives and his clan." Not only would this person not know how to act toward others, but others would not know how to act toward him. Clan exogamy also extends the network of

peaceful social relations within a society as different clans are allied through marriage.

Patrilineal Descent Groups. In societies with patrilineal descent groups, an individual (whether male or female) belongs to the descent group of the father, the father's father, and so on (see Figure 11.1). Thus, a man, his sisters and brothers, his brother's children (but not his sister's children), his own children, and his son's children (but not his daughter's children) all belong to the same group. Inheritance moves from father to son, as does succession to office.

The degree to which a woman is incorporated into the patrilineage of her husband varies in different societies. In some cases, a woman may retain rights of inheritance in her father's lineage. In general, however, in a patrilineal system a man gains some degree of control over his wife and children. Great care is taken in patrilineal societies to guarantee the husband's rights and control over his wife (wives) and children, because the continuity of the descent group depends on binding the wife and children to the husband. Patrilineal systems most often have patrilocal rules of residence, so a wife may find herself living among "strangers" (this of course would not be the case in societies where cousin marriage is practiced), and this undermines female solidarity and support. Because marriage in patrilineal systems is generally surrounded by strict sanctions and tends to be more stable than in matrilineal systems, anthropologists have tended to neglect the potential for disruption that derives from the discontent of women in these societies. In fact, women are not always as submissive as they have been portrayed in the anthropological lit-

Figure 11.1 *Membership in a patrilineal descent group. In societies with patrilineal descent groups, membership is based on links through the father only. Sons and daughters are members of their father's descent group, as are the children of sons, but* not *of daughters.*

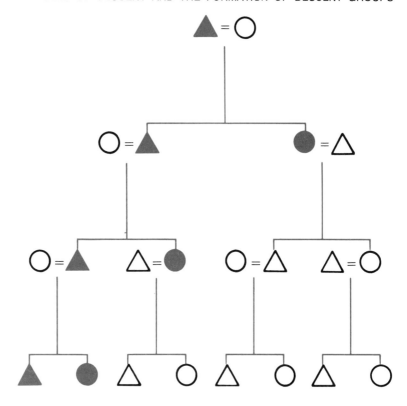

erature on patrilineal societies, and their struggles against control by the husband's group is an important theme in both the reality of domestic life and in mythology and literature (Denich 1974).

The Nuer, a pastoral group that lives in the Sudan in East Africa, are a patrilineal society. Among the Nuer, all rights, privileges, obligations, and interpersonal relationships are regulated by kinship: One is either a kinsman or an enemy. Membership in a patrilineal descent group is the most significant fact of life, and the father, his brothers, and their children are considered the closest kin. Membership in the patrilineage confers rights in land, requires participation in certain religious ceremonies, and determines political and judicial obligations, such as making alliances in feuds and warfare.

The patrilineage has important political functions among the Nuer. Lineage membership may spread over several villages and thus help create alliances between otherwise independent villages that contain members of several different lineages. Related lineages form still larger groups, or clans. Clans are viewed as composed of lineages, not of individuals. Each Nuer clan has its members spread out over many different villages. Because an individual cannot marry someone from within his/her own lineage or clan, or from the lineage of the mother, kinship relations extend widely throughout the tribe. In the absence of a centralized system of political control, kinship-based alliances are an important mechanism for keeping the peace, in view of the Nuer belief that kin should not fight with each other.

Matrilineal Descent Groups. Two fundamental ties recognized by every society are those between a woman and her children, and that between siblings (brothers and sisters). In all societies males have the responsibility for providing and protecting the mother-child unit, and control over women and their children. In patrilineal societies, this control falls to the man who is designated as the child's father. In matrilineal societies, however, the major protecting, providing, and controlling male is the brother of a woman rather than her husband. A man gains sexual and economic rights over a woman when he

marries her, but he does not gain rights over her children. Children belong to the mother's descent group, not the father's. Thus, the membership of a matrilineal descent group consists of a woman, her brothers and sisters, her sister's (but not her brother's) children, her own children, and the children of her daughters (but not of her sons) (Figure 11.2).

Matrilineal systems tend to be correlated with a matrilocal rule of residence; a man goes to live with or near his wife's kin after marriage. This means that in the domestic group it is the man who is among "strangers," while his wife is surrounded by her kin. The inclusion of a husband in the household is of less importance in a matrilineal system than in a patrilineal one, and marriages in mat-

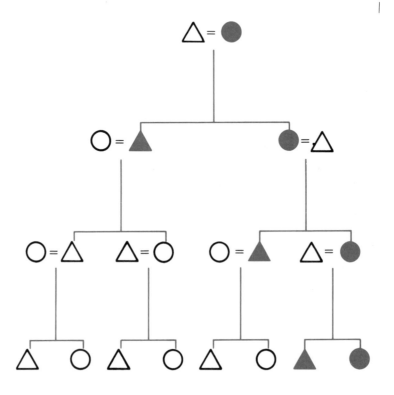

Figure 11.2 *Membership in a matrilineal descent group. In a society with matrilineal descent groups, membership in the group is defined by links through the mother. Sons and daughters are members of their mother's descent group, as are the children of daughters, but* not *the children of sons.*

rilineal societies tend to be less stable than in other kinds of systems. As we saw among the Nayar of India, it is possible for a matrilineally organized group to do away with the presence of husbands and fathers altogether, as long as there are brothers who assume responsibilities. It is important to remember that although women usually have higher status in societies where there is a matrilineal reckoning of descent, matrilineality is not the same as matriarchy. With a few possible exceptions (Wallace 1970), the most important resources and highest political positions are in the control of males, although the male with the most power and control in matrilineal societies is not the husband/father but the brother/uncle. The role of the mother's brother is an important or special one even in patrilineal societies, but in matrilineal societies it is particularly important. The mother's brother is a figure of authority and respect, and it is the children of a man's sister rather than his own who are his heirs and successors.

In a matrilineal society, the relationship between a man and his son is likely to be affectionate and loving because it is free of the problems of authority and control that exist between fathers and sons in a patrilineal society. A man may feel emotionally close to his sons, but he is committed by the matrilineal kinship ideology to pass on his knowledge, property, offices, and so on to the sons of his sister. With these individuals (his "nephews") he may have less friendly relations or even conflicts, as they are subject to his control. Thus, in a matrilineal system a man's loyalties are split between his own sons and the sons of his sister; in a patrilineal system, this tension does not occur as part of the kinship structure.

The Hopi, a Pueblo group in the American Southwest, are a matrilineal society. The matrilineage is conceived of as timeless, stretching backward to the beginnings of the Hopi people and continuing into the future. Both male and female members of the lineage consider their mother's house their home, though men move out to reside with their wives after marriage. They return to this home for many ritual and ceremonial occasions, however, and also in the case of separation or divorce. The relationship of a man with his father's lineage and household is affectionate, involving some economic and ritual obligations but little direct cooperation or authority.

In addition to lineages, the Hopi also have matrilineal clans that extend over many different villages. A Hopi must not marry within his own clan, or the clan of his father or his mother's father. Marriage thus results in a wide range of relatives in addition to those an individual acquires through birth through the clan he (and his mother) belongs to. A Hopi has obligations to the clan of the father as well as to that of the mother and also to the clans of the person designated as the ceremonial father. Kinship terms are extended to all these individuals, leading to a vast number of potential sibling relationships and a lateral integration of a great number of separate lineages and clans. This extension of Hopi kinship relates a Hopi in some way to almost everyone in his/her village, in other villages, and even to individuals in other Pueblo groups who have similar clans. Whereas the lineage group is of particular importance to women, these larger clan groups are the arena of male activities. Here men play important political and religious roles, in contrast to the marginal positions they have in domestic life. The Hopi also extend kinship ideology to the world of nature. The sun is called "father," the earth and corn are called "mother."

DOUBLE DESCENT: THE YAKO OF NIGERIA*

When descent is traced through a combination of matrilineal and patrilineal principles, a system of **double descent** exists. In societies with double descent systems, the individual belongs both to the patrilineal group of the father and the matrilineal group of the mother. Such societies are relatively rare, about 5 percent of the world's known cultures. In systems of double descent, matrilineal and patrilineal descent both operate as principles of affiliation, but the descent groups formed by these rules tend to operate in different areas of life.

The Yako of Nigeria are a society with a system of double descent. The Yako have full development of both patrilineal and matrilineal corporate kin groups. Cooperation in daily domestic life and continuous association is strongest among a group of patrilineally related kinsmen who live with or near each other. These men jointly control and farm plots of land, and membership in the patriclan is the source of rights over basic economic resources—farmland and forest products. Patriclan obligations include providing food at funerals; inheritance of membership in the men's associations and the right to fruit trees are also transmitted in the male line. The arbitration of disputes is in the hands of senior patriclan members, and cooperation in ritual as well as succession to some religious offices are also derived from clan membership.

Matrilineal bonds and clan membership are also important in Yako society, despite the fact that matriclan members do not live near each other and do not cooperate as a group in everyday activities. The rights and duties of matrilineal kinship are different. Practical assistance to matrilineal kin, the rights and obligations of the mother's brother and his sister's sons, and the authority of the priest of a matrilineal clan are based on mystical ideas regarding the perpetuation and tranquillity of the Yako world. The Yako believe that the fertility of crops and beasts, as well as that of humans, and peace between individuals and within the community as a whole are associated with and passed on through women. Life comes from the mother; it is by a wife that children are produced. The children of one mother are bound to mutual support and peaceful relations. The matrilineage is thus held together by mystical bonds of common fertility, and anger and violence between its members are considered sinful. These sentiments are expressed and reinforced in the cult of the matriclan spirits, whose priests are ritually given the qualities of women.

*Daryll Forde, "Double Descent Among the Yako," in *African Systems of Kinship and Marriage*, ed., by A. R. Radcliffe-Brown and Daryll Forde, pp. 285–332. London: Oxford University Press, 1967 (orig. 1950).

Despite their isolation from each other by the rule of patrilocal residence, matriclan relatives have specific mutual obligations. Rights in the transfer of accumulated wealth, as opposed to basic economic resources, belong to the matrilineal kinship group. It is the members of a matriclan that supervise a funeral and arrange for the disposal of the dead person's property. All currency and livestock customarily pass to matrilineal relatives, who also receive the greater share of tools, weapons, and household goods. The movable property of women passes to their daughters. Matriclans also have the responsibility for the debts of their kin, for making loans to each other at reasonable rates, and for providing part of the bridewealth transferred at the marriage of a sister's son. Thus, for the Yako, paternity and maternity are both important in descent; each contains inherently different qualities from which flow the rights, obligations, and benefits, both practical and spiritual, by which individuals are bound to each other and through which the continuity of the society is ensured.

Those phenomena in nature, such as plant and animal species that serve as clan names are also referred to by kinship terminology, such as "mother" or "mother's brother." (Eggan 1950).

A variety of different explanations have been given by anthropologists in their attempts to understand the evolution of unilineal descent groups. Many of these explanations fail to take into account the diversity of the systems that have been lumped together as unilineal. The contemporary anthropological approach is not so much to ask "What kind of kinship system exists in a particular society?" but rather to ask "What are the common interests that give people a reason for joining together and defining themselves as a collective entity justified by reference to kin ties?" These interests *may* be economic, such as land or cattle or gardens; they may also be political or religious, or involve warfare within the society or with other societies. As older theories of kinship lose their explanatory power under the weight of new data, rethinking kinship has become an important new focus in anthropology.

Bilateral Descent

In systems of bilateral descent, an individual is considered to be related equally to other kin through both the mother's and the father's side, although in our own society, which is bilateral, the patrilineal principle is dominant in the handing down of family names. In a unilineal kinship system, an individual is affiliated with a large number of lineally extended relations through time, but only on one side of the family. A bilateral group extends along lines established by links through both males and females, but incorporates only relatively close biological relatives.

In bilateral (or cognatic) systems of descent, there are no clear descent groups formed in the way described for unilineal systems. The kin network formed by a bilateral reckoning of descent is called a **kindred.** With the exception of brothers and sisters, every individual's kindred is different from every other individual's. Since kindreds are actually overlapping categories of kin (which is why the term kin network rather than group is used), they cannot be the basis for the formation of corporate groups. This is the major functional weakness of the kindred as a cooperative, kin-based collectivity. Since it is not a group, but rather an ego-centered network, it cannot own land or have continuity over time. On the other hand, bilateral systems have great flexibility. An individual can mobilize a number of relatives from either the father's or the mother's side (or both), depending on the particular enterprise being undertaken. Bilateral kinship systems appear to be particularly adaptive in societies where mobility and independence are important, and predominate among hunters and gatherers and in modern industrial societies.

THE CLASSIFICATION OF KIN

In all societies, kin are referred to by special terms. The total system of kinship terms and the rules for using these terms make up a kinship classification system. An understanding of these systems is more than an interesting anthropological game: The ways in which kin are classified are associated with the roles they play in society. If, for example, an individual (called **Ego**) refers to his father and his father's brothers by the same term, the roles he plays in relation to these kin will tend to be generally similar. By the same token, if Ego's father and father's brothers are referred to by different terms, it is expected that these males will be in a somewhat different relationship to Ego. Kinship classification systems not only structure perception of the social universe; they also

regulate behavior. As with other cultural norms, kinship has both an idea and a real component. Not all individuals act according to cultural norms, and special circumstances as well as individual personality differences modify the actual relationship individuals have with their kin.

No kinship classification system has a different term of reference for each position in the kinship structure. This would require far too many terms to remember. In every kinship terminology, therefore, some relatives are classed together—that is, referred to by the same kinship term. In our own terminology, we use the term "aunt" to refer to both our father's and our mother's sisters, as well as women who marry the brother of either father or mother. In other societies, these women may be referred to by different terms. In our kinship terminology we lump together our mother's sister and our father's sister, as well as the wives of our "uncles," because their roles in relation to Ego are generally similar. In societies where the mother's sister and the father's sister have very different rights and obligations with respect to Ego, they will be distinguished in the kinship terminology.

Principles for Classifying Kin

Societies differ in the categories of relatives they distinguish and in the principles by which kin are classified. Some of the most important principles used to separate and lump together different categories of kin are the following:

1. *Generation.* In English, the kinship terms that refer to generation are those such as "father," "uncle," "aunt." These terms refer to relatives who belong to the parental generation. "Grandfather" and "grand-

mother" are in the generation before that. "Brother" and "sister" refer to individuals in Ego's generation; and "son," "daughter," "niece" and "nephew" are in the generation below Ego.

2. *Relative age.* This criterion for classifying kin is not used in the English kinship terminology, although it is used in many other kinship systems. In North India, Ego uses different terms to refer to older brother's wife and younger brother's wife. These differences reflect the important differences in behavior that exist between Ego and these two kinds of kin. An Indian woman is expected to avoid or act with great reserve toward her husband's older brother (referred to as jait), but is allowed great freedom, affection and even sexual joking with her husband's younger brother (referred to as deva).

3. *Lineality vs. collaterality.* Lineal kin are related in a single line, such as grandfather-father-son. **Collateral kin** are related through a linking relative. An example of a collateral relation is that between Ego and father's brother or sister or mother's brother or sister. In many societies, collaterality is not distinguished in the kinship terminology. Ego refers to the father and the father's brothers as "father." The mother and her sisters may similarly be referred to as "mother." In these systems, parallel cousins may also be referred to by the same terms as those for brother and sister.

4. *Sex.* In English, some of our kinship terms differentiate by sex; for example, "aunt" and "uncle," "brother" and "sister." The term "cousin," how-

ever, does not distinguish the sex of the relative.

5. *Consanguineal vs. affinal kin.* Some people related to Ego by blood (consanguinity) are distinguished from similar relationships by marriage. In our own society, we have "daughter" and "daughter-in-law," "sister" and "sister-in-law," and so forth. We do not, however, distinguish between a male of our father's generation (one ascending) in terms of blood or marriage tie. An "uncle" refers to both the brother of our father and mother, and also a man who marries the sister of either parent.

6. *Sex of linking relative.* Where collaterality is important, the sex of the linking relative may be distinguished in the kinship terminology. For example, parallel cousins are distinguished from cross cousins. Distinguishing between these types of cousins is important in societies where Ego may not marry a parallel cousin but may be allowed, or even obliged, to marry a cross cousin.

7. *Side of the family.* This basis of classification, called **bifurcation,** means that the kinship terms used for the mother's side of the family are different from those used for the father's side of the family. In societies with this principle, the mother's brother would be referred to differently from the father's brother.

Types of Kinship Terminologies

Systems of kinship terminology reflect the kinds of kin groups that are most important in a society. Anthropologists have identified six different systems of kinship terminology: Hawaiian, Eskimo, Iroquois, Omaha, Crow, and Sudanese.

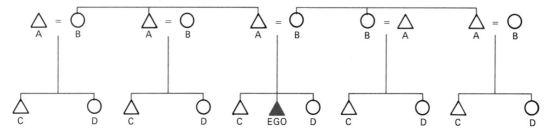

Figure 11.3 *Hawaiian terminology. Symbols with the same letters underneath are referred to in the same way by Ego.*

Hawaiian. As its name suggests, this system is found in Polynesia. It is relatively simple in that it uses the least number of kinship terms. The Hawaiian system emphasizes the distinctions between generations and reflects the relative equality between the mother and the father's side of the family in relation to Ego. All relatives of the same generation and sex are referred to by the same kinship term—for example, "father," "father's brother," and "mother's brother." Male and female kin in Ego's generation are distinguished in the terminology, but the terms for sister and brother are the same as those for the children of one's parents' siblings (Figure 11.3). This system correlated with ambilineality and ambilocality, which means that an individual may choose which descent group he or she wishes to belong to and will live with after marriage. By using the same terms for parents and their siblings, a closeness is established with a large number of relatives in the ascending generation, allowing a wide choice for Ego in deciding which group to affiliate and live with.

Eskimo. The Eskimo terminology is correlated with bilateral descent. It is found among hunting and gathering peoples and also in our own society. The Eskimo system emphasizes the unit of the nuclear family by using terms for its members (mother, father, sister, brother, daughter, son) that are not used for any other kin. Outside the nuclear family, many kinds of relatives that are distinguished in other systems are lumped together. We have already given the examples of aunt and uncle. Similarly, all children of our kin in the parental generation are called "cousin," no matter what their sex or who the linking relative is. The Eskimo system singles out the biologically closest group of

Figure 11.4 *Eskimo terminology.*

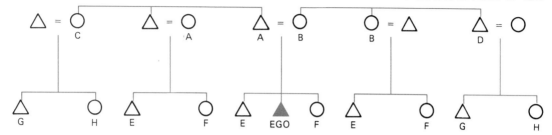

Figure 11.5 *Iroquois terminology.*

relations (the nuclear family) and treats more distant kin more or less equally (Figure 11.4).

Iroquois. The Iroquois system is associated with matrilineal or double descent and emphasizes the importance of unilineal descent groups. In this system the same term is used for mother and mother's sister, and a common term also applies to father and father's brother. Parallel cousins are referred to by the same terms as those for brother and sister. Father's sister and mother's brother are distinguished from other kin, as are the children of father's sister and mother's brother (Ego's cross cousins) (Figure 11.5).

Omaha. The Omaha system is found among patrilineal peoples, including the native American group of that name. In this system, the same term is used for father and father's brother and for mother and mother's sister. Parallel cousins are

equated with siblings, but cross cousins are referred to by a separate term. A man refers to his brother's children by the same terms he applies to his own children, but he refers to his sister's children by different terms. These terms are extended to all relations who are classified as Ego's brothers and sisters (Figure 11.6). In this system there is a merging of generations on the mother's side. All men who are members of Ego's mother's patrilineage will be referred to as "mother's brother" no matter what their age or generational relationship to Ego. Thus, the term applied to mother's brother is also applied to the son of mother's brother. This generational merging is not applied to relations on the father's side. Although father and his brothers are referred to by the same term, this does not extend to the descending generation. The differences in terminology as applied to the father's patrilineal and the mother's patrilineal group reflect the different position of Ego in relation to these kin. Generational differences are im-

Figure 11.6 *Omaha terminology.*

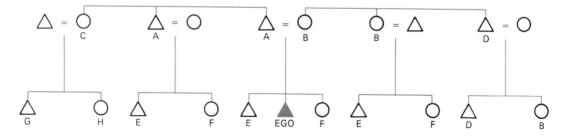

portant on the father's side because members of the ascending generation are likely to have some authority over Ego (as his father does), and be treated differently than patrilineage members of Ego's own generation. Since the mother's patrilineage is relatively unimportant to Ego in this system, this is reflected in lumping them all together in the terminology.

Crow. The Crow system, named for the Crow Indians of North America, is the matrilineal equivalent of the Omaha system. This means that the relations on the male side (Ego's father's matrilineage) will be lumped together, while generational differences will be recognized in the mother's matrilineal group (Figure 11.7). In both the Omaha and Crow systems, the overriding importance of unilineality leads to the subordination of other principles of classifying kin, such as relative age or generation.

Sudanese. The most extremely descriptive terminological systems are sometimes called Sudanese systems, after the groups in Africa, primarily Ethiopia, that use this system. The terminological types included here use different terms for practically every relative—siblings, paternal parallel cousins, maternal parallel cousins, paternal cross cousins, and maternal cross cousins. Ego refers to his/her parents by distinct terms and uses separate terms for father's brother, father's sister, mother's sister, and mother's brother (Figure 11.8). Although most groups using this system tend to be patrilineal, there is also evidence of ambilineality. This distinguishes these kinship systems from other patrilineal systems described here, and may account for this distinctive and relatively rare type of terminology.

The great variety in kinship terminologies calls attention to the fact with which we began this chapter: Kinship systems reflect social relationships and are not based simply on biological relations between people. Kinship classification systems are part of the totality of a kinship system. Each of the types of classification described above emphasizes the most important kinship groupings and relationships in the societies in which they are found. Thus, the Eskimo system emphasizes the importance of the nuclear family, setting it apart from the more distant relations on the maternal

Figure 11.7 *Crow terminology.*

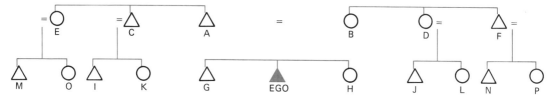

Figure 11.8 *Sudanese terminology.*

and paternal side. The Iroquois, Omaha, and Crow systems, found in unilineal societies, emphasize the importance of lineage and clan. In the Hawaiian system, the relative simplicity of terms leaves the way open for flexibility in choosing one's descent group. At the other extreme, the Sudanese system, with its highly descriptive terminology, may in fact have the same function. In making sense out of kinship, including our own system, anthropologists attempt to understand the relationship between terminologies, rules of descent, and the formation of groups based on kinship, and the particular ecological, economic, and political conditions under which different kinship systems emerge.

NONKIN FORMS OF ASSOCIATION

Although kinship is of great importance in structuring social relations and as a basis for the formation of groups in all societies, other principles of association are also important. In this section, we will look at nonkin groups and relationships, including the roles such associations play in traditional and changing societies.

Groups Based on Age

All societies recognize at least three social categories based on age: children, adults,

and the aged. Each category has its own role, and in some societies, groups based on age are extremely important. Age as a basis of social groups reaches its most elaborate development among certain tribes in Africa. Most of these age-based groups are made up of males and have military and political functions, such as among the Karimojong, the Masai, and the Nandi of East Africa. A society for which age is the most important principle of social organization are the Nyakyusa, who have been studied by Monica Wilson (1963).

Associations Based on Sex

Sex—that is, being male or female—provides an obvious basis for solidarity. In some societies sex is a very important principle upon which associations are formed. Most anthropological attention has been paid to male associations, probably because more societies have such groups than have comparable ones for females. Age grading, for example, is largely a male phenomenon, with women apparently tacked on through marriage.

In Melanesia, Australia, and among some South American Indian groups, men's associations and cults are prominent in social and religious life. Adolescent boys are initiated into the men's cult and thereafter spend most of their lives in the men's house, only visiting their wives, who live with the children in their own huts in the village. These men's cults are closed to women and surrounded by great secrecy.

AGE VILLAGES AMONG THE NYAKYUSA*

The Nyakyusa are cattle owners and cultivators living in the Great Rift Valley at the north end of Lake Nyasa in southeastern Africa. Before the coming of the Europeans in the late nineteenth century, they had no centralized political authority, and were divided up into a number of small, independent chiefdoms. The Nyakyusa are patrilineal and patrilocal. Although the patrilineage is important as a group which has a common interest in cattle, patrilineal kinsmen do not live together. Rather, the Nyakyusa village consists of a group of age mates with their wives and young children. It is the formation of age villages that distinguishes the Nyakyusa from other culturally similar African groups who also have age-based forms of organization.

The age village starts when a number of boys about 10 years old build huts together at the edge of their fathers' village. The boys go to live in their new huts, sleeping and spending their spare time in them as well. They continue to eat in their mothers' huts. A group of boys will eat together, taking turns visiting the mother of each member of the "gang." For the Nyakyusa, eating with one's age mates is highly valued, and a boy who often comes home to eat by himself will be severely scolded. The boys' village starts out small, with perhaps a dozen members, but it grows larger as young boys from the fathers' village or other villages in the neighborhood become old enough to join it. When the original members are about 15 years old, the village is closed to any more 10-year-olds, who will then form a new village on their own. The boys in an age village live together throughout their lives. When they marry, they bring their wives to the village. As their sons grow up, they form new villages. Daughters may move out if they marry men in other villages, but since they frequently marry one of their father's age mates, they may remain within the village in which they were born.

Once in each generation there is a great ritual at which the elders hand over administrative power and military leadership to the younger generation. At this time, land is also transferred from the village of the fathers to the village of the sons. One of the members of the sons' village is appointed headman by the retiring chief and the headmen of the villages of his generation. At any one time, then, Nyakyusa social organization includes three different age grades: the old men, who are retired from administra-

*Monica Wilson. *Good Company: A Study of Nyakyusa Villagers.* Boston, Beacon Press (1963).

tion and military duties; the ruling generation, which is responsible for administration and defense; and the young men and boys, who have not yet "come out" but who may be called upon to fight.

The age village is the group around which the good life is organized for the Nyakyusa. The good life consists of the enjoyment of the company of equals. A man learns law, logic, and manners in the company of his peers, and a social isolate is likely to be accused of witchcraft or think himself betwitched. Because kinsmen of different generations cannot communicate easily due to the respect juniors must show for their elders, it is the age village, not the kin group, that is the most important center of sociability. Nor can the nuclear family be the center of the good life: women are fit for lovemaking, not for friendship.

This unusual form of social organization raises some questions about its origin and functions. The Nyakyusa explanation is that age village organization inhibits incest between father-in-law and daughter-in-law. "Once, they say, a certain chief looked upon his son's wife and saw that she was beautiful and said, 'she is fit to be a queen,' and took her; and men thought that was very bad and said henceforth fathers-in-law should never see their daughters-in-law lest they be tempted to commit incest with them. and so fathers and sons live in different villages". Furthermore, the Nyakyusa believe that sex activities of parents should be kept separate from children. This is a common belief in many societies, including our own, and is particularly prominent among East African peoples (see the description of Kaguru initiation rites in Chapter 6). The Nyakyusa have reached a solution to these two problems that seems quite reasonable to them, although it represents a rare case from a cross-cultural perspective.

Wilson suggests that the regulation of sex may indeed play a role in Nyakyusa social organization. The Nyakyusa do not have male initiation rites or any formal recognition of male adulthood. Therefore, any young man past puberty is a potential mate for a woman of his own age. Since the Nyakyusa are polygynous, a grown son may be a potential lover of his father's junior wives. Furthermore, the Nyakyusa, who practice the levirate, permit a son to inherit his father's wives when his father dies (with the exception of his own biological mother). These cultural patterns give some basis to the jealous fears fathers have of their sons in this society, a source of potential disruption for which age villages are a solution.

The men's house itself is usually the most imposing structure in the village, and in or near it are kept the sacred musical instruments and paraphernalia of the cult. The musical instruments, which are often flutelike (shaped like the male genitals) are the symbolic expressions of male dominance and male solidarity in opposition to women. Often, and especially in Australia, these cults are associated with circumcision rites for newly initiated boys, after which they are considered men and introduced to the secrets of the cult. Frequently associated with these cults is a mythology of how the cults came into being, and an "explanation" of why women are not allowed in them. These myths may also "explain" why women are socially inferior to men and why men and women have different roles in society.

Some social scientists give psychological interpretations of these cults. They are seen as unconscious defenses against the males' recognition of their own vulnerability in relation to women. Men, after all, are born of women and nurtured by them; only women have the creative power of childbirth. Many of the rituals associated with men's cults appear to be reenactments of childbirth. The very secrecy with which men's cults are surrounded, the phallic shape of the musical instruments, and the associated mythology seem to make sense as an expression of the ambivalence men have toward women, who give them life and from whom they must ultimately break away if they are to become truly men. (Murphy 1974; Bettelheim 1962)

A men's house in Ponape, Micronesia. In societies with men's cults the men's house is often the most imposing structure in the village. (Raymond Kennedy)

The solidarity of women in these societies is not formalized in cults or associations, but is based on the actual cooperation of domestic life and strong interpersonal bonds between female kin.

In many native American societies, associations based on sex were also prominent. A few of these associations were exclusively for women, and their activities involved the performance of rituals to make the corn grow and to increase the buffalo herds. Most of the clubs were for men, however, although they had purposes and social functions different from those of the men's cults described above. Typical were the military associations among the Crow and Cheyenne. For the individual, the association was like a social club; many of its activities were recreational. These societies fostered the ideal of the brave warrior and membership was limited to those of outstanding military achievement. Exceptionally brave men were chosen as officers and were allowed to wear special ornaments and dress as a sign of their bravery. Although the activities of these societies provided public entertainment, they also had more important functions. At the time of the communal buffalo hunts, when bands gathered together, the military societies acted as police, keeping order and punishing those who broke the law (Lowie 1963).

In West Africa, many different kinds of associations with important social functions existed for both males and females. Two of the most well documented of these societies are the Poro and the Sande, which are the male and female associations among the Kpelle of Liberia. Both societies had the initiation of the young as one of their primary purposes, but had many other functions as well. The Poro (male) society had important political functions beyond the local community, and extends even today into national politics. Although

Sande power was more limited, there was in the past a female head of the entire tribal Sande. In Sierra Leone, where the Sande organization includes over 90 percent of rural women, men are discouraged from marrying uninitiated women. The Sande organization has power through its transformation of girls into marriageable women. Madam Yoko, a woman who became very powerful in Sierra Leone in the late nineteenth century, effectively utilized her role within the Sande organization to build the political network on which her leadership was based. Sande dancers achieve great prestige, and Madame Yoko was an outstanding dancer. She also sponsored the initiation of many girls into Sande and arranged marriages for them in ways that would advance her own political career. Even today, women in Africa use the Sande organization to establish alliances and further their political careers (Hoffer 1974).

In relatively small and technologically primitive societies, associations such as we have been describing appear to be organized for recreation and the distinction of rank. They also may have religious functions. In some cases, these societies are for healing, and only individuals who have recovered from serious illness can become members and are then called upon to practice their arts on others. In tribal societies, associations that go beyond kinship as a basis for membership have important political functions. Among the Plains Indians, they keep the peace during communal hunts, and also provide entertainment. In other cases they resolve disputes, protect members against both supernatural and human harm, and integrate different segments of a tribe beyond the local level. The presence of societies in West Africa, for example, corresponds with an absence of age-group organizations; where one is

False-face dancers : two are doorkeepers

A drawing by Jesse Cornplanter of the False Face Society among the Iroquois. Such associations had important religious and political functions among many native American peoples and served as mechanisms of pan-tribal integration. (Courtesy of Museum of the American Indian Heye Foundation)

Urbanization and Voluntary Associations

absent, the other fulfills similar political and social functions. Many of these associations are based on ascribed statuses such as sex or age, but others are voluntary, and still others require certain achievements for membership. It is under conditions of modernization and urbanization that voluntary associations increase dramatically and play important roles in social change.

With urbanization, a great variety of social groups based on voluntary membership develop. These groups are generally called **voluntary associations.** Voluntary associations are adaptive in helping people organize to achieve their goals in complex and changing societies, and especially in helping migrants make the transition from traditional, rural-based society to a modern, urban, industrial life style. Although not all voluntary associations formed in newly urbanized societies have goals that are directly economic or political, these associations frequently serve as vehicles through which such goals can be achieved.

Voluntary associations that emerge among newly urbanized populations may serve as mutual aid societies, lending money to members, providing scholarships for students, arranging funerals, and taking care of marriage arrangements for urban migrants. Some of these voluntary associations develop along kinship or tribal lines that were relevant in the traditional culture, but others, such as labor unions, are based on relationships deriving from new economic contexts and have no parallel in traditional rural society. Voluntary associations help migrants adjust to city living, and provide the basis for political organization through which the interests of different groups in newly emergent states can be served. Such associations are also training grounds for new skills that are useful in industrial and urban contexts, such as electing officials, practice in speaking before a group, and use of a language other than one's native tongue. Because these associations often award prestige based on modern rather than traditional role achievements, they ease the transition from traditional to modern identities.

Voluntary associations can also help members move beyond narrow local identities based on kinship, village, caste, and tribe to wider identifications more relevant in modern nation-states, such as those of citizen or worker. Some urban voluntary associations are based on traditional statuses. These include tribal and regional associations found in West Africa, caste associations in India, and the kinship-based associations found among the Batak peoples who have migrated to cities in Indonesia. These associations have a dual function, however. On the one hand, they provide continuity with traditional sources of identity and culture; on the other, they

also socialize their members into city ways, serving as a link between traditional and modern structures.

During my fieldwork in India, I studied a voluntary association in Bombay formed by women who had originally come from villages and small towns in northern India. These women were drawn together by their common language and culture, which was distinct from that of the majority ethnic group in Bombay. They belonged to the same category of high castes and were upper-middle class; their husbands were professionals and businessmen. The women began their group about twenty years ago, meeting once a week mainly for the purpose of holding religious ceremonies and participating in the devotional singing that is an important feature of contemporary Hinduism. In their ritual activity they attempted to re-create the social and religious life in their native region. Although this is the reason they organized, their association now has other purposes and functions as well. Through the informal exchange of gossip in the group, new patterns of behavior are introduced, discussed, evaluated, and diffused. For example, if a woman's son marries a Westerner, the group will discuss this and its implications for their own lives. In this way, the association provides a kind of emotional support system that helps the women adjust to change. Through informal discussion, new fashions and new ideas are introduced and slowly become part of an upper-middle-class urban life style.

Because high-caste Indian women are not encouraged to work, women's associations play a very important role in widening their cultural horizons and their social circle within the appropriate caste, ethnic, and class groups to which they belong. Women's groups in urban India tend to be age-graded; through participation in such a group, a young daughter-in-law can escape, at least temporarily, from the supervision of her mother-in-law and find solidarity with other women of her own age. For older women whose sons and daughters are ready to be married, these associations provide access to a network among whom marriages can be arranged with some confidence.

Voluntary associations are an important part of the adaptive strategies of urban migrants because they can be based on an almost infinite number of interests and serve a wide range of purposes. In West Africa, for example, urban women's associations are much more directly concerned with political goals and economic interests, reflecting the fact that their membership is made up of working women. The importance of these associations reflects the important economic and political roles women in West Africa traditionally play. The importance of voluntary associations in the nations of Asia, Africa, and Latin America is paralleled by the importance of similar associations among immigrant groups in the urban centers of the United States.

Informal Association in Complex Societies: Social Networks

A **social network** refers to a set of both direct and indirect links between an individual, who is at the center of a network, and other people. Unlike a social group, such as the voluntary associations discussed above, a social network is really a framework for understanding social relationships imposed by the outsider. Networks are a useful way to study social organization in cities and in complex societies, where social organization consists less of closed, kin-based, corporate groups, and includes more links between individual actors who share only a part of their lives with a great many other individuals in a number of different situations.

One of the important points of comparison among networks is the degree of connectedness or density of the network. In a highly connected or dense network, the individuals with whom Ego is connected are also connected to one another. In a low-density or dispersed network, Ego is connected to other people who do not know one another (see Figure 11.9). Comparison of network density and structure has been used to explain a number of different kinds of social behavior—for example, communication of gossip, diffusion of norms, and pressures for social control. One of the earliest uses of social networks was in the study of urban families in England (Bott 1957). Among other things, **network analysis** showed that although many urban families are not contained within organized groups (like a corporate kin group, for example), they do have many external relationships with individuals and institutions who are not, however, linked. Network analysis opens up a new perspective on the urban family; it allows us to see that the urban family is not necessarily isolated, as is often claimed, but rather is involved in a more or less dispersed network of social relations without which it could not survive.

Not all the individuals with whom Ego is connected have the same relationship to him/her. In some of the relationships, Ego will be related to an individual in a number of ways—friend, kin, neighbor, co-worker. In other relationships, Ego may be linked to an individual in one role only, say as a co-worker. Furthermore, Ego uses different parts of his/her network depending on the situation. Some individuals may be mobilized when it comes to finding a job,

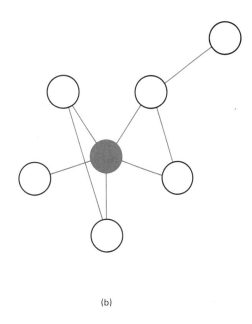

Figure 11.9 *A comparison of a highly connected network (a) and a dispersed network (b).*

others in times of personal crisis, still others in building up a power base.

As people in traditional societies move out of their relatively self-contained communities of kinship and local groups and expand their social ties in new situations, new methods of anthropological analysis become appropriate. Network analysis is one of these methods. Its increasing use is an example of the ways in which anthropology is adapting to social change in the contemporary world.

SUMMARY

1. Kinship systems are cultural creations that define and organize relatives by blood and marriage. A kinship system includes the kinds of groups based on kinship and the system of terms used to classify different kin.

2. The functions of kinship systems are to provide continuity between generations and to define a group of people who may depend on one another for mutual aid.

3. In traditional societies, kinship is the most important basis of social organization. This contrasts with industrial states, in which principles of social organization, such as citizenship, social class, and common interests, become more important than kinship.

4. In many societies, descent is important in the formation of corporate social groups. In societies with a unilineal rule of descent, descent group membership is based on either the male or female line. Unilineal systems are found among pastoral and horticultural societies.

5. A lineage is a group of kin whose members can actually trace their descent through a common ancestor. A clan is a group whose members believe they have a common ancestor but cannot trace the relationship genealogically. Lineages tend to have domestic functions, clans to have political and religious functions. Both lineages and clans are important in regulating marriage.

6. In patrilineal systems, a man's children belong to his lineage, as do the children of his sons but not of his daughters. Husbands have control over wives, and children and marriage are surrounded by strong sanctions. The Nuer and the Rajputs of India are patrilineal.

7. In matrilineal systems, a woman's children belong to her lineage, not that of their father. The mother's brother has authority over his sister's children, and relations between husband and wife are more fragile than in patrilineal societies. Matrilineal systems contain a contradiction in that men are reluctant to give up control over their sons to the lineage of their wives. The Hopi and the Nayar are matrilineal societies.

8. Patrilineality grows out of patrilocality, which is based on the common economic interests of brothers. Matrilineality grows out of matrilocality, which arises under special circum-

stances; when these conditions disappear, the kinship system tends to change.

9. In systems of double descent, Ego belongs to both the patrilineage of the father and the patrilineage of the mother. Each group functions in different social contexts. The Yako of Nigeria have a system of double descent.

10. In bilateral systems, Ego is equally related to mother's and father's kin. A bilateral rule of descent results in the formation of kindreds, which are ego-centered kinship networks, rather than a permanent group of kin. Bilateral kinships is found predominantly among foragers and in modern industrialized states.

11. Kinship terminology lumps together and distinguishes relatives according to various principles such as generation, relative age, lineality or collaterality, sex, consanguinity or affinity, bifurcation and sex of the linking relative. Different societies may use all or some of these principles in classifying kin.

12. The six types of kinship classification systems defined by anthropologists are the Hawaiian, Eskimo, Iroquois, Omaha, Crow, and Sudanese. Each reflects the particular kinship group that is most important in the society.

13. Although kinship groups dominate in most structurally simpler societies, other forms of association are also found. Some of the nonkin groups in tribal societies are based on age. One example is the age villages found among the Nyakyusa of East Africa.

14. Groups based on sex may also be important. In many parts of Melanesia and South America, men spend most

of their time in association with other men, and live in a special men's house. In other societies, notably those of West Africa, men's and women's associations are also important in religious, political, and social life.

15. In complex societies and those undergoing social change, kinship groups often become weaker and voluntary associations, based on economic and political interests, become more important, though kinship relationships are still relevant.

16. Anthropologists have developed a method called network analysis to study some of the informal social relationships that become increasingly important in contemporary societies. In network analysis, the links between Ego and other individuals, some of whom are in contact with one another, are examined.

SUGGESTED READINGS

Bohannan, P., and Middleton, J., eds.
1968   *Kinship and Social Organization.* Garden City, N.Y.: The Natural History Press. Classic articles on kinship and kinship terminology.

Little, Kenneth
1965   *West African Urbanization: A Study of Voluntary Associations in Social Change.* London: Cambridge University Press. The study of voluntary associations and their functions in contemporary Africa.

Schusky, E. L.
1965   *Manual for Kinship Analysis.* New York: Holt, Rinehart and Winston. An introduction to the basics of kinship, including exercises for the student in analyzing kinship terminology.

Schneider, David M.
1968   *American Kinship: A Cultural Account.* Englewood Cliffs, N.J.: Prentice-Hall. A look at our kinship and terminology in the United States and what it suggests about our culture.

Schneider, David M., and Gough, Kathleen, eds.
1961   *Matrilineal Kinship.* Berkeley: University of California Press. An examination of a variety of matrilineal systems and how matrilineality may be related to subsistence, productivity, and political organization.

Wilson, Monica
1963   *Good Company: A Study of Nyakyusa Age-Villages.* Boston: Beacon Press (orig. 1951). An interesting study of an African society with an unusual form of social organization.

United Nations

12
Political Systems
and Social Control

Regulating Human Behavior
Political Organization
Law
Kinds of Political Organization
Band Level Societies
Political Integration
Leadership
Social Control
Conflict Resolution
Tribal Societies
Political Integration
Leadership
The Tribal Big Man
Social Control and Conflict Resolution
War in Tribal Societies: The Yanomamo
Chiefdoms
The Regulation of Behavior and Conflict Resolution
State Societies
Social Stratification
Centralized Government
The Monopoly of Force
The Rise of State Societies
Summary
Suggested Readings

248

All human societies must coordinate and regulate the behavior of their members; all need mechanisms for making and enforcing decisions. In this chapter we will look at two ways in which societies organize and regulate themselves. One is **political organization,** the patterned ways in which legitimate power, or authority, is used to coordinate and regulate behavior. The other is law. In this chapter we will look at the different kinds of political organization found at different levels of social complexity: band societies, tribals societies, chiefdoms and states.

REGULATING HUMAN BEHAVIOR

Political Organization

In most societies, the authority to make decisions that affect the public interest is placed is some part of the social system, such as kinship, economics, or religion. Group leaders can rule by virtue of their positions as heads of families, lineages, or clans. In other cases, rulers base their claim on divine ancestry. In some societies, the coordination and regulation of behavior may be in the hands of a religious practitioner. If supernatural intervention is an important part of the decision-making process—where to hunt, when to move camp, finding a thief—those who have access to supernatural power will have important political roles in society. If political authority is based on the distribution of goods and services, as it frequently is, leadership will be embedded in economic roles and modes of exchange.

Legitimate power, or authority, means power exercised with the approval of the community. In cases of the legitimate use of power, people obey because they expect that eventually they will benefit from the exercise of that power. We may not like to pay taxes, but we do recognize the right of our government to collect taxes and consider it one of the prices we have to pay for the benefits of government in general. The shared values and beliefs that legitimatize the distribution and uses of power in a particular society make up its **political ideology.** If power is not legitimate, it is coercive; people obey because they are afraid of some immediate, direct, and specific punishment. Although some political systems rest more on coercion than others, both coercion and political ideology play a role in maintaining order in a society.

Up until 1940, anthropologists were primarily interested in how political institutions—the structure of status roles through which legitimate power was exercised in a society—worked to maintain stability. More recently, they have turned their attention to **political processes,** the ways in which different groups and individuals mobilize support and use power to achieve a variety of public goals. These goals include changing the relationships between different groups in society—for example, the redistribution of material resources, or the right of access to political office. Another goal may be changing the relationship of the group to its environment, such as building a road or clearing public land. Political goals may also involve changing the relationship of the group to other groups, such as waging war or making peace, or gaining independence from a colonial power. The motivations behind these goals are many; although all political behavior affects the public interest, it is not always in the public interest. Groups and individuals may be motivated by self-interest, economic gain, or prestige; they may also be motivated by altruism and idealism.

The study of political processes focuses on political activities and events and the ways in which different groups compete with one another for control. Anthropologists look for sources of power outside formal political institutions. One is factions, informal systems of alliance within well-defined political units such as lineages or villages. Another is leadership, which may depend partly on political office, but may also depend on the manipulation of kinship networks, or wealth, in order to build a following. The study of political processes emphasizes how power may change hands in society, and how new kinds of political organization may develop.

Political processes are thus not just activities that support the social order, avoid or resolve conflicts, and promote the general welfare. The political goals of a group within a society may, in fact, be to promote conflict, change some of the basic aims of existing political institutions, or even destroy the existing social order. Groups or factions within a society may use illegal or informal means to gain their ends—terrorism, for example—but this does not make these activities any less political. On the other hand, conflict and violence are not *necessarily* destructive. In many societies, violence is a legitimate means of dealing with conflict, as in the case of blood feuds in tribal societies. Conflict may actually support the social order; competition for legitimate goals makes those goals seem worth fighting over. The violent conflict that may occur over succession to office does not destroy the power of the office being sought. The struggle itself emphasizes that the conflicting groups see the office as something worth struggling for. Thus, there is a difference between **rebellion,** the attempt of one group to reallocate resources *within* the existing po-litical structure, and **revolution,** an attempt to overthrow the existing form of political structure and put another type of political structure in its place.

Law

In no human society does life move along in peace and harmony at all times. Individuals do not always do what they are supposed or expected to do, and they frequently act in ways that disrupt the social order. For a society to function adequately, there must be some conformity among its members. An important— perhaps major—basis for conformity in most societies is the internalization or learning of norms and values. Most people comply with authority, and most societies do not rely on force to maintain order.

But what happens when people do not want to conform, or rather want to do things that do not follow the norms and values of their society? Every society has developed mechanisms to deal with this situation. Many of these mechanisms are informal; gossip and ridicule, for example, are important ways of regulating human conduct. Since most individuals value the esteem of others, the fear of being gossiped about or made fun of is a powerful way of ensuring conformity. Witchcraft accusations are another control mechanism. Anyone who stands out in society, or is malicious or has a nasty temper, may be accused of being a witch and suffer punishment. Just the fear of being accused exerts pressure on individuals to conform. Avoidance is another informal way of dealing with social deviants. In small societies, where activities are cooperative, an individual who is shunned by others is in a very bad way, both psychologically and economically. Even in our own society, avoidance is a powerful way to get people to conform. One of the strongest expressions of anger, and one often used by small children who have few resources at their command with which to control others, is to say "I'm not going to talk to you anymore."

Supernatural sanctions are also important in regulating human behavior. Sins are kinds of deviant behavior that are believed to call forth punishment by supernatural forces. In the Trobriand Islands, incest is a sin; an individual who engages in this behavior is punished by a divinely imposed skin affliction. Supernatural forces

The village court in Sierra Leone is administered by a tribunal of local leaders headed by the chief. The defendant (center with a shaved head) faces the tribunal on the charges of possessing stolen goods at the time of his arrest. The Chief's police officer (left, with white skull cap) acts as defender for the accused. In this case, the defendant was given three months hard labor and a fine. (United Nations)

who punish social deviants are found in every culture: there are ghosts, spirits, giants who eat little children—even a Santa Claus who does not give presents to children who do not behave.

But what of those who just will not conform? Every society has such people. What is to be done with them? This is where law comes in. In *The Law of Primitive Man* E. Adamson Hoebel (1974) defines **law** as "those social norms whose neglect or infraction is regularly met, in threat or in fact, by the application of force by an individual or group who have the socially recognized privilege of acting this way." In every society, some offenses are considered so disruptive that force or the threat of force will be applied. It may be applied by official representatives of the community, such as judges, courts, police, jails. It may also be done by individuals with community approval, such as where kin of a murdered man may be allowed, or even expected, to revenge him by killing someone from the murderer's kin group. The control of deviant behavior is therefore a major function of law in all societies.

Law also operates to resolve conflicts that would otherwise be disruptive to community life. In politically complex societies such as modern states, crimes against the state are differentiated from grievances individuals have against one another. In structurally simpler societies, disputes between individuals may be handled by the community in the interests of maintaining order. Conflicts between individuals may involve the whole community as judge, as in the Eskimo song duels, or a go-between may try to get the complainants to settle. In some societies, go-betweens have the authority to enforce their decisions; in others, they can only persuade the parties to resolve their differences peaceably. In still other cases, supernatural powers are called upon, for example in cases of trial by ordeal.

The anthropology of law, like political anthropology, has also redefined its emphasis in the last fifteen years. Now the focus is more on the informal and formal ways in which behavior is regulated and conflicts are resolved in a society than on the formal legal institutions with which we are familiar. At one time, there were heated arguments over whether or not primitive societies, with no formal institutions for regulating behavior, could be said to have law. Such questions are no longer of interest to most anthropologists. All societies have "trouble cases," incidents of individual behavior that contradict important social norms, or conflicts between individuals that cannot be settled informally between themselves. Every society includes patterned ways of responding to these

cases, and it is in this response that law is found. Because political organization includes both the ways in which public policy is made and the ways in which it is enforced in a society, our study of political organization also includes the study of law.

KINDS OF POLITICAL ORGANIZATION

Political organization and law exist in all societies, but not all societies have specialized, formal mechanisms through which authority is exercised and law enforced. The main point about variation in political organization is, in fact, the degree to which political roles, institutions, and processes are differentiated from other aspects of social organization. A second important aspect of variation is the degree to which authority is centralized or diffused throughout society. Both aspects of political variation, in turn, are related to social complexity, the number of different *kinds* of groups in a society and the ways in which they are connected to one another. Using social complexity as a standard, anthropologists have defined four major types of political organization (Service 1971). In order of their complexity, these are band societies, tribal societies, chiefdoms, and states. Each type tends to be correlated with a particular way of making a living, population size and density, economic system, and pattern of social ranking. Of course, these exact types are not always found in the real world; many societies will have some but not all the characteristics of an ideal type.

BAND LEVEL SOCIETIES

Band organization, which is the least complex type of society, is characteristic of hunters and gatherers. Reciprocity is the dominant economic pattern in band societies. There is no concept of private ownership of basic resources, such as land or water, although bands may be loosely identified with certain territories. Band societies are egalitarian; there is little role specialization and little difference among the members in terms of wealth, prestige, or power.

Political Integration

A **band** is a relatively small group of people (20 to 50) made up of nuclear families who live together and are loosely associated with a territory on which they hunt and gather. Bands are relatively independent of one another. There are few higher levels of control or centralized mechanisms of leadership.

Bands are exogamous (people must marry out), and ties between bands are established mainly by marriage. Because a bilateral kinship system is characteristic in band societies, an individual is linked to many different bands through ties of blood and marriage. Bands may also be linked through the trading relations of some of their members. Membership in bands is quite flexible, and individuals may change their residence from one band to another fairly easily. The flexibility of band organization is particularly adaptive for the hunting and gathering way of life and low population densities.

Leadership

There is no formal leadership in band societies. Leaders in foraging bands are usually older men whose experience, knowledge of group traditions, and success in hunting is the source of their re-

spect by others. Leaders have no way of enforcing their views; decisions are usually made by all adult men in the group, and leaders can only persuade. Others follow them if they have been successful in the past. Among Eskimo groups, for example, the local level leader is called "The one to whom all listen," "he who thinks" or "he who knows everything best." Successful Eskimo whaling captains who do not generously distribute their accumulated wealth among the group are called merely "rich men" and distinguished from those whose superior ability and generosity make them respected leaders in the village.

The African Bushmen also have headmen, and among some groups this office is passed from father to son. The band headman is not necessarily the group leader, however; members may turn to any individual of intelligence and skill for guidance. Neither headman nor leaders gain any political or economic advantage from their position: "Every person does his own work, carries his own load and shares meat." Nothing special in the way of wealth or status marks them out from others. The main duty of a !Kung headman is to manage the band's resources, primarily water and vegetable foods, and to plan where the band will migrate within its territory. Visitors to the band must ask his permission before gathering plant foods and taking water, although, as one informant told Laura Marshall, an anthropologist who worked among the !Kung, "If you are very thirsty, you have no time to ask permission" (1967).

Social Control

In band societies, social order is maintained informally by gossip, ridicule, and avoidance. In extreme cases, an individual may be killed or driven out of the community. Among the Bushmen, for example, the sharing of meat is so strongly established that they can hardly conceive of an individual not doing this. When Marshal tried to suggest that an individual could hide with his family in order not to share meat with others, the !Kung "howled with laughter. They said that a man would be very bad to do that. He would be like a lion. They would have to treat him like a lion by driving him away or teach him manners by not giving him any meat. . . . not even a tiny piece." Stealing is another crime among the !Kung, although it occurs rarely. An individual's footprints are as recognizable as his face, and a thief can easily be detected. In the one case of stealing recounted to Marshall, a man who stole another's cache of honey was killed by the owner.

Although theft and the refusal to share food are serious offenses in most band societies, not all are as successful as the Bushmen in regulating them. The Siriono, a hunting society of the Amazon, have a similar norm, but it is recognized more in the breach. Siriono frequently attempted to hide food, and families would steal off to the forest in the night to eat in order to avoid sharing. Unlike the Bushmen, however, the Siriono live in a difficult environment and are constantly on the brink of starvation (Holmberg 1969). Where food is very scarce, social norms about sharing may break down altogether, as illustrated by the selfishness of the Ik of Uganda, described by Colin Turnbull (1972). Theirs is a truly frightening story of a society in which almost perpetual starvation led children to take food from the mouths of their old parents, and people who shared were ridiculed as fools.

Among the Eskimo, supernatural sanctions are an important means of social control. Violations of norms are considered sins, and offenders may be controlled through ritual means. Public confessions are directed by the shaman. The offender is defined as a patient, rather than a criminal, and is led to confess all the taboos he or she has violated. The local villagers form the audience and participate as a background chorus. These confessions are mainly voluntary, although a forceful shaman may denounce a member of the community he feels has engaged in acts repulsive to the spirits, and is therefore dangerous to the whole group. A person who fails to obey the orders of the shaman may be driven from the community.

Conflict Resolution

Although the need for cooperation and reciprocity minimize conflicts between individuals in band societies, they do occur and may even become quite violent. Under the conditions of band society, where the effective social unit is a small group of persons in face to face contact, quarrels and conflicts between individuals have a way of involving many other group members. Though few formal institutions exist for resolving conflicts, social mechanisms do operate to prevent them from seriously threatening the social order.

The Pygmies of the Ituri forest, for example, have a process called flux (Turnbull 1968). Among the Pygmies, there is great flexibility in the composition of local groups; individuals may change their residence quite easily, and bands regularly break up into smaller units and reform into larger ones throughout the year. Breaking the band down into smaller units always separates individuals who have been in conflict with each other, thus preventing prolonged hostilities.

Among some Eskimo groups, disputes between individuals are resolved through various kinds of contests. Some of these are physical, such as head butting or a kind of boxing. Others are verbal, like the famous song duels, where the weapons are words—"little, sharp words like the wooden splinters which I hack off with my ax" (Hoebel 1974:93). Although murder is normally resolved by a killing, a man may choose to revenge his kin in a song duel if he feels too weak to kill his opponent, or if he knows he will win the song contest. Each contestant in a song duel tries to deliver the traditional compositions with the greatest skill. The one for whom the audience claps the loudest is the winner. Winning the song duel has little to do or nothing to do with the facts of a dispute. But it does resolve the quarrel and restore normal relations between those who have become hostile toward each other. The original complaint is laid to rest, and a "judgment" is laid down that is accepted by the contestants.

There is fighting in band societies, both verbal and physical. Violent aggression of an individual nature is not infrequent, and can and does result in death or serious injuries. But warfare or armed conflict between socially defined groups of people is not formalized in most band societies due to the low level of technology and simple political organization. Among band level hunting and gathering societies, war usually takes the form of family feuding that may continue for generations. There is no formal organization for war and no position of warrior. Military activity is contained within the patterns of kinship. There is little production for warfare, and little organized social mobilization to support armed combat. In band societies, the primary objectives of war are likely to be personal; the motivations for fighting are the personal grievances of one individual or a small group of people. Fighting takes place in short skirmishes. Where band societies come in contact with technologically and culturally more dominant groups, the bands tend to retreat into marginal areas rather than fight. They isolate themselves or form peaceful relations with their neighbors (Harrison 1973:42).

TRIBAL SOCIETIES

A **tribe** is a culturally distinct population whose members think of themselves as descended from the same ancestor, or as part of the same "people." Tribes occur primarily among pastoralists and horticulturalists, and are integrated economically by both reciprocity and redistribution. Like bands, tribes are basically egalitarian, with no important differences among members in wealth, status, and power. Also like bands, tribes do not have a separate and distinct set of political roles and institutions. Tribes are usually organized by unilineal kin groups. It is these groups that are the units of political activity, as well as the "owners" of basic economic resources. The emergence and importance of local kin groups larger than the nuclear family goes with the larger populations that develop in horticultural and pastoral societies.

The effective political unit in these societies is a shifting one. For most of the time, local units of a tribe operate independently. They come together in response to external conditions—either the threat of attack or the opportunity to attack others. Otherwise, little tribal-level organization exists. In fact, under certain conditions, segments of a tribe may be in a state of perpetual violent conflict. Like bands, tribal political organization and mechanisms of social control are embedded in institutions like kinship or religion. Political functions and roles are not specialized.

Political Integration

The major difference between band and tribe is that a tribal society contains mechanisms which integrate the local segments of the society. Age grades are one kind of association; military societies (clubs) or secret societies also cut across and integrate the segments that make up a tribe. The clan is a form of tribal association based on kinship, and clans may even link members of different tribes.

One form of tribal integration that clearly shows the shifting nature of the po-

litical unit in tribal society is a **segmentary lineage system.** In this system, individuals belong to multiple descent units, or segments, that form at different geneological levels and function in different contexts. Among the Nuer of East Africa (Figure 12.1), for example, there are about twenty clans, each of which is divided into lineages. Below the level of the clan are segments called maximal lineages, which are themselves broken down into major lineages. Major lineages are in turn subdivided into minor lineages, and minor lineages are made up of minimal lineages. The minimal lineage contains three to five generations and is the basic permanent descent group that functions in day-to-day

Figure 12.1 *The location of the Nuer.*

It may be that native American tribal "chiefs" were created by Europeans who projected their own systems of centralized political office on groups with whom they came in contact. Dealing with one leader was easier than dealing with a collective body. (Courtesy of the American Museum of Natural History)

activities. Members of a minimal lineage live in the same village and regard each other as the closest relatives. The minimal lineages are politically independent, and there is no formal or centralized leadership above this level.

Only when there is conflict between two minimal segments does the higher order of lineage structure come into play. Minor, major, and maximal lineages are not groups: they are alliance networks that emerge only in opposition to each other.

In a serious dispute between members of different minimal lineages, other groups take the side of their nearest kin. The conflict thus becomes one that matches the highest-order lineages involved. Anthropologists call this kind of political structure complementary opposition (Evans-Pritchard 1968). Marshal Sahlins (1961) suggests that the segmentary system allows stronger tribes to expand into nearby desirable territories held by weaker groups. Complementary opposition directs the energies of the society upward, away from the competition between kin, to the outside enemy. Lineage segments on the borders of other tribes know that if they attack an enemy, they will be helped by other lineages related to them at the higher levels of organization.

Tribes with segmentary lineage systems are expanding populations. The Nuer have expanded at the expense of the Dinka, a neighboring pastoral group who originally inhabited the grasslands desired by the Nuer for pasturing their livestock. Because the Dinka were the first in this area and had neither enemies to fight nor neighbors to push back, they did not develop strong mechanisms of tribal integration. The Nuer were the invaders in this area. Their segmentary lineage system developed in response to the need for expansion, and they have, in fact, been successful in pushing the Dinka off much of their land.

Leadership

Like bands, tribal societies have leaders but no centralized leadership and no formal offices that are a source of political power. Among the Nuer, for example, the head of the minimal descent group can use his authority to threaten members of the local group with banishment if they do not agree to settle a dispute. Among many native American populations, there were different kinds of leaders for different kinds of activities. The Cheyenne had war chiefs and peace chiefs. Among the Ojibwa of Canada, there were war leaders, hunting leaders, ceremonial leaders, and clan leaders. Europeans who first came in contact with the Ojibwa frequently misinterpreted the system and imposed on the Ojibwa the concept of a supreme leader or chief. A much better translation of tribal leader in many of these groups is "big man." When the Canadian government insisted that the Ojibwa must have a chief, the Ojibwa coined a native word, *okimakkan,* which is best translated as "fake chief."

Under certain ecological and social conditions, a more substantial kind of political leadership may emerge in tribal societies. In areas with predictable climate and relatively abundant resources, strong authority roles or true chiefs emerge. The Basseri of Southern Iran are a tribe of pastoral nomads with a strong chieftaincy. On their migrations, the Basseri move through areas used by other tribes. To avoid exhaustive grazing of an area, famine of the flocks, and intertribal fighting, the Basseri must stick to their migration schedules and fixed routes. One of the important functions of the Basseri chief, therefore, is to coordinate the movements of the tribe.

The Basseri chief's strength rests not only on the need for a strong authority to coordinate migration movements, but also on the role he plays in mediating between the tribe and the settled agricultural populations with whom the Basseri interact. The Basseri must pass through land inhabited by farmers under centralized bureaucratic control. They negotiate contracts with these agriculturalists for using pastureland, and they also exchange products with them. These interactions can result in conflicts—for example, a nomad's herds may damage a farmer's crops. Because the nomad and the farmer operate within two different social systems, informal mechanisms of conflict resolution cannot be used to settle their differences. Furthermore, the nomad, because he must be on the move, cannot take the time to become involved in lengthy court proceedings, which are a regular way of settling disputes among farmers. The nomad may not even be able to respond to a court summons without hardship. Violence is, of course, a solution, and one that has been used frequently in the past. But for peaceful resolution of farmer-nomad conflicts, other political mechanisms must come into play. This is provided by the institution of centralized chieftaincy. The chief represents a fixed point in the nomadic community on which the farmer can fix his grievance. Because a chief has a domestic staff and is relieved from the actual duties of pastoralism, he has the time to work at conflict resolution and can represent the interests of his tribe. Nomads recognize the need for a chief in these situations and have a great feeling of respect for and awareness of their dependence on him, all of which strengthen his power (Barth 1964).

Social Control and Conflict Resolution

Tribes, like bands, depend a great deal on informal ways of controlling deviant be-

---

The Tribal Big Man

In Melanesian horticultural societies, the role of big man as leader is particularly interesting. The Melanesian big man is a self-made leader who gains power through personal achievements rather than from holding office. He begins his career as the leader of a small, localized kin group. Through a series of public actions, such as generous loans, the big man attracts followers within the community. He skillfully builds up his capital and increases the number of his wives. Since women take care of pigs, he can increase the size of his pig herds. He distributes his wealth in ways that build his reputation as a rich and generous man: by sponsoring feasts, paying subsidies to military allies, purchasing high ranks in secret societies, and paying bridewealth for young men seeking wives. By giving generously, he places many other people under obligation to him. Big men command obedience from their followers through this personal relationship of gratitude and obligation.

The activities of big men do provide leadership above the local level, but this integration is fragile. It depends not on the creation of permanent office, but on the personality and constant striving of an individual. Big men rise and fall. With their deaths, their faction may dissolve, or other ambitious men may undermine their power. Most important, however, the big man must spur his local group on to ever greater production if he is to hold his own against other big men in the tribe. To maintain prestige, he must give his competitors more than they can give him. This means the big man must begin to withhold gifts to the followers who are producing for him. The discontent this brings may lead to the defection of the followers or even the murder of the big man. A big man cannot pass on his status to others; each individual must begin anew to amass the wealth and forge the internal and external social relationships on which big man status depends (Sahlins 1971).

havior and settling conflicts, but they have also developed more formal mechanisms of control. The Cheyenne were particularly successful in peacefully resolving intra-tribal conflict and in controlling individual behavior when this was necessary for the common good. Their relatively formal structure of social control came into play during the summer season, when Cheyenne bands came together for great communal buffalo hunts and tribal ceremonies. Order was necessary to prevent disputes, and strict discipline was required on the buffalo hunt. An individual hunter could ruin the hunt for others by alarming and scattering the buffalo. These tribal gatherings and communal hunts were policed by members of military associations. The associations not only punished offenders, but also tried to rehabilitate the guilty parties by bringing them back within the tribal structure. The function of the police was not revenge, but getting the deviant to conform to tribal law in the interest of the welfare of the tribe. Individuals were punished by a variety of methods. Sometimes their teepees were ripped to shreds, or the ears of their horses were cut off, a mark of shame. Offenders might also be whipped. If they resisted, they might be killed on the spot. If, however, the person accepted the punishment and appeared to have learned a lesson, he was accepted back into the group and his belongings often replaced. But the Cheyenne military societies operated only during the hunt period. At other times, more informal sanctions and leadership operated at the band level.

Another means of regulating behavior in tribal societies is through the use of go-betweens. Among the Nuer, a Leopard Skin chief acts as a mediator, particularly in cases where a killing takes place. As in other tribal societies, when one person kills another, retaliation can be expected from the dead person's kin and may begin a true feud. After a killing, the killer may seek sanctuary in the home of the Leopard Skin chief. The chief goes to the home of the slayer's family and gets the family to promise to pay a certain number of cattle to the dead person's family. He then goes to the family of the victim and tries to get them to accept this compensation. The Leopard Skin chief can only mediate, however; he cannot compel either of the families to accept the settlement. In the case of other kinds of disputes, such as that over ownership of cattle, the chief and perhaps other respected elders in the community may attempt to get the two sides to make a settlement through public discussion. There is no means of enforcing their suggestions, however. Although go-betweens have little or no authority to enforce their decisions, they express the general interest of society in ending tension, punishing wrongs, and restoring social stability. Go-betweens, with the power of public opinion behind them, are usually effective. But if a settlement cannot be agreed upon, a feud will begin, undertaken by the aggrieved party.

Formal, complex, and specialized systems for resolving conflicts and regulating behavior are particularly well developed in West Africa. Among the Ibo, for example, the body of elders met in a central council to act as mediators and referees in settling disputes. In these courts, or councils, the senior elder opened the proceedings by a prayer to the gods to enable them to come to the right decisions and punish anyone who attempted to pervert justice or any witness who gave false evidence. In some towns, a council elder was first made to swear that he would not make decisions in secret, take sides in disputes, appropriate communal or other property by force, or use public monies for his own purposes.

All offenses did not result in a trial. A criminal might be punished by the family, or by the person against whom he or she had committed the crime. A murderer could hang himself or get a relative to substitute for him, and the case would be considered closed. Trials were held when a case was in doubt. The elders who tried cases took into account the social position of the accused, the strength of his kin relations, and whether he was a useful member of society or not, as well as the seriousness of the offense. If after the evidence was heard the case was still in doubt, it was decided by an oath or an ordeal. An **ordeal** is a means of determining guilt or innocence by having the accused submit him- or herself to dangerous or painful tests believed to be under supernatural control. Among the Ibo, the drinking of poison was an ordeal. The use of ordeals

means that judges do not have to put their own prestige on the line in every judgment. Where there is no central political authority to enforce decisions, mediators need the extra weight of supernatural backing to ensure that people will comply (Meek 1972).

Nomadic pastoralists, like horticulturalists, also have a tendency to engage in feuding and warfare. Warfare among pastoralists is most frequently associated with raiding other groups for animals, a way of bringing about a balance between population and resources. The approach to warfare that stresses the interrelationship among ecology, social structure, level of sociocultural complexity, and conflict is a good example of the kinds of understanding anthropologists seek. The studies of Harris, Vayda, and others indicate that warfare can be explained *not* by attributing it to some human instinct for aggression, but rather by understanding its rela-

WAR IN TRIBAL SOCIETIES: THE YANOMAMO

Because of the relatively low level of sociocultural integration and the absence of strong centralized authority in tribal societies, violence frequently erupts between individuals and groups. This violence characteristically takes the form of a blood feud. The kin group of an individual who is offended, either by verbal insult, property loss, physical injury, or death, is expected to avenge the wrong. The distinction between feuding and warfare is one of scale and organization. Feuding usually involves relatively small numbers of people and contains an element of surprise. War involves more people and has an element of planning and organization.

Feuding and warfare appear to be constant in many tribal societies. Among the Yanomamo (Figure 12.2, p. 262), intertribal hostility and warfare are almost a way of life. Yanomamo villages organize and conduct war parties against each other not for land, but to steal each other's women. In a Yanomamo raid, as many men as possible are killed and as many women as possible are captured.

Figure 12.2 *The location of the Yanomamo.*

According to their ethnographer, Napoleon Chagnon (1977), the constant warfare and militant ideology of the Yanomamo is a way of preserving village autonomy. Because the Yanomamo have not been able to control conflict within villages, fights often break out among individuals. This leads to the division of villages into independent and mutually hostile camps. In order to be able to survive as an independent unit in an environment of constant warfare, members of a village adopt a hostile and aggressive stance toward other villagers. Yanomamo aggressiveness is encouraged from childhood and reinforced by a cultural pattern that demands a display of ferocity on the part of males. This ferocity is demonstrated not only in the fights between men, but also in the way husbands treat their wives.

Warfare among the Yanomamo, as well as among other horticultural groups, has been explained as a way of controlling population. William Divale and Marvin Harris (1976) argue that war regulates population indirectly by leading to female infanticide, not by causing deaths in battle. In societies where warfare is constant, there is a cultural preference for fierce and aggressive males who can become warriors. Since male children are preferred over females, female infants are frequently killed. Among the Yanomamo, the shortage of women that results from female infanticide appears as a strong *conscious* motivation for warfare, thus providing a continuing "reason" for the Yanomamo to keep fighting among themselves. In the absence of effective contraception and abortion, the most effective and widespread means of regulating population growth is reducing the number of fertile females.

However persuasive Divale and Harris's argument is for the Yanomamo, it is not necessarily valid for all tribal groups in which war is a predominant feature. Andrew Vayda (1976) has suggested that a critical factor is the fact that most of these societies practice slash and burn horticulture. Because it is much harder to clear forest for cultivation than to work land which has already been used, a local group may prefer to take land from other groups, by force if necessary, rather than expand into virgin forest. This sets up a condition in which warfare is a way for societies that have experienced a decrease in food supplies due to population increase, or that have reached the limits of expansion into unoccupied land, to expand. Where there are effective nonwarlike ways in which population can be redistributed within the total territory of the tribe, tribes may not be warlike, or may direct their aggressive activities outward toward other tribes. According to Vayda, the Maori of New Zealand are an example of the first model, and the Iban of Sarawak are an example of the second.

tionship to other ecological and sociocultural factors—that is, as part of a total sociocultural system.

The function of warfare in regulating the balance between population and resources in tribal populations is related to the absence of strong mechanisms for tribal integration through peaceful means, and to the absence of strong motivations to produce food over and above immediate needs. An economic surplus, which can support more specialized and centralized political authority really emerges with the level of sociocultural integration called a chiefdom.

CHIEFDOMS

Two main characteristics distinguish chiefdoms from tribes. Unlike a tribe, in which all segments are structurally and functionally similar, a **chiefdom** is made up of parts that are structurally and functionally different from one another. A ranking system means that some lineages, and the individuals in them, have higher or lower social status than others. As we saw for Polynesia and the Northwest Coast of America, rulers, nobles, and commoners may be distinguished from one another by genealogical closeness to the chief. There may also be geographical units within a chiefdom, each of which has its own chief or council.

The second difference between tribes and chiefdoms is that a chiefdom has centralized leadership which consists of an *office* of chief (as opposed, for example, to the individualistic and self-made leadership provided by a Melanesian "big man"). The rise of a centralized governing center—that is, the chief and his political authority—is closely related to redistributive exchange patterns. Goods move into the center (the chief) and are redistributed through the chief's generosity in giving feasts and sponsoring rituals. The economic surplus created by the chief level of organization is used to benefit the whole society, though at the same time it is the primary support of the chief's power and prestige.

An economic surplus gives members of a chiefdom a greater measure of security than is possible in a tribal society. The chief can distribute labor as well as food.

In addition, centralized authority prevents the outbreak of violence between segments of the society, and at the same time gives the society a greater degree of military power vis-à-vis other societies than tribes are able to muster. Chiefdoms are found mainly in pastoral societies, or those in which intensive agriculture is practiced, though they also existed among the hunting and fishing societies of the Northwest Coast of America.

The Regulation of Behavior and Conflict Resolution

Internal violence within chiefdoms is reduced because the chief has authority to make judgments, to punish deviant individuals, and to resolve disputes. In the Trobriand Islands, the power of a chief to punish people is achieved partly by hiring sorcerers to kill the offender by black magic. The greatest power of the Trobriand chief lies in his power to control garden magic. As "garden magician" he not only organizes the efforts of the villagers under his control, but also performs the rituals considered necessary for success at every step—preparing the fields, planting, and harvesting. The ultimate power of the chief is his magical control of rain: If he wishes, he can produce a prolonged drought, which will cause many people to starve. This power is used when the chief is angry as a means of collective punishment and enforcement of his will.

Among the Basseri, the chief, or *khan*, has great power in settling disputes. Disputes come to the chief only after informal methods within the camp have failed to achieve a settlement. Once a dispute is brought to the chief, he can dispose of the case at his will. His decisions must be obeyed, and an individual who does not comply is beaten with a pole. In other so-

Among pastoral tribes the office of chief is an important one. This Bedouin shaikh is shown with his two sons. (United Nations)

cieties, even where chiefs have equally strong powers, they choose to rule with tact and kindness, rather than by the use of force. Clellan Ford (1938) describes the actions of a wise Fijiian chief in the following case:

A woman had gotten angry at her husband, who had failed to fix their leaky roof. One rainy night she threatened to kill him with a knife. She chased him around the room and finally aimed a blow at his head. The husband grabbed a mat from the floor to use as a shield. The knife struck the mat and rebounded on the woman's head, resulting in a deep cut. On hearing of this, the chief called both parties together, and listened with great seriousness to their arguments. The wife complained her husband was lazy and spent all his time drinking *kava*. The husband complained his wife neglected her duties and seldom cooked for him. The chief could easily have disposed of the matter by fining the husband and the wife for causing trouble. Instead, he sensed an underlying tension in the relationship, of which this fight was only a symptom. He called members of the village and heard their testimony. It appeared that the woman thought herself too good for her husband, and he felt and resented this. The chief got the husband and wife to admit this. He then ordered the woman to be a better spouse and sent the man off to work in his garden, warning him that any future trouble would result in his exile from the village. The chief then gave a gift to the male members of the village and asked them to repair the roof. After settling the dispute, the chief held a feast for the village.

Social order in chiefdoms is maintained through fear and through the genuine respect for and loyalty of the people to the chief. As our examples illustrate, the chief's authority is backed by his control of symbolic, supernatural, administrative, economic, and military power. This permits more stability in chiefdoms than in tribes, though sometimes violent competition for the office of chief occurs. Chiefs generally suppress any attempt at rebellion or threats from competitors, and deal harshly with those who try to take their power. To emphasize the importance of this office for the society, offenses against the chief are punishable by death.

STATE SOCIETIES

The most complex kind of political organization is the state. A **state** may be defined as a hierarchical, centralized form of political organization in which a central government has the legal monopoly over the use of force. In addition to the emergence of central government, states are also characterized by social stratification. In most cases state societies rest on a system of intensive agriculture, whose productivity allows for the development of cities, economic and occupational specialization, and the development of extensive trade. It has

In a state society monopoly over the use of legitimate force rests in the hands of the state. (United Nations)

been suggested that one of the most important characteristics of the state is its ability to expand indefinitely without splitting, through the incorporation of a variety of political units and ethnic groups. Thus states can become much more populous, heterogeneous and powerful than any other kind of society.

Social Stratification

As with chiefdoms, the rise of a centralized ruling authority creates an economic surplus. But in state societies only a part of the surplus created by intervention in the economy goes back to the people directly; some is used to support the activities of the state itself, such as maintaining administrative bureaucracies, standing armies, artists and craft workers, and a priesthood. Part of the wealth produced in states is also used to support the ruling class in a luxurious style. Only the ruling classes have unlimited access to basic resources. The power of the state is used to maintain this unequal access and to collect food surpluses through taxation.

Unlike chiefdoms, in which ranking is based on kinship, in state societies kinship does not regulate relations between the different social classes. Instead, each class marries within itself, and kin ties no longer extend throughout the whole society. This contributes to the widening of the gap between the classes.

Centralized Government

The state as a form of political organization is characterized by a high degree of functional specialization. Social order is maintained through government, an interrelated set of status roles that became separate from other aspects of social organization, such as kinship. The components of a state are no longer kinship groups; other kinds of groups and relationships, particularly those based on territory, become more important. A person becomes a member of the society through citizenship rather than kinship, and the sense of being "one people" is no longer limited to those who recognize ties of blood and marriage. The administrative divisions of a state are territorial units, cities, districts, and so on. Each unit has its own government, though these governments are not independent of the central government.

In state societies, government performs the functions that keep the society going. The state, for example, intervenes in every aspect of the economic process. Through taxation, it stimulates the agricultural production of households. It also controls labor; it can order people to work on roads and building and to serve in armies, thus affecting the work force available for agriculture. The state also intervenes in the exchange and distribution of goods and services through complex market networks. It protects the distribution of goods by making travel safe for traders as they move their goods from one place to another and by keeping peace in the marketplace. The state may also intervene in the consumption process. It can pass laws about which people are allowed to use which goods, reserving for the elite such items as gold, silk, or other costly material symbols of high status. These complicated exchanges and rules brought a need for recordkeeping. Systems of writing arose in some states, as well as systems of weights and measures. In some states, cities arose as administrative, religious, and economic centers. It was in these centers that important cultural achievements in science, art, architecture, and philosophy were stimulated.

The Monopoly of Force

The major defining characteristic of state societies is the government's monopoly over the use of force. A state uses a code of law to make clear how and when it will use force and forbids individuals or groups to use force by interfering in their disputes. Written laws are passed by authorized legislative bodies and enforced by formal and specialized institutions of law enforcement. Courts and police forces, for example, have the authority to impose all kinds of punishments: jail, confiscation of property, fines, and even death.

In state societies, the fact that only the state has the authority to use force does not mean that force is used only by the state. In fact, many states are plagued by illegal use of force and violence, which may take many different forms: Sometimes it occurs as disputes between individuals; sometimes as the terrorizing of the population by bandits or outlaws, sometimes as rebellion directed at overthrowing those who control the government, and sometimes as revolutionary attempts to overthrow the entire structure of government. The state is constantly on the alert to ward off threats to depose the government or outbreaks of violence that may result in civil war. To the extent that a state wins the loyalty of its people by its ideology and effective protection of their economic and political rights, the constant use of force will not be necessary. It is always there in the background, however, as an instrument of social control. In addition to suppressing internal disorder, the state also defends itself against external threats. More than any other form of political organization, the state can mobilize to carry out military action or war for both defensive and offensive purposes.

The Rise of State Societies

The formation of a state is the result of a number of interrelated events feeding back on one another in complex ways. Ecological and historical circumstances, population pressure, long-distance trade, warfare and military organization, conquest, internal competition between groups, the maintainance of private property and the privileges of elite classes, and the necessity for more integrated management of public works such as irrigation all may play a role in the emergence of the state (Cohen and Service 1978).

Theories of state formation tend to emphasize either conflict or integration as the dominant factor. A conflict theory approach proposed by Morton Fried (1967) focuses on the centralization of government power as a response to social stratification. In Fried's view, as population increases different parts of a population begin to compete for access to scarce resources. Ultimately one group becomes dominant, and that group then wants to protect its superior position. In order to do this, it centralizes the institutions of government, particularly those that give a monopoly on the use of force. For Fried, the function of the state is first and foremost to protect the system of social stratification.

Elman Service (1978), on the other hand, stresses the integrative functions of the state. He emphasizes the positive benefits of the state as a form of sociopolitical integration and points out that all its citizens tend to regard it as legitimate and even good. There are many examples in history of states ruled by a monarch who was despotic and even cruel, and who nevertheless was perceived by the people as deserving of respect and loyalty. For Service, the main functions of the state are

A view of Machu Picchu, a pre-Columbian Peruvian state, showing the setting in which such states developed. (United Nations/A. Jongen)

protection of the rights of citizens, providing effective mechanisms for the peaceful settlement of disputes, and an ability to increase substantially food production, thus providing a greater measure of economic security than other forms of organization. Social stratification, in Service's view, is a result rather than a cause of state formation; conditions leading to centralized government bring with them the development of a ruling class.

Within this opposition of what may be called the conflict or integrative approaches to state formation are theories that emphasize more specific factors.

V. Gordon Child, an archeologist, sees the state developing automatically with the invention of agriculture. As the domestication of plants increases the surplus of food, some individuals are able to take on full-time occupational specialties. This creates a more complex division of labor, out of which develops the complex form of political integration called the state. One criticism of this view is that increased food production does not automatically create a surplus. Rather, a food surplus tends to be created by social mechanisms, such as the rise of centralized political institutions or the introduction of a cash economy.

Another theory stresses large-scale irrigation as the main factor leading to development of the state. This theory attempts to demonstrate that under certain ecological conditions, large-scale irrigation is perceived as conferring definite economic advantages on a population. But building irrigation projects and keeping them in repair requires much coordination as well as more complex decision-making processes, because conflict can easily arise over who receives what benefits. The need to regulate rights to water and to manage human labor leads to the centralization of political power and ultimately results in the formation of a state. Critics of this theory point out that although large-scale irrigation does lead to some political centralization, it does not necessarily lead to formation of a state. Furthermore, a number of large-scale states, such as China, Mesopotamia, and Mexico, developed before the development of large-scale irrigation. On the whole, however, centralized political authority does seem to be adaptive in an economy dependent on irrigation.

Another theory developed by Robert Carneiro (1970) sees the state resulting from warfare under certain ecological conditions—where there is a limit on the agricultural land available to expanding populations. As an example of this theory, Carneiro describes the rise of the state in pre-Columbian Peru. The independent dispersed farming villages of Peru were confined to narrow valleys bounded by the sea, the desert, or mountains. As the population grew, villages split and population dispersed until all the available agricultural land was used up. At this point, more intensive methods of agriculture were applied to land already being farmed, and previously unusable land was brought under cultivation by means of terracing and irrigation. As population continued to increase, more pressure was brought on the land and war over land was the result. Because of the environment, villages that

lost wars had nowhere to go. The price of a defeated population remaining on its land was acceptance of a politically subordinate role. As a number of villages were defeated, the political organization of these areas became more complex and developed into chiefdoms. The warring units were now larger. As conquest of larger areas continued, centralization of authority increased, until finally the entire area was under the control of one chief. The next step was the conquest of weaker valley chiefdoms by stronger ones until powerful empires emerged. The Inca Empire of Peru is a notable example of this process of state formation.

As a form of sociopolitical organization, the state is one of humankind's most important cultural achievements. Philosophers as well as anthropologists have been fascinated by what induces human beings to give up part of their freedom to the control of the state. In seeking the answer to this question, anthropologists have examined the available evidence, both for ancient and contemporary states, and have developed various theories. It is now generally agreed that no theory which limits state formation to one single chain of cause and effect is a sufficient explanation. A newer approach sees the origin of the state as involving a different interaction of factors in different circumstances. Prestate societies in various situations respond to different selective pressures by changing some of their internal structures, by subduing a competing group, by gaining control of water resources, or by establishing themselves as dominant in a region. This initial shift sets off a chain reaction of other changes that leads ultimately to the state. The state thus emerges as a cultural solution to various kinds of problems that demand more centralized coordination and regulation of human populations.

SUMMARY

1. Political systems, which include law, function to solve the problems of coordinating and regulating human behavior. The major political processes in any society are making and enforcing decisions affecting the common good, and resolving conflicts.

2. Both informal and formal mechanisms of social control regulate human behavior. Informal social control is achieved through gossip and ridicule. Formal sanctions include exile, death and punishment as meted out by judges, courts, and police.

3. Political organization varies according to the degree of specialization of political functions and the extent to which authority is centralized. These, in turn, vary with the degree of social complexity. Four basic types of political organization are bands, tribes, chiefdoms, and states.

4. In a band society there is little integration of groups at a level higher than the band, and no centralization of leadership or social control. Band-level political organization is characteristic of hunting and gathering societies.

5. Tribal organization occurs mainly among horticulturalists and pastoralists. Most frequently localized kin groups, which are the typical political units in tribal society, act independently. But under certain social conditions, such as the threat of attack, these units may come together in collective action. Tribal societies contain some mechanisms of organization, such as age groups, clans, and associations that integrate all the local segments of the tribe.

6. Although tribal societies often have some centralized form of social control that inhibits violent conflict between segments, warfare is frequent. Warfare may be adaptive in these societies as a way of limiting population growth or redistributing land.

7. In a chiefdom, kinship is the most important principle of social organization. Unlike tribes, there is an office of chief, which is a socially recognized position of leadership and authority. An important support of the chief's power is his role in the redistribution of goods through feasting.

8. A state, which is a hierarchical, centralized form of organization in which a central government has a legal monopoly over the use of force, is the most complex of the four types of political organization. States are characterized by social stratification. But unlike chiefdoms, in which social ranking is based on kinship, the state incorporates groups and classes that have no kinship ties with one another.

9. A number of theories deal with the rise of the state. Some emphasize the conflict created by the existence of social classes; others emphasize the integrative functions of the state, such as protecting the rights of citizens, providing for the peaceful resolution of conflict, and promoting increased food production.

10. If we examine the various factors associated with the rise of states in different parts of the world and at different times, it appears that the state is a cultural solution to a number of *different* problems, all of which demand more centralized coordination and regulation of human populations.

SUGGESTED READINGS

Barth, Fredrik
    1964 *Nomads of South Persia.* New York: Humanities Press. Economics, politics, and social life in a chiefdom.

Chagnon, Napoleon
    1977 *Yanomamo: The Fierce People* (2nd ed.). New York: Holt, Rinehart and Winston. A fascinating ethnography about a people who are still practicing constant warfare.

Cohen, Ronald, and Service, Elman R.
    1978 *Origins of the State: The Anthropology of Political Evolution.* Philadelphia Institute for the Study of Human Issues.

    A series of articles on the rise of the state in different parts of the world. A good introduction summarizes anthropological theories of state formation.

Harris, Marvin
    1977 *Cannibals and Kings: The Origins of Cultures.* New York: Random House. In his usual interesting style, the author discusses, among other things, the rise of states and warfare in preindustrial societies.

Hoebel, E. A.
    1968 *The Law of Primitive Man.* New York: Atheneum (orig. 1954). Interesting ethnographic material showing the relationship of law to other aspects of society among groups at different levels of sociocultural integration.

Kiefer, Thomas M.
    1972 *The Tausug: Violence and Law in a Philippine Moslem Society.* New York: Holt, Rinehart and Winston. An ethnography of a society in which both violent dispute and legal processes are embedded in the social structure.

Dittmann/Foxx

13
Religion

Our discussion in this chapter will view religion as "the beliefs and practices concerned with supernatural beings, powers and forces" (Wallace 1966). Supernatural refers to those powers, events, and experiences that are beyond ordinary human control and the laws of nature, and outside reality as normally experienced. Every society has some set of beliefs and practices that center on the relationship of humans to the supernatural. Religion, which goes back to the beginnings of the human species, is a true cultural universal. The antiquity and universality of religion has led many anthropologists to speculate about its origins and functions. Although the search for origins no longer dominates anthropological thinking as it once did, anthropologists are still interested in the many functions religion serves in human society. Some of the most important functions of religion will be discussed in the following section. They will come up again as we look at the variety of religious beliefs and practices throughout the world's cultures.

THE FUNCTIONS OF RELIGION

The Search for Order and Meaning

One of the most important functions of religion is to give meaning to and explain those aspects of the physical and social environment that are not fully understood through normal experience and thought. In every society religion deals with the nature of life and death, the creation of the universe, the origin of society and groups within society, the relation of individuals and groups to one another, and the relation of humankind to nature. This whole cognitive system is called a **cosmology**, or

world view. In the absence of full understanding about themselves and the world, humans create an image of reality peopled with supernatural beings and supernatural forces. This image serves as a framework for interpreting events and experiences, particularly those that are out of the ordinary, or "unnatural." Where humans reach the limits of their intellectual capacities, their powers of endurance, or the limits of their understanding the relation between what they try to do and the success they have, beliefs and practice relating to the supernatural emerge as a way of imposing order on the universe, of giving humans the feeling they have some measure of control.

Science and religion are similar in that both involve "the quest for unity underlying apparent diversity; for simplicity underlying apparent complexity, for order underlying apparent disorder; for regularity underlying apparent anomaly" (Horton 1973). But there is also a major difference between science and religion. Science is an open system of thought, religion a closed system. Science provides explanations that are not considered to be absolutely valid, but rather are open to new data. In science there is an awareness of alternative theories or explanations; ideally, as old explanations are found to be invalid, new ones will be accepted. Religion, on the other hand, is a closed system of beliefs. Religious beliefs are sacred; they are not to be questioned and are not open to empirical testing.

The separation between religion and science in our own society corresponds to our sharp separation of the supernatural and the natural. In other societies, these two concepts are less sharply separated. The supernatural may be seen as part of the natural, and intervenes in all aspects of life. Thus, the kin group includes both living relatives and dead ancestors; power and leadership are often believed to have divine origins; rules of behavior are given divine sanction, and breaches are punished by the gods. The success of even ordinary undertakings in the physical world is ensured by enlisting the help of supernatural powers. Natural disasters, illness, and misfortune are believed to be caused by extrahuman or supernatural spirits. Natural and supernatural, man and nature, past, present, and future, may be perceived as a unity in a way that violates the logic of Western thought. This makes it difficult for us to understand many non-Western religions and accounts for our ethnocentric labeling of them as "irrational," "contradictory," or the products of faulty thinking.

Reducing Anxiety and Increasing Control

Many religious practices are aimed at ensuring success in carrying out a wide variety of human activities. Prayers and offerings are made to supernatural beings in the hope that they will aid a particular individual or community. Rituals are performed to call on supernatural beings and to control forces that appear to be unpredictable, such as those in the natural environment upon which humans depend for survival. One of the widespread practices used to control supernatural forces is magic. Although magical practices exist in many societies, magic seems to be more prominent in those in which there is less predictability in the outcome of events and thus less feeling of being in control of the social and physical environment. In the Trobriand Islands, for example, magic is not used for ordinary canoe trips within the lagoons, but only when the Islanders undertake the long-distance and danger-

ous canoe trips to other islands in their Kula trade. Magic is also prevalent in sports and games of chance.

Even if magic cannot "work" from the standpoint of Western science, it may be effective in achieving results indirectly, mainly by reducing the anxiety of the individuals and groups who practice it. This reduced anxiety allows them to proceed with more confidence, and the confidence may lead to greater success. Where technological advance and science are able to increase predictability and control over events and human relations, magic tends to become less important.

Maintaining the Social Order

Religion has a number of important functions that either directly or indirectly help maintain the social order and the survival of a society. To begin with, religious beliefs about good and evil are reinforced by supernatural means of social control. Thus, religion is a powerful force for conformity in a society. Furthermore, through myth and ritual, social values are given sacred authority and provide a reason for the present social order. Religious ritual also intensifies solidarity by creating an atmosphere in which people experience their common identity in emotionally moving ways. Religion is also an important educational institution. Initiation rites, for example, almost always include the transmission of information about cultural practices and tradition.

By supporting the present social order and defining the place of the individual in society and in the universe, religion also provides people with a sense of personal identity and belonging. When individuals have lost a positive identity or life has no meaning because of the disintegration of a traditional culture, religion can supply a

RELIGIOUS RITUAL AND ADAPTATION

Recent research has shown that religious belief and ritual not only indirectly contribute to the survival of a society but may also directly affect the relationship between a social group and its physical environment. A study by Roy Rappaport (1967) of the Tsembaga of New Guinea shows how religious belief and ritual may produce "a practical result on the external world."

The Tsembaga, who live in the valleys of a mountain range in New Guinea are swidden cultivators who also raise pigs. Small numbers of pigs are easy to keep, as they eat anything and help keep residential areas free from garbage. Although pigs can ruin gardens in the early stages of planting, after the trees are well established, pigs are allowed to root in the gardens where they actually help cultivation by eating seeds and tubers (sweet potatoes). If pig herds grow very large, however, feeding them becomes a problem and it becomes necessary for extra food to be harvested just to feed the pigs. Furthermore, when pig herds become too large, they are more likely to invade gardens and require more supervision. The Tsembaga kill pigs only on ritual occasions: either at pig feasts or in times of misfortune such as illness, death, or warfare.

The Tsembaga have a ritual cycle which they say they perform in order to rearrange their relationships with the supernatural world. This cycle may be viewed as beginning with the rituals performed during warfare. In Tsembaga warfare opponents generally occupy territories next to each other. After hostilities have broken out, each side performs certain rituals which formally designates the other group as the enemy. Fighting may continue on and off for weeks, sometimes ending with one group being routed. In this case the survivors go to live with their kinsmen, and the victors destroy the losers' gardens, slaughter their pigs, and burn their houses. The victors do not occupy their land, however, as this is believed to be guarded by the ancestors of the defeated group.

Most Tsembaga warfare ends in truce, however, with both groups remaining on their territory. When truce is declared, each group performs a ritual called "planting the rumbin." The rumbin is dedicated to the ancestors who are thanked for helping in the fight. At this ritual planting there is a wholesale slaughter of adult pigs. Some of the meat is eaten by the local group itself, while the rest is distributed to other groups who have helped them fight. After this feast there is a period in which the fighting groups are still considered to be in debt to their allies and their ancestors.

This period will not end until the rumbin plant is uprooted. This ritual also requires a pig feast and occurs when there are sufficient pigs.

The question is: How many pigs are sufficient? It is when pig herds reach over four per woman who takes care of them that they become too troublesome to manage and begin to compete with humans for food. Thus, it is the wives of the owners of large numbers of pigs who begin to start agitating for the ritual to uproot the rumbin. This ritual, which is followed by a pig festival lasting about a year, involves much entertaining among villages. Food is exchanged and hosts and guests spend the nights dancing. At this time, future alliances may be set up between hosts and guests. At this time, also, much trade takes place, involving such items as axes, bird plumes, and shell ornaments. For one festival, Rappaport observed that between 4500 and 6000 pounds of pig meat were distributed over 163 occasions to between 2000–3000 people in seventeen local groups. The pig festival ends with another pig slaughter and the public presentation of salted pig belly to one's allies. This concludes the ritual cycle. A local group would now consider itself free to attack its neighbors knowing that assistance from both human allies and ancestors would be forthcoming because their obligations to feed them pork have been fulfilled.

This ritual cycle among the Tsembaga shows a number of different functions of religion. It adjusts the man-land ratio, as survivors in a defeated group seek refuge in other local groups. It also facilitates trade through the markets and exchanges which take place during the year of the pig festival. Most directly in terms of survival, however, it assures the distribution of local surpluses of pig meat, which is a source of high quality protein throughout the whole Tsembaga region. The ritual cycle also helps to maintain an undegraded environment, as pigs are killed when there get to be too many of them and when they threaten the source of human food.

new and more positive identity and become the basis for a new and better culture. Religion can also provide an escape from reality; in the religious beliefs of an afterlife or the coming of a Messiah, powerless people who live in harsh and deprived circumstances can create an illusion of power through the manipulation of religious symbols. Religion in these circumstances is an outlet for frustration, resentment, and anger, and is a way of draining off energy that might otherwise be turned against the social system. In this way, religion indirectly contributes to maintaining the social order.

In summing up some of the various functions of religion, we may say that it has both instrumental and expressive aspects. The instrumental aspect of religion has to do with actions performed in the belief that if people do certain things, they can influence the course of natural or social events to their advantage. The expressive aspect of ritual refers to the ways in which religious symbolism is used to express ideas about the relation of humans to nature, self to society, or group to group. In its expressive aspect, religion is an important force for social integration.

RELIGION AND SYMBOLISM

Because religious ideas are always expressed through symbolism, anthropologists today are also interested in studying and understanding the meanings of religious symbolism and the logic which connects symbols to religious beliefs. Religious symbols may be verbal, such as the names for gods and spirits, certain words, phrases or songs, which are believed to contain some supernatural power. **Myths,** or sacred narratives which tell how the world came to be created through the agency of semi-divine heroes, are powerful symbolic communications of religious ideas. Myths are not merely explanatory stories of the cosmos, but rather have a sacred power in themselves which is evoked by telling the myths or acting them out ritually. Myths may tell of what *really* happened, though they are clothed in poetic and sometimes esoteric language. Religious symbolism may also be expressed in material objects; in masks, statues, paintings, costumes, body decorations or in objects in the physical environment.

Religious ideas are also acted out, in dance, drama, and physical movements. In religious ritual all these symbolic means are used to express religious ideas. It is because religious ideas are so complex and abstract that they require symbolic representation in order to be grasped by the ordinary person. The Christian ritual of the communion service, for example, itself symbolizes the New Testament myth of the Last Supper, which communicates the difficult idea of "communion with God." This idea is present in other religious, but is represented by different symbolism. In Hinduism, for example, one of the most popular representations of communion with God is the love between the divine Krishna in the form of a cowherd, and the gopis, or milkmaids who are devoted to him. In the dramatic enactment of the stories of Krishna, and in the singing of songs to him, the Hindu religion offers a path to communion with God that can be understood by ordinary people.

One anthropological approach which is particularly interested in religious symbolism is called **structuralism.** Structuralists, among whom the most well known is Claude Lévi-Strauss, aim to discover the rules by which meanings are attached to symbols and ultimately to discover the laws of human thought. Because the freest thought takes place in myth, and ritual, these are the main materials analyzed by structuralists.

Structuralists hold that human experience is fundamentally conceived of as contrasts—between life and death, male and female, nature and culture, man and God. The function of myth, ritual, and other elements of culture, particularly religion, is to re-establish a bridge between the opposi-

Statue of Ganesh, a Hindu deity who has the head of an elephant and the body of a human baby. He symbolizes the connection between humans and the divine. (Serena Nanda)

tions. This bridge is established by the introduction of a third category which partakes of both of the oppositions and is thus in itself abnormal. It is this mediating category that is the focus of religious awe and all ritual and taboo. A structural analysis of the Hebrew taboo on pork, for example, centers on the pig as an animal that partakes of two animal categories; it has cloven hoofs like cattle, but does not chew cud as cattle do. Being neither here nor there,

it is unclean (in a spiritual or symbolic sense) and thus tabooed (Douglas 1970). The structuralist approach also helps explain the widespread use of such symbols as hair (which is both part of the human body but can be separated from it), ashes (which are both matter and non-matter), the color white (which is all colors and no color), and the mythological use of "monsters" or figures with bodies of animals and heads of humans. The worship of Ganesh (left), an elephant-headed deity in the Hindu pantheon, is an example of the use of figures in this mediating category. Such figures, which make connections between the human and the supernatural, are often used in religious ritual.

KINDS OF BELIEFS: ANIMISM AND ANIMATISM

A basic distinction in types of religious beliefs is that between animism and animatism. **Animism** is the belief that not only living creatures, but also inanimate objects have life and personality; these supernatural persons are referred to as spirits, ghosts, or gods. Such beings are believed to behave like people; they are conscious, they have will, and they feel the same emotions as human beings do. Such spirits may reside in features of the physical environment, such as trees or stones, or they may reside in animals. In hunting societies, for example, the Lele of Africa and the Eskimo, the spirits of animals are worshipped because it is believed that a hunt will be successful only if an animal allows himself to be killed. Souls, which may also reside in human bodies, are believed to be able to leave the body at will, temporarily during sleep, or permanently as in death.

Spirits or souls that leave the body at death turn into ghosts, who come in a variety of forms and relate in various ways to the living in different cultures.

The distinction between a spirit and a god is mostly one of scale. A god is a supernatural being of great importance and power; a spirit is a lesser being. **Polytheism** is the term used for a religion with many gods; **monotheism,** for a religion with only one god. Things are not quite this clear in real cultures, however. In so-called polytheistic religions, the many gods may be just so many aspects of the one god. In India, for example, it is said that there are literally millions of gods; yet even an uneducated Indian will understand that in some way (which does not confuse him or her though it may confuse us), these are all aspects of one divine essence.

The Nuer are another culture in which the distinction between the great spirit and lesser spirits is fuzzy to the outsider. The Nuer, of course, have no difficulty in understanding the different contexts in which different aspects of the Great Spirit are invoked. E. E. Evans-Pritchard (1968) describes a ceremony held to end a blood feud. All the speakers, representing both clans and including the Leopard Skin chief, addressed the various gods: Great Spirit, spirit of the sky, spirit of our community, spirit of the flesh (this refers to the divine power of the Leopard Skin chief), and spirit of our fathers. Each clan representative appealed to God not only as God, but also as God in relation to the group he represented. The Leopard Skin chief referred to God in his special relation to his religious role as mediator, as well as to the priestly lineage he belonged to.

Just as in polytheistic religions, where all gods and spirits may be reflections of one god, so in monotheistic religions the one god may have several aspects. In the Catholic religion, for example, there is God the Father, the Son, and the Holy Ghost, in addition to a number of lesser supernatural spirits such as the saints, ghosts, the devil, and the souls of people in heaven as well as the souls of those living on earth.

Animatism is the belief in an impersonal supernatural power. *Mana* is perhaps the most widely known term for this power. **Mana,** or supernatural power, may be inherent in the universe, but can also be concentrated in individuals or in objects. We have seen earlier that Polynesian chiefs had a much higher degree of *mana* than ordinary people. *Mana* is the key to success, but it can also be dangerous. That is why the belief in *mana* is so frequently associated with an elaborate system of taboos, or prohibitions. *Mana* is like electricity; it is a powerful force but it can be dangerous when not approached with the proper caution.

A cross-cultural approach seems to indicate that *mana* or power is very often found in those areas (spatial, temporal, verbal, or physical) which are the boundaries between clear-cut categories. Hair, for example, is believed to contain supernatural power in many different cultures (remember the Old Testament story of Samson and Delilah). Hair is a symbol of the boundary between the self and the not-self. It is both part of a person, and can be separated from the person. Hence its ambiguity, and its power. Doorways and gates are also familiar symbols of supernatural power. They separate the inside from the outside, and can thus serve as a symbol of moral categories such as good and evil, pure and impure. Because these symbols of boundaries contain supernatural power, they are frequently part of religious ritual and surrounded by religious taboos.

PRACTICES AND RITUALS

A religious **ritual** is a patterned act that involves the manipulation of religious symbols. Most religious rituals use a combination of the following practices to contact and control supernatural spirits and powers: prayer, offerings and sacrifices, manipulation of objects, telling or acting out of myths, altering the physiological state of the individual (as in trance and ecstatic experiences or through drugs), music, dance, and drama (Wallace 1966).

Offerings to the gods are frequently used to gain their helpful intervention in human affairs. Here a Ponapean pounds the root for making kava, a ceremonial drink that is offered to the deities. (Raymond Kennedy)

Prayers and Offerings

Prayer is any conversation held with spirits and gods. Prayer can involve a request or a pleading; it can be in the form of a bargain or consist of merely praising the deity. In many religions it is common to make a vow in which the individual promises to carry out a certain kind of behavior, such as going on a pilgrimage or building a temple, if the gods will grant a particular wish. Other forms of prayer are less familiar to the Westerner. In some cultures gods can be lied to, commanded, or ridiculed. Among the many Northwest Coast tribes of North America, the insulting tone used to one's political rivals was also used to the gods. In these ranked societies, the greatest insult was to call a man a slave; when calamities fell or their prayers were not answered, people would vent their anger against the gods by saying "You are a great slave" (Benedict 1961:221). Making offerings and sacrifices to supernatural beings is also a widespread religious practice. Sometimes these offerings consist of the first fruits of a harvest—grain, fish, or game. Sometimes the offering of food is in the form of a meal for the gods; among the Hindus, the gods are given food which they eat behind a curtain. After the gods have eaten, this food is distributed among the worshippers.

In some societies, animals or humans may be sacrificed as an offering to the gods. Among cattle pastoralists of East Africa, such as the Nuer and the Pokot, cattle sacrifices are an important part of religious practices. The essence of the East African "cattle complex" is that cattle are killed and eaten only in a ritual and religious context, which seems to be an inefficient use of resources. This ritual use of cattle in sacrifice has always been of interest to anthropologists, and at one time it was given as a common example of how religious practices interfere with rational exploitation of the environment. More recent research has shown, however, that the sacrifice of cattle in a ritual context may be quite adaptive. Cattle sacrifices are offered in community feasts that occur on a fairly regular schedule, averaging out to once a week in any particular neighborhood. The feasts are thus an important source of meat in the diet. Furthermore, the religious taboo that an individual who eats ritually slaughtered meat may not take milk on the same day has the effect of making milk more available to those who have no meat, or conserving milk which can be consumed as sour milk on the following day. In addition, the Pokot prefer fresh meat, which is also healthier than meat which is not fresh.

Since one family could not consume a whole steer by itself, the problem of how to utilize beef most efficiently without refrigeration techniques is solved by offering it to the community in a ceremonial setting. In this way, meat can be shared without fighting over the supply, because the portions are distributed according to age and sex by a rigid formula (Schneider 1973).

In cultures where animal sacrifice occurs, only certain animals are considered appropriate offerings. Among the Nuer, for example, only animals that have been neutered, particularly oxen, are used in religious ritual. In sacrificing an ox, a parallel is being made between symbolic and social categories. Among the Nuer, certain problems involve the restraint of sexuality and the role of women. The ideal norms of Nuer society require loyalty of brothers to the patrilineage. In reality, however, it is the brothers by the same mother who are most loyal to each other and may be in competition with their half-brothers (the Nuer are polygynous). An important source of conflict in Nuer society thus centers on women. Furthermore, there is conflict between the cooperation demanded by loyalty to the patrilineage versus the individual ambitions a man can realize through his wife and his sons. Thus, Nuer women are divisive on two counts—as wives and as mothers. These conflicts are projected onto women, and women are blamed for the conflicts between men. The aggressive aspects of sexuality are seen as responsible for the failure of Nuer men to live up to their moral obligations. Cattle are important religious symbols for sexuality and social relations. Bulls represent the attributes of maleness and vitality which are admired, but which, it is recognized, contain elements of ambition and aggression that are socially disruptive. The castrated ox, on the other hand, represents the subordination of sexuality and disruptiveness to social ends and thus symbolizes the Nuer moral ideal. This makes the ox the most suitable animal for ritual sacrifice (Beidelman 1966).

Human sacrifice has also been a widespread practice, although it was often stamped out by European colonial governments. The Aztecs of Mexico, for example, had a religion in which human sacrifice was an important element. The Aztec gods, such as the jaguar and the serpent, were bloodthirsty and fierce, and required human victims to appease their appetites. The victims, most of whom were captured in war, were ritually killed at the top of a pyramid built for this purpose. Their hearts were torn out and offered to the sun, and their blood offered to the idols representing gods. The corpse was then tumbled down the pyramid, which with its very steep steps was efficient for this purpose. An attendant dismembered the body, and the arms and legs of the victim became the central dish in a feast hosted by the man who had captured him. Although Aztec cannibalism was limited to the ruler, nobles, and those who had captured victims in war, it was practiced on a rather grand scale, perhaps totaling about 20,000 victims a year.

Michael Harner (1977) has recently proposed an ecological interpretation of Aztec sacrifice and cannibalism. He holds that human sacrifice was a response to certain diet deficiencies in the population. In the Aztec environment, wild game was getting scarce and population was growing. Although the maize-beans combination of food that was the basis of the diet was usually adquate, these crops were subject to seasonal failure. Famine was frequent in the absence of edible domesticated animals. To meet essential protein requirements, cannibalism was the only solution.

Although only the upper classes were allowed to consume human flesh, a commoner who distinguished himself in war could also have the privilege of hosting a cannibalistic feast. Thus, although it was the upper strata who benefited most from ritual cannibalism, members of the commoner class could also benefit. Furthermore, as Harner explains, the social mobility and cannibalistic privileges available to the commoners through warfare provided a strong motivation for the "aggressive war machine" that was such a prominent feature of the Aztec state.

Other interpretations of Aztec cannibalism have also been offered. To begin with, although there is little question that the Aztecs practiced ritual cannibalism, there is no agreement about the extent of this practice. Harner, for example, bases his arguments on the evidence from early Spanish chroniclers such as Cortez, who wrote journals and letters describing Mexican customs. But as one critic (Ortiz de Montellano 1978) points out, the Spanish conquistadors did not necessarily write straightforward accounts of what they saw; they slanted their descriptions to make the Aztecs seem like barbarians in order to convince the king of Spain to support the conquest and undertake a large conversion effort by the Church. Ortiz de Montellano further argues that Aztec cannibalism can be fully explained by religious ideology and the desire to achieve status. He holds that neither the need for a dietary supplement nor the significance of the dietary contribution of human flesh have been convincingly demonstrated by Harner. The point here is not to prove one side of the argument or the other, but to indicate some of the ways in which even the most bizarre religious practices can be made to "make sense" in terms of sociocultural system of which they are a part.

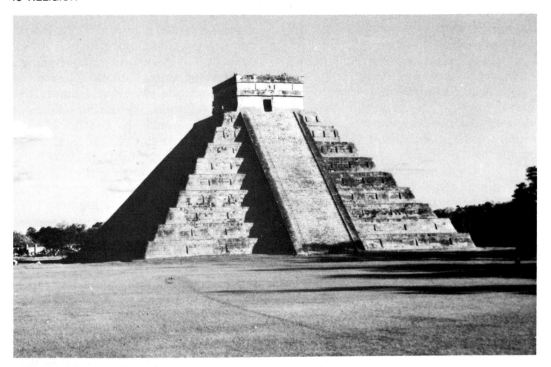

The religion of post-classic Maya, like the Aztec, involved human sacrifice. Pictured is a temple at the Mayan site of Chichen-Itza, in Yucatan, showing vividly the steep steps from which the sacrificial victims were thrown to the bottom. (Serena Nanda)

Magic

Magic is an attempt to mechanistically control supernatural forces. In performing magic, human beings are expressing their belief that they may directly affect nature and each other, for good or ill, by their own efforts. Magic is thus different from other religious practices, such as prayer and offerings, in which the gods are *asked* to help bring about some condition. Magic involves specific ritual procedures, which if done correctly will compel a specific and predictable result. In imitative magic, the procedure performed resembles the result desired. Imitative magic may go back thousands of years; pictures of bleeding animals painted on cave walls suggest that imitative magic was used to ensure success in hunting. Imitative magic may make use of verbal elements as well. Among the Cherokee, a spell for minor burns is

Water is cold
Ice is cold
Snow is cold
Rime is cold
"Relief!" I will be saying.

Here the spell invokes four cold things. Along with saying the spell, cold water is also blown onto the burns, and this probably has some healing power of its own. Contagious magic uses something that has been in contact or will be in contact with whatever the magician wishes to influence.

In contagious magic, the part may represent the whole; for example sorcerers will use the hair or fingernails of their intended victims to work their magic against them.

In many cultures, magical practices are part of most human activities. Among the Asoro of New Guinea, when a child is born its umbilical cord is buried so that it cannot later be used by a sorcerer to cause harm. In order to prevent the infant's crying at night, a bundle of sweet-smelling grass is placed on the mother's head, and her wish for uninterrupted sleep is blown into the grass. The grass is then crushed over the head of the child who, in breathing its aroma, also breathes in the mother's command not to cry. When a young boy kills his first animal, his hand is magically "locked" into the position of the successful kill. When he later tries to court a girl, he will use love magic, which in a particularly powerful form will make him appear in front of her with the face of another man to whom she is known to be attracted. Both magical and technical skills will be used to make gardens and pigs grow. One technique is to blow smoke into the ear of a wild pig to tame it. This is based on the belief that the smoke cools and dries the pig's "hot" disposition. Magical techniques are used for serious illness; blowing smoke over the patient to cool a fever (which is hot); administering sweet-smelling leaves with a command for the illness to depart.

Divination, a magical practice directed toward obtaining useful information from a supernatural authority, is found in many societies. Flipping a coin is an example of divination in our own culture. Divination is magical in that it is a mechanical procedure for picking one of a set of alternative solutions, no one of which appears on the basis of available evidence to be preferable to the other. The practice of divination makes people more confident in their choices when they do not have all the information they need, or when several alternative courses of action appear equal. Divination may also be practiced when a group decision has to be made and there is disagreement. If the choice is made by divination, no member of the group feels rejected.

Among the Naskapi, who hunt caribou on the Labrador penisula, a form of divination called scapulomancy is used for hunting. In the divination ritual, a shoulder blade (scapula) of a caribou or other animal is scorched by fire. The scorched bone is used as a map of the hunting area, and the cracks in the bone are read as giving information about the best place to hunt. Naskapi scapulomancy may be adaptive because it randomizes the choices of location, a strategy that modern game theorists know results in the least chance of repeated failures.

Some farmers in the United States use a divination technique called "water-witching" or "dowsing" to find sources of well water where scientific opinion offers no certainty about where water will be found. In one technique, the dowser holds a forked willow branch (a willow is a tree found by river banks and is "sympathetic" to water) in his hands as he walks over a property. When he stands above water, the wand is supposed to bend downward. The effect of this ritual is to help a homesteader make a decision and be able to move forward confidently in developing his farm. In fact, because of the great variability of the water table, the method of the dowser appears to be no more or less reliable than scientific techniques in determining which spots will have water.

Sorcery

Magic may be used to benefit the community or an individual, or for antisocial purposes. **Sorcery** is the use of magic with the intent of harming another person. Bone-pointing is a magical technique of sorcerers in Melanesia and is described by Malinowski for the Trobriand Islands. The sorcerer ritually imitates throwing a magical stick, either an arrow or the spine of some animal, in the direction of the person the magic is intended to kill. For the magic to work, the sorcerer must perform the procedure with an expression of hatred. He thrusts the bone in the air, twists it as if in anger in the wound, and then pulls it out with a sudden jerk. Both the physical act and the emotional state of passion have to be imitated to achieve results.

Cases of magical death, or death from sorcery, have been observed by anthropologists in a number of different parts of the world. A classic case is that described by Cannon (1942), in which he observed an Australian aborigine who sickened and died after believing himself the victim of sorcery. Sorcery, like the other forms of magic discussed above, achieves its results indirectly by affecting the individual's emotional state. The effectiveness of sorcery depends on the awareness of the victim that a magical ritual is being performed against him or her. If the victim is psychologically vulnerable to begin with and believes in the effectiveness of sorcery, he or she may exhibit a stress reaction that consists of the disordering of various physiological functions. The intended victim may despair, lose his or her appetite, and slowly starve to death, unable to overcome the inertia caused by realizing he or she is a victim.

The use of magic and sorcery appears to be attracting an increasing following in our own society, where it also achieves its results through exploiting the vulnerability of people who feel they have little control over their lives. Edward J. Moody (1974) describes a witch cult in San Francisco in which a great many ritual and magical practices are believed to give the cult members control over others and help them achieve success in life. A frequently used magical ritual is the "curse." If a member of the cult feels he has been hurt by another individual, he can bring his case to the high priest and the congregation. If they agree he has been unjustly treated, they will perform a ritual curse on the offender. The name of the intended victim is written on the skin of an unborn lamb and burned in the altar flame while the member speaks the curse, commanding that his victim be tormented in a variety of horrible ways. In one case described by Moody, a letter was sent to the victim informing him that a curse had been placed on him, and then a death certificate filled out in his name was mailed to him. After several weeks, the man in fact entered the hospital with a bleeding ulcer and when he recovered left San Francisco permanently. Although this victim may not have believed in the power of magic, he already had a bleeding ulcer, a failing business, and hypertension, a combination that made him vulnerable to the cult's efforts against him. Moody's description of the cult members suggests that where people feel they are losing control over their lives and are unable to make changes through manipulation of the real world, they will turn to the manipulation of the supernatural. Marvin Harris (1975) has also suggested that this is one explanation of the increase in the popularity of magic and witchcraft in contemporary American society.

Witchcraft

Witchcraft, like sorcery, is an attempt to harm another person through supernatural means. Unlike sorcery, which requires actual material substances, witchcraft is a quality of an individual, and witches operate only through psychic means. Sorcerers consciously undertake the kinds of actions they know will harm another; the power of witches may be an involuntary one. Our understanding of witchcraft will best be furthered by looking at the way it operates in a particular human society, in this case the Azande of Africa, who have been intensively studied by the anthropologist E. E. Evans-Pritchard (1958).

The Azande believe witchcraft to be a physical condition of the intestines that allows the soul of the witch to go out at night and harm others. Although the Azande believe that witchcraft can enter into every misfortune that befalls them, they do not live in the constant terror of witches. After some misfortune occurs, they blame it on a witch. The Azande know that misfortunes are part of life: canoes are overturned, people become ill, houses burn down. The question the Azande asks, which is the basis of the belief in witchcraft, is "Why me?" and "Why now?" Witchcraft in one sense is thus a theory of causation; what Americans might attribute to coincidence or bad luck, the Azande blames on the activities of a witch. Where a belief in witchcraft pervades a society, it

Divine intervention may be invoked to cure illness. The Navajo curer, Grey Squirrel, attempts to cure a patient by administering herbs, which is one element in the curing ceremony. The patient sits on a sand painting. (Museum of the American Indian, Heye Foundation)

becomes the first explanation when misfortune occurs. The Azande understand perfectly well that sometimes a lack of skill or a lack of morality are the cause of misfortune. A careless potter whose pots break will have a hard time getting others to accept witchcraft as the cause. Similarly, the Azande do not believe that witchcraft causes a person to lie or steal, and they hold the individual responsible for such moral lapses.

The Azande believe that witches are motivated by hate, envy, and spite against a specific person. Thus, an Azande man who believes that witchcraft has been worked on him looks around for the person with whom he has quarreled, or who may have reason to be jealous of him. If the misfortune is a significant one, such as an illness or blight on his crops, the man will take action in a number of ways. He may try using magic to stop the witchcraft or call in a diviner to find out who the witch is so that he or she can be persuaded to call off the evil. In extreme cases, he may kill the alleged witch.

Witchcraft as it operates among the Azande indirectly helps to maintain the social order. It provides an explanation for what would otherwise be unexplainable and therefore gives support to the established pattern of culture. The procedures involved in handling witchcraft also help prevent the open disruption of established social relations, since an oracle must be consulted to divine who the witch is. Action is taken only with the support of the group; one person does not carelessly accuse another of being a witch. Witchcraft also serves as a leveling mechanism among the Azande, as it does in other societies. Since it is primarily a man who has repeated good fortune or who acquires more than the normal amount of wealth who is believed to become the target of witchcraft, individuals rarely attempt to outdo their neighbors by producing more than is required for their own needs. Furthermore, witchcraft helps reinforce Azande ideas about morality; it defines the good man and the evil man. The person who is jealous, spiteful, and envious knows that he is most likely to be accused as a witch, and this expectation will bring his behavior more into conformity with the norms. In this way, witchcraft is a means of controlling behavior considered harmful and disruptive to the society. These functions of witchcraft are not unique to Azande society; they have been found to operate in many other societies as well.

THE ORGANIZATION OF RELIGION

Like other human behavior, religious behavior is patterned and organized. A useful way of examining religious organization is in terms of the degree of specialization of religious personnel—those who conduct ceremonies and perform rituals. On this basis, Anthony Wallace identifies four patterns of religious organization: individualistic cults, shamanistic cults, communal cults, and ecclesiastical cults. Although all patterns may be found in complex societies, simpler hunting and gathering societies may only have individualistic and shamanistic cults. Communal cults are characteristic of horticultural and tribally organized societies, and ecclesiastical cults are found in state societies.

Individualistic Cults

In **individualistic cults** each person may be a religious specialist, seeking contact with the supernatural directly according to his or her own experience and psychic needs. An example of an individualistic religious cult is the *vision quest*, a pattern of seeking contact with the supernatural found among many Indian groups of North America. In these cultures, an individual was able to develop a special relationship with a particular spirit that would give the person power and knowledge of specific kinds. The spirit acted as a personal protector, or guardian. The vision seeker was under a strong emotional impulse and by various means, such as fasting, isolation in a lonely spot, or self-mutilation, intensified his or her emotional state.

The Thompson Indians of western Canada had a vision quest that included most of the traits typical of this pattern. When a boy, usually between the ages of 12 and 16, became old enough to dream of an arrow, a canoe, or a woman, he began his search for a guardian spirit. Before the actual quest itself, the boy had to run, with bow and arrow in his hands, until he was exhausted. Then he was made to plunge into cold water. He did this four times a day for four days. His face was painted red, and he put on a headband of cedar bark and tied ornaments made of deer hoof to his knees and ankles. He also wore a skin apron decorated with symbols of the life occupation for which he sought the spirit's assistance. The nights prior to undertaking the quest were spent in dancing, singing, and praying around a fire on some nearby mountain peak.

The boy then went on lonely pilgrimages into the mountains, eating nothing for several days on end. He intensified his physical suffering by sweating himself with heated rocks over which he threw water, and also by whipping his body with nettles. During all this time he also threw rocks and ran for miles to ensure against disease, laziness, and bad luck. This strenuous

regime continued until the boy had a dream of some animal or bird and received the inspiration for a spirit song that he would then always use to call upon his protector. He also prepared a medicine bag of the skin of the spirit animal and filled it with a variety of objects that had taken on symbolic significance for him during his quest. These became the symbols of his power (Pettitt 1972).

Although the vision quest was an intensely individual experience, it was nevertheless shaped by culture in a number of ways. Among the Crow Indians, for example, several informants related the same vision and interpretation to the anthropologist, Robert Lowie. They told of how on their lonely vigil they saw a spirit or several spirits riding along, and how the rocks and trees in the neighborhood turned into enemies who attacked the horsemen but were unable to inflict any harm. They interpreted this to mean that the spirits were making the visionary invulnerable. This motif is part of Crow mythology and is unconsciously worked into their experience by the vision seekers. Another cultural influence is that most Crow Indians obtained their spiritual blessing on the fourth night of their seclusion, and four is considered a mystical number among the Crow.

Shamanistic Cults

A **shaman** is a person who is socially recognized as having special supernatural powers that are used on behalf of human clients for a variety of activities: curing, divination, sorcery, and reading fortunes, among others. Among Eskimo coastal communities, the shaman's most important service is to make a yearly spiritual trip to the bottom of the sea to persuade the sea goddess (Sedna), who is the keeper of the sea animals, to release the game so that the Eskimo can live through one more year. Eskimo shamans are also frequently called upon to cure illness; this is done by discovering which supernatural being has been offended by a broken taboo and caused the illness. Frequently the illness will be treated by extracting a confession from the victim, and through a ritual procedure the possessing spirit will then be exorcised.

A typical shamanistic curing performance among the Netsilik Eskimo is described by the ethnographer Asen Balicki (1963):

> The shaman, adorned with his paraphernalia, crouched in a corner of the igloo . . . and covered himself with a caribou skin. The lamps were extinguished. A protective spirit called by the shaman entered his body and, through his mouth, started to speak very rapidly, using the shaman's secret vocabulary. While the shaman was in trance, the *tupiliq* (an evil spirit believed to be round in shape and filled with blood) left the patient's body and hid outside the igloo. The shaman then dispatched his protective spirits after the *tupiliqs;* they, assisted usually by the benevolent ghost of some deceased shaman, drove the *tupiliqs* back into the igloo through the entrance; the audience encouraged the evil spirits, shouting: "Come in, come in, somebody is here waiting for you." No sooner had the *tupiliqs* entered the igloo than the shaman, with his snow knife, attacked them and killed as many as he could; his successful fight was evidenced by the evil spirits' blood on his hands.

In case the patient died, it was said that the *tupiliqs* were too numerous for the shaman to kill or that after the seance evil spirits again attacked the patient.

Shamanistic activity has important therapeutic effects for individual clients, who are often relieved of illness through the cathartic effects of the ritual. Shamanism also has important integrating functions for the society. Through a wide variety of symbolic acts, shamanistic performances bring together various beliefs and religious practices in a way that dramatically expresses and reinforces the values of a culture and the solidarity of a society. Such performances frequently involve participation by the audience, whose members may experience various degrees of ecstasy themselves. These performances are cathartic in the sense that they release the anxiety caused by various disturbing events affecting individuals or the community as a whole. The forces of nature and the supernatural, which have the power to do evil in a society, are brought under control; seemingly inexplicable misfortunes are given meaning within the traditional cultural pattern; and the community is better able to carry out its normal activities.

Communal Cults

In **communal cults,** groups of ordinary people hold rituals or ceremonies for the total community or parts of it—for example, age groups, sex groups, kinship groups, castes, or neighborhoods. These ceremonies may use ritual specialists, but the basic responsibility lies with ordinary people who on this occasion take on specialized sacred roles and perform sacred acts. Communal cult institutions include many different kinds of rituals. Some are not connected with the supernatural, such as Fourth of July celebrations in the United States. Most of these rituals can be conveniently divided into rites of passage and rites of intensification.

Rites of Passage. **Rites (rituals) of passage** mark the transition of an individual from one social status to another. One of the most important functions of religion is to help individuals and society deal with the crises of life. In almost all societies, transitions in social status—conception, birth, puberty, marriage, death—are surrounded by religious ritual. Rites of passage tend to have three phases: separation, transition, incorporation. In the separation phase, the individual is removed from his/her old group or status. The rituals of this phase symbolize the loss of the old status or personality—having the head shaved, or casting off one's old name. In the transition stage, the individual is between stages; although he/she has been cut off from the old status, he/she has not yet

been incorporated into the new one. At this point the individual may be treated as sacred, in recognition of the power and the danger of this in-between position. In the third stage, the individual is incorporated into the new group or status. The rituals and symbols of this stage frequently are those of rebirth.

Funerary rites from our own and other societies indicate that death is a rite of passage. Rituals of the first stage, in which grief may be demonstrated by family and friends, mark the loss of the social person. In this stage the remains of a deceased person may be buried. In the transitional period, the soul of the dead, as well as the corpse itself, is believed to be dangerous. It can take the form of a ghost and can wander among the living and cause illness and other misfortunes. In the third stage, the deceased is ritually removed from iso-

Initiation rituals use many kinds of religious symbolism. Here white pipe clay is being applied as part of an Australian ritual. (American Museum of Natural History)

lation or "limbo" and incorporated into its new status, perhaps as an angel in heaven, or as reunited with ancestors. This stage is marked in some societies by unearthing the bones of the dead, ritually treating them, and burying them again. With this phase of the ritual the deceased is no longer dangerous to the living.

Rites of Intensification. **Rites of intensification** are directed toward the welfare of the group or community, rather than the individual, and have rather explicit goals: increasing the fertility of the land in agricultural societies, or the availability of game among hunting and fishing groups. These rites are also performed when there is a crisis in the life of the group, as in the transfer of power or in the loss caused by death. Funerary rites directed at moving the deceased individual from death to a new life have corresponding rituals that must be observed by the survivors. In the first stage, the survivors ritually express their bereavement for the loss of the deceased; in the interim stage they are in a period of limbo (mourning); finally, with the performance of rituals that end the mourning period, they resume normal social activity. Rites of intensification are also carried out to maintain the ties between the dead and the living, as in the case of ancestor worship, or to express the unity between humans and nature, as in the case of totemism.

Totemism is a prominent feature of the religion of the Australian aborigines, who believe that people and nature share a common life and belong to one moral order. Just as human society is divided into mutually dependent and reciprocating groups, so too is nature. Each human group is linked with some species or object in the natural environment, which is its totem and with which it is mutually inter-

dependent. By rules of birth and locality, people are grouped into "societies" or "lodges," each of which is associated with a different totem. This totem is their Dreaming. The Dreaming refers to the name of the totem species, to a cult hero, to the myths that tell of the deeds and sacred places of the totem species or hero, and to the rituals organized to represent the myths. In order to join the cult for which he is eligible, each male must undergo an initiation symbolizing death and rebirth. Only after this is knowledge of the myth, ritual, and sacred objects that make up the Dreaming gradually given to him. The chief object is the bull-roarer, the symbol and voice of the sky hero or of the totemic Dream Time heroes. In desert areas, the most important rites are for the increase of the totemic species. These rites are connected with centers associated with the cult heroes. Natural objects, mostly rocks, are said to be transformed bodies or parts of heroes or totemic species that appear in the cult myths. Myths are sung, actors re-create the heroic scenes, and human blood is applied to the stone symbol. As a result, the natural species increases, as the spirits of the species go forth to be reincarnated. Except for an annual ritual occasion, the members of a totemic group do not eat its totem species, although members of other totem groups are allowed to do so. Thus, each group denies itself one type of food and depends on other groups for the ritual increase of foods it does eat. In addition to increasing rites, there are also ceremonies held at temporarily sacred places. Here the past of the Dream Time heroes is reenacted. As they realize the presence of the Dreaming, onlookers and performers become carried away in a state of ecstasy. Through these rituals, the community maintains continuity with the past, enhances the feeling of social unity in the present, and renews the sentiments on which cohesion depends (Elkin 1967).

The totem rites of the aborigines clearly point up the social functions of religion. According to Emile Durkheim, a French sociologist, it was this function of religious ritual that was most important. When people worship their totem, which is a symbol of their common social identity, they are actually worshipping society—the moral and social order that is the foundation of social life. Durkheim believed that totemism was the origin of religion because the aboriginal populations of Australia are technologically among the world's simplest societies. Although this aspect of his theory is no longer thought to be correct, his analysis of the social function of religious rites in terms of heightening social solidarity is an important contribution to anthropology.

Religious ritual can also promote social solidarity by channeling conflict so that it does not disrupt the society. In all societies there are conflicts of interest and unconscious hostility between different groups who are in unequal power relationships. Many societies have *rituals of reversal* during which people in the different groups ritually reverse their relationships. In the Zulu society in Africa, one day in the year women act as men and men act as women. The women chase and beat the men and act sexually aggressive toward them. In India, the celebration of Holi, which is primarily a harvest festival, includes a ritual reversal between dominant and inferior castes, as well as between men and women.

We are familiar with such reversals in Sadie Hawkins Day and Leap Year rituals, when in our own society it is considered permissible for women to ask men to marry them. In many high schools and colleges one day is set aside when freshmen are allowed to harass the senior class, or students take over the classrooms and teachers take the role of students. Rituals of reversal contribute to social stability by allowing the channeled release of tensions that build up when one group of people is in a permanently subordinate position to another.

Ecclesiastical Cults

An **ecclesiastical cult** has a professional clergy that is formally elected or appointed and that devotes all or most of its time to a specialized religious role. These people, called priests, are responsible for performing certain rituals on behalf of individuals, groups, or the entire community. Individuals have access to supernatural power only through these intermediaries. Where ecclesiastical cults exist, there is a rather clear-cut division between the lay and priestly roles. Laypeople participate in the ritual largely as passive respondents or audience, rather than as managers or performers. Ecclesiastical cults are most frequently associated with gods who are believed to have great power; these cults may be part of a religion that worships several such high gods, as in the religion of the ancient Greeks, Egyptians, and Romans, or just one high god, as in the Judeo-Christian tradition and Islam. Ecclesiastical cults are usually found in politically complex state societies. In these socially stratified societies, the elite may invoke religious authority in order to control the lower classes. The priesthood and religion act not only as a means of regulating behavior, which is a function of religion in all societies, but also as a way of maintaining social, economic, and political inequalities.

In societies where an ecclesiastical cult is the established religion of the state or the upper classes, the religious practices and

In ecclesiastical religions, priests and other kinds of intermediaries are required to carry out religious ritual. These specialists are also more knowledgeable than the ordinary person and act as teachers, as well as ritual leaders, such as this Buddhist priest in Katmandu, Nepal. (United Nations)

beliefs of the poor or lower classes may be quite different from those of the elite. Powerless segments of society may use religion to rationalize their lower social position, and place more emphasis on an afterlife in which they will be rewarded more than those who have power. Sects and cults among the poor may have a millenarian outlook—they may be focused on the coming of a messiah who will usher in a utopian world. In many of these cults, members participate in rituals that give individuals direct access to supernatural

power by experiencing states of ecstasy heightened by singing, dancing, handling of dangerous objects such as snakes, or the use of drugs. There are many such sects and cults in the United States.

One of the most well known is that of the serpent-handlers whose churches are spread over Southern Appalachia. Serpent handling is justified in these fundamentalist congregations by reference to Mark 16:17–18, in the King James Bible:

And these signs shall follow them that believe: In my name shall they cast out devils; They shall speak with new tongues; *They shall take up serpents;* and if they drink any deadly thing, it shall not hurt them; They shall lay hands on the sick, and they shall recover.

For those who are the members of these churches, the above signs are demonstrations of the power of God working in those individuals who, through their belief, become his instrument. When a person receives the power of the Lord he or she is able to handle poisonous snakes without being bitten. In these church services, members of the congregation pick up handfuls of poisonous snakes, thrust them under their shirts or blouses, hold on to them while dancing ecstatically, and even wrap them around their heads and wear them like crowns. The ritual of serpent handing takes up only part of the service, which includes in addition the singing of Christian hymns, dancing, spontaneous sermons, faith-healing and "speaking in tongues," all of which are part of the Holiness movement in Appalachia.

Weston LaBarre (1969) writing about these churches in *And They Shall Take Up Serpents* suggests that to the extent that these religious experiences create an illusion of power and stop people from making real changes in their lives, these sects and cults are maladaptive. They are adaptive at the level of the whole society, however, because they channel dissatisfaction and anger so that the larger social structure is left intact.

REVITALIZATION MOVEMENTS

In many parts of the world, groups of people have experienced rapid disintegration of their culture through contact with the West. Culture loss, and the subsequent loss of a positive personal identity, have led to the emergence of **revitalization movements,** consciously organized efforts to construct a more satisfying culture. Some of these movements aim to restore a golden age believed to have existed in the past; others look toward a utopian future in which roles will be reversed and the lowly will be in power. Sometimes these movements reject all elements of the old cultural systems under which they suffer; in other cases, they attempt to combine new customs with the old and dissolve the social boundaries between the dominant

THE BLACK MUSLIMS: A REVITALIZATION MOVEMENT IN CONTEMPORARY AMERICA

In our own society, cultural loss, economic oppression, and powerlessness experienced by different lower-class and minority groups have also led to religious revitalization movements, such as the Ghost Dance among the Native Americans in the 1880s and the Black Muslim movement in contemporary America. Two hundred years of slavery and 150 years of prejudice and discrimination have left blacks in America economically deprived and burdened with a sense of racial inferiority. Various religious revitalization movements have appeared from time to time in the black community as a response to the stress of deprivation and the inability to forge a positive identity within American culture and society. The Nation of Islam, also known as the Black Muslims, is a contemporary revitalization movement that appears to be somewhat successful, both in attracting members and in changing their lives (Parenti 1967).

The Black Muslims advocate racial separation in a nation of their own and obedience to the messianic and authoritarian leadership of the "messenger," Elijah Mohammed. The movement contains many religious elements drawn from Islam, and rejects many cultural patterns that are part of black life in the United States. According to the Muslim vision, the first man whom God (Allah) created was black, and "blackness" was the true expression of beauty and virtue. Then came the Fall, in which the black man was enslaved by the Devil, in the form of the white man. But then came the Message; a Messiah and his followers, armed with the truth of Islam, purged themselves of the white man's corruption. The Muslims will lead the chosen people, the heretofore rejected and despised, from their present bondage to paradise on this earth, a separate Muslim nation. The "blue-eyed white devil" will fall in the Battle of Armageddon, and nonwhites will rule the earth.

The Black Muslims did not for the most part seek violent confrontations with whites in order to create their new world, but rather attempted to change the behavior of blacks in a way that would endow their life with meaning and purpose. The movement offered hope in a future in which blackness would no longer be despised. It expressed the nationalist's need to attach him/herself in a positive way to something worthy and esteemed, some center of power and some tradition, a central ideal capable of endowing life with meaning and purpose.

The success of this movement with blacks for whom all hope of rehabilitation had been dismissed—drug addicts, criminals, alcoholics, unemployed slum dwellers—has been impressive. They have become obedient to the teachings of Elijah Muhammad, abstaining from drink, drugs, tobacco, gambling, promiscuity, stealing, and idleness. Muslims are forbidden to spend money frivolously, and are committed to pooling their resources to help themselves and each other. They have created Muslim-owned schools and businesses. Muslim men must dress conservatively in suits and ties. Muslim women are supposed to wear a full white robe covering their arms and legs, and a white headdress. The dress of both men and women represents a break with the stereotype of the flamboyantly dressed lower-class black in America. The woman's dress in particular symbolizes a new relationship between men and women; women are protected, secluded, and obedient to males, and are expected to be devoted to their homes and families.

The foods prescribed by the Nation of Islam are wholesome (whole wheat rather than white bread), and those that are forbidden include both the traditional Islamic taboos on pork and sea food, as well as "soul food" or the standard southern fare reminiscent of the past, such as corn bread, black-eyed peas, collard greens, and possum. There is only one daily meal, which the family eats ceremoniously together. These patterns do not merely symbolize a new and positive identity for Black Muslims; they also have had a strengthening effect on health and family life.

The Black Muslim movement is a clear example of the ways in which the construction of a collective identity through the use of myth, symbol, and organization revitalizes the identity of the individual. The movement suggests that the seeking of change through secular political organization has not made a sufficient impact in restructuring American society to include a positive identity for all its citizens. Where politics fails, religious revitalization movements fill the gap.

and powerless groups in society. Even when a revitalization movement may be relatively ineffectual in bringing about the desired changes, it can still bring a sense of salvation and a more positive identity to people afflicted with feelings of conflict, inadequacy, and alienation from themselves and society.

This discussion of the Black Muslims again raises the question of whether religion may be more adaptive for some groups in society than for others. Where religious myths justify social stratification, elite groups obviously benefit more than others. Where the resentment of oppressed or subordinate groups is drained off in religious ritual, the resulting social stability would seem to be most advantageous to those already in the dominant positions. Although religion allows an illusion of control, this illusion may not be adaptive for many peoples in the long run. It remains to be seen whether political revitalization and participation will undermine the power of religious beliefs and rituals to alleviate the stresses caused by culture contact, modernization, and social inequality in the contemporary world.

SUMMARY

1. Religion is the beliefs and practices of a society concerned with supernatural beings, powers, and forces. Religion is a universal culture pattern and goes back to the beginnings of the human species.

2. Religion has many functions. Some of the most significant are explaining aspects of the physical and social environment, reducing anxiety in risky situations, increasing social solidarity, education, ensuring confor-

mity, maintaining social inequalities, and regulating the relationship of a group of people to their natural environment.

3. Religious ideas are always expressed through symbols in which things stand for other things. Religious ideas are also acted out in ritual, and ritual reinforces beliefs.

4. Two widespread kinds of religious beliefs are animism and animatism. Animism is the belief that inanimate objects as well as living creatures have life and personality. Animatism is the belief in an impersonal supernatural power.

5. Many different kinds of religious rituals are used to manipulate and control supernatural powers: prayer, offerings and sacrifices, telling and acting out of myths, and altering emotional states through music, physical suffering, and drugs.

6. Magic is an attempt to control supernatural forces mechanically. Magic may be used for good or antisocial purposes; sorcery, however, is the use of magic with the intent of harming another person.

7. Witch beliefs have a number of different functions in society. They ensure conformity, explain unpredictable events, prevent open social conflict, and act as a leveling mechanism.

8. Religious behavior is almost always organized. Four types of organization have been defined based on the degree of specialization of religious personnel.

9. In individualistic cults, each individual may be his/her own religious specialist and have direct contact with supernatural power.

10. Shamanistic cults involve the use of shamans, people who are socially recognized as having special powers which they exercise on behalf of their clients and groups in society.

11. In communal cults, groups of ordinary people hold rituals for the welfare of the whole community, or of groups within the community. Two kinds of communal rituals are rites of passage, which mark the transition of individuals from one social status to another, and rites of intensification, which are directed toward the welfare of the community.

12. Ecclesiastical cults are characterized by a professional group of religious specialists who are responsible for performing rituals on behalf of individuals or the community. Only these specialized practitioners have access to supernatural power. This kind of religious organization is characteristic of complex and socially stratified societies.

13. Religious revitalization movements are consciously organized efforts to construct a new culture and personal identity. These movements arise in situations in which a group of people has been oppressed and has suffered cultural loss and loss of personal identity.

SUGGESTED READINGS

Daner, Francine
1976   *The Children of Krishna.* New York: Holt, Rinehart and Winston. An anthropologist looks at the Hari Krishna cult in the United States and some of the ways it has adapted to Western culture and the identity needs of young adults who are alienated from the larger society.

Leslie, Charles, ed.
1960   *Anthropology of Folk Religion.* New York: Random House. A collection of interesting articles on religious beliefs and ritual from Africa, India, the South Pacific, and Mexico.

Lessa, W. A., and Vogt, E. Z., eds.
1971   *Reader in Comparative Religion: An Anthropological Approach* (3rd ed.). New York: Harper and Row. An excellent collection of articles on many different aspects of religion.

Malinowski, B.
1954   *Magic, Science and Religion, and Other Essays.* Garden City, N.Y.: Doubleday. A discussion of some theoretical issues, using data from the Trobriand Islands.

Turner, Victor
1967   *The Forest of Symbols: Aspects of Ndembu Ritual.* Ithaca, N.Y.: Cornell University Press. Fascinating and detailed accounts of a variety of rites of passage and communal rites among a south-central African people. The emphasis is on the meaning of the symbols and the function of ritual; the author is a leading figure in symbolic anthropology.

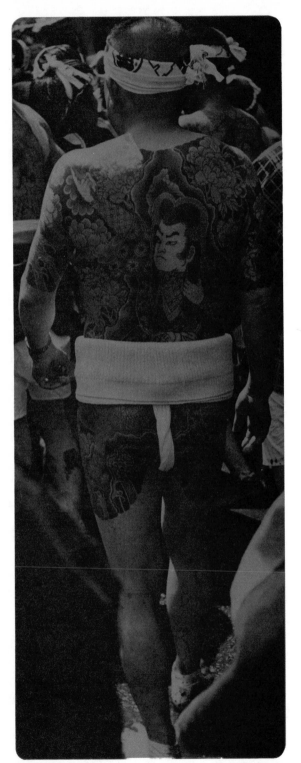

Sheldon Brody

14
The Arts

Much of what human beings do, as we have seen, they do to survive. And yet it is also true that human life everywhere consists of more than just survival. In every society, people apply imagination and skill to matter, movement, or sound to express emotions and values and to give one another pleasure. The forms of this creative activity may be plastic arts, such as painting, sculpture, carving, pottery, or weaving; the structured use of sound in music, song, and poetry, and in myths, storytelling, folklore, and word play. In the movements of the human body—in dance, sport, and games—we also see the application of imagination, beauty, skill, and style that goes beyond the merely practical. **Art,** then, refers to both the process and the products of human skill applied to any activity that meets the standards of preferred form or beauty in a particular society. In this sense, for example, tea drinking is an art form in Japan, but not in the United States. This kind of broad definition of the arts allows us to consider games and other forms of popular entertainment in some of the same ways we consider arts in the more traditional sense.

ANTHROPOLOGICAL PERSPECTIVES

Because art in its broadest sense is a universal aspect of human experience, it is worthy of study by anthropologists, and by those who wish to understand our species more completely. It is also the great variety of artistic forms and styles that characterize human cultures which makes the study of the arts so rewarding. Because artistic endeavors express some of the basic themes and values of a culture, they are an important way to gain insight into cultural patterning in different societies, and into the different ways in which peoples perceive reality.

Anthropological discussion of the arts ordinarily divides them into four types; plastic and graphic arts; music; dance; and folklore (consisting mainly of oral tradition). Certain general approaches in cultural anthropology can be applied to the study of all these arts, but because of their different natures, they are usually studied by specialists. Some of the generalized approaches to the study of the various arts consider (1) content, themes, or subject matters; (2) style; (3) changes over time; (4) social and psychological functions; (5) relationship with other aspects of culture and society; (6) the creative process and the interaction of the artist and his/her audience. Before looking at the various forms of human art, we will look first at the functions of art in society and at the place of art within culture.

The Symbolic Nature of Art

One way of analyzing art is in terms of how it functions as a form of symbolic communication in society. In the first place, art can be seen as communicating direct meaning. For example, some dance movements attempt to imitate the movements of animals, while the contents of some paintings are believed not merely to represent, but to *be*—to partake of the spirit of—the thing visualized. Masks used in ritual are often believed to take on the supernatural power of the spirits or beings they represent. By being given a form, as in a mask, a painting, or a sculpture, the spirit may be more easily manipulated and controlled by humans. Among the Kalabari of Africa, for example, spirit beings are represented by sculptures. Offerings are made to them, and the sculptures are the center of ritual action. The more sophisticated individuals in the culture recognize that the statue is not the actual spirit; they consider it a confinement of the spirit. The point of confining, or localizing, the spirit in material form is to manipulate it for human ends.

A second way in which art is symbolic is that particular artistic elements reflect particular emotions or meanings. In this case, the symbolism is culturally specific, and one needs a knowledge of the particular cultural meanings assigned to a particular artistic element. In Western music, for example, the use of the minor scale conveys the emotion of sadness, and various other musical forms are traditionally associated with particular emotions. The traditional element is important in evoking the emotion, because individuals in that culture have been taught the association. In our own culture, the phrase "Once upon a time" signals to us that this is not going to be a story about "real" events and people and sets the stage for us to respond emotionally in certain ways.

A third way in which the arts are symbolic is that they reflect certain kinds of social behavior or social structure: the totem poles of the Northwest Coast Indians reflect the importance of social hierarchy; stories of traditional dance dramas deal with religion; the organization of ritual utilizing dance and music reflects the division of society into various kinship units or ethnic groups. Art styles may also reflect cultural values or patterns. In a study of Navajo music, for example, David McAllester showed that the music reflected their values in several ways. The characteristic Navajo cultural value on individualism is reflected in the attitude that what one does with one's music is one's own affair. Second, the Navajo are essentially a conservative people and believe that "foreign music is dangerous and not for Navajo." Third, the Navajo value of formalism is expressed in the belief that there is only one right way to sing every kind of song (one can contrast this with the value of innovation expressed in improvisation in music—for example, jazz).

The arts may also be symbolic on a deeper level: that is, they represent certain universal aspects of human thought, needs, and emotions. Freudian psychology, for example, assigns certain universal meanings to certain kinds of symbols. The widespread plots of myths having to do with incest might appear to reflect the unconscious working out of the Oedipal complex; the shape of the flute as a musical instrument, and its association with men's cults in many culture areas, has been interpreted as having phallic significance; certain colors have been interpreted as expressing universal physiological processes: red for blood, or white for semen or breast milk.

The Integrative Function of the Arts

The symbolic nature of the arts in communication is related to what is undoubtedly their most important function—that of integration. Through the arts, the beliefs, values, ethics, knowledge, emotions, and ideology and world view of a culture are expressed and communicated. The art forms of a society do not merely reflect culture and society. Participation in cultural performances fosters the unity and harmony of a society in a way that is intensely *felt* by its members. It is perhaps the primary social function of the arts to produce this condition. The art forms of a society take up cultural themes and individual emotions—death, masculinity, pride, chance, relations between male and female, aggression, social cooperation—and present them in ways that make their essential nature understandable, even if it cannot be consciously articulated. Art makes dominant cultural themes visible, tangible, and thus more real. Thus, art is a means of expression that not only heightens emotions associated with cultural themes, values, and goals, but also serves to display them in ways that are emotionally compelling.

In many cultures, including our own, games and sports are emotionally compelling and symbolic in a way that make us think of them, at least in their function, as like traditional art forms. Using this perspective, let us look at the American game of football and see what it may symbolize about our society.

The Arts in Cultural Context

The study of art largely divorced from its cultural context reflects to some extent an ethnocentric point of view that "art for

FOOTBALL IN THE UNITED STATES

According to Arens (1976), the popularity of football in the United States (which is unique among the countries of the world in its attachment to this game) derives from the fact that football contains characteristics particularly important in our society: technological complexity, coordination and specialization, as well as the tendency to violence, although that violence is expressed within the framework of teamwork, specialization, and mechanization. From this view: "The football team looks very much like a small scale model of the American corporation: compartmentalized, highly sophisticated in the coordinated application of a differentiated, specialized technology, turning out a winning product in a competitive market" (Montague and Morais 1976:39). Thus, the football game is a model of the most important productive unit in our society—the business firm. By watching football, we are watching a model of the way our world works. It is because football is a small-scale model of our world that it allows us to understand that world. It "renders visible and directly comprehensible a system that is far too large and complex to be directly comprehended by any individual." How many of us can understand the interconnections between all aspects of the American economic system?

Beyond this, however, football is a model of the traditional route to success in our society. Dedication, hard work, and self-sacrifice for the good of others (here, the football team) are held up as the basic principles on which success is based, and are the characteristics most praised in individual players. Football is the staging of a real event in which the principles of success are shown to work. The success model is also illustrated in football commentary or sportscasting. The accomplishments of each player are compared with those of others, and the rewards of the system—money and recognition—are then extended to the players on the basis of their performances. To the extent that football is a model of the real world, the audience sees the actors being evaluated according to objective criteria and rewarded according to performance. It is this process that is at the ideological core of the traditional culture of the United States, and that is ultimately related to the productive process in our society. Surely football is an example of the statement that "art" serves to display the cultural themes of a society in ways that make them emotionally compelling. As for its integrative function, Arens notes at the very beginning of his article that 79 percent of American households were tuned in to the first Super Bowl game on TV, indicating that this entertainment cuts across all the divisive aspects of our social structure—race, ethnicity, income, political affiliation, and regionalism.

art's sake" exists in all cultures. In fact, the opposite is true. Art in most societies is in fact *not* manufactured (or performed) solely for the purpose of giving pleasure. The separation of art from other activities, and the separation of a class of objects or acts labeled "art," is characteristic only of modern societies, and an extension of their tendency toward less cultural integration than is generally true of preindustrial societies. In modern societies, for example, even bad art is distinguished from other cultural products. In preindustrial societies, art is embedded in all aspects of culture; no separate class of materal products, movements, or sounds are created solely to express esthetic values.

The Eskimo, for example, who are considered by anthropologists to have a highly developed artistic skill, do not themselves have a separate word for art. Rather, all "artificial" objects are lumped together as "that which has been made," regardless of the purpose of the object. This does not mean that Eskimos do not have esthetic values, but rather that their plastic art is applied to the manufacture of objects which have primarily instrumental value, such as tools, amulets, or weapons. It should not surprise us, then, that the Eskimo, like most other preindustrial societies, do not make a distinction between artist and craftworker, a distinction which does exist in our society. Similarly, many skills—dancing, weaving, singing, playing a musical instrument—that in our own society are performed as a special category of behavior called the arts in other societies are skills most people learn and use in everyday life. In all societies, some individuals are recognized as more competent in these skills than others, but this competence does not necessarily translate itself into the specialized role of artist.

Because art is so embedded in cultural

A typical house style with rather elaborate decoration in a Paramacca Maroon village in Surinam, South America. Each man ideally carves his own house decoration, and the excellence of the craftsmanship is a source of prestige. (John Lenoir)

traditions, many anthropologists tend to believe it may be difficult to measure esthetic values and styles according to any universal standard. What is beautiful in one culture may not be in another. Each culture has developed its own traditions of content and style to which individuals in that culture conform in their application of creative imagination and skill. The appreciation of art in terms of values and forms that are not our own is difficult to achieve, although this can partly be overcome by attempting to understand the cultural context of art. One of the difficulties is that in the United States today, originality and innovation are an important part of our artistic standards. But art, which is a creative process, is not necessarily an innovative one. Artists in other societies may be very conservative, and archeologists provide evidence that the artistic styles of cultures remain stable over very long periods of time. Furthermore, the integration of art with religion in non-Western societies may limit the range of variation that individual artists display. Where religion and art have become separated, as is now true in much of the contemporary world, experimentation, innovation, and real change in artistic endeavor is much more likely to occur.

Cultures differ not only in their esthetic preferences, but also in the attention they give to various types of art. In some cultures masks and painting are the most important media for the expression of esthetic values and technical skill; in other cultures verbal skills are more important. They will have a wealth of myths, folktales, and word games and relatively little painting, sculpture or pottery. Although every culture has dramatic performances as part of its religion, some cultures have developed this skill more than others. We do not know of any human culture, no matter how simple its technology or how difficult its environment, that does not have any

form of art. In fact, when we look at cultures in which making a living is not easy and in which social structure is relatively simple, such as among Eskimo and aboriginal Australian groups, we find that art has an important place in the culture and that skill in a variety of art forms is of a very high level. We may thus speculate that art is essential in human society, and may even have very important adaptive functions.

GRAPHIC AND PLASTIC ARTS

Many different kinds of skills come under the heading of graphic and plastic arts: painting; sculpture and carving in wood; work in precious metals, bone, ivory, and horn; pottery and work in clay; basketry; weaving and embroidery; architecture; the tailoring of skins and other materials for clothing; and tattooing and other kinds of body ornamentation. The major anthropological emphasis on the arts in small-scale societies has been on the study of graphic and plastic arts. This may be due to the fact that such arts result in products which can be dealt with on their own, removed from their cultural setting, in a way

---

ART IN CULTURE: INTERPRETING ICE AGE ART

One early anthropological interest in these arts was an attempt to apply to them the evolutionary perspective that was being applied by nineteenth-century anthropologists to other aspects of culture. One of these evolutionary theories held that there was a progression from abstract art, characteristic of "primitive" cultures, to the naturalistic or realistic art found in Western civilizations. This theory was undermined by the discovery of Paleolithic or Ice Age art, much of which consists of paintings of animals on cave walls. The images are realistic and complex, and show a high degree of delicacy, skill, and stylistic variation. When this art was first discovered in France and Spain, it was hard to believe it had been created by human beings living 30,000 to 15,000 years ago. The fact that this art was in no way primitive and yet was made by the earliest modern ancestors of our species underlines the difficulty of trying to establish an evolutionary perspective in the development of art styles. Contemporary anthropologists have thus attempted to study this art from a different perspective: What it can tell us about the ideology and life styles of the humans who created it.

Although it is impossible to know for certain, comparison with the art of contemporary hunting and gathering societies suggest that some Ice Age art had a close association with hunting ritual and with a world view that is particular to hunting societies (Levine 1957). In these societies, dependence on nature leads to an intense and intimate relationship with the natural setting. Given the technology of hunting peoples, the hunt is difficult and killing big animals may even be dangerous. Although hunting peoples are extremely knowledgeable about their environment, unexpected natural phenomena can produce crises in their lives. Even when the food supply is abundant, unpredictability and the resistance of

Figure 14.1 *Analysis of this horse, found in a cave in France and dated about 14,500 B.C., indicates that the outline was filled with spots over a period of time, and the hand prints above the horse, and more spots, were added later. These kinds of superimpositions support the argument that such paintings had ritual value for the peoples who made them.*

game to the hunter's purpose create anxiety. This anxiety and uncertainty is expressed by an ideology that perceives nature as active and personal. The peopling of the universe with gods or spirits that can take helping action allows hunting societies to have some control over their situation. It is believed that nature can be appealed to, by humans. One of the ways this is done is by ritually compensating nature for what humans must take from it.

These themes are associated with certain attitudes and patterns of behavior toward art. The main belief in this connection is that a work of art *is* what it represents. From this belief stems the idea that art objects themselves have *mana*-like power. Thus, hunting peoples who make artistic products often do so ritually—that is, as a way of satisfying and appealing to nature. Some aspects of Ice Age art may be interpreted in this way. Many of the drawings of animals, for example, show signs of having been superimposed; it is possible to interpret this superimposition as being part of a restitution ritual (Figure 14.1). Whenever an animal was killed, its essence was restored to nature by a ritual drawing of the animal's image at a sacred spot. If restitution to nature is believed not only possible but necessary, drawing images is one way this may be accomplished. Taking a life is dangerous; ritual art, dedicated to the powerful spirits who protect life, is one way of lessening the danger.

that nonmaterial products such as dance or musical performance cannot. Plastic and graphic forms of art, for example, can be collected and exhibited in museums and art galleries, illustrated in books, and photographed easily. This allows them to be fairly easily compared with each other—in chronological sequences, in terms of stylistic variation, or as representative of the work of individual artists. An artistic product has a permanence a performing art does not have, and this also makes it easier to study.

Style and Society

Interpreting Ice Age art is just one example of how art may lead us to an understanding of culture, and how culture may influence art. Another fascinating attempt in this direction is the work of John Fischer (1961). Fischer's theory is that certain aspects of artistic style "say something" about sociocultural reality, and that this reality in turn shapes the kinds of fantasies which provide psychological security and thus esthetic satisfaction for the artist. Using a cross-cultural sample of relatively homogeneous societies, Fischer tested several hypotheses relating artistic style to the development of social hierarchy. First he distinguished two major types of societies: in "authoritarian" societies, social hierarchy is positively valued. Society is viewed as divided into groups in higher and lower statuses. Each group has a set of rights and responsibilities in relation to those above and below. Those lower than Ego serve him and he must help and protect them; Ego must serve those higher than he, who will in turn help and protect him.

The opposite ideal type is the egalitarian society, in which hierarchy as a principle of organization is rejected. Although differences of prestige do exist, these are not emphasized or even explicitly recognized. Work is seen as cooperative, rather than involving power differences between people working together. Individuals who attempt to control others are not valued as leaders; in fact, they are likely to be seen as a threat to society. Fischer hypothesized that hierarchical and egalitarian societies would have different art styles, and he specifically related four aspects of style to the emphasis on social differentiation.

1. Designs that included the repetition of a number of simple elements would be characteristic of egalitarian

societies, whereas designs integrating a number of unlike elements would be characteristic of hierarchical societies. This hypothesis was based on the idea that security in egalitarian societies depends on the number of comrades (equals in social status) that Ego has. The multiplying of the same design elements is the symbolic representation of peers. In the hierarchical society, security depends on relationships with individuals in a number of differentiated positions. In design, these are symbolized by the integration of a variety of distinct elements.

2. Designs with a large amount of empty (irrelevant) space should characterize egalitarian societies; designs with little irrelevant space should characterize hierarchical societies. This hypothesis was based on the as-

Traditional art forms may use contemporary subject matter. Here a lady driver is expressed in the x-ray style characteristic of much of Australia and New Guinea. Note the repetition of simple elements in the art of egalitarian societies. (Serena Nanda)

sumption that in egalitarian societies people relate to others as equals or do not relate at all. Security in egalitarian societies is found in isolation from other groups. In hierarchical societies, security is produced by incorporating strangers into the hierarchy in a position of relative dominance or submission. This tendency for incorporation would be expressed in designs having little empty space.

3. Symmetrical designs should characterize egalitarian societies; the designs of hierarchical societies should tend to be asymmetrical. Symmetry is a special case of repetition; asymmetry expresses difference.

4. Figures without enclosure should characterize egalitarian societies; enclosed figures should predominate in the designs of hierarchical societies. The lack of enclosure in egalitarian societies symbolizes their face-to-face interaction on an equal basis. The enclosures in the designs of hierarchical societies symbolize the importance of social boundaries between individuals of different ranks.

Fischer's hypotheses were all supported, and this suggests he is indeed on to something in his view that in the field of visual design, at least, art styles may be seen as "cognitive maps" of a sociocultural system.

MUSIC

The Conceptual Basis of Music

All cultures have their own traditional way of using the voice and instruments in structured ways to produce song and music. But the variety in musical systems is not limited to the different ways in which sound is structured; different conceptualizations underlie and shape musical systems. Although music is sound, not all sounds are music. It requires knowledge of a culture from the inside to understand its conceptualizations, which are part of its musical behavior. A description of the conceptual basis of music of the Basongye people of the Republic of the Congo by Alan Merriam (1964) serves as an excellent example. The Basongye see music as something uniquely human. They do not consider the sounds made by birds or animals as music, nor the sounds of nature, such as the wind whistling through the trees. But all human sound is not music either. The Basongye say: "When you are content, you sing; when you are angry, you make noise." "When one shouts, he is not thinking; when he sings, he is thinking." "A song is tranquil; a noise is not." Furthermore, the Basongye consider that in order to be music, sound must be organized. Thus, a single tap on a drum is not considered music, but when the drums play together in the traditionally patterned form drummers use, this is music. For sound to be considered music, it must continue over time. Thus, all drums struck once together are not music.

Focusing on the conceptualization of music in a particular culture leads us to understand why some avant-garde or controversial music elicits such resistance, even in our own culture. In a book significantly called *Silence* (1961), John Cage, a composer who is original, even "shocking" in his conception of music, advocates some new understandings. Cage, unlike the Basongye, wants to work out compositions according to the idea that "nothing takes place but sounds"; he wants to include in musical compositions those sounds that just happen to be in the environment. A composer who makes a musical composition out of twelve radios playing simultaneously challenges us to consider our own conceptualization of music in the same way as musical behaviors from another culture do.

Variation in Culture Areas

Although the variety of conceptualizations of music has not been explored by anthropologists, the variety of musical forms and instruments has been well documented. We are fond of saying that music is a universal language, but it may be more correct to say that music is a language consisting of a number of dialects, some of them mutually unintelligible. Several musical culture areas of the world may be differentiated, though all culture areas show significant internal differences in details and have several rather than only one musical tradition.

The Northeast Asia area includes China, Mongolia, Korea, and Japan. The music of this area is essentially melodic rather than harmonic. Melodic instruments in the early Confucian orchestra consisted of sets of like units; a set of tuned metal bells for chimes, stone slabs for stone chimes, a set of strings on a zither. In contrast to the Western idea of an ensemble in which all instruments sound together as one, each instrument in this music maintains its own identity. Divergence in time, pitch, and ornamentation of several instruments simultaneously playing the same basic melody gives the music a highly stylized quality.

In the Southeast Asian area, percussion, made with gongs, xylophones, cymbals, and bells, predominates. Here the orchestra is not a group of musicians, but a set of instruments unified by their physical appearance and common tuning system. In Indonesia, for example, the *gamelan* (orchestra) is unified by the proper relative sizes of the instruments, the themes and motifs of the decorative carving, and the particular color combinations of paints on the instruments. There is no standard tuning; only instruments belonging to the same orchestra or made by the same maker are in tune with one another. Thus, unlike in the West, musicians do not bring their own instruments to a concert. Each instrument has a function in the orchestra; some may lead, others carry the theme, others accentuate the theme. This is also in contrast to the Western symphony orchestra, in which one instrument may do several of these things at various times during the performance.

In South Asia (India and Ceylon), there are many traditions: tribal music, folk music, commercial film music, and a classical tradition that grows out of religion and philosophy of the Vedic period, going back several thousand years. In the classical tradition, music is seen as a path to self-realization; the texts of classical songs are prayers to the gods. The human voice is the primary instrument. Vocal style is basic to all melody, whether sung or played on an instrument. If an ensemble includes a vocalist, her/his role is preeminent: What is sung is more important than how it is sung. The music is essentially melodic and improvisation has a significant place in performance.

Music in Africa is part of community life. The most important general characteristics of African music are its rhythmic complexity, a call and response pattern, the constant use of percussive devices such as hand clapping and foot stomping, improvisation, interesting vocal effects such as falsetto, and the simultaneous sounding of different pitches by singers or instrumentalists. A great variety of materials is used for musical instruments—clay, metal, gourd, bamboo, tortoise shell, hides, skins, seeds, stones, and palm leaves. Wind and string instruments are found in Africa, but it is the drum that has always attracted the attention of students of African music. Drums are used to talk to spirits, to communicate between people and provide accompaniment for dancing. The important factor in the "talking drums" for which Africa is famous is that the drums create a sound that will carry for long distances. Although in some tribes arbitrary signals are used to symbolize

words and concepts, more frequently the sound system of the drum is tied into the pitch structure of a language. Most African languages are tonal, which means that each syllable of a word has a prescribed tone or pitch. In order to be understood, a speaker must use the proper pitch and syllable. With drums on which the pitch can be changed, the tones and rhythms of these languages can be played and understood.

Among the Indians of North America, music is essentially used in connection with religious ceremonies. It is largely vocal, with flutes, drums, and rattles used to accompany the voice. There is a wide variety of vocal styles. The Pueblos of the Southwest prefer deep male choruses; Plains tribes and the Navajo have a piercing falsetto tradition. In South America, where

Among tribal nomadic peoples of North Africa and Western Asia, major musical forms include the solo song, recitation of epics, and group dances with modest instrumental accompaniment. Women use tamborines to accompany their own songs, as these women of Targuist, Morocco, singing the song of the Rif. (United Nations)

complex civilizations developed, orchestras and musical drama predate the Spanish conquest. Some of these forms spread into the countryside in the form of folk versions of urban music. Orchestral and choral effects are quite unlike anything in North America. Contemporary urban music often includes aboriginal influences in both melody and instruments.

In contemporary music in the Americas, the influence of the African tradition is important—particularly rhythmic sophistication, call and response patterns, and the use of improvisation. African musical styles have continued with the least change in the dance and cult music of Brazil and the Caribbean, and blends in with Hispanic styles in the rhumba and conga of Cuba and the steel band music of Trinidad. The steel band instruments, however, are a local invention, and use a previously unknown principle of instrument construction. In the United States, spirituals and blues and jazz, from which rock and roll is derived, also have their origins in Afro-American music.

The music of the islands of Polynesia shows great variation, with a few common stylistic features. For the most part, traditional music was restricted to chantlike recitations and employed relatively few pitches. The complex manner of singing used trills, different tempos, shouts, and variations in breathing that were often more significant than tonal range or song structure. Traditional chant songs consisted of genealogies, accounts of mythological events, war songs, and love songs. The number of instruments was relatively small: drums, slit-gongs, and bamboo pipes. For making the rhythm of dance movements audible, shells or animal teeth were strung together and worn on the body. Before European contact, stringed instruments were scarce: today two imported string instruments—the ukulele and the guitar—are among the most popular in all Oceania.

Music and Human Adaptation

Documenting the wide variety of musical styles and instruments is, of course, only the beginning in the science of ethnomusicology. Music, like the other arts, may be said to represent the "soul" or cultural identity of a people in a highly condensed and emotional form. An important aspect of studying music, then, is in an attempt to understand the culture of a particular people. And like other art forms, music plays an important indirect role in human adaptation, primarily perhaps by contributing to the integration of society.

One of the most ambitious attempts to document the more direct ways in which music enters into human adaptation has been carried out by Alan Lomax and his colleagues (1968). One obvious relationship is the way in which music is used as an accompaniment for the procurement of food and natural resources and the processes of preparing them for human use. Lomax demonstrates that there is a direct correlation between the ways in which people work and their song style. Individualized song performances are correlated with several kinds of work situations: the voluntary and temporary work teams found in simple band societies and the small family work teams found in societies with plow agriculture. In horticultural societies, where work groups are relatively permanent, cohesive groups of age mates, clan brothers, or extended families, group singing predominates. Thus the individualism characteristic of many aspects of life in hunting societies has its correlate in individualized song performance. The solidarity and cohesiveness of kin groups in

Aboriginal music makers with Didgeridoo and Tapping Sticks. (Courtesy of the American Museum of Natural History)

horticultural societies is reflected in the communal or group nature of their singing. In industrial societies, where the individual and/or individual family is separated from others, individualized song performance again emerges as important.

DANCE

Dance is a form of human behavior composed of culturally patterned, purposeful, and intentionally rhythmical nonverbal body movement and gestures that are not part of ordinary motor activities and that have an esthetic value. Dance appears in every human culture and is also universally combined with other kinds of media—music and song, for example. It also involves supplementary kinds of materials added to the human body, such as decoration, costume, and masks.

Dance, like the other arts, is also symbolic behavior. It carries meanings that are arbitrary and culturally specific in the same way as human speech does. In dance, as in other kinds of human behavior, social learning is important. It is this aspect of human dance which differentiates it from biologically programmed ritual movements among nonhuman animals, such as the "dance" of honeybees or the mating movements of birds. Dance in human societies is used to communicate a variety of ideas and emotions (information), but the meaning of human dance is not self-evident; it depends primarily on the meanings assigned to it in different societies.

Because of its physical nature and its ability to elicit intense emotions, dance is often associated with the kind of excitement that signals special events in the lives of individuals or groups. Thus, dance is often involved in rites of passage, which mark changes in social status. Because the physical behavior involved in rhythmic and energetic dance may alter various physiological processes, such as the production of adrenalin, dance is also an important way of altering states of consciousness. In this connection it may be part of rituals that involve trance and other states of emotion which transcend everyday experience. Through dance, an individual and a group can *feel* the qualitative shift in the normal pattern of mental functioning through a disturbed sense of time, a loss of control, perceptual distortion, a feeling of rejuvenation, a change in body image, or hypersuggestibility.

The study of dance suggests that it appears to be rooted in human capabilities for imposing order on the universe, and may be adaptive for human societies as a way of conveying information about this universe. Dancing may also be adaptive in that, like the other arts, it is a form of exploratory, novel, even playful behavior. Novelty and play are also important adaptive aspects of other primate species. Dance teaches coordination and the skills that are involved in hunting, agriculture, and war. Ordinary movements used in procuring food may be incorporated into dance. Dance (and music) can be, and in many cultures are, used to stir up feelings that may then be directed toward dealing more effectively with one's environment, or coping with particular social problems. War dances, for example, may rouse men to the proper pitch of excitement and confidence so that they may act more effectively in battle. Dance also provides a protected situation in which human beings can experience forms of disorientation that could not be tolerated in everyday life. These may keep alive the capacity for new orientations to reality that at some point may be critical in a group's ability to adapt and thus to survive.

FOLKLORE: FORMS AND FUNCTIONS

Folklore is an inclusive term that includes myths, which are stories about supernatural characters and events; legends, which concern historical persons and events; and other kinds of oral traditions such as riddles, proverbs, poetical compositions, and word play.

Myth

Myths are "sacred narratives" telling of supernatural beings and heroes and of the origin of all things. By explaining that things came to be the way they are through the activities of sacred beings, myths validate or legitimatize beliefs, values, and customs, particularly those having to do with ethical relations. As Bronislaw Malinowski pointed out over half a century ago, there is an intimate connections between the sacred tales of a society on the one hand, and its ritual acts, moral deeds, and social organization on the other (1926). "Myth is not [merely] an idle tale," wrote Malinowski, "but a hard-worked active force; the function of myth, briefly, is to strengthen tradition and endow it with a greater value and prestige by tracing it back to a higher, better, more supernatural reality of initial events."

A clear example of what Malinowski

JACK AND THE BEANSTALK

In the contemporary study of folklore, the emphasis is on understanding the processes of change—the spread and patterns of acceptance and remolding of tales in terms of cultural values, and the processes by which features of styles change from one culture to another. An example of this type of study is illustrated in the comparison of the English and American versions of Jack and the Beanstalk (Wolfenstein 1965). Martha Wolfenstein compares the version of Jack and the Bean Tree told in the mountains of North Carolina with the typical English version of the tale. In America, the plot is retained. Jack climbs the wonderful beanstalk, gets to the giant through his wife, and is in danger of being eaten by the giant. The wife hides Jack; Jack steals three things from the giant, is chased by the giant, and chops down the beanstalk, causing the giant's fatal fall. In the English tale, however, Jack and his mother are very poor, and Jack is reproached by his mother for not being able to hold a job and for carelessly spending the family's resources, as in his seemingly foolish bargain in trading their only cow for a handful of beans. Jack is viewed as making his mother suffer, and she is in despair and rages against him. He then frees himself from this burden of guilt by his heroic feats and the gifts he brings his mother at the end of the story.

In the North Carolina version, Jack is a small boy following his mother around the house as she sweeps. She finds a big bean, and to keep Jack out of her way, tells him to go plant it outside. He does, and each day tells his mother how high his beanstalk has grown. She slaps him each time for telling a lie, but when she sees it for herself, makes it up to him by giving him something to eat. In this version, it is Jack, not his mother, who is wronged. According to Wolfenstein, this scene embodies a major theme in American fantasy in which the hero, who is actually innocent, appears guilty and has to clear himself of false suspicions. In the European version, the hero redeems himself from sin. The English and American versions also differ in what Jack steals from the giant. Instead of the moneybags and the hen that lays the golden eggs, the American Jack steals a gun and a knife. These are definitely masculine things, which a person can use in an active way to do something. This contrasts with the magical sources of supply, like the hen that lays the golden eggs, in which the owner is relatively passive. Again, this difference points up the importance of the American value of actively seeking success on one's own, particularly in relation to masculinity.

meant is provided by the origin myth of the Yanomamo described by Napoleon Chagnon. The Yanomamo call themselves "the fierce people"; not only do warfare and other forms of violence such as club-fights and wife beating play an important role among them, but they also make frequent reference to their masculine cultural ideal as one of aggressiveness and fearlessness. They justify both this ideal and the violent activity in which they engage in terms of their origin myth.

According to Yanomamo belief, Periboriwa, the spirit of the moon, had a habit of coming down to earth to eat the souls of children. One day, two brothers, Uhudima and Suhirina, who lived on earth, got so angry at Periboriwa for doing this they decided to shoot him. One of the brothers shot a bamboo-tipped arrow at Periboriwa while he was overhead and hit him in the stomach. Blood spilled from the wound, and as it hit the earth it changed into men. This was the beginning of the Yanomamo population; it is because they have their origin in blood that they are so fierce and are continuously making war on each other (1977:48). It is easy to see how this myth functions as a "social charter" for society. In the telling of such myths, and in the ritual reenactments that often accompany them, social tradition is reinforced and solidarity enhanced.

Folktales

Although folktales may contain a supernatural element, they are not sacred in the same way as myths. Folktales are told mainly for enjoyment, although they often have important educational functions. Most folktales and other verbal arts, such as riddles and proverbs, have a moral. Oral traditions are thus important in the socialization process of every society, and especially in societies without writing. Folklore can tell us much about the cultural values of a society, because it reveals which actions are approved and which are condemned. The heroes in folktales give us clues to characteristics considered admirable in a particular culture. The audience is always led by the way the tale is told to know which characters and attributes are a cause for ridicule or scorn, and which are to be admired. Thus, in studying folklore, the cultural context of its telling is an important clue to understanding the tale itself.

Folklore and Social Protest

Another important way of understanding folklore is in terms of its psychological and social functions in society. Folklore provides a socially acceptable outlet for emotions that might otherwise be disruptive to the social order. Through humor, fantasy, and the creative use of imagination, oral traditions provide a channel through which hostility, ambivalence, distress, and conflict can be released. Thus, folklore is an important channel of social protest.

Folktales often embody conflicts that are part of a shared experience; the conflict of heroic folk figures symbolically touches on and communicates what the audience feels but cannot articulate. Folklore resolves in fantasy issues that are problems in real life. This function is illustrated by Roger Abrahams' (1970) studies of the various oral traditions among urban blacks in the United States. One of the most common figures in this oral tradition is the "trickster" or "clever hero." The trickster, who is usually smaller and weaker than those against whom he is matched, triumphs through his wits rather than through force. This folklore hero is known in the United States through the Brer Rabbit

Figure 14.2 *Humor in folklore is one way of releasing tension when protest cannot be expressed openly. This anonymous bit of folklore from urban life is a protest against the unfairness of the system of rewards in contemporary bureaucracies.*

Be good, loyal and work hard
and you will get your just reward !!!

tales—a set of stories in which small animals are constantly getting the better of larger ones. The popularity of trickster tales in the Old South seems to have an obvious relationship to social relations between blacks and whites before the Civil War. The trickster tales can be seen as a veiled reaction or protest against domination, and as a way of presenting feelings of protest in a nonthreatening way. For blacks in the United States, the trickster may represent the hero who can be in control of his world only through cleverness. The humor of these tales serves to release tension in a situation in which open rebellion seems futile.

Abrahams points out that as the social situation has changed for blacks in the United States, their folklore has also changed. In urban black ghettos, the "badman" has supplanted the trickster as a hero. The badman, unlike the trickster, is consciously rebelling against authority. He is arrogant and virile, and unlike the manipulative and sly trickster, the badman is manliness openly displayed. The emergence of the badman hero would appear to relate to the recognition of a more open environment in the urban North, and of the greater possibility of resisting authority than was true in the old South.

THE ARTIST IN SOCIETY

In studying the artist in society, anthropologists have been somewhat limited by the relative lack of good ethnographic data. Part of the reason for this is that in many small-scale societies, the artist as a specialist does not exist. Even if certain individuals are recognized as exceptionally skilled, they may not be full-time artists, but rather combine artistic specialties with other kinds of activities. As already noted, artistic skill may be applied to the manufacture of objects for everyday use. Various other artistic skills, such as in dance and music, are usually embedded in the role of religious specialist.

Furthermore, in Western society we tend to define the artist as an innovator. The importance we place on being "original" has blinded us to some extent to the role of the artist in societies where the artistic product appears to conform much more to cultural tradition and is less likely to stand out than is true in our own society. The emphasis on innovation and difference has led us, in general, to see the artist as a special person, often a deviant, working alone and often in opposition to rather than in harmony with his/her society. Artists in other societies do not always have this deviant or marginal status; their personalities may also be much closer to the cultural norm than is true in the West. The importance of designating a particular individual as the creator of a particular work of art is also not universal. Much artistic production in non-Western societies has a collective and thus anonymous quality. Folk art has traditionally been defined, in fact, as productions in which the individual creator is not known, or has faded out of memory. As folk art becomes commercialized, however—as is the case all over the world today in places where there are tourist markets—individual artists have emerged as specialists. They have been created by market forces: the work of certain individuals is in greater demand than that of others.

In an ambitious attempt to explore the role of the artist in society, Dennison Nash (1968) has developed a model that raises some questions which lend themselves to cross-cultural research. Although Nash was specifically interested in the role of the composer in society, his framework can be applied to other kinds of artists as well. Nash concentrated on the social factors operating in recruitment to the artistic role, personality, and the role of the audience.

Although persons with artistic talent may appear in either sex and in any social class, societies, through their cultural definitions of ascribed status, may inhibit or prevent these talents from developing and thus not use the gifts of talented individuals to their full potential. Art, for example, is often limited to either males or females in a particular society. Kinship status may define who fulfills artistic roles. Artistic roles may be inherited in families, clans, or castes. Where art is family property, such as in the songs owned by kinship groups among Northwest Coast Indians, the singing of these songs is limited to members of the kinship group. In India, to give another example, certain art forms are practiced only by the members of certain castes. For a long time in India, certain forms of a classical dance called *bharatnatyam* could be performed only by women of a particular caste. These women were called *devadasis*, and they were attached to temples and ceremoniously married to temple deities. Their female children also became *devadasis*, while their male children became musicians and music teachers. Often people who are marginal in a culture are its performers. In Europe and Asia, for example, gypsies play an important role in musical performances. It is possible that marginal peoples are more able to be innovative because of their marginality.

Where religious activity, such as shamanism, incorporates artistic performance, it may be that essentially unstable personalities are attracted to artistic roles. The idea of the artist as separated from, and at odds with, the world, is a Western conception. We might expect to find,

Tourism stimulates artistic innovations and leads to the development of artistic specialization. (United Nations)

therefore, that the personality of the Western artist does differ in important respects from that of the nonartist. A study of avant-garde painters in the United States in the 1960s showed that they had a variety of personality characteristics, but a common thread was a profound quest for autonomy and alienation from middle-class life. Perhaps only when music or the other arts become vehicles for altered states of consciousness do the arts attract particularly unstable personalities, although they may always attract those with an exceptional innate talent and a drive that sets them apart from others in the culture.

The widespread Western idea that the

essence of art consists in the artist "expressing her-/himself" in some unique and innovative way appears to contain a culturally specific value of individualism. Certainly, the situation for some kinds of art among the Tiv of Africa would be very foreign to us. According to Paul Bohannan (1971), art among the Tiv is a secondary aspect of other facets of life—play, religion, social status. Much of Tiv art is communal; the artist, as an individual, is unimportant. In making various products out of wood, such as walking sticks or stools, one man may start a design or carving. If for some reason he has to leave it for a while, another person may add a few strokes, and then in turn hand the object to a third person. It may take several people to finish it. In Tiv society, then, the audience, or critics, of some kinds of art may also play a role in creating it. This situation contrasts with our view that art should be a thoroughly individual product.

In music, dance, and drama, the communal nature of the arts is much more apparent in traditional, small-scale societies than in modern industrial nations. Creation, performance, and audience reaction tend to merge and feed back into each other. For a performer's activity to be socially significant it must carry some meaning to an audience, and thus such performances are always carried out within certain musical traditions. Even in the West, however, where innovation is an important artistic value, composers and musical performers have written and performed largely for their own times and within the framework of the musical conventions of their culture. If there is no writing system for recording or notating music, dance, and drama, this is even more likely to be true. If the audience does not understand or like one's artistic activity, there will be little chance for it to become part of the culture; and without becoming part of the culture, there is little chance of its being preserved for posterity.

SUMMARY

1. Art refers to both the process and products of human skill applied to any activity that meets the standards of beauty in a particular society. For convenience, the arts may be divided into the graphic and plastic arts, music, dance, folklore, and games and sports.

2. Art is a symbolic way of communicating. One of the most important functions of the arts is to communicate, display, and reinforce important cultural themes and values. The arts thus have an integrative function in society.

3. The arts should be studied in their cultural context; the separation of a class of objects or activities labeled "the arts" is mainly characteristic of modern societies and reflects the general tendency toward the separation of many kinds of activities from one another.

4. The comparative evaluation of esthetic values and artistic styles is difficult, if not impossible. Each culture has its own standards of beauty and its own artistic traditions. Cultures also differ in the degree to which they have developed different art forms. It is thus generally agreed by anthropologists that art should be studied in its cultural context.

5. Because they are easily separated from their cultural context, most attention has been given to the study of

the graphic and plastic arts. These arts may be examined in terms of their stylistic variation, as a way of understanding a particular culture, or as a cognitive map of a sociocultural system.

6. Music is a universal language with many different dialects. Each musical culture area of the world has its own characteristic way of structuring voice and instrument sound. Music has many functions in culture, and may have a directly adaptive role in its relation to the nature of work in different societies.

7. Dance is a universal form of human behavior in which meaning is attached to specific nonverbal movements. Dance and music are frequently associated with altered states of consciousness, and are used in ritual and other performances that mark exceptional events in the life of the individual and the group. Both are frequently associated with religion.

8. Dance may also be directly adaptive in teaching physical coordination and in building skills necessary in productive work and in warfare.

9. Folklore refers to oral traditions, particularly myth and folktales. Myths are sacred narratives that function as social charters, validating the beliefs and social structure of a society. Folktales, though told primarily for entertainment, also have important functions in society. They serve to educate, to release tension and act as a channel for social protest, and to integrate society by displaying cultural themes in a dramatic setting.

10. In small-scale societies, the artist is rarely a full-time specialist, and art is much more of a communal or anonymous endeavor. The importance of innovation as a part of artistic judgment is more characteristic of Western culture than of other cultures.

11. Although persons with artistic talent may appear in any segment of society, most societies restrict the artistic role to certain individuals, using criteria of sex, kinship status, or social class. Sometimes those who fill artistic roles are cultural outsiders or members of culturally marginal groups.

12. Where art is a vehicle for altered states of consciousness—for example, where it is tied in with religion—the artist may have a personality that is strikingly different from that of other members of society. Even where the artist is an exceptional personality, however, in all cultures most artists tend to operate within the traditions of their society.

SUGGESTED READINGS

Dundes, Alan, and Pagter, Carl R.
1975   *Urban Folklore from the Paperwork Empire.* Austin: American Folklore Society. A very funny book that looks at the typewritten and Xeroxed folklore which emerges as a way of protesting against the urban bureaucracy.

Graburn, Nelson H. H., ed.
1976   *Ethnic and Tourist Arts: Cultural Expressions from the Fourth World.* Berkeley: University of California Press. An extremely interesting collection of articles on various kinds of folk art that have become popular commercially. Very good illustrations.

Keil, Charles
1966   *Urban Blues.* Chicago: University of Chicago Press. An outstanding book on the blues and bluesmen favored by black urban audiences, and the ways in which such music relates to urban culture and society.

Marriott, Alice
1948   *Maria: The Potter of San Ildefonso.* Norman: University of Oklahoma Press. A book based on first-person observations and interviews with a well-known native American potter, written in a personal way that will capture the beginning student's attention.

Otten, Charlotte M., ed.
1971   *Anthropology and Art: Readings in Cross-Cultural Aesthetics.* Garden City, N.Y.: The Natural History Press. Covers all areas of the plastic and graphic arts, with articles ranging from those that are a good introduction for the beginning student to those that require some background in the field.

15
Culture Change in the Contemporary World

Our world is one of rapid change. Although culture change has been a continuous fact in the history of the human species, the *rate* at which changes are occurring today is faster than in any earlier period of human existence. With the exception of a few small populations in remote regions, no society today is unaffected by other social groups and the stream of current events. Furthermore, the very attitudes toward change itself are changing among many traditional and peasant populations. Although adherence to tradition and reluctance to take risks are still strong, some of the changes introduced by modern industrial nations have been welcomed. Whether welcome or not, however, the initial changes have almost always had an impact on traditional peoples far beyond what was anticipated, both by the people themselves and by those who brought the changes.

CULTURE CONTACT AND CULTURE CHANGE

In Chapter 3 we discussed the idea that cultures are always changing, if they are to survive, in response to changes in the physical and social environment. We also introduced some of the processes by which cultures change, notably **innovation** and **diffusion.** If the contact between two societies is prolonged, so that one or both change substantially, we use the term **acculturation** to describe what happens. Acculturation did not begin with the age of Western exploration and colonialism, but the impact of these encounters on non-Western societies has been more radical in its consequences than anything previously known. The West, too, has been affected by contact with other cultures, though in less drastic ways. The channels through which culture contact has occurred and the processes of acculturation have not been the same everywhere. In some cases the agents of cultural change have been primarily Christian missionaries; in other cases commercial interests have brought traditional peoples into a world market economy. Industrialization and urbanization have been greatly accelerated since World War II, and the military operations of this and other wars have also played their role in culture change. Since World War II, we may also include tourism as an important form of culture contact.

Not all traditional cultures have been equally affected by contact, nor have the cultural responses been identical. In some cases, as we have seen with the Yir Yiront, native cultures just disintegrated. In other cases revitalization movements arose, as with the cargo cults of New Guinea.

Some tribal peoples have been relatively successful in keeping their traditional systems almost intact, or have been able to synthesize new elements with the old in ways that have minimized personal and cultural disorganization. A case of successful resistance to the impact of Western culture is described by Robert Tonkinson (1974) for a group of Australian aborigines called the Jigalong Mob, who live around the Jigalong Mission Station in western Australia. The Jigalong had traditionally lived as hunters and gatherers, moving around in pursuit of the game and roots and fruits that formed the basis of their subsistence. With the establishment of the mission station, some of the group settled down nearby to work for wages and to be near their children, whom they sent to the mission school. Although this led to some changes in local organization and economic life, the Jigalong Mob continued their traditional religious rituals and their complex kinship system. They exploited

CARGO CULTS IN MELANESIA

The anthropologist Peter Worsley has described cargo cults as they have operated in Melanesia (1959). For the last 400 years, Western culture has been spreading through the islands of Melanesia. Initially the Melanesians were receptive to Western culture, which primarily reached them through trade goods, called "cargo" in Pidgin English, and Christianity, which was introduced by missionaries. At first the natives believed they would receive cargo and the riches of the Europeans through the missions, but they found that accepting Christianity did not bring the cargo any nearer. The Melanesians were discriminated against because of their color, and they realized that the preaching of Western religion was different from its practice.

With the expansion of the plantation economy in the islands, the enthusiasm of the Melanesians for Western culture began to wane. The Europeans removed men from their villages to work on plantations in Fiji and Australia. This trapped them into a worldwide commodity market in copra and rubber in which the prices, and thus wages, changed every month. These tribal peoples searched for an answer to the power of the white man and concluded that it rested on magic, which was the basis of power in their own societies. This made sense in terms of their observation of the whites: Whites did not work; they merely wrote "secret signs" on scraps of paper for which they were given shiploads of goods, while the Melanesians, who worked so hard, got nothing. Plainly the whites who knew the secret of cargo were keeping it from the islanders.

Cargo cults began to appear in all parts of Melanesia. The central theme of the cults was based on the Christian idea of the millennium: in native belief, the world was about to end in a terrible catastrophe. Then God (or the ancestors, or some local culture hero) would appear, and a paradise on earth would begin. The riches (cargo) of the white man would come to the Melanesians. When Australian government patrols arrived in one part of the New Guinea highlands in 1946, they found themselves viewed as the fulfillment of a prophecy—the sign that the end of the world was at hand. The natives butchered all their pigs in the belief that after three days of darkness, "great pigs" would appear from the sky. Food, firewood, and other necessities were stockpiled to see the people through until the great pigs arrived.

In other places, native prophets announced that Europeans would soon leave, abandoning their property to the natives. In Guadalcanal, native peoples were preparing airfields, roads, and docks for the magic ships and planes they believed were coming from

America. In Dutch New Guinea, where the Dutch had been driven out by the Japanese, it was believed that on the return of Mansren, the native culture hero, the existing world order would be reversed. White men would turn black like the Papuans, Papuans would turn white, root crops would grow in trees, and coconuts would grow on the ground. In some cults, the believers would sit around tables dressed in European clothes, making signs on paper, in the belief that these mysterious customs were the clue to the white man's extraordinary power over goods and people.

Worsley emphasizes that although the Europeans viewed these cult activities as "madness," they were rational attempts to make sense out of a seemingly chaotic and senseless social order, whose economy, politics, and society were beyond the comprehension of the tribal peoples caught up in them. The cargo, of course, never arrived, and old cults and leaders gave way to new ones. With the incorporation of Melanesian cultures and peoples into the political life of their newly independent nations, and their participation in political institutions such as trade unions and native councils, the cargo cults died out.

---

the opportunities to earn a living afforded by the mission, expending as little effort as possible and working only to satisfy their limited wants. Communication between missionaries and aborigines was limited; the missionaries visited the aborigine encampment only for prayer meetings, and the aborigines excluded the missionaries from their own religious ceremonies. The mutually unfavorable conceptions each group had of the other also acted as a barrier to meaningful social interaction. The aborigines associate the fundamentalist Christian missionaries with the absence of smoking, drinking and sexual joking, while the missionaries see the aborigines as children of the Devil and stereotype them as lazy, deceitful, and depraved.

A number of different factors help explain the successful resistance of the Jigalong Mob to cultural change. Their relative isolation at the mission contributed to their feeling of group solidarity, and they made a self-conscious effort to maintain their cultural traditions. In rural Australia, there is a generally laissez-faire attitude toward the activities of the aborigines outside the work situation, and this too contributed to the maintainence of the aborigines' cultural autonomy. Furthermore, because of their geographical isolation, this particular group had not been subject to the racial prejudice of white Australians, which has led to feelings of inferiority and loss of identity among other aboriginal populations.

The experience of this particular group under the impact of culture contact is instructive because it shows that contact does not affect every population in the same way. Neither, it might be added, does it affect every individual in the society in the same way. The physical location of a population, the nature of its traditional relationship with its environment, the degree to which the traditional culture is highly or loosely integrated, the nature of the contacting institution, and the mechanisms that stimulate or inhibit meaningful social contact between the populations must be considered before making any grand generalizations about the impact of culture contact. Where traditional cultures are able to withstand disintegration and resist change, a number of different factors may be at work. As we saw for the Amish in Chapter 3, it was also a particular combina-

tion of factors that has allowed this group to resist change relatively successfully in spite of strong pressures from United States culture and society.

MODERNIZATION AND CHANGE

Modernization refers to processes by which traditional societies move in the direction of taking on the technological and sociocultural systems characteristic of industrialized nations. Modernization includes advanced machine technology, industrialization of the production process, urbanization, a market economy, centralized and bureaucratic structures of political administration, a growth of nonkinship social groupings, and an attitude that favors innovation and change. Whereas in-

A feature of change in contemporary life in the United States is the joining of religious cults which have their origin in Eastern culture. Here, some members of the Hare Krishna organization prepare for a public celebration in New York City. (Serena Nanda)

dividuals in traditional societies are most often conservative and innovation is inhibited both because of traditional values and the leveling mechanisms of the society, modernization requires a more open attitude toward change. The typically fatalistic and conservative attitude toward experimentation that characterizes peasant and tribal societies gives way, although in most cases very slowly, to an achievement orientation, as it becomes more and more possible to acquire newly created wealth and status in the wider society through the changes modernization brings.

The response of a society to modernization depends on complex interrelationships among the physical environment, the traditional sociocultural system, and the particular modernizing influences it experiences. Although many of the changes that are part of modernization tend to occur together, they need not necessarily do so. Industrialization may occur without large-scale urbanization, and urban migrants may be attracted to cities even in the absence of enough industrialization to give them employment. Entry into the market system may also be achieved without local industrialization—as, for example, in the case of tribal peoples who are induced by worldwide market demands for local natural resources, such as rubber, to produce for the market, while not themselves becoming factory workers. Because change in one part of the sociocultural system leads to changes in other parts, many of the results of specific social changes that accompany the entry of traditional peoples into the modern world are unanticipated. These results are also not always positive for the society. But whether through the gradual voluntary acceptance of industrialization and urbanization under capitalism, or through rapid reorganization under totalitarian state control, the traditional social and cultural orders of peasant and tribal societies are being changed, often drastically and irreversibly.

Technology, Economy, and Change

The essential element in modernization is the application of machine technology and scientific knowledge to the production process. Along with modern technology come changes in the traditional patterns of work: an increase in occupational specialization, the separation of production from kinship units, and the substitution of cash wages for traditional forms of exchange. As a result, social inequalities frequently develop where they had not existed or been important. In socially stratified societies, technological improvements often lead to even wider gaps between different social classes as the benefits of technology are not equally realized by all groups within the society.

Entry into World Markets

In the desire for manufactured goods made available by industrialization, many preindustrial peoples are drawn into worldwide market economies. Consumer goods such as electrical appliances, new clothing, bicycles, and many other gadgets become available to tribal and peasant populations, stimulating them to look for new economic opportunities. The market economy, with its commercialization of exchange and the use of all-purpose money, penetrates the tribal and peasant household or subsistence economy. Soon, even the most geographically remote peoples become caught up in market networks that extend not only to nearby urban centers, but to other societies thousands of miles away. In order to obtain the cash necessary

THE SKOLT LAPPS An excellent study of some of the kinds of changes that result from technological improvements is presented by Pertti J. Pelto, who studied the effects of the snowmobile on the sociocultural system of the Skolt Lapps of northern Finland (Pelto 1973). Lapp economy is based on reindeer herding·and reindeer were important for both subsistence and transportation in this Arctic environment. Skolt Lapp males took great pride in their abilities as reindeer herders. The society was basically egalitarian, as most individuals had equal access to basic economic resources and there was little opportunity for social and economic differences to develop. Although they had obtained some material goods, such as flour, sugar, and various metal objects, from the outside world for centuries, the energy sources on which subsistence depended were locally available, and the Lapps were essentially an autonomous society.

Snowmobiles were first introduced in Finland in 1962. They caught on like wildfire, and by 1971 practically all Lapp households owned at least one snowmobile and used it for transportation, hauling, and herding reindeer. Reindeer-drawn sleds, the traditional means of transportation, had completely disappeared. Many families sold their sled reindeer to finance the purchase of snowmobiles. Mechanized reindeer herding appeared to be a success; it made herding physically easier and economically more productive for the families who were the first to take advantage of the new technology.

The snowmobile has brought significant changes in Skolt life, most of which, from the point of view of Pelto, the anthropologist, are not without great disadvantages to the society as a whole. From being economically independent, the Skolt Lapps are now dependent on external and commercially distributed sources of energy for transportation, which is the critical factor in the reindeer herding economy. The management of resources now requires new skills, including reading and writing, and the use of money, as well as the technical skills involved in repairing and maintaining the snowmobiles. These skills were not equally present in all Skolt Lapp families.

Because of the initial cash outlay required to purchase a snowmobile, the families who were somewhat better off had a head start in making the transition to mechanized herding. They also gained additional income by providing transportation to families without snowmobiles. This initial advantage was a critical factor in subsequent economic success. The accumulation of resources could be used to expand into other opportunities, such as acting as tourist guides, or even freeing adult males for wage work. Not all families are equally able to keep up in the snowmobile revolution. Those with lesser skills, cash, and flexibility have dropped out of herding altogether and have become dependent on the Finnish government for welfare payments and training for new kinds of employment. Although no strong system of social stratification has yet developed, Pelto predicts that the social differentiation between successful snowmobile herders and families marginal to the herding economy will become greater.

Pelto concludes that although the snowmobile revolution has brought some economic advantages for some families, it has substantially increased dependency for all families. Even those that are succeeding are dependent on external sources of credit, for example. With the loss of the old skills involved in non-mechanized reindeer herding, the diminished prestige accorded traditional herding activities and skills, the complete abandonment of sled reindeer for transportation, and the loss of control over the reindeer themselves, which have become more fearful of humans as a result of the noise and speed of the snowmobile, a complete return to the presnowmobile economy is not feasible. The Skolt Lapps themselves are somewhat divided on how they view the changes in their society. Those in the younger generation and those older men who have been successful tend to regard the snowmobile revolution positively. Looking at it in a more objective light, and with an eye to the long-run changes, Pelto concludes that it has substantially decreased the autonomy and adaptive flexibility of the Skolt Lapp sociocultural system as a whole.

for participation in the market economy, agriculture becomes commercialized. Production of cash crops equals or even outdistances production for use. We have already seen that participation in world markets they neither controlled nor understood was one of the factors that led to the rise of cargo cults among various peoples of New Guinea. This is but one of many examples of the effects of such participation on local economies.

Another example, with somewhat different effects, was the introduction of the growing of sisal in the Sertao in northeastern Brazil (Gross 1973). Peasants in the interior of northeastern Brazil had traditionally subsisted on cattle raising and small-scale growing of beans and maize. In the 1930s sisal, which is used to make rope, was introduced as a cash crop. When World War II cut off the supply of hemp from the Philippines, the price of sisal rose dramatically in the world market. Sisal was hailed as "green gold," and both large and small landholders in northeastern Brazil planted all their land with sisal in the expectation of great profits.

Sisal crops take four years to harvest, however. The world price for sisal dropped dramatically after the war, and many small landholders found they could not realize a profit on their harvest. As they no longer had any land to use for the growing of traditional crops with which to feed themselves, many small landowning peasants were forced to work for wages processing sisal for the large landowners who had bought processing machines and thus could still make a profit. Machine processing of sisal involves enormous amounts of manual labor, including shifting thousands of pounds of fiber per hour. Because the workers were paid on a production basis, they worked long hours to make ends meet in order to buy the food they

could no longer grow. Food had to be imported into the region, which now produced only sisal, and a new social class of well-to-do shopkeepers grew up upon whom the peasants were economically dependent.

A study of the economic and social changes resulting from sisal growing was made by Daniel Gross, an anthropologist, in collaboration with a nutritionist. These researchers studied household budgets and caloric intake and measured physical growth and health among peasant families. They found that households which depended on wages from sisal work spent nearly all their money on food, most of which was needed to sustain the energy level of the wage earner so that he could adequately perform his demanding job. As a result, children in the households of sisal

Many non-Western nations have become dependent on one crop that is produced for a world market. Coffee is one of the most important cash crops in Ruanda-Urundi and most of it is grown by individual farmers. The farmer shown here is putting coffee beans out to be dried by the sun.
(United Nations)

workers were being deprived of sufficient calories to maintain good health and normal rates of growth. The economic gains of the higher social classes, on the other hand, were manifested in a marked improvement in their nutritional state and that of their children. Sisal had brought prosperity to only a favored few; for most peasants, it only increased their poverty and intensified their misery.

Urbanization and Change

In many of the nations of Asia, Africa, and Latin America, spontaneous and voluntary migration of peasants to urban centers is one of the most, if not the most, important mechanisms of change. Although cities had important cultural roles in preindustrial societies, in the contemporary world urban migration has increased dramatically. Rural people come to cities seeking jobs and the social, material, and cultural advantages they perceive to be related to urban living. There are many different ways in which urbanization affects traditional societies. One anthropologist has characterized the adaptations of traditional societies to urbanization as a "three-ring circus," referring to the three arenas within which adaptations to urbanization take place: among the members of the home community left behind, among the urban migrants themselves, and within the urban host community to which the migrants go (Graves and Graves 1974).

Many of the migrants who leave their local communities do so only temporarily. They return to their places of origin to participate in a variety of economic and/or social activities and maintain important ties with those left behind. The degree to which urban migration is permanent depends partly on the personal involvements of the migrating individual within the local rural community, partly on the ability of the local community to reabsorb its returning migrants, and partly on the barriers to assimilation the migrant group meets in the urban area.

In a study of outmigration from Vasilika, a Greek village, Ernestine Friedl (1974) showed how a variety of factors led to a high degree of permanent migration to Athens, the Greek capital. Vasilika, like other peasant villages all over the world, had a labor surplus. At the same time, there were job opportunities in Athens. Furthermore, Vasilikans had a positive view of living in Athens; city living carried more prestige than village life. Rural families would support one of their sons who went to Athens to get an education, a usual first step toward obtaining a job in government service. In return for the family's support, the migrant generally gave up his rights to his share of village land, an economic benefit for those who remained. This loss of one's share in village property is a strong factor in permanent migration. Furthermore, since Vasilikans were not an ethnic or racial minority group in Athens, there were few barriers to assimilation. The Vasilikans lived throughout the city, and had a wide range of social contacts with urban people. Many of them married nonvillagers, which also contributed to the permanence of urban migration. Unlike migrants in many developing nations, the Vasilikans did not form voluntary associations. These associations, as we have seen, serve many functions for rural migrants, but they also serve to isolate them socially from other segments of urban populations.

Whether temporary or permanent, however, urban migration is both a direct and an indirect source of change in traditional societies. Not only are urban migrants themselves changed in the process of adapting to urban life, but the communities of origin are also changed. Most modern influences enter the countryside through urban centers, either by mass communication, as radios and movies become available in villages, or through the links between urban migrants and those who remain at home. Not only modern consumer goods, but new ideas, knowledge, and values are passed on to villagers through urban migrants. These modern influences permeate the village only slowly, however; material culture is affected first, and then social organization and ideology.

Ruth and Stanley Freed (1978), who studied a village close to New Delhi, the Indian capital, found that in spite of the large numbers of villagers who worked in the city, village social organization and culture remained largely traditional. Although some urban-oriented men were more relaxed about requiring the isolation of women and *purdah* (veiling), role behavior in the family did not change substantially. The basic features of the caste system were also not much changed. Two important changes which did occur were that the prohibitions on lower caste use of public facilities had decreased, and *jajmani* relationships were transformed into "fee for service" arrangements. The prohibitions on untouchability were due more to new laws passed by the national government than urbanization itself, but the transformation of the *jajmani* system was clearly the result of the alternative of urban jobs for landless laborers who preferred to work for cash.

In summing up the trends they believed were due to urbanization, the Freeds listed the following factors, which would probably apply in a general way to other urbanizing societies as well: (1) increasing modernization of material culture; (2) increasing number of villagers earning a living from modern industrial and commercial jobs instead of traditional crafts and farming; (3) landless laborers becoming less dependent on large landowners; (4) more casual social interactions taking place across caste boundaries; (5) an emphasis on various features of Hinduism more in accord with city life than rural life; (6) a rising level of education; and (7) more exposure to the wider world through mass communications.

Political Modernization and Planned Change

Politically, modernization refers to the growth of centralized and bureaucratic structures of political administration and law that extend down to local levels, both undermining local and traditional mechanisms of social control and filling in where such control mechanisms have been eroded by other processes of social change. New political ideologies emerge as the nation-state becomes the overriding structure of social integration. Previously autonomous cultural groups are drawn into national networks and brought (with varying degrees of success) under control by the state. The elite groups that control new nation-states in Asia, Africa, and Latin America are committed to ideas of progress and development, and are deliberately trying to transform their rural populations through programs of planned change.

The ways in which this happens are extremely variable and do not allow precise formulas to be very useful. As Clifford Geertz points out, modernization is not just the replacement of the traditional and obsolete with the imported and up-to-date.

Traditional forms of communication are also used to convey new ideas. Here a traditional Balinese song and dance drama presents the theme of family planning. (United Nations/Ray Witlin)

The new nations of the world have the double goal of seeking to remain themselves and at the same time to adapt to the requirements of the twentieth century: "There is no simple progression from 'traditional' to 'modern,' but a twisting, spasmodic, unmethodical movement, which turns as often toward repossessing the . . . past as disowning [it]" (Geertz 1973:319).

In some cases, the social changes planned by modern governments may take place through peaceful democratic means. The transformation of peasant societies may also occur through more violent alternatives, as in the case of revolutionary movements in China, the Soviet Union, North Korea, North Vietnam, and Cuba, in which peasants took an active part. These movements or revolutions are quite different from the peasant rebellions of the past, in which peasant uprisings were violent outbursts that did not fundamentally change the social structure of the larger society. In modern peasant revolutions, which are supported by a coherent ideology and an effective organizational framework, the social structures of some traditional societies have been almost completely destroyed and new socialist states created in their place.

William Geddes and other observers of

REVOLUTIONARY CHANGES IN CHINA

The most dramatic example is the People's Republic of China. A concise view of these changes is presented by Jack M. Potter (1967). In 1949, when the Chinese Communist part took power, China was an overpopulated, poverty-stricken country with more than 80 percent of its people living in rural villages. Many farms were small and inefficient, and technology had changed little in two thousand years. Most villagers made hardly enough to meet their basic needs, and any surplus went into the ceremonial activities—funerals and marriages—necessary to maintain a family's status. Much of the surplus capital was siphoned off by landlords in the form of rents and exorbitant interest rates on loans. The landlord-scholar-government official class dominated the entire society. Traditionally, government intervened little in village life; its primary functions were maintaining order and collecting taxes. The nation was exploited economically by foreign powers and almost totally disrupted by the Japanese invasion in the late 1930s. An important basis of the achievement of the Communist government in reorganizing the society was the view that only through modernization and industrialization could China regain its national dignity.

The new government intervened in every aspect of peasant life in order to control the peasants and mobilize them to work in the interest of the state. The first order of business was land reform. Through government-supervised peasant associations, land and property were taken from wealthy landlords and redistributed to the peasants. The destruction of the landlord class, which had been the main buffer between the peasants and the government, now left the way open for direct government intervention in the villages. The ultimate aim was the establishment of total collectivization of village life. This process was to be achieved by stages. The first involved the reorganization of peasants into mutual aid teams in which villagers retained absolute control over their property, but worked together, pooling farm tools, draft animals, and labor. In the second stage land was still privately owned but placed in a collective pool along with farm equipment, cattle, and labor, and worked on a collective rather than an individual field basis. When crops were harvested, some was set aside for taxes, some for the collective purchase of fertilizer, machinery, and so on, and the remainder divided among the members in proportion to their investment through a point system. In the third stage, the village was turned into social cooperative: Tools, animals, and land were made the permanent property of the cooperative; members received no compensation for what they contributed,

Material changes as well as extensive political education, especially of young people has contributed to the remaking of Chinese society since 1948. (Bernhard Krauss)

but derived their income only from labor points. In every stage of reorganization, there were heavy propaganda campaigns and educational meetings in order to commit the peasant to the goals of the government and a collectivized society.

By 1958, when almost all peasants had been organized into socialist cooperatives, the Great Leap Forward into the commune stage began. These communes were multifunctional organizations covering an area including about twenty villages. The communes operated small factories, and ran banks, commercial enterprises, schools, and the local government. In this stage, houses, trees, domestic animals, and garden plots, which the peasants had earlier been allowed to own and work privately, were confiscated. Women were mobilized to work alongside men and common mess halls, kindergartens, and old age homes were built to take over many functions previously performed by the family.

The Great Leap Forward is now acknowledged to have failed in its objectives. The labor resources devoted to industry left a shortage of agricultural labor; confiscation of garden plots substantially decreased production due to a lack of incentive on the part of peasants; communal family activities demoralized the population.

The government began a retreat to less radical forms of collective organization, and since the end of 1960 private garden plots have been returned to the peasants, along with their houses and kitchens and domestic animals. Industry is giving greater attention to producing consumer goods. With these modifications, economic conditions seem to have improved considerably.

The lack of anthropological studies in China after 1945 has hindered our ability to understand fully many of the changes that have occurred there. In 1956, an anthropologist named William Geddes got permission to visit a village in the People's Republic that had been studied prior to the revolution. Comparing what he was able to observe and the information gained through intensive questioning in the few days he was there with the earlier study, Geddes (1963) summarized the changes in the following ways: Women had generally achieved a higher status, and now voted; marriages were no longer arranged; there was a lessening of the importance of kinship ties beyond the household, and a decline in the authority and status of the aged. This correlated with the decline of the ancestor cult, which had been at the center of Chinese religion and kinship. The government did not encourage religion, but had substituted new collective festivals that had a political orientation for the traditional village activities. The government had made strong efforts to promote literacy, for both children and adults, and Geddes estimated that most adults could probably now read and write at a simple level. The changes initiated by the government were organized around improving the economic conditions of the population; all aspects of the new social order serve this goal. In this area the government has been successful, although Geddes reminds us that the peasant acceptance of government control was prepared by armed revolution and sustained to an unknown degree by force and interference with basic freedoms.

contemporary Chinese society, point out that the success of the Communist system as it has worked in China is due to the completeness of reorganization and change; material changes and ideological commitment were mutually reinforcing. The very completeness of the system raises questions that ultimately have to do with values: To what extent does the new system allow for freedom and individuality and artistic creativity? How important is this to the people themselves compared to the dramatic inprovement in the material conditions under which they live? But however we evaluate the changes that have occurred, an understanding of them would seem essential to our understanding of the transformation of peasant societies generally. This understanding has direct relevance to the formation and execution of public policy in the United States regarding its political and economic commitments to developing nations. It is to be hoped that anthropologists, who are trained to look at whole systems, can make an important contribution to these policies which ultimately involve questions of culture change.

SUMMARY

1. The contemporary world is affected by rates of change unlike those in any earlier period of human existence. An important source of this change is the contact between modern industrial nations and traditional nonindustrial societies.

2. One important aspect of change in the contemporary world is the application of machine technology and scientific knowledge to the production process. These technological changes can lead to significant changes in culture and social organization, many of which are unanticipated. An example is the effect of the snowmobile on the society of the Skolt Lapps in Finland.

3. Entry into worldwide market systems is another powerful factor of change in the contemporary world. Although such participation may increase the number of consumer goods available to tribal and peasant peoples, it does not necessarily raise their basic standard of living. Furthermore, it leads to a dependence on often unstable world markets over which traditionally autonomous populations have no control.

4. Urbanization is yet another important process of change. The migration of rural peasants to cities affects not only the lives of those who migrate, but also the culture and social structure of the rural areas they leave. Because of the rapid rate of urbanization in the contemporary world, the study of urban adaptations has become an important subject of anthropological research.

5. Although much contemporary change is unplanned and unanticipated, many politically modernizing nation-states are also attempting to introduce planned changes consistent with ideas of progress and development, while at the same time retaining aspects of traditional culture that are important in forming national identities and ideologies.

SUGGESTED READINGS

Brady, Ivan, and Isaac, Barry
1975 *A Reader in Culture Change.* Volume II: Case Studies. Cambridge, Mass.: Schenkman. An anthology of readings on culture contact and planned change in a wide variety of societies in the contemporary world.

Hopkins, Nicholas
1972 *Popular Government in an African Town.* Chicago: University of Chicago Press. An excellent study of political modernization in Kito, Mali.

Murphy, Yolanda, and Murphy, Robert
1974 *Women of the Forest.* New York: Columbia University Press. An account of how rubber tapping has changed the lives of a group of horticulturalists in South America, and particularly how these changes have affected the lives of women.

Nader, Laura, and Maretzki, Thomas W.
1973 *Cultural Illness and Health.* Washington. D.C.: American Anthropological Society. An outstanding collection of articles dealing with contemporary problems in the United States studied by a number of leading anthropologists.

Spindler, Louise S.
1977 *Culture Change and Modernization: Mini-Models and Case Studies.* New York: Holt, Rinehart and Winston. An introduction to the subject that includes discussion of theories of change and case studies of change among particular human populations both within and outside the United States.

Glossary

Acculturation   The process that takes place when contact between two societies is so prolonged that one or both cultures changes substantially.

Achieved status   A social position an individual chooses or achieves on his or her own.

Adaptation   The ways in which living populations relate to the environment so that they may survive and reproduce.

All-purpose money   Money that serves as a means of exchange, a standard of value, and a means of payment for a wide variety of goods and services.

Animatism   The belief in impersonal supernatural power (sometimes called mana).

Animism   The belief that living creatures and also inanimate objects have life and personality, referred to as spirits, ghosts, or gods.

Anthropology   The comparative study of humankind.

Applied anthropology   The organized interaction between professional anthropologists and both private and public policy-making bodies.

Archeology   A specialized field of cultural anthropology focused on human cultures that have existed in the past and for which there are no written records.

Art   The process and products of human skill applied to any activity that meets standards of beauty in a particular society.

Ascribed status   A social position an individual is born into.

Authority   Power exercised with the consent of the members of the society (legitimate power).

Avunculocal residence rule   Where a married couple resides with the husband's mother's brother.

Balanced reciprocity   An exchange, in which there is a clear obligation to return within a specified time limit, of goods of nearly equal value.

Band   The basic social unit in many hunting and gathering societies, made up of less than 100 people related to each other through blood ties or marriage.

Behavioral norms   The typical behavior people who share a culture actually engage in.

Bifurcation   A principle of classifying kin where different kinship terms are used for the mother's side of the family and the father's side of the family.

Bilateral descent rule   Both maternal and paternal lines are used in reckoning descent.

Bilocal residence rule   Where a married couple has the choice of living with the husband's or wife's family.

Bride service   Work that the groom performs for his bride's family for a variable length of time either before or after the marriage is finalized.

Bridewealth   Goods presented by the groom's kin to the bride's kin, to legitimatize a marriage.

Call system   Form of communication among nonhuman pimates composed of a limited number of sounds that are tied to specific stimuli in the environment.

Capital   Goods used to produce other

goods, or wealth invested to purchase capital goods.

Capitalist society A society in which people work for wages; land and capital goods are privately owned; and capital is invested for individual profit.

Caste system A system of stratification based on birth and in which movement from one strata (caste) to another is not possible.

Chiefdom A society with social ranking where political integration is achieved through an *office* of centralized leadership.

Clan A unilineal kinship group whose members believe themselves to be descended from a common ancestor but who cannot trace this link genealogically.

Class system A form of social stratification in which the different strata form a continuum and where social mobility is possible.

Cognition The ways in which human beings perceive, understand, and organize their responses to the universe.

Cognitive anthropology A theoretical approach that defines culture in terms of the rules and meanings underlying human behavior, rather than behavior itself.

Collateral kin Kin related through a linking relative, such as the relationship between an individual and his father's brother.

Communal cult A type of religious organization in which ordinary people hold rituals for the community or segments of it.

Communication The act of transmitting information that influences the behavior of another organism.

Composite (or compound) family An aggregate of nuclear families linked by a common spouse.

Configurationalism The theory that holds that each culture is a unique configuration or pattern of elements and values.

Conflict theory A theory of social stratification that holds that the natural condition of society is constant change and conflict. The inequality in systems of social stratification are considered evidence of this conflict.

Controlled cross-cultural comparison An anthropological method that uses comparable ethnographic data from many different societies and tests particular hypotheses.

Cosmology The system of beliefs that deals with fundamental questions in the cosmic and social order.

Cross cousins Individuals related through siblings of the opposite sex at the parental generation.

Cultural anthropology The study of human behavior that is learned, rather than genetically transmitted and that is typical of a particular human group.

Cultural ecology A theoretical approach that regards cultural patterns as adaptive responses to the basic problems of human survival and reproduction.

Cultural evolution The process by which new cultural forms emerge out of older ones.

Cultural integration The tendency of the parts of a culture to be consistent or in harmony with each other.

Cultural relativity An attempt to understand cultural patterns from the "inside" and to see the traits of a culture in terms of the cultural whole.

Culture (general) The learned and shared kinds of behavior which make up the major instrument of human adaptation.

Culture (particular) The way of life characteristic of a particular human society.

Culture area A broad geographical area in which a number of different societies make similar adaptations to a particular ecological zone and through diffusion come to develop similar cultural patterns.

Culture of poverty The name given by Oscar Lewis to the constellation of cultural traits that emerge as a reaction and an adaptation of the poor to their poverty and lack of power in the larger society.

Descent The culturally established affiliation between a child and one or both parents.

Descent group A group of kin who are lineal descendents of a common ancestor, extending beyond two generations.

Deviance Departures from cultural norms regarded negatively by society.

Diffusion The spread of cultural elements

from one culture to another through cultural contact.

Divination   A magical practice directed at obtaining useful information from a supernatural authority.

Domestic group   A household unit that usually, but not always, consists of members of a family.

Double descent   Where descent is traced through both matrilineal and patrilineal links, each of which is utilized for different purposes.

Dowry   Presentation of goods by the bride's kin to the family of the groom or to the couple.

Ecclesiastical cult   A type of religious organization in which access to supernatural power is mediated by a professional and specialized clergy.

Economic system   The norms governing production, distribution, and consumption of goods and services.

Economizing   Choosing a course of action that maximizes the well-being and material profit of the individual.

Ecosystem   The term referring to the interaction between human populations and their environment.

Egalitarian society   A society in which no individual or group has more privileged access to resources, power, or prestige than any other.

Enculturation   A term referring to the specific ways in which human infants and children learn to be adult members of their particular society.

Endogamy   The rule prescribing that marriage must be *within* a particular group.

Ethnocentrism   Perceiving and judging other cultures from the perspective of one's own culture.

Ethnography   The major research tool of cultural anthropology that includes both fieldwork among people in society and the written results of fieldwork.

Ethos   The dominant theme or value of a particular culture.

Exogamy   A rule that specifies that an indi-

vidual must marry outside any particular group covered by the rule.

Extended family   Family based on blood relations extending over three or more generations.

Folklore   Primarily oral traditions that have anonymous authorship and include at least two variations of the same form.

Formal economics   The theory that holds that human material wants are unlimited but the means for achieving these wants is finite, and that people make choices among alternative courses of action in a rational manner.

Functionalism   The anthropological theory that culture functions to serve the needs of individuals in society.

Gender   The social classification of masculine and feminine.

Generalized reciprocity   A distribution of goods where no immediate or specific return is expected.

Government   A social institution specifically concerned with making and enforcing public policy.

Horticulture   Production of plants using a simple, nonmechanized technology, and where fields are not used continuously.

Hunting and gathering   A food-getting strategy that does not involve food production or domestication of animals. Also called foraging.

Ideal norms   The ideas a society has about what *ought* to be done.

Ideology (political)   The shared values and beliefs that legitimatize the distribution and use of power in a particular society.

Incest taboos   Prohibitions on sexual relations between relatives or persons classified as relatives.

Independent invention   The process whereby similar cultural features develop without involving cultural exchange.

Individualistic cult   A form of religious organization in which each person may be her or his own religious specialist.

Initiation rite   A ritual that marks the passage from childhood to adult status.

Innovation   A new variation on a pre-existing cultural pattern that is subsequently accepted by other members of the society.

Intelligence The many different skills and capacities that are part of the adaptive responses human beings make to their environment.

Intensive agriculture A form of food production in which fields are in permanent cultivation using plows, draft animals, and/or techniques of soil and water control.

Invention New combinations of pre-existing cultural elements.

Kindred A descent group made up of all the people related to an individual.

Kinship A culturally defined relationship established on the basis of blood ties or through marriage.

Kinship system The totality of kin relations, kin groups, and system of classifying kin in a particular society.

Kula A pattern of exchange among trading partners in the Trobriand Islands and other islands that are part of the Kula ring.

Law Those social norms whose neglect or infraction is regularly met by the application of force by those in a society who have the socially recognized privilege of doing so.

Leveling mechanism A practice, value, or form of social organization that results in an evening out of wealth within a society.

Levirate The custom whereby a man marries the widow of a deceased brother.

Life chances The opportunity of an individual to fulfill his or her potential in society.

Lineage A group of kin whose members trace descent from a known common ancestor.

Linguisics A field of cultural anthropology that specializes in the study of human languages.

Magic An attempt to mechanistically control supernatural forces.

Market exchange A system of exchange in which goods and services are bought and sold at a money price determined by the impersonal forces of supply and demand.

Marriage The customs, rules, and obligations that establish a special relationship between a sexually cohabiting adult male and female, between them and any children they produce, and between the kin of the bride and groom.

Matrilineage A lineage formed by descent in the female line.

Matrilineal descent A rule that affiliates an individual to kin related through the mother only.

Matrilocal residence rule A rule that states that a husband goes to live with his wife's family.

Modernization The process in which traditional societies move technologically and socially in the direction of industrialized nations.

Monogamy The rule that permits only one person to be married to one other person at a time.

Monotheism The belief in one god.

Morpheme The smallest unit of a language that has a meaning.

Myth Narratives that tell of the creation of the universe through the agency of supernatural beings.

Neolocal residence rule The rule that specifies that a couple establishes an independent household after marriage.

Network analysis An approach to understanding the informal and fluid social relations that are typical in complex societies, by mapping the links individuals have with others.

Niche Specialized adaptation to a local environment by a particular group of people.

Nomadism The constant mobility of human groups in pursuit of food (as in foraging) or a form of pastoralism in which the whole social group (men, women, and children, and animals) move in search of pasture.

Norm An ideal cultural pattern or behavioral expectation in a culture.

Nuclear family The family organized around the conjugal tie (the relationship between husband and wife). A nuclear family consists of a husband, a wife, and their children.

Ordeal A means of determining guilt or innocence by having an accused party submit to tests believed to be under supernatural control.

Paleontology   The discipline that traces the evolution of humankind in the fossil record.

Parallel cousins   The children of siblings of the same sex at the parental generation.

Pastoralism   A food-getting strategy that depends on the care of domesticated herd animals. It occurs in areas where, for a variety of reasons, large human populations cannot be supported through agriculture.

Patrilineage   A lineage formed by descent in the male line.

Patrilineal descent rule   A rule that affiliates children with kinsmen of both sexes related through males only.

Patrilocal residence rule   The rule stating that a bride goes to live with her husband's family.

Peasants   Food-producing populations that are incorporated politically, economically, and culturally into nation states.

Phoneme   The smallest significant sound unit in a language. A phonemic system is the sound system of a language.

Phonetic laws   Regularities in sound changes that can be traced by linguists.

Physical anthropology   The study of human evolution and the biological processes involved in human adaptation.

Political organization   The patterned ways in which authority is used to coordinate and regulate human behavior in the public interest.

Political process   The ways in which individuals and groups use power to achieve public goals.

Polyandry   The rule permitting a woman to have more than one husband at a time.

Polygamy   The general term for the rule allowing more than one spouse.

Polygyny   The rule permitting a man to have more than one wife at a time.

Polytheism   The belief in many gods.

Potlatch   A form of competitive giveaway practiced by the Kwakiutl and other groups of the Northwest Coast of North America.

Power   The ability to produce intended effects on oneself, other human beings, and on things.

Prestige   Social honor or respect.

Primate   The *order* within the mammalian *class,* which includes among other forms, monkeys, apes, and humans.

Psychic unity   The anthropological proposition that all human groups have the same mental capacities and ability to think logically.

Races   Human populations that differ in the relative frequencies of some genes.

Racism   The belief that some human populations are superior to others because of inherited, genetically transmitted, characteristics.

Rank society   A society in which there are institutionalized differences in prestige, but no important restrictions on access to basic resources.

Rebellion   The attempt of a group within society to force a redistribution of resources and power.

Reciprocity   A mutual give and take among persons of equal status.

Redistribution   A form of exchange in which goods are collected or contributed from members of the group and then redistributed to the group, often in the form of ceremonial feasts.

Religion   The beliefs and practices concerned with supernatural beings, powers, and forces.

Religious revitalization movements   A consciously organized effort to construct a more satisfying culture based on religious beliefs and practices.

Revolution   An attempt to overthrow the existing form of political organization.

Rites of intensification   Religious rituals directed toward the welfare of a group or society.

Rites of passage   Rituals that mark the transition of an individual from one social status to another.

Ritual (religious)   A patterned act that involves the manipulation of religious symbols.

Segmentary lineage system A form of sociopolitical organization in which multiple descent groups (usually patrilineages) form at different levels and function in different contexts.

Semantics The subsystem of a language that relates form to meaning.

Sex The biological difference between male and female.

Shaman A person who is socially recognized as having special supernatural power that they use on behalf of human clients for a variety of activities.

Social function The contribution a cultural trait makes to the maintenance and solidarity of a social system.

Social mobility Movement from one social class to another.

Social network A set of direct and indirect links between an individual and other people.

Socialization The learning processes through which human cultural traditions are passed on from one generation to the next.

Social stratification A system of institutionalized inequalities of wealth, power, and prestige.

Society A group of people who are dependent on each other for survival and/or well being and who share a particular way of life.

Sociobiology A new interdisciplinary field that attempts to apply the perspective of evolutionary biology to human behavior.

Sociocultural system The social enactments of designs for living (culture) in particular environments; incorporates both behavior and the rules of behavior as the subject matter for cultural anthropology.

Sociolinguistics An anthropological specialty interested in speech performance

Sorcery The use of magic with the intent of harming another person.

Sororate The custom whereby when a man's wife dies her sister is given to him as a wife.

State A hierarchical and centralized form of political organization in which the central government has a legal monopoly over the use of force.

Status A social position within a social structure.

Stimulus diffusion When the general idea of an alien culture trait is borrowed, but the specific form of the trait is a local invention.

Structural-functionalism An anthropological theory developed by A. R. Radcliffe-Brown that emphasizes the ways in which different structural elements in a social system contribute to social solidarity.

Structuralism A theoretical perspective in anthropology that attempts to analyze the deep meanings underlying cultural elements and the rules by which cultural meanings are produced.

Subculture A system of perceptions, values, beliefs, and customs that are significantly different from the larger, dominant culture.

Substantive economics The study of economic systems as part of a total sociocultural system.

Swidden A form of cultivation in which a field is cleared by felling the trees and burning the brush (sometimes called slash and burn cultivation).

Symbolic anthropology An approach that focuses on culture as a system of shared meanings and symbols.

Syntax That part of grammar that has to do with the arrangements of words to form phrases and sentences.

Theory A general idea that attempts to explain and ultimately predict the interrelationships among phenomena in any scientific discipline.

Totem A plant or animal considered to have an intimate relationship with a human group, sometimes as an ancestor.

Transformational generative grammar A model of language that focuses on the relationship of deep structure of sentences to surface structures, and the rules that relate the two.

Transhumance A pastoralist pattern in which herd animals are moved regularly throughout the year to different areas as pasture becomes available in different climatic zones.

Tribe   A culturally distinct population, the members of which consider themselves to be descended from the same ancestor.

Unilineal descent rule   A rule that specifies that membership in a descent group is based on links through either the maternal or paternal line, but not both.

Vocabulary   The total stock of words in a language.

Voluntary association   Social groups based on voluntary membership, typically found in complex and modernizing societies.

Wealth   The accumulation of material resources or access to the means of producing these resources.

Whorf–Sapir hypothesis   The hypothesis that perceptions and understandings of time, space, and matter are in part conditioned by the structure of a particular language.

Witchcraft   The attempt to harm people through supernatural means and powers, which uses only psychological processes and not any material objects.

References

Aberle, David F., et al.
1963   "The Incest Taboo and Mating Patterns of Animals." *American Anthropologist* 65:253–65.

Abrahams, Roger, D.
1970   *Deep Down in the Jungle.* Chicago: Aldine.

Alland, Alexander, Jr.
1972   *The Human Imperative.* New York: Columbia University Press.

Allen, J. P. B. and van Buren, Paul, eds.
1971   *Chomsky: Selected Readings.* London: Oxford University Press.

Arens, W.
1976   "Professional Football: An American Symbol and Ritual." In *The American Dimension.* W. Arens and Susan P. Montague, eds. Pp. 3–14. Port Washington: Alfred.

Baal, J. van
1966   *Dema: Description and Analysis of Marind-anim Culture* (South New Guinea). The Hague: M. Nijhoff.

Balicki, Asen
1963   "Shamanistic Behavior Among the Netsilik Eskimos." *Southwestern Journal of Anthropology* 19:380–96.

Barth, Fredrik
1964   *Nomads of South Persia.* New York: Humanities Press.
1956   "Ecologic Relationships of Ethnic Groups in Swat, North Pakistan." *American Anthropologist* 58:1079–89.

Bascom, William
1970   "Ponapean Prestige Economy." In *Cultures of the Pacific: Selected Readings.* Thomas G. Harding and Ben J. Wallace, eds. Pp. 85–93. New York: Free Press.

Beidelman, Thomas O.
1971   *The Kaguru: A Matrilineal People of East Africa.* New York: Holt, Rinehart and Winston.
1966   "The Ox and Nuer Sacrifice." *Man* (new series) I:453–67.

Benedict, Ruth
1961   *Patterns of Culture.* Boston: Houghton Mifflin (first publ. 1934).
1946   *The Chrysanthemum and the Sword.* Boston: Houghton Mifflin.
1938   "Continuities and Discontinuities in Culture Conditioning." *Psychiatry* 1:161–67.
1934   "Anthropology and the Abnormal." *Journal of General Psychology* 10:791–808.

Benet, Sula
1976   *How to Live to Be 100: The Life Style of the People of the Caucasus.* New York: Dial Press.

Berreman, Gerald D.
1959   "Caste in India and the United States." *American Journal of Sociology* LXVI:120–27.

Berry, J. W.
1974   "Ecological and Cultural Factors in Spatial Perceptual Development." In *Culture and Cognition: Readings in Cross-Cultural Psychology.* J. W. Berry and P. R. Dasen, eds. Pp. 129–40. London: Methuen (first publ. 1971).

Bettelheim, Bruno
1962   *Symbolic Wounds.* Rev. ed. New York: Collier.

Boas, Franz
1940   *Race, Language, and Culture.* New York: Free Press.

REFERENCES

Bohannan, Paul
    1971   "Artist and Critic in African Society." In *Anthropology and Art.* Charlotte M. Otten, ed. Pp. 172–81. Garden City: The Natural History Press.

Bott, Elizabeth
    1957   *Family and Social Network: Roles, Norms and Extended Relationships in Ordinary Urban Families.* London: Tavistock.

Bronfenbrenner, Urie
    1974   "The Origins of Alienation." *Scientific American* 2:53–61.

Cage, John
    1961   *Silence.* Middletown: Wesleyan University Press.

Cannon, Walter B.
    1942   "The 'Voodoo' Death." *American Anthropologist* 44:169–80.

Carneiro, Robert
    1970   "A Theory of the Origin of the State." *Science* 169:733–38.

Caudhill, William
    1973   "Psychiatry and Anthropology: The Individual and his Nexus." In *Cultural Illness and Health.* Laura Nader and Thomas W. Maretski, eds. Pp. 67–77. Washington, D.C.: American Anthropological Association.

Chagnon, Napoleon
    1977   *Yanomamo: The Fierce People.* 2nd ed. New York: Holt, Rinehart and Winston.

Chodorow, Nancy
    1974   "Family Structure and Female Personality." In *Women, Culture, and Society.* Michelle Rosaldo and Louise Lamphere, eds. Pp. 43–66. Stanford: Stanford University Press.

Chomsky, Noam
    1965   *Syntactic Structures.* London: Mouton.

Clark, Margaret
    1973   "Contributions of Cultural Anthropology to the Study of the Aged." In *Cultural Illness and Health.* Laura Nader and Thomas W. Maretski, eds. Pp. 78–88. Washington, D.C.: American Anthropological Association.

    1970   *Health in the Mexican American Culture.* Berkeley: University of California.

Cohen, Ronald and Service, Elman R., eds.
    1978   *Origins of the State: The Anthropology of Political Evolution.* Philadelphia: ISHI.

Cohen, Yehudi, ed.
    1971   *Man in Adaptation: The Institutional Framework.* Chicago: Aldine.

Cole, M. and S. Scribner
    1974   *Culture and Thought.* New York: Wiley.

Conklin, Harold C.
    1969   "An Ethnoecological Approach to Shifting Agriculture." In *Environment and Cultural Behavior.* Andrew P. Vayda, ed. Pp. 221–33. Garden City: The Natural History Press.

Dalton, George
    1967   Primitive Money." In *Tribal and Peasant Economies.* George Dalton, ed. Pp. 254–81. Garden City: The Natural History Press.

Damas, David
    1972   "The Copper Eskimo." In *Hunters and Gatherers Today.* M. G. Bicchieri, ed. Pp. 3–50. New York: Holt, Rinehart and Winston.

D'Andrade, Roy, G.
    1974   "Sex Differences and Cultural Conditioning." In *Culture and Personality.* Robert A. LeVine, ed. Pp. 16–37. Chicago: Aldine.

Denich, Betty
    1974   "Sex and Power in the Balkans." In *Woman, Culture and Society.* Michelle Rosaldo and Louise Lamphere, eds. Pp. 243–62. Stanford: Stanford University Press.

Dentan, Robert
    1968   *The Semai: A Nonviolent People of Malaya.* New York: Holt, Rinehart and Winston.

Divale, William Tulio and Marvin Harris
    1976   "Population, Warfare and the Male Supremacist Complex." *American Anthropologist* 78:521–38.

Dollard, John
    1937   *Caste and Class in a Southern Town.* New Haven: Yale University Press.

Douglas, Mary
1970   *Purity and Danger.* Baltimore. Penguin Books.

Draper, Patricia
1974   "Comparative Studies of Socialization." In *Annual Review of Anthropology.* Bernard J. Siegel, ed. Pp. 263–78. Palo Alto: Annual Reviews.

Drucker, P. and Heizer, R. F.
1967   *To Make My Name Good.* Berkeley: University of California Press.

Dumont, Louis
1970   *Homo Hierarchicus: An Essay on the Caste System.* Chicago: University of Chicago Press.

Edgerton, Robert
1971   *The Individual in Adaptation.* Berkeley: University of California Press.

Edgerton, Robert and Dingman, H. F.
1964   "Good Reasons for Bad Supervision: 'Dating' in a Hospital for the Mentally Retarded." *Psychiatric Quarterly Supplement* 38:221–33.

Eggan, Fred
1950   *The Social Organization of Western Pueblos.* Chicago: University of Chicago Press.

Ekman, Paul
1977   "Biological and Cultural Contributions to Body and Facial Movement." In *Anthropology of the Body.* John Blacking, ed. Pp. 34–89. New York: Academic Press.

Elkin,
1967   "The Nature of Australian Totemism." In *Gods and Rituals.* John Middleton, ed. Pp. 159–76. Garden City: The Natural History Press.

Ember, Melvin and Ember, Carol R.
1971   "The Conditions Favoring Matrilocal vs. Patrilocal Residence." *American Anthropologist* 73:571–94.

Evans-Pritchard, E. E.
1968   *The Nuer.* Oxford: Clarendon Press.
1967   "The Nuer Concept of Spirit in Its Relation to the Social Order." In *Myth and Cosmos.* John Middleton, ed. Pp. 109–26. Garden City: The Natural History Press.
1958   *Witchcraft, Oracles, and Magic among the Azande.* Oxford: Clarendon Press.

Fallers, Lloyd
1955   "The Predicament of the Modern African Chief: An Instance from Uganda." *American Anthropologist* 57:290–305.

Fischer, John
1961   "Art Styles as Cognitive Maps." *American Anthropologist* 63:79–93.

Flannery, K.
1973   "The Origins of Agriculture." *Annual Review of Anthropology.* Bernard J. Siegel, ed. Pp. 271–310. Palo Alto: Annual Reviews.

Ford, Clellan S.
1938   "The Role of a Fijian Chief." *American Sociological Review* 3:542–50.

Forde, Daryll
1950   "Double Descent Among the Yako." In *African Systems of Kinship and Marriage.* A. R. Radcliffe-Brown and Daryll Forde, eds. Pp. 285–332. London: Oxford University Press.

Foulks, Edward F.
1974   *The Arctic Hysterias.* Washington, D.C.: American Anthropological Association.

Frake, Charles O.
1964   "The Diagnosis of Disease among the Subanum of Mindanao." In *Language in Culture and Society.* Dell Hymes, ed. Pp. 192–210. New York: Harper and Row.

Freed, Ruth S.
1977   *Space, Density, and Cultural Conditioning.* Annals of the New York Academy of Sciences 285:593–604.

Freed, Stanley A. and Freed, Ruth S.
1978   "Shanti Nagar: The Effects of Urbanization in a Village in North India. 2. Aspects of Economy, Technology and Economy." *Anthropological Papers of the American Museum of Natural History* Vol. 55, Part I. New York: American Museum of Natural History.

Fried, Morton
1967   *The Evolution of Political Society.* New York: Random House.

Friedl, Ernestine
1975 *Women and Men: An Anthropologist's View.* New York: Holt, Rinehart and Winston.
1974 "Kinship, Class and Selective Migration." In *Family in the Mediterranean.* J. Peristiany, ed. London: Cambridge University Press.

Gardner, B. T. and Gardner, R. A.
1967 "Teaching Sign Language to a Chimpanzee." *Science* 165:664–72.

Gardner, Peter
1966 "Symmetric Respect and Memorate Knowledge: The Structure and Ecology of Individualistic Culture." *Southwestern Journal of Anthropology* 22:389–413.

Gay, John and Cole, Michael
1967 *The New Mathematics and an Old Culture.* New York: Holt, Rinehart and Winston.

Geddes, William
1963 *Peasant Life in Communist China.* Society for Applied Anthropology, Monograph No. 6. Ithaca: Society for Applied Anthropology.

Geertz, Clifford
1973 *The Interpretation of Culture.* New York: Basic Books.
1963 *Agricultural Involution: The Process of Ecological Change in Indonesia.* Berkeley: University of California Press.

Gorer, G. and Rickman, J.
1949 *The People of Great Russia.* London: Cresset.

Graves, Nancy B. and Graves, Theodore D.
1974 "Adaptive Strategies in Urban Migration." In *Annual Review of Anthropology.* Bernard J. Siegel, ed. Pp. 117–51. Palo Alto: Annual Reviews.

Gross, Daniel
1973 "The Great Sisal Scheme." In *Man's Many Ways.* Richard Gould, ed. Pp. 371–79. New York: Harper and Row.

Hall, Edward
1959 *The Silent Language.* Greenwich, Conn.: Fawcett.

Hanna, Judith
1977 "To Dance Is Human." In *The Anthropology of the Body.* John Blacking, ed. Pp. 211–32. London: Academic Press.

Harlow, Harry
1962 "Social Deprivation in Monkeys." *Scientific American* 206:1–10.

Harner, Michael
1977 "The Ecological Basis for Aztec Sacrifice." *American Ethnologist* 4:117–33.

Harris, Marvin
1975 *Cows, Pigs, Wars, and Witches: The Riddles of Culture.* New York: Random House (Vintage).
1968 *The Rise of Cultural Theory.* New York: Crowell.
1966 "The Cultural Ecology of India's Sacred Cattle." *Current Anthropology* 7:51–66.

Harrison, Robert
1973 *Warfare.* Minneapolis: Burgess.

Hart, C. W. M.
1967 "Contrasts Between Pre-pubertal and Post-pubertal Education." In *Personality and Social Life.* Robert Endelman, ed. Pp. 275–90. New York: Random House.

Hart, C. W. M. and Pilling, Arnold R.
1960 *The Tiwi of North Australia.* New York: Holt, Rinehart and Winston.

Heider, Karl
1970 *The Dugum Dani.* Chicago: Aldine.

Henry, Jules
1963 *Culture Against Man.* New York: Random House.

Herskovitz, Melville
1965 *Economic Anthropology.* New York: Norton.

Hockett, C. F. and Ascher, R.
1964 "The Human Revolution." *Current Anthropology* 5:135–68.

Hodges, Harold M. Jr.
1963 "Peninsula People: Social Stratification in a Metropolitan Complex." In *Education and Society.* Harold M. Hodges, Jr. and W. Warren Kallenbach, eds. Pp. 389–420. Columbus: Charles E. Merrill.

Hoebel, E. Adamson
1960 *The Cheyennes: Indians of the Great Plains.* New York: Holt, Rinehart and Winston.
1974 *The Law of Primitive Man.* New York: Atheneum (first publ. 1954).

Hoffer, Carol
1974 "Madam Yoko: Ruler of the Kpa Mende Confederacy." In *Women, Culture, and Society.* Michelle Zimbalist Rosaldo and Louise Lamphere, eds. Pp. 173–88. Stanford: Stanford University Press.

Hoijer, Harry
1964 "Cultural Implications of Some Navajo Linguistic Categories." In *Language in Culture and Society.* Dell Hymes, ed. Pp. 142–60. New York: Harper and Row.

Holmberg, Allan R.
1969 *Nomads of the Long Bow: The Siriono of Eastern Bolivia.* Garden City: The Natural History Press.

Holtzman, Wayne H., Diaz-Guerrero, Rogelio, and Swartz, Jon D.
1975 *Personality Development in Two Cultures.* Austin: University of Texas Press.

Horton, Robin
1973 *Modes of Thought: Essays on Thinking in Western and Non-Western Societies.* Robin Horton and Ruth Finnegan, eds. London: Faber.

Hymes, Dell
1972 *Reinventing Anthropology.* New York: Random House (Vintage).

Itard, Jean-Marc-Gaspard
1962 *The Wild Boy of Aveyron.* Englewood Cliffs: Prentice-Hall (trans. George and Muriel Humphrey).

Kardiner, Abram, Linton, Ralph, Dubois, Cora, and West, James
1945 *The Psychological Frontiers of Society.* New York: Columbia University Press.

Kinsey, Alfred C., Pomeroy, Wardell B., and Martin, Clyde E.
1948 *Sexual Behavior in the Human Male.* Philadelphia: W. B. Saunders.

Kroeber, Alfred L.
1939 "Cultural and Natural Areas of Native North America." *University of California Publications in American Archeology and Ethnology,* Vol. 38. Berkeley: University of California Press.

LaBarre, Weston
1969 *And They Shall Take Up Serpents.* New York: Schocken Books.

Labov, William
1972 "On the Mechanisms of Linguistic Change." In *Directions in Sociolinguistics.* John J. Gumperz and Dell Hymes, eds. New York: Holt, Rinehart and Winston.

Leach, Edmund
1976 *Culture and Communication.* New York: Cambridge University Press.

Lee, Dorothy
1959 *Freedom and Culture.* Englewood Cliffs, N.J.: Prentice-Hall.

Lee, Richard
1974 "Eating Christmas in the Kalahari." In *Conformity and Conflict.* James Spradley and David W. McCurdy, eds. Pp. 14–21. Boston: Little, Brown and Company.
1968 "What Hunters Do for a Living, or, How to Make Out on Scarce Resources." In *Man the Hunter.* Richard B. Lee and Irven DeVore, eds. Pp. 30–48. Chicago: Aldine.

Lehnert, Martin
1960 *Poetry and Prose of the Anglo-Saxons* Vol. I: Texts. 2nd ed. rev. Verlag/Halle, Germany: Vebmax Niemeyer.

Levi-Strauss, Claude
1969 *The Elementary Structures of Kinship.* Boston: Beacon Press (first publ. 1949).
1967 *Structural Anthropology.* Garden City: Doubleday.

Levine, Morton
1957 "Prehistoric Art and Ideology." *American Anthropologist* 59:949–62.

Lewis, Oscar
1966 *La Vida.* New York: Random House.
1960 *Tepoztlan, Village in Mexico.* New York: Holt, Rinehart and Winston.

Liebow, Elliot
1967 *Tally's Corner.* Boston: Little, Brown and Company.

Lomax, Alan
 1968   *Folk Song Style and Culture*. American Association for the Advancement of Science Publication No. 88. Washington, D.C.

Lowie, Robert H.
 1963   *Indians of the Plains*. Garden City: The Natural History Press (first publ. 1954).
 1948   *Social Organization*. New York: Holt, Rinehart and Winston.

Lynch, Owen K.
 1969   *The Politics of Untouchability*. New York: Columbia University Press.

Lynd, Robert and Lynd, Helen
 1937   *Middletown in Transition*. New York: Harcourt, Brace and World.

McNetting, Robert
 1977   *Cultural Ecology*. Menlo Park: Cummings.

Malinowski, Bronislaw
 1961   *Argonauts of the Western Pacific*. New York: E. P. Dutton (first publ. 1922).
 1953   *Sex and Repression in Primitive Society*. London: Routledge and Kegan Paul (first publ. 1927).
 1954   *Magic, Science, and Religion*. Garden City: Doubleday (first publ. 1926).
 1944   *A Scientific Theory of Culture and Other Essays*. Chapel Hill: University of North Carolina Press.
 1929   *The Sexual Life of Savages*. New York: Harcourt Brace and World.

Marshall, Donald
 1971   "Sexual Behavior on Mangaia." In *Human Sexual Behavior: Variations in the Ethnographic Spectrum*. Donald S. Marshall and Robert C. Suggs, eds. Pp. 103–62. New York: Basic Books.

Marshall, Laura
 1967   "!Kung Bushman Bands." In *Comparative Political Systems*. Ronald Cohen and John Middleton, eds. Pp. 15–44. Garden City: The Natural History Press.

Mauss, Marcel
 1954   *The Gift*. New York: MacMillan.

Mayer, Philip and Mayer, Iona
 1970   "Socialization by Peers: the Youth Organization of the Red Xhosa." In *Socialization: the Approach from Social Anthropology*. Philip Mayer, ed. Pp. 159–89. London: Tavistock Publications.

Mead, Margaret
 1963   *Sex and Temperament in Three Primitive Societies*. New York: Dell (first publ. 1935).
 1961   *Coming of Age in Samoa*. New York: Dell (first publ. 1928).
 1942   *And Keep Your Powder Dry: An Anthropologist Looks at America*. New York: Morrow.

Meek, Charles K.
 1972   "Ibo Law." In *Readings in Anthropology*. Jesse D. Jennings and E. Adamson Hoebel, eds. Pp. 247–58. New York: McGraw-Hill.

Mencher, Joan
 1965   "The Nayars of South Malabar." In *Comparative Family Systems*. M. F. Nimkoff, ed. Pp. 162–91. Boston: Houghton Mifflin.

Merriam, Alan P.
 1967   "The Arts and Anthropology." In *Horizons of Anthropology*. Sol Tax, ed. Pp. 224–36. Chicago: Aldine.
 1964   *The Anthropology of Music*. Evanston: Northwestern University.

Messenger, John C.
 1971   "Sex and Repression in an Irish Folk Community." In *Human Sexual Behavior: Variations in the Ethnographic Spectrum*. Donald S. Marshall and Robert C. Suggs, eds. Pp. 3–37. New York: Basic Books.

Montague, Susan and Morais, Robert
 1976   "Football Games and Rock Concerts: The Ritual Enactment." In *The American Dimension*. W. Arens and Susan P. Montague, eds. Pp. 33–52. Port Washington: Alfred.

Moody, Edward J.
 1974   "Urban Witches." In *Conformity and Conflict*. James P. Spradley and David W. McCurdy, eds. Pp. 326–36. Boston: Little, Brown.

Munroe, Robert L. and Munroe, Ruth H.
 1977   *Cross-Cultural Human Development*. New York: Aronson.

Murdock, George
 1949   *Social Structure*. New York: The Free Press.

Murphy, Robert
1964   "Social Distance and the Veil." *American Anthropologist* 66:1257–73.

Murphy, Yolanda and Murphy, Robert
1974   *Women of the Forest.* New York: Columbia University Press.

Nash, Dennison
1968   "The Role of the Composer." In *Readings in Anthropology.* Vol. II. *Cultural Anthropology.* Morton H. Fried, ed. Pp. 746–48. New York. Thomas Y. Crowell.

Nash, Manning
1967   "The Social Context of Economic Choice in a Small Society." In *Tribal and Peasant Economies.* George Dalton, ed. Pp. 524–38. Garden City: The Natural History Press.

Nimkoff, M. F. and Middleton, Russell
1960   "Types of Family and Types of Economy." *American Journal of Sociology* LXVI:215–25.

Ogbu, John
1978   "African Bridewealth and Women's Status." *American Ethnologist* 5:241–60.

Oliver, Symmes C.
1965   "Individuality, Freedom of Choice, and Cultural Flexibility of the Kamba." *American Anthropologist* 67:421–28.

Ortiz de Montellano, Bernard R.
1978   "Aztec Cannibalism: An Ecological Necessity?" *Science* 200:611–17.

Parenti, Michael J.
1967   "Black Nationalism and the Reconstruction of Identity." In *Personality and Social Life.* Robert Endelman, ed. Pp. 514–24. New York: Random House.

Pelto, Pertti
1973   *The Snowmobile Revolution: Technology and Social Change in the Arctic.* Menlo Park: Cummings Publishing Company.

Pettitt, George A.
1972   "The Vision Quest and the Guardian Spirit." In *Readings in Anthropology.* Jesse Jennings and E. Adamson Hoebel, eds. Pp. 265–71. New York: McGraw-Hill.

Pfeiffer, John
1972   *The Emergence of Man.* New York: Harper and Row.

Polyani, Karl
1944   *The Great Transformation.* New York: Holt, Rinehart and Company.

Pospisil, Leopold
1963   *The Kapauku Papuans of West New Guinea.* New York: Holt, Rinehart and Winston.

Potter, Jack M.
1967   "From Peasants to Rural Proletarians: Social and Economic Change in Rural Communist China." In *Peasant Society: A Reader.* Jack M. Potter, May N. Diaz and George M. Forster, eds. Pp. 407–18. Boston: Little, Brown.

Queen, Stuart and Habenstein, Robert W.
1974   *The Family in Various Cultures.* New York: J. B. Lippincott.

Radcliffe-Brown, A. R.
1965   *Structure and Function in Primitive Society.* New York: The Free Press.
1964   *The Andaman Islanders.* New York: The Free Press (first publ. 1922).

Rappaport, Roy A.
1971   "The Flow of Energy in an Agricultural Society." *Scientific American* 225:116–32.
1967   "Ritual Regulation of Environmental Relations among a New Guinea People." *Ethnology* 6:17–30.

Redfield, Robert
1971   "Art and Icon." In *Anthropology and Art.* Charlotte M. Otten, ed. Pp. 39–65. Garden City, N.Y.: The Natural History Press.

Reynolds, Vernon
1965   *Budongo: An African Forest and Its Chimpanzees.* Garden City: Doubleday.

Rohner, Ronald and Rohner, Evelyn
1970   *The Kwakiutl: Indians of British Columbia.* New York: Holt, Rinehart and Winston.

Rosaldo, Michelle Z., and Lamphere, Louise
1974   *Women, Culture and Society.* Stanford: Stanford University Press.

REFERENCES

Rosenfeld, Gerry
1971   *Shut Those Thick Lips: A Study of Slum School Failure.* New York: Holt, Rinehart and Winston.

Sahlins, Marshall
1972   *Stone Age Economics.* Chicago: Aldine.
1971   "Poor Man, Rich Man, Big Man, Chief." In *Conformity and Conflict.* James P. Spradley and David W. McCurdy, eds. Pp. 362–76. Boston: Little, Brown.
1961   "The Segmentary Lineage: An Organization of Predatory Expansion." *American Anthropologist* 63:332–45.
1957   "Land Use and the Extended Family in Moala, Fiji." *American Anthropologist* 59:449–62.

Salzman, Philip C.
1972   "Multi-Resource Nomadism in Iranian Baluchistan." In *Perspectives on Nomadism.* William Irons and Neville Dyson-Hudson, eds. Pp. 61–69. Leiden: E. J. Brill.

Sapir, Edward
1949   "The Status of Linguistics as a Science." In *The Selected Writings of Edward Sapir in Language, Culture and Personality.* David Mandelbaum, ed. Pp. 160–66. Berkeley: University of California Press.

Schneider, Harold K.
1973   "The Subsistence Role of Cattle Among the Pokot and in East Africa." In *Peoples and Cultures of Africa.* Elliott P. Skinner, ed. Pp. 159–87. Garden City: The Natural History Press.

Schwartz, Gary
1972   *Youth Culture: An Anthropological Approach.* Reading: Addison Wesley.

Schwartz, Theodore
1976   *Socialization as Cultural Communication.* Berkeley: University of California Press.

Service, Elman
1971   *Profiles in Ethnology.* New York: Harpers.

Sharma, Ursula
1979   "Segregation and Its Consequences in India." In *Women United, Women Divided.* Patricia Caplan and Janet M. Bujra, eds. Pp. 259–82. Bloomington: University of Indiana Press.

Sharp, Lauriston
1952   "Steel Axes for Stone Age Australians." In *Human Problems in Technological Change.* Edward H. Spicer, ed. Pp. 69–90. New York: Russell Sage Foundation.

Singer, Milton
1968   "The Indian Joint Family in Modern Industry." In *Indian Society: Structure and Change.* Milton Singer and Bernard Cohn, eds. Pp. 432–52. Chicago: Aldine.

Southworth, F. C. and Daswani, C. J.
1974   *Foundations of Linguistics.* New York: The Free Press.

Spiro, Melford
1974   "Is the Family Universal?—the Israeli Case." In *The Sociological Perspective.* Scott G. McNall, ed. 3rd. ed. Pp. 509–20. Boston: Little, Brown and Company.
1958   *Children of the Kibbutz.* Cambridge: Harvard University Press.

Spitz, Rene A.
1975   "Hospitalism: The Genesis of Psychiatric Conditions in Early Childhood." In *The Human Life Cycle.* William C. Sze, ed. Pp. 29–44. New York: Aronson.

Spradley, James
1970   *You Owe Yourself a Drunk.* Boston: Little, Brown.

Stack, Carol
1974   *All Our Kin.* New York: Harper & Row.

Steward, Julian
1972   *The Theory of Culture Change: The Methodology of Multilinear Evolution.* Urbana: The University of Illinois Press.

Sturtevant, Edgar H.
1947   *An Introduction to Linguistic Science.* New Haven: Yale University Press.

Talmon, Yohina
1964   "Mate Selection in Collective Settlements." *American Sociological Review* 29: 491–508.

Tonkinson, Robert
  1974   *The Jigalong Mob: Aboriginal Victors of the Desert Crusade.* Menlo Park: Cummings.

Turnbull, Colin
  1972   *The Mountain People.* New York: Simon and Schuster.
  1968   "The Importance of Flux in Two Hunting Societies." In *Man the Hunter.* Richard B. Lee and Irven DeVore, eds. Pp. 132–37. Chicago: Aldine.
  1961   *The Forest People.* New York: Simon and Schuster.

Tylor, Edward
  1920   *Primitive Culture.* 2 vols. New York: G. P. Putnam's Sons (first publ. 1871).

Valentine, Charles
  1971   "The 'Culture of Poverty': Its Scientific Significance and Its Implications for Action." In *The Culture of Poverty: A Critique.* Eleanor Burke Leacock, ed. Pp. 193–225. New York: Simon and Schuster.

Valentine, Charles A. and Valentine, Betty Lou
  1970   "Making the Scene, Digging the Action and Telling It Like It Is: Anthropologists at Work in a Dark Ghetto." In *Afro-American Anthropology.* Norman E. Whitten, Jr. and John F. Szwed, eds. Pp. 403–18. New York: The Free Press.

Vayda, Andrew P.
  1976   *War in Ecological Perspective.* New York: Plenum.

Wagner, Roy
  1975   *The Invention of Culture.* Englewood Cliffs, N.J.: Prentice-Hall.

Wallace, Anthony
  1970   *Death and Rebirth of the Seneca.* New York: Knopf.
  1966   *Religion: An Anthropological View.* New York: Random House.

Warner, Lloyd
  1963   *Yankee City.* Abridged ed. New Haven: Yale University Press.

White, Leslie A.
  1949   "Energy and the Evolution of Culture." In *The Science of Culture.* Leslie A. White, ed. Pp. 363–93. New York: Farrar Strauss and Cudahy.

Whiting, Beatrice, ed.
  1963   *Six Cultures: Studies of Child Rearing.* New York: Wiley.

Whiting, John and Child, Irvin L.
  1953   *Child Training and Personality: A Cross-Cultural Study.* New Haven: Yale University Press.

Whiting, John and Whiting, Beatrice
  1973   "Altruistic and Egoistic Behavior in Six Cultures." In *Cultural Illness and Health.* Laura Nader and Thomas W. Maretski, eds. Pp. 56–66. Washington, D.C.: American Anthropological Association.

Whiting, John, Kluckhohn, Richard, and Anthony, Albert
  1967   "The Function of Male Initiation Ceremonies at Puberty." In *Personality and Social Life.* Robert Endelman, ed. Pp. 294–308. New York: Random House.

Whorf, B. L.
  1956   *Language, Thought and Reality.* Boston: M.I.T. Press.

Whyte, William F.
  1955   *Street Corner Society.* Chicago: University of Chicago Press.

Wilson, Monica
  1963   *Good Company.* London: Oxford University Press.

Wissler, Clark
  1926   *The Relation of Man to Nature in Aboriginal North America.* New York: Appleton.

Witkin, H. A.
  1974   "Cognitive Styles Across Cultures." In *Culture and Cognition: Readings in Cross-Cultural Psychology.* J. W. Berry and P. R. Dasen, eds. Pp. 99–118. London: Methuen.

Wolf, Arthur
  1968   "Adopt a Daughter-in-Law, Marry a Sister: A Chinese Solution to the Incest Taboo." *American Anthropologist* 70: 864–74.

Wolf, Eric B.
  1966   *Peasants.* Englewood Cliffs, N.J.: Prentice-Hall.

Woodburn, James
  1968   "An Introduction to Hadza Ecology." In *Man the Hunter.* Richard

356
REFERENCES

B. Lee and Irven DeVore, eds. Pp. 49-55. Chicago: Aldine.

Worsley, Peter M.
  1959   "Cargo Cults." *Scientific American* 200: 117–28.

Wolfenstein, Martha
  1965   "Jack and the Beanstalk: An American Version." In *The Study of Folklore*. Alan Dundes, ed. Pp. 110–14. Englewood Cliffs, N.J.: Prentice-Hall.

Index

Page references in italic type refer to illustrations and photographs; page references in bold type refer to Suggested Readings at the ends of chapters.